Mergers and Acquisitions

Third Edition

Subscriber Update Service

BECOME A SUBSCRIBER!
Did you purchase this product from a bookstore?

If you did, it's important for you to become a subscriber. John Wiley & Sons, Inc. may publish, on a periodic basis, supplements and new editions to reflect the latest changes in the subject matter that you *need to know* in order to stay competitive in this ever-changing industry. By contacting the Wiley office nearest you, you'll receive any current update at no additional charge. In addition, you'll receive future updates and revised or related volumes on a 30-day examination review.

If you purchased this product directly from John Wiley & Sons, Inc., we have already recorded your subscription for this update service.

To become a subscriber, please call **1-800-225-5945** or send your name, company name (if applicable), address, and the title of the product to:

mailing address: **Supplement Department**
John Wiley & Sons, Inc.
One Wiley Drive
Somerset, NJ 08875

e-mail: **subscriber@wiley.com**
fax: **1-732-302-2300**
online: **www.wiley.com**

For customers outside the United States, please contact the Wiley office nearest you:

Professional & Reference Division
John Wiley & Sons Canada, Ltd.
22 Worcester Road
Rexdale, Ontario M9W 1L1
CANADA
(416) 675-3580
Phone: 1-800-567-4797
Fax: 1-800-565-6802
canada@jwiley.com

John Wiley & Sons, Ltd.
Baffins Lane
Chichester
West Sussex, PO19 1UD
ENGLAND
Phone: (44) 1243 779777
Fax: (44) 1243 770638
cs-books@wiley.co.uk

Jacaranda Wiley Ltd.
PRT Division
P.O. Box 174
North Ryde, NSW 2113
AUSTRALIA
Phone: (02) 805-1100
Fax: (02) 805-1597
headoffice@jacwiley.com.au

John Wiley & Sons (SEA) Pte. Ltd.
2 Clementi Loop #02-01
SINGAPORE 129809
Phone: 65 463 2400
Fax: 65 463 4605; 65 463 4604
wiley@singnet.com.sg

MERGERS AND ACQUISITIONS

BUSINESS STRATEGIES FOR ACCOUNTANTS

Third Edition

WILLIAM J. GOLE

JOSEPH M. MORRIS

1807
WILEY
2007

JOHN WILEY & SONS, INC.

This book is printed on acid-free paper. ∞

For general information on our other products and services, or technical support, please contact our Customer Care Department within the United States at 800-762-2974, outside the United States at 317-572-3993 or fax 317-572-4002.

Wiley also publishes its books in a variety of electronic formats. Some content that appears in print may not be available in electronic books.

For more information about Wiley products, visit our Web site at http://www.wiley.com.

Library of Congress Cataloging-in-Publication Data:

Gole, William J.
  Mergers and acquisitions : business strategies for accountants / William J. Gole, Joseph M. Morris. —3rd ed.
      p. cm.
  Prev. ed. entered under title: Mergers and acquisitions
  Includes index.
  ISBN 978–0–470–04242–7 (cloth : acid-free paper)
  1. Consolidation and merger of corporations—Accounting. I. Morris, Joseph M., 1949- II. Title.
  HF5686.C7M673 2007
  657′.96—dc22

                                                                                 2006036658

Printed in the United States of America.

10 9 8 7 6 5 4 3 2 1

CONTENTS

ABOUT THE AUTHORS

William J. Gole is a business consultant, educator, and author of professional books and continuing professional education courses for accountants and other financial professionals. From 1986 to 2003, he was a senior executive at a number of operating companies affiliated with The Thomson Corporation. Most recently, he was senior vice president, Planning and Business Development, at Thomson Healthcare, a $500 million information company serving healthcare professionals with database, newsletter, and medical education products. In that capacity he had responsibility for strategic planning and M&A activity, and managed the acquisition and divestiture of over 50 properties. Prior to that assignment, he was senior vice president for Worldwide Sales and Services for Thomson Scientific, an internationally renowned scientific database publisher with offices in Philadelphia, San Diego, London, Tokyo, Seoul, and Singapore. In that role, he had responsibility for international sales, customer education, and customer service. He has also held positions as president and chief executive officer of Frost & Sullivan, an international market research publisher; as publisher at the American Institute of CPAs; and as senior auditor with Coopers & Lybrand.

Mr. Gole has authored or co-authored several books, including *Guide to Small Business Consulting Engagements* and *Guide to Construction Contractors,* published by Practitioners Publishing Company, and over 20 continuing professional education courses on accounting and consulting services. He has also taught accounting and business courses at a number of colleges and universities in the New York metropolitan area, and currently teaches a course on International Business at Molloy College in Rockville Centre, New York.

Joseph M. Morris is an accounting, tax, and general business consultant and an author of professional books for practicing accountants and other financial professionals. From 1988 to 1990, he was a project manager for the Financial Accounting Standards Board. At the FASB, Mr. Morris was responsible for the major project on consolidations and related matters, which included accounting for consolidated financial statements and parent-subsidiary relationships, accounting for acquisitions, and accounting for joint ventures. He was also the FASB staff specialist in accounting for the software industry.

From 1966 to early 1999, he was senior vice president and chief financial officer and a member of the board of directors of ITEX Corporation, a publicly traded company, which provides diversified financial services and operates the largest organized commercial barter exchange. Previously, he was vice president and corporate controller of Scientific Software-Intercomp, Inc., a publicly traded Nasdaq company. Earlier in his career, Mr. Morris worked extensively on acquisitions in private industry while with Lone Star Industries, Inc., and in public accounting while with Coopers & Lybrand LLP.

Mr. Morris has authored several other Wiley books, including *Software Industry Accounting,* which received the Association of American Publishers award for Best New Professional Book in Accounting Practice for 1993. The first edition of his book, *Mergers and Acquisitions,* received the Association of American Publishers award for Best New Professional Book in Accounting Practice for 1995.

PREFACE

In 2005, a record number of Merger and Acquisition (M&A) transactions were announced. As this work goes to press, it is a virtual certainty that this record will be surpassed in 2006. And, the forces driving M&A activity—technological change, low interest rates, globalization, and an environment conducive to business consolidation—are expected to persist unabated into the second half of the decade. One result of this increased activity is that corporate accountants and financial managers are being called upon more often than ever to play important roles in M&A transactions, often with little in the way of preparation and resources. *Mergers and Acquisitions: Business Strategies for Accountants*, 3rd edition, has been revised and updated to be responsive to the needs of these financial professionals.

When confronted with the challenge of managing various aspects of M&A transactions, financial professionals require a broad range of referential and application resources. The contents of the 3rd edition attempt to strike a balance between guidance on practical application of M&A principles and best practices, while also providing access to important referential information. The earlier chapters of the new edition focus on transaction structure and management, with a strong emphasis on thoughtful planning and disciplined execution. This discussion is supported by a rich set of appendices that contain documents, forms and exhibits that illustrate important M&A concepts and procedures. The later chapters focus on the areas of federal taxation, regulation, and purchase accounting. These discussions deal with those laws and regulations that establish the boundaries within which M&A transactions are executed, and provide the financial professional with important guidance in structuring and finalizing transactions.

Chapters 1 through 7 discuss the acquisition process at a very granular level. Chapter 8 provides a detailed discussion of the sales and divestiture process. Chapter 9 provides a thorough review of the relevant areas of the federal tax code. Chapter 10 contains detailed guidance on acquisition accounting. And, Chapter 11 reviews the major regulatory considerations applicable to mergers, acquisitions, and sales.

As M&A activity continues to escalate in the coming years, this 3rd edition of *Mergers and Acquisitions* is designed to equip accountants and financial managers of all types with a combination of practical and theoretical guidance when pressed into duty to manage important aspects of these transactions.

William J. Gole
Lake Placid, New York
April 2007

CHAPTER 1

MERGER AND ACQUISITION OVERVIEW

The author would like to thank James R. Krendl, who wrote the version of this chapter that appeared in the last edition.

1

1.1 INTRODUCTION

Historically, mergers and acquisitions (M&As) have always been a factor in the expansion and consolidation of the modern industrial base of the United States and other advanced economies. However, over the last decade or so, M&As have emerged as a particularly significant market force. This trend is reflected in the volume of M&A activity, measured in terms of both dollars and the number of transactions consummated. The dollar volume of M&A activity in the United States exceeded $1 trillion in 1998 and has reached or exceeded that benchmark almost every year since. During that same period, the number of announced M&A transactions has consistently exceeded 7,500 annually.

Understandably, the largest of these transactions, large public company combinations, have been the most visible. These large transactions typically entail enormous transfers of value and affect thousands of employees and hundreds of thousands of investors. However, smaller transactions, such as those involving the sale of closely held businesses and the divestitures of business units—usually to larger, publicly traded companies—dwarf the number of combinations involving publicly traded entities.

Although these smaller transactions generally fall under the radar of the financial press and the casual business observer, they have consistently accounted for over 90% of all transactions by volume for the last several decades. They are clearly an important source of growth for publicly traded companies and, more relevantly, they are the types of transactions that are very likely to be encountered by business professionals, especially financial professionals, in the course of their careers.

Not only do these transactions differ in terms of size and visibility, they also differ significantly in terms of dynamics and process. The remainder of this chapter discusses these differences and other important factors that provide background and context for the more fulsome discussions of the acquisition and sales process that appear in the chapters that follow. This initial foundational discussion focuses on:

- The role of M&A activity in the context of overall corporate strategy
- Important definitions of, and distinctions among, the various types of M&A transactions
- Descriptions of the various types of transactions, highlighting differences in the nature of their execution
- An overview of the central role the financial manager generally plays in the various types of M&A transactions

1.2 CENTRAL ROLE OF STRATEGIC PLANNING IN THE MERGER AND ACQUISITION PROCESS

(a) GENERAL. Any meaningful discussion of M&As should start with an understanding of the role of strategic planning in the corporate decision-making process. Most companies reinforce or update their business development strategy annually. Typically, the end product of this planning process is the articulation of a limited number of strategic objectives whose implementation begins with translating them into concrete investment activities. The categories of the investment options available are limited. They take the form of internal development (build), acquisition (buy), or strategic partnership (ally).

It should also be understood that, even in those cases in which a formal, structured strategic planning process is not employed, a company will still be guided by a stated or implied business strategy that is broadly understood within the organization. That strategy may result in a planning document, or it may simply be a shared understanding within a business of the need and intent to fill important gaps in the company's portfolio and infrastructure.

An expansive description of the strategic planning process is beyond the scope of this discussion. Suffice it to say that companies typically chart a strategic direction that is expressed in the form of long-term objectives and that the realization of those objectives must be driven by specific investment activities. These objectives typically fall into these broad categories:

- Developing or acquiring new products for current markets
- Expanding the distribution channels for existing products
- Developing or acquiring new products for new markets
- Achieving economies of scale in order to lower production costs
- Increasing brand recognition of products and/or services
- Developing or acquiring new technology, intellectual property, or research and development (R&D) capability
- Establishing control over sources of supply by expanding operations toward suppliers' markets (backward integration)
- Expanding operations toward customers' markets (forward integration)

(b) INVESTMENT CONSIDERATIONS.   Frequently, the approach employed to accomplish strategic objectives is purely acquisition-based, but, as noted, acquisitions are just one of the three broad investment options (build, buy, or ally) available to further these objectives. These options are significantly different from one another in terms of risks, benefits, advantages, and disadvantages. The differences revolve around the trade-offs among a number of variables, particularly those of strategic fit, speed of implementation, cost of implementation, and anticipated synergistic benefits.

(i) Strategic Fit.   It is axiomatic that the investment option must support the entity's strategic objective. Internal development generally provides the greatest potential for control and customization, and often the greatest assurance of strategic fit. Acquisitions and strategic alliances, when they can be implemented, generally will provide an *approximate* fit. However, occasionally the assets needed to accomplish a key strategic objective are unique, that is, truly one of a kind.

If such an asset does not exist in the marketplace (e.g., customized infrastructure technology), then acquisition can be automatically ruled out as an option. Alternatively, the unique assets coveted (e.g., intellectual property assets) may be owned by another entity, and acquisition of that entity or strategic partnership with it may be the only options available.

(ii) Speed of Implementation. One of the primary factors an enterprise must consider when making an investment decision is the importance of speed in accomplishing the strategic objective at hand. If speed is a primary consideration, acquisition is likely to be the most attractive alternative, assuming some or all of the assets acquired are a good strategic fit. This is particularly the case when market entry or market expansion is the objective. Internal development may provide a more precise fit, but the market opportunity may have passed by the time an internally developed initiative is implemented. Strategic alliances may also be a viable option, but execution can be difficult and time-consuming and, by definition, requires a sharing of the benefits derived.

(iii) Cost of Implementation. Cost is clearly a key consideration. Strategic alliances can be attractive because their costs (as well as their benefits) are shared. Acquisition, however, is generally the most expensive option, because it will often entail paying a premium over the cost of internal development.

(iv) Synergistic Benefits. When acquisition or strategic alliance is the option exercised, there is generally a presumption that, by combining assets and/or capabilities, benefits can be realized that are greater than what would be expected if the two companies operated independently. In the case of an acquisition, these anticipated synergies must be considered in the context of any purchase premium paid by the acquiring company. (Purchase premiums are discussed in greater detail in section 3.2(c).)

The investment option chosen will involve the weighing of these, and perhaps other, variables specific to the facts and circumstances of a given situation. Frequently, acquisition is the favored option, because it best satisfies the company's objectives in the context of these decision variables—or at least appears to do so.

(c) IMPACT OF GLOBALIZATION. The recent, accelerated pace of globalization has had a significant impact on strategic thinking and strategic plan implementation in the corporate world. Driven primarily by technological innovation, competition has intensified in many industries. To a greater extent than ever, this has led to strategic initiatives that focus on more aggressive market expansion and on rapidly attaining economies of scale and substantially enhanced efficiencies. This in turn has placed increased emphasis on the rapid implementation of strategic initiatives.

(d) ENHANCED RISK. Arguably, the interplay of the factors just noted has given primacy to speed of implementation and provided significant impetus to acquisition as an investment option in many cases. In situations where acquisitions are the chosen path to achieving strategic objectives, this choice is generally accompanied by increased risk. That risk derives from the likelihood of imperfect strategic fit, the high probability of paying a premium for the assets acquired, and the exposure inherent in integrating the purchased properties into the fabric of a separate business. *For these reasons, a thoughtful, well-planned, and disciplined approach to acquisitions is critical, if these risks are to be mitigated.*

1.3 TYPES OF M&A ACTIVITY

(a) GENERAL. M&A transactions can be characterized in a number of ways. These different characterizations provide important context for discussions of the transaction process, regulatory compliance, and the strategic and financial impact of the different types of transactions. The major categories of transactions are described in sections 1.3(b) through (g).

(b) MERGERS VERSUS ACQUISITIONS. The term "merger" technically means the absorption of one corporation into another corporation. Typically, in a merger, the selling corporation's shareholders receive stock in the buying corporation. However, the term "merger" is frequently used more loosely—for example, to include a consolidation that is technically the combination of two or more corporations to form a new corporation.

In a true merger (as opposed to an acquisition), the acquirer becomes directly liable for all the liabilities of the acquired corporation, often an undesirable result. In a pure stock purchase or *acquisition*, the acquired company can be kept as a separate subsidiary and, while its liabilities continue to exist, they do not become legal claims against the assets or earnings of the acquirer. However, assumption of liabilities by the acquirer can be avoided by a special structure known as a *triangular merger,* in which the acquirer sets up a subsidiary and then merges it with the acquired company. The more significant issue is often not whether the transaction is a merger or a stock acquisition, but whether it qualifies for tax-free treatment under Section 368 of the Internal Revenue Code. (The tax treatment of M&As is discussed in greater detail in Chapter 9.)

(c) LARGE PUBLIC VERSUS SMALL PRIVATE ACQUISITIONS. Arguably, the most important distinction among types of acquisitions revolves around size. Mergerstat data confirms that a reasonable dividing line between large, public company acquisitions and small, nonpublic acquisitions, as determined by magnitude of purchase price, is $500 million. This is because the vast majority of transactions that are larger than $500 million involve the sale of a public company, and those falling below that benchmark are sales of private companies or divestitures of business units by larger companies. This distinction is important because large transactions have dynamics and requirements that are substantially different from those of smaller transactions, and those differences have a significant impact on the acquisition process for each. These differences and their impact are briefly described in the paragraphs that follow and are illustrated in Exhibit 1.1.

(i) Strategic Impact.   Large public transactions are almost invariably transformational in nature. They involve the combination of two large entities that can be expected to have strong positions in the same or adjacent markets. Such combinations generally result in an entity of great size, with substantially expanded product breadth and depth, market reach, and overall capabilities. In contrast, smaller transactions are generally nontransformational in nature and fulfill important, but limited, strategic objectives. While they may materially advance the strategic position of the acquirer, they rarely are significant enough to *transform* the acquirer's business.

Characteristics	Large Transactions ($500 million or greater)	Smaller Transactions (less than $500 million)
Parties to the Transaction	Predominantly two publicly traded companies	Predominantly a private company acquired by a large (frequently publicly traded) company
Strategic Impact	Transformational, resulting in a quantum leap in size, product breadth, market reach, and other capabilities	Usually nontransformational, improving strategic position but rarely significant enough to change business fundamentals
Regulatory Requirements	Substantial, including SEC filings, Hart-Scott-Rodino filings	Minimal under $53 million; Hart-Scott-Rodino filings over $53 million
Stock or Asset Purchases	Almost invariably stock	Both stock and asset purchases common
Leverage of the Parties	Tilted toward seller and reflected in premiums paid over preacquisition market price	Tilted toward buyer, especially when there is a thin market for the company being sold
Risk Profile	Substantial, due to premiums paid, the lack of recourse on breaches of representations and warranties, and challenges of integration	Moderate, due to ability to conduct in-depth due diligence, greater leverage on price, occasional ability to purchase just selected assets, and greater recourse on breached of reps and warranties
Volume of Transactions	Less than 10% of transactions executed	More than 90% of transactions executed

Exhibit 1.1   Comparison of Deals by Size of Purchase price

(ii) Regulatory Requirements.   The acquisition of a publicly traded company is heavily regulated by the Securities and Exchange Commission (SEC), state law, and federal antitrust statutes, specifically the Hart-Scott-Rodino (HSR) Act. (See section 11.5 for a discussion of relevant SEC regulations and a summary of HSR provisions.) Nonpublic transactions, in comparison, are minimally regulated. However, those with a purchase price of more than $53 million (periodically adjusted for inflation) may be subject to the provisions of the HSR. In any

event, the greater the need for regulatory compliance, the greater the need for additional expertise and resources and the greater the length of time needed to execute the transaction.

(iii) Stock or Asset Purchases. As noted, when publicly traded companies are acquired, it is the shares of those companies that are almost invariably purchased. As a result, all the liabilities of the acquired company are assumed as well. Although the acquirer may be able to shield itself from direct exposure to those liabilities, the acquired entity is still liable for all obligations known and unknown to the acquirer. Frequently, in contrast, selected assets of nonpublic companies are acquired, in lieu of stock. This may enable the buyer to pay for only those assets it truly wants and to avoid assuming many of the target company's liabilities.

(iv) Leverage of the Parties to the Transaction. In acquisitions of publicly traded companies, pricing leverage will generally reside with the seller. Even as rumors that the target company is being pursued by a suitor emerge, the value of its stock will invariably increase. This among other factors will affect the negotiated price of the shares. If successful in executing a transaction, the acquirer will pay a premium that historically has been within a range of from 30 to 40% above the preacquisition price. In contrast, transaction leverage is generally tilted toward the buyer at the small end of the market, particularly when the field of potential buyers is small. This has significant implications regarding price as well as other major terms of the transaction.

(v) Risk Profile of the Transaction. There is an inverse relationship to leverage and risk. Accordingly, the risk profile of the acquisition of a publicly traded company is quite high. A large body of research has been conducted that indicates that a high percentage of public transactions never generate returns that would justify the price paid. This fact is generally attributable to two factors: synergies generated from the combination are not sufficient to justify the purchase premium paid, and the challenges of integration associated with a transaction of this magnitude are frequently not fully anticipated, adequately prepared for, and effectively executed. In addition, transaction risk is elevated because the acquirer has no recourse for breaches of representations

and warranties subsequent to the consummation of the transaction. (For a more detailed discussion of representations and warranties, see section 5.2(b).) Private transactions generally allow for a much greater mitigation of risk. This includes measures such as the ability to negotiate price and minimize premiums, the possibility to purchase only selected assets, the ability in many cases to perform more intensive due diligence, and much greater recourse in the case of breached representations and warranties.

It is particularly noteworthy that less than 10% of the transactions executed are those in which a publicly traded company is purchased, with smaller, private transactions accounting for the rest. The differences cataloged in the preceding paragraphs make it clear that transaction characteristics are strongly influenced by the size and nature of the entity being acquired. They potentially impact most major aspects of the acquisition process—ranging from negotiation of terms, to regulatory compliance, financing, due diligence, and contract and close.

(d) STRATEGIC VERSUS FINANCIAL ACQUISITIONS.   The discussion to this point has focused on strategic acquisitions, those involving a buyer motivated by strategic considerations, such as the objectives listed in the introductory section of this chapter. However, when investment capital is plentiful, venture capital firms (i.e., financial buyers, to be distinguished from strategic buyers) are very likely to become major competitors in the acquisition arena. Rather than buy with the intent to build an enterprise for the long term, these private equity firms acquire properties for the short to midterm and, after investing, repositioning, and combining them with other synergistic assets, will resell them to strategic buyers. Although the discussion herein is biased toward strategic acquisitions, many of the same principles and procedures presented have equal application to financial acquisitions.

(e) PORTFOLIO ACQUISITIONS OF HOLDING COMPANIES.   Acquisition-based holding companies buy companies in diverse industries, based more on the quality of the company, its products, and its management than any overriding strategic approach to a specific market. Although more common in the 1960s, a time when the concept of the "conglomerate" was in vogue, such organizations are relatively rare in the current environment. By definition, such organizations make acquisitions with no expectation of realizing synergies and no intent to integrate operations. The properties are generally acquired along with their management teams and are run with the intent of building value over the long term. A notable (and extremely successful) example of such an organization is Berkshire Hathaway, the company founded and built by Warren Buffett.

(f) OTHER CHARACTERIZATIONS OF ACQUISITIONS.   Other characterizations of acquisitions cross the lines established by the distinctions just made. There are "roll-up" strategies employed by both strategic and financial buyers wishing to expand size and reach, and realize greater scale and efficiency, in a particular niche market. Similarly, there are also "fold-in" strategies employed by buyers, whether strategic or financial, wishing to fill gaps in their offerings by acquiring relatively small companies (or their assets) that can be easily assimilated into the buyer's operation, while shedding the support infrastructure of the company being acquired.

(g) DIVESTITURES VERSUS SALES OF AN ENTIRE BUSINESS.   It is important to distinguish between divestitures and sales of entire enterprises, because they have substantially different transaction dynamics. Divestitures entail disposals of a segment of a business such as a business unit, a product line, or even an individual product. They are made either for strategic reasons or for financial reasons. In the case of the former, the unit being sold is deemed by the parent company to no longer be compatible with its strategic direction and therefore not a candidate for continued investment. In the latter case, the sale is invariably made to generate needed cash and is generally executed by a parent that is under financial duress. The sale of a business in its entirety is simply the sell side of an acquisition of a standalone company as described in section 1.4.

1.4 TRANSACTION OVERVIEWS

(a) GENERAL.   This section provides overviews of the transaction process for acquisitions, for sales of an entire business, and for divestitures (i.e., sales of portions of a business). Chapters 2 through 6 discuss the various phases of the acquisition process in great detail, and Chapter 8 provides a similarly detailed discussion of the sales process. This summary provides a view of the staging, process flow, and event sequencing of these transactions as well as overall context for those more detailed accounts.

(b) ACQUISITION PROCESS.   The acquisition process begins with the search for, and identification of, a target company that will fulfill certain strategic objectives of the acquirer and ends with the acquisition and integration of that company into the acquirer's operation. The entire process is made up of a number of discrete steps that can be grouped into five major phases:

1. From process initiation through target qualification
2. From valuation through preliminary agreement
3. From due diligence through approval to finalize the transaction
4. From contract to close
5. Postacquisition integration

(i) From Process Initiation through Target Qualification.   This initial phase of the process begins with the creation of a core team to manage the process and the identification of a target company and confirmation that the targeted company is a viable candidate for acquisition. The actual process by which this is accomplished can vary significantly from company to company and from one situation to the next. It may be readily apparent that a target company provides an excellent strategic fit and is the optimal candidate to fulfill the acquirer's objectives. Alternatively, a screening process may be employed to identify potential candidates before they are approached. In still other cases, a candidate may make its availability known either through an intermediary, such as a business broker or investment banker, or through direct contact with executive management of the acquirer's organization. Assuming that the process proceeds, the core team would ensure that a confidentiality agreement is executed; it would arrange a formal meeting with the principals of the target company to confirm their interest; and it would request sufficient preliminary information to perform a meaningful analysis and valuation of the target company.

The identification and qualification process for both public and private company acquisitions is similar but can differ in a number of important respects. When a public company is the target, the direct involvement of the acquiring company's chief executive officer (CEO) early in the process is almost a certainty, whereas with a smaller, private company acquisition, there is a much greater probability that the

CEO would delegate negotiations to a core team of senior managers who will keep him or her informed on an as-needed basis. In addition, the board of the acquiring company is likely to be advised by its management of its intentions to pursue a transaction. Smaller transactions generally do not warrant early board notification, especially at more acquisitive companies, where there may be many such preacquisition discussions in progress at any given time. Although relatively rare and often unsuccessful, an acquirer of a publicly traded company may pursue a transaction on a nonnegotiated basis, that is, a hostile bid that is opposed by the target company's board, an option generally not available in private company acquisitions.

(ii) From Valuation through Preliminary Agreement. Based on the information provided, the acquirer will perform a preliminary analysis of the potential acquisition. This analysis would be used as the basis for internal discussions about the advisability of acquiring the target company and would include a preliminary valuation as well as the consideration of acceptable terms under which the acquirer would execute a transaction. Once internal agreement is reached on price range, other major terms, and negotiating strategy, the core acquisition team under the leadership of the CEO would negotiate basic terms of the transaction with the target company principals. These terms would generally be documented in the form of a letter of intent (LOI). It is during this phase of the process that the acquirer would also determine whether it needed outside financing to consummate the transaction and, if so, would initiate the process to raise the necessary capital.

If the transaction involves publicly traded companies, the agreement to pursue a transaction puts into motion a number of additional activities. The boards of both companies would most certainly be apprised of discussions and, typically, a host of legal, business, and financial advisors would be brought into the process in anticipation of drafting a definitive agreement (contract) and a fairness opinion (a letter that will eventually be sent to shareholders opining on the fairness of the purchase price and other aspects of the transaction). The valuation arrived at will invariably result in a share price that is substantially higher than market value prior to these discussions. This premium assumes that the performance of the combined companies will yield synergies materially in excess of that premium. The extent of the typical premium paid in the acquisition of a public company is one of the features that set it apart from a private company purchase. That does not mean that purchasers of private companies do not pay premiums. However, whether one is paid and its magnitude is much more of a controllable variable in a private transaction.

(iii) From Due Diligence to Approval to Proceed to Contract.   Once the parties have agreed to the basic terms of the transaction, the acquirer would proceed to the due diligence phase of the process. This would entail fleshing out the core acquisition team with additional internal staff and external experts to assist in due diligence, thoroughly briefing team members, developing a due diligence program, conducting the due diligence review, and reporting on its results. Assuming that no evidence of material impairment of the value of the target company is uncovered, the process would proceed to the contract phase. If major issues affecting value are uncovered, the transaction may be terminated or the purchase price may be renegotiated.

This would be a period of particularly intense activity if the transaction is between two public companies. The boards of both companies would be actively involved in discussions with their respective managements and their advisors, and the drafting of the definitive agreement and fairness opinion would have commenced.

(iv) Contract and Close.   Negotiation of the granular terms of the agreement would follow successful due diligence. Private company acquisitions may involve the sale of stock or the sale of assets. The form of the transaction would have a significant impact on the content of the contract, specifically the nature of the representations, warranties, covenants, and conditions contained therein. If the transaction is for a purchase price of more than $53 million, there will almost certainly be a need for an HSR antitrust filing with the Department of Justice (DOJ) and the Federal Trade Commission (FTC). Assuming that the transaction will not result in an anticompetitive combination, the HSR filing will generally delay closing for about one month. In addition, a large private company acquisition may require the approval of the acquiring company's board; even if it does not, management may still present the transaction to the board for comment.

If the transaction involves public companies, the process from due diligence to close is much more complex and lengthy. The definitive agreement will require the affirmative approval of the target company's board and usually the approval of the acquiring company's board. Securities regulations would require public disclosure of the impending transaction. In addition, a combination of this size and nature will undoubtedly require an HSR filing and may, in fact, require the divestiture of selected properties to satisfy the anticompetition concerns of the DOJ and the FTC. Shareholder approval will also be required, and steps leading up to such approval (possible prospectus preparation, SEC approval, proxy statement preparation, and proxy solicitation) will generally take several months to implement. Once all of these requirements are met and approvals are obtained, the transaction would proceed to closing.

(v) Postacquisition Integration. There is virtually universal agreement among students and practitioners of M&As that poorly planned and executed postacquisition integration is one of the primary causes of acquisitions not meeting pretransaction expectations. Integration planning should begin at the early stages of the acquisition process, and those who are charged with integrating the businesses should have strong representation on the acquirer's due diligence team. Aggressive timetables for accomplishing integration objectives should be set in advance of close, and the integration process should start immediately after the deal has been finalized.

The challenges associated with integration are the same for large and small companies, and any differences generally lie in the order of magnitude of those challenges. Integration is predominantly about the realization of synergies and the standardization of policies, processes, and procedures. The areas of synergistic opportunity are generally distribution, operations, systems, facilities, and infrastructure personnel.

Timely implementation is a key to the success of integration efforts. Implementation should be substantially accomplished within the first three to six months following the close of the transaction. Effective implementation is enabled by establishing clear objectives and assigning unambiguous accountability and authority to a team leader whose efforts are regularly monitored by an engaged CEO. However, clear and thoughtful objectives and rapid implementation are necessary, but not sufficient, components of a successful integration plan. Employee buy-in is also a critical factor in maintaining productivity, retaining talent, and ensuring that the integration is effective in the long term. Key to establishing buy-in is clear, candid, and continuous communication. To the greatest extent possible, employees must be made to feel as if they are part of the process and the future vision of the organization.

(c) SALES PROCESS. In contrast to an acquisition, the process associated with selling a business is considerably more reactive. However, it too can be broken down into several distinct phases, specifically:

- Prenegotiation preparation
- Negotiation
- Due diligence
- Contract and close

(i) Prenegotiation Preparation. The seller of a private company often has no prior experience in navigating the issues encountered in such a sale. Once serious discussions with a prospective buyer begin, the seller should enlist the assistance of a number of advisors. This should include an attorney with M&A experience and some combination of business, tax, and financial professionals who are skilled in the M&A field. The primary area of focus for the inexperienced seller should be an understanding of the value of the business being sold, the tax impact of the terms of the sale, and how the transaction will unfold. Accordingly, the professionals engaged should provide expertise in these areas. In addition, the seller will want to mobilize a limited number of internal managers to assist in early-stage discussion and data assembly. To minimize the potential for business disruption and reduced productivity, it is generally advisable to keep this group small and to impress upon them the importance of strict confidentiality. One other potential member of the seller's team may be a business broker or investment banker. Their understanding of the market and the sales process can be of significant value. However, the seller must determine whether that value is likely to be in excess of the commissions paid for their services.

Public company sales, as noted earlier, are considerably more complex than private sales. Similar to the private seller, the management of a public company will seek out M&A expertise. However, at this stage of the process, management will also maintain an ongoing dialogue with its board as the transaction takes shape.

(ii) Negotiation.   There are a number of major elements to be considered in structuring the transaction: price, the form of the sale (stock or assets), the form of the consideration (cash, debt, stock, or a combination), tax implications, the ongoing role of the seller (if any), and, possibly, the impact of the sale on the seller's employees. As a result, the negotiation process can be expected to be iterative and protracted. Expert input in the areas of greatest importance and an understanding of interrelationships (e.g., tax and valuation implications on the form of the transaction) are critical. From a strategic perspective, the seller, with the assistance of his or her team, should identify deal breakers and establish a walkaway position and be prepared to discontinue discussions if issues critical to the seller cannot be resolved.

The negotiation process is not necessarily different in concept for a publicly traded company. The major difference lies with the number of individuals involved in the process. A public company will enlist a substantial number of advisors and will involve the close participation of board members as well as the most senior members of its management team. In sharp contrast to a smaller transaction, especially one in which there is owner management, the communication and decision-making process can be quite byzantine.

(iii) Due Diligence.   The parameters of due diligence are negotiable but, under any circumstances, preparation for and administration of due diligence requires the dedication of a substantial amount of company resources. Due diligence consists of extensive document review and analysis, management presentations, interviews of key personnel, and tours of facilities. Creation of a data room (the locus of document review) is a labor-intensive activity, and preparation of management presentations can be expected to tie up key managers and their staffs for substantial periods of time.

The length of the formal on-site due diligence process varies but will generally span several days to several weeks, depending on the size and complexity of the company being reviewed. Clearly, review of large public companies with multiple locations will require more time and staffpower than review of small closely held businesses. In addition, there is a vast amount of historical financial and business information available in the public domain for publicly traded companies. In the broadest terms, due diligence includes analysis of such information outside the framework of formal on-site diligence.

Although these activities have no impact on seller's resources, it is worth noting that, from the buyer's perspective, they may in fact dwarf the efforts associated with the formal, on-site due diligence review.

(iv) Contract and Close.   Negotiation of the final contract (or definitive agreement) can be a lengthy, iterative process. Even for small deals, the final contract may take in excess of a month to negotiate. Typically, the seller is supported by his or her M&A attorney, a financial advisor, and/or the company's chief financial officer (CFO). This is the point in the process where the attorney is of greatest assistance and value. Negotiation of the granular detail of the transaction requires someone who is intimately familiar with the process, the associated documents, and the issues. By virtue of training and experience, a good M&A attorney will have mastered the first two of these items. Participation in the acquisition process from the beginning will have provided the attorney with the basis for dealing with the issues. That said, the active participation of the seller and his or her financial advisor is critical to ensure that business and financial issues are quickly and properly resolved.

In the case of private companies, contract and close can occur simultaneously, unless there has to be an HSR filing. As noted earlier, closing on public company acquisitions is more complex, and the time from contact to close is substantial and requires an affirmative vote by the board and, ultimately, the approval of the stockholders.

(d) DIVESTITURE PROCESS.   Divestitures are sales of a segment of a company's business, such as a business unit, a product line, or even an individual product. Divestitures historically have accounted for a sizable percentage of all M&A transactions executed (estimated to be about 25% in recent years). Decisions to divest or dispose of a segment of a business generally originate once it becomes evident that the unit in question is no longer compatible with the strategic direction of the parent company. Divestitures are generally proactive initiatives that lend themselves to detailed planning and execution. Management of these transactions can be broken down into three distinct phases:

1. Divestiture planning
2. Transaction preparation
3. Transaction execution

(i) Divestiture Planning.   Divestiture planning begins with the development of a paper that lays out the rationale for disposal. That document becomes the basis for corporate approval (from the CEO or the board), which is the trigger event for launching the initiative. Approval will be followed by the development of a retention plan (with incentives) for key personnel associated with the property being divested, to minimize business disruption and loss of productivity. At about the same time, a team charged with responsibility for the transaction should be assembled. The first priority of that team should be to develop a detailed divestiture plan that would identify objectives, assign responsibilities, outline the sales process, and establish a timeline for implementation. The final element of the planning process should be the creation of a communication plan for announcing the prospective sale and its rationale to the employee populations (those of the parent company and those of the business being divested) and external constituencies, such as customers, suppliers, contractors, and, if appropriate, shareholders and the investment community.

(ii) Transaction Preparation.   The vast majority of divestitures are made by large businesses, frequently publicly traded companies. These companies usually opt to use a business broker or investment banker to assist in the sale. In these situations, the first step in this phase of the process will be to engage the broker or banker. If the business unit to be sold is of substantial size and is integrated into the infrastructure of the parent company, the seller might also engage an accounting firm to "carve out" dedicated financial statements that fairly represent the historical performance of the unit being sold.

   With assistance of the broker or banker, and under the direction of the divestiture team, the key managers of the business being divested would develop an offering memorandum or prospectus that would eventually be sent to possible buyers. In a similar manner, management presentations would be developed to be used by the management team to describe the business to a limited number of qualified, potential buyers after the field is pared down. Concurrently, business, legal, and financial documents of interest to a buyer would be assembled in a data room, a location where the information would be stored and indexed awaiting buyer review. During this phase, a list of potential buyers would be created by the broker or banker and vetted by the divestiture team. Once all of these tasks have been completed, the process would be ready to move to the execution stage.

(iii) Transaction Execution. The execution phase of the process begins with the announcement of the prospective sale. This announcement is essentially the implementation of the communication plan. Shortly thereafter, the seller would solicit initial bids from the list of potential buyers. Generally, a limited number of qualified buyers would be invited to participate in due diligence, and, ultimately, the field would be narrowed down to the final buyer. The parties would then proceed to contract and close.

(e) IMPORTANCE OF PROPER PLANNING AND DISCIPLINED IMPLEMENTATION. The transactions just outlined are generally of a material nature and entail significant risk for the participants. Although proper planning and disciplined execution cannot eliminate the risk inherent in such transactions, attention to preparation and execution can serve to substantially mitigate that risk. Although there is tremendous variability among and within the types of transactions described, several principles worth noting should be adhered to by those who manage M&A activities. They are:

- *Leave as little as possible to chance.* Establish clear objectives and develop detailed plans to attain them.
- *Ensure that transactions are properly resourced.* Draw on internal and external capabilities as needed and consider them investments, not expenses.
- *Respect the importance of staging and event sequencing within a transaction.* Transactions may differ in many respects, but they all follow a logical and natural process. Remember the adage, "Nine women can't make a baby in a month."
- *Do not be afraid to walk away from a transaction.* Do not give in to the temptation to salvage a transaction that does not make strategic or financial sense. At any point in time, the costs—both financial and psychological—should be considered sunk costs.

1.5 ROLE OF THE FINANCIAL MANAGER IN MERGERS AND ACQUISITIONS

(a) GENERAL. Financial professionals play a critically important part in all M&A activities. Often CFOs, controllers, and their functional equivalents (throughout this chapter referred to as financial officers) are logical candidates to play a central role in the acquisition process, and invariably should be involved in the transaction from beginning to end.

Although executed for strategic purposes, acquisitions are essentially financial transactions. As such, a fundamentally sound acquisition process typically draws on these skills and expertise of the financial manager:

- The ability to apply rigorous financial analysis to ensure sound decision making
- An understanding of the tax implications associated with the various forms a transaction may take
- An understanding of the applicable regulatory requirements
- The ability to model and/or critically evaluate business valuations
- Familiarity with the various financing options available as well as the ability to take a leadership role in structuring a financing package, if necessary
- Familiarity with the principles of acquisition accounting and their application
- The ability to plan, coordinatc, and execute an efficient and effective due diligence review

In addition to these financial/accounting capabilities, the senior financial officer involved in the acquisition process should also have strong leadership, organizational, and communication skills. A successful acquisition requires a substantial amount of cooperation and coordination among professionals and experts, both financial and non-financial, within and outside the acquiring company. It is imperative that those providing leadership ensure that the process is rationally structured (i.e., that the steps in the process are properly sequenced) and that the efforts of all those involved are not compartmentalized (i.e., that individual efforts are integrated and that all valid inputs are synthesized).

Capabilities the financial officer should bring to the acquisition process are discussed in detail in sections 1.5(b) through (e).

(b) COORDINATION. As a member of the core team managing an acquisition, the financial officer will have responsibility for coordinating much of the planning and execution of internal and external team members. This includes various line managers within the acquiring organization, as well as accounting, tax, and legal and other specialists who may reside outside the organization and/or in corporate headquarters in the case of larger, multilayered organizations.

(i) Internal Coordination.   The financial officer within the acquiring organization will generally be a co-equal partner with the business executives tasked with evaluating the merits of a transaction, making recommendations whether or not to proceed, and developing a plan of action, if the transaction is to be pursued. Additionally, he or she would play an important role in determining what internal resources would be needed to further evaluate the target company, to perform due diligence and, ultimately, to execute the transaction.

(ii) Coordination of External Experts.   The financial officer is the logical point of contact in dealing with a wide range of accounting, tax, legal, and regulatory issues and processes. Outside accounting and auditing resources may be accessed to conduct preliminary assessments and financial due diligence. The financial officer must also interface with the target company's internal and outside accountants. And, he or she will have responsibility for ensuring that acquisition accounting is properly implemented.

The financial officer is also the logical coordinator of input from internal tax professionals or external tax advisors. Tax expertise is drawn on early in the acquisition process to determine the tax ramifications in structuring the transaction and is involved in the post–due diligence stage to ensure optimal tax treatment prospectively.

Financial and legal considerations intersect frequently throughout the acquisition process. The financial officer is the logical individual to coordinate with legal counsel to ensure compliance with regulatory requirements and coordination of tax and legal issues, including the drafting of the Letter of Intent, ensuring compliance with SEC regulations, state law, and antitrust statutes, and negotiation of the final Purchase Agreement.

The financial officer also has a role to play in the financing process. This can range from the simplest type of involvement for a large company, such as notifying the corporate treasury function that money has to be wired to the bank of the sellers at closing date, to very complex negotiations with those funding the acquisition for a smaller organization.

(c) FINANCIAL ANALYSIS.   Not surprisingly, the financial officer plays an important role in analyzing the transaction and modeling the target company's business. This includes, among other things, evaluating the target company's business model and financial dynamics in the context of the acquirer's investment objectives and establishing the value of the target company.

(i) Financial Criteria and Metrics.   The financial officer provides critical input on the appropriateness of strategic fit, the reasonableness of projections of growth and profitability and assumed synergies and efficiencies, as well as comparisons of the acquiring company's projected performance before and after the proposed acquisition (to measure such things as potential accretion and dilution). These are important judgments and measurements for establishing a basis for a preliminary decision to proceed with a transaction.

(ii) Valuation.   Establishing a preliminary view of value and updating that view as additional information becomes available is a major role of the finance function in the evaluation of an acquisition. There is a variety of valuation methods used in the acquisition process, but larger, acquisitive organizations generally have a standard approach and models that are used to determine value, returns on invested capital, and other investment hurdles. Smaller, less acquisitive organizations may engage a valuation expert on a consulting basis. In either case, development of a credible valuation model requires a detailed understanding of the financial dynamics of both the acquiring and target companies and how synergies and efficiencies can be realized (and quantified) by the two. The financial officer is, unquestionably, in the best position to make these determinations.

(d) DETERMINATION OF DEAL STRUCTURE.   The financial officer is a key player in determining how the transaction can optimally be structured. Some of the major aspects of the potential structure he or she would consider are:

- Assets versus stock
- Earn-outs
- Working capital adjustments

(i) Assets versus Stock.   Almost invariably, the buyer will prefer to buy specific assets (vs. the stock) of the target company, because it enables the buyer to be selective about which assets are purchased and reduces the buyer's exposure to hidden liabilities and generally reduces its tax liabilities. Conversely, the seller will prefer a sale of stock, so that unfavorable tax treatment can be avoided and all assets and all liabilities are included in the transaction. There are special situations in which the seller can treat a stock sale as an asset sale and the buyer can realize some of the benefits of an asset sale. The financial officer, often in combination with tax specialists, can determine the range of acceptable options and quantify their costs and benefits.

(ii) Earn-Outs.   Earn-outs are an approach to risk sharing between the buyer and the seller. They provide the seller with upside potential in the form of additional consideration tied to company's post-acquisition performance above a defined level (usually measured by revenue and/or profit). The financial officer is in the best position to determine if the use of an earn-out makes strategic and economic sense and, if so, how the earn-out should be structured.

(iii) Working Capital Adjustments.   Letters of Intent will frequently require that sufficient working capital is left in the business at the point of the acquisition to fund ongoing requirements. In such cases, if the working capital falls below that level, then the purchase price would be adjusted downward accordingly. These adjustments are designed to offset any unusual removals of cash from the business. An analysis of the working capital dynamics over time by the financial officer is necessary to determine a fair and suitable working capital target, if a working capital adjustment is contemplated.

(e) DUE DILIGENCE.   Clearly, the lead financial officer involved in the acquisition should have responsibility for financial due diligence. This would include establishing due diligence objectives, managing the process, and reporting on its results. These functions are briefly discussed below.

(i) Establishing Due Diligence Objectives.   Although the due diligence process varies from transaction to transaction, there are some aspects of the process that are standard, regardless of the size and nature of the transaction. This includes the overarching objectives

of the review, which are to verify historical results and to validate forecasts and key assumptions (such as synergies, growth rates, and anticipated efficiencies) related to the valuation that the acquirer has established. The financial officer should be the primary architect in establishing these objectives.

(ii) Managing the Due Diligence Process.   By virtue of expertise and experience, the finance function is a logical one to take a lead role in structuring the due diligence program and process. A due diligence review is by no means the same as an audit. Constraints on time and resources limit the depth of the evaluations conducted. However, a due diligence review is analogous to an audit, and the types of procedures that should be reflected in the program are not unlike what one would find in an audit program. The financial officer and his or her staff will generally have the experience and expertise to shape the program and coach non-accountants in performing the review.

(iii) Reporting on Results.   Finance professionals are co-equal commentators, along with the business managers involved in the process, on the results of the due diligence. Because an acquisition is fundamentally an investment decision, recommendations to proceed or to disengage will largely be based on whether due diligence supports or contradicts the valuation that has been established. The financial officer is clearly in the best position to make such determinations.

CHAPTER 2

CANDIDATE SEARCH AND QUALIFICATION

2.1 INTRODUCTION

(a) STRATEGIC CONSIDERATIONS.   Merger and acquisition (M&A) activity has its roots in the strategic planning process. An output of that process is the identification and articulation of specific strategic objectives. These objectives typically reflect the need to enhance the company's product portfolio and/or improve its infrastructure capabilities and efficiencies. (The strategic planning process may also identify business units that no longer fit or support the company's strategy, and these units may be earmarked for divestiture. See Chapter 8 for a more expansive discussion of divestitures.)

Specific strategic objectives are peculiar to the individual company but, generically, they focus on these areas:

- Developing or acquiring new products for current markets
- Expanding the distribution channels for existing products
- Developing or acquiring new products for new markets
- Achieving economies of scale in order to lower production costs
- Increasing brand recognition of products and/or services
- Developing or acquiring new technology, intellectual property, or research and development (R&D) capability
- Establishing control over sources of supply by expanding operations toward suppliers' markets (backward integration)
- Expanding operations toward customers' markets (forward integration)

Once its strategic objectives are articulated, the company must decide whether those objectives will be pursued organically (i.e., through internal development) or inorganically (i.e., through acquisition or strategic alliance with another entity). The decision to pursue strategic objectives via acquisition should be based on a rigorous analysis to confirm that acquisition is the optimal investment alternative to pursue. At a minimum, this would entail consideration of all investment options and the trade-offs among them, including cost, timing (i.e., opportunity cost), synergistic benefits, and strategic fit.

(b) PHASES OF THE ACQUISITION PROCESS.   When inorganic development through acquisition is the choice, the acquisition process typically proceeds through five phases:

1. Search and qualification

2. Valuation and preliminary agreement
3. Due diligence
4. Contract and close
5. Postacquisition integration

The comprehensive, step-by-step approach presented in this and the chapters that follow illustrates transaction flow and sequencing as well as the interrelationships among the various steps in the process. It also reinforces the importance of the principles of planning, structure, and discipline in the execution of M&A transactions. Adherence to these principles will not guarantee a successful transaction, but the lack thereof is likely to result in an inefficient, or possibly even a failed, transaction.

2.2 OVERVIEW OF THE SEARCH AND QUALIFICATION PROCESS

(a) GENERAL.   The initial phase of the acquisition process generally follows the sequence of the steps listed next and discussed in detail throughout the remainder of this chapter. (A complete overview of this initial phase of the process and where it fits into the overall acquisition process is illustrated in Exhibit 2.1.)

Creation of a core acquisition team
Search for potential acquisition candidates
Screening of possible candidates
Identification of an acquisition target
Contact with the targeted company
Meeting with the principals of the targeted company
Qualification of the target company
Mutual agreement to proceed with the sale/acquisition discussion

(b) EARLY IDENTIFICATION OF AN ACQUISITION CANDIDATE.
The prospecting phase of the process assumes some degree of uncertainty about the universe of potential acquisition candidates to achieve a specific strategic objective. That uncertainty, combined with the desire to find the optimal candidate, drives the need for an extensive search. However, in some instances, the acquirer may have set its sights on a particular target company very early in the planning stages of the

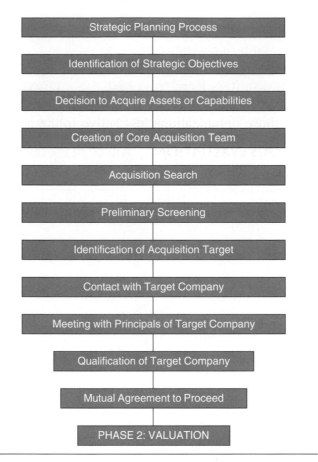

EXHIBIT 2.1   ACQUISITION PROSPECTING AND QUALIFICATION

process, thereby leapfrogging the search and identification aspects of the prospecting phase of the process.

(c) IMPORTANCE OF STRUCTURE AND DISCIPLINE.   This prospecting phase of the acquisition process has the potential to be chaotic. The net is cast broadly and inputs are sought from a variety of sources. For each candidate that is seriously pursued, often dozens or scores of candidates eventually fall by the wayside. Because of the large volume of leads generated, it is important that structure and discipline are brought to bear on the search and qualification effort. In this phase of the process, each successive step is designed to continually narrow the field of possible candidates and ultimately qualify the most attractive target or targets.

Understandably, the level of existing formal structure is generally greater—both organizationally and procedurally—with larger, acquisitive companies than with smaller, occasional acquirers. Simply stated, frequent acquirers learn from each transaction. This makes the process described in the remainder of this chapter especially relevant and helpful to those organizations less active in the acquisition arena.

(d) CONTINUOUS EVALUATION. Although the due diligence phase of the acquisition process is the one most closely associated with analysis and validation of assumptions, it is important to understand that *the acquisition process is one of continuous evaluation.* Candidate evaluation begins in the prospecting phase of the process with the accumulation of foundational information, the performance of preliminary analysis, and the formulation of initial insights. Although the view of the candidate will be refined as more information becomes available, early impressions should be documented. They represent the starting point of the evaluation process and the foundation upon which the final view of the candidate company will be built.

2.3 CREATION OF A CORE ACQUISITION TEAM

(a) GENERAL. Once a decision is made to aggressively pursue acquisition as the investment option, responsibility for the management of the acquisition process should be assigned to a core team of managers. This core team will shepherd the process along until such time that a transaction appears likely. Occasionally the team may draw on other managers to provide input or analysis on an as-needed basis, but expansion of the core team would generally not occur until it becomes apparent that a transaction will take place and formal due diligence is imminent.

The constitution of this core team will vary depending on a number of factors, most importantly the size and structure of the acquiring company and the anticipated size and strategic importance of the company to be acquired. Many larger companies are staffed with a planning officer (typically titled Senior Vice President [SVP] of Strategic Planning or SVP of Planning and Business Development), who would be the logical choice to take a lead role in the process. In smaller companies, the chief executive officer (CEO) would generally assign executives based on the nature of the acquisition. For example, if the target company is being acquired to supplement or expand the acquirer's product line or enhance its marketing capabilities, the assignment may go to the executive in charge of product development, or product management or marketing. Alternatively, if the target company is being acquired to enhance technical or technological capabilities, the assignment may go to the executive in charge of technology.

It is worth noting though that, even in the case of a large company with a business development function, the involvement of line executives who will inherit responsibility for the acquired company is extremely desirable. Their involvement is advantageous for purposes of establishing strong support for the transaction as well as developing an understanding of strategic and operational issues important to the successful integration of the new business, if the company is acquired.

(b) ROLE OF THE CEO.   The role of the CEO in the transaction will vary, based on the magnitude of the anticipated transaction and the style and preferences of the individual CEO. Large, transformational acquisitions typically will require the CEO's intense involvement. This may cause the CEO to take a leadership role within the core acquisition team. If not, day-to-day responsibility would be delegated to a senior executive who would maintain close contact with the CEO as the process progresses. Delegation of responsibility is generally the approach employed for smaller transactions that do not warrant the ongoing involvement of the CEO. However, when responsibility is delegated, it is critical that the assigned individuals are empowered by the company's CEO to make tactical judgments and decisions relative to the transaction and that they have ready access to the CEO to ensure that he or she is informed and able to make strategic decisions as the need arises. Regular contact between the CEO and the assigned team leader and periodic, scheduled meetings between the CEO and the core acquisition team are effective mechanisms for assuring the appropriate level of communication.

(c) NEED FOR THE INVOLVEMENT OF THE CFO.   Invariably, the chief financial officer (CFO) or a senior finance executive would be intimately involved in the acquisition process from inception. The importance of the financial aspects of the transaction makes such participation imperative. (See section 1.5 for a more detailed discussion of the financial officers' role in the acquisition process.) Typically, the finance executive would work closely with the lead business executive and provide key financial inputs as well as much of the analysis used for decision-making purposes. In larger, tiered organizations, the senior financial executive involved would also act as liaison with corporate tax, finance, legal/regulatory, and treasury functions. In smaller organizations, he or she would coordinate with outside specialists in these areas.

(d) ROLE OF THE M&A ATTORNEY. Arguably, the most important member of the acquisition team is a seasoned M&A attorney. The attorney should participate in the acquisition process from beginning to end. A knowledgeable and capable M&A attorney will help the team avoid critical mistakes as well as provide invaluable positive input while protecting the interests of the buyer throughout the transaction process. Internal counsel assigned to (and/or outside counsel engaged for) the transactions should be consulted early and often by the core team. Although the attorney or attorneys need not attend every meeting or be involved in every discussion of the core team, they must be kept abreast of developments and should provide input on all major decisions affecting the transaction.

2.4 SEARCH EFFORT

(a) GENERAL. The objective of the search effort is to identify the largest number of truly relevant candidates for acquisition. The effort should be anchored by a clear statement of the strategic objectives driving the acquisition and general guidance relative to the characteristics (e.g., nature, size, and market position) of the ideal target. This may exist in the acquirer's strategic plan or it may be expressed in a separate document (see Appendix 2.A for an example of such a document). Whatever its source or form, it is extremely important that the core acquisition team is provided with clear direction to guide its efforts.

The search effort is essentially one of intelligence gathering, and it can be broken down into two basic components: research and networking (see Exhibit 2.2 for a listing of the major intelligence-gathering resources). It should also be noted that intelligence gathering, to be effective, is an ongoing activity. Accordingly, research and networking should not be seen in the context of a single transaction; rather, they should be seen as continuous processes integral to the

Internal Data Resources

- Competitor files
- Acquisition targeting files

External Data Sources

- Annual reports
- SEC filings
- Analyst reports
- Trade and business periodicals
- Industry market research reports
- U.S Industrial Outlook
- Standard & Poor's industry data
- Dun & Bradstreet industry data
- Ward's Business Directory of U.S. Public and Private Companies
- Value Line Investment Survey
- The Directory of Corporate Affiliations
- Internet resources, such as Factiva, Lexis-Nexis, and Hoover's Online
- Company Web sites
- Company Webcasts

Networking Resources

- Trade association membership
- Trade show attendance
- Business brokers
- Investment bankers
- Industry consultants
- M&A attorneys

EXHIBIT 2.2   INDUSTRY AND COMPANY INFORMATION SOURCES

organization's ongoing acquisition efforts. This may create a challenge for the occasional acquirer, which might be unwilling or unable to maintain a robust intelligence-gathering capability. In such cases, the most effective use of resources is to ensure that internal records and industry relationships, particularly relationships with business brokers, are leveraged and that use of the Internet is optimized. These resources are discussed in detail in the sections that follow.

(b) RESEARCH. Research draws on a range of information sources, some of which may be housed internally and some of which may be available from external repositories. Internal records and analysis are generally extremely valuable intelligence sources. Most companies maintain files to track the behavior and intentions of competitors, and many companies also maintain files of some sort on potential acquisition candidates. These internal records are foundational to the search process and can be easily supplemented by readily available business, industry, and specific company information from a wide array of resources. A rich universe of relevant, easily accessible databases can enhance a company's research efforts. For example:

- *Dun & Bradstreet (D&B)* maintains one of the largest business information databases in the world, with risk and market information on more than 100 million businesses in almost 200 countries.
- *Standard & Poor's Stock Reports* contains information on 5,000 publicly traded companies with brief profiles and analysts' evaluations.
- *Value Line Investment Survey* covers 1,700 stocks in almost 100 industries and contains extensive analyst research and commentary.
- *Ward's Business Directory of U.S. Public and Private Companies* lists over 100,000 companies, the vast majority of which are privately held.

The contents of information databases such as these can be supplemented by other resources, such as industry publications, industry and company analyst's reports, and filings with the Securities and Exchange Commission (SEC) (in the case of publicly traded companies). Industry publications, such as trade journals and newsletters, are a valuable complement to such statistical and descriptive data. They provide ongoing, current views of developments in the industry and at individual companies within that industry. In addition, most industries are closely followed by analysts, market research firms, and industry experts or consultants. These industry monitors produce research reports, industry overviews, market trends, and company profiles that further supplement information that can be gleaned from databases and industry publications. SEC filings and annual reports also provide an extremely broad and deep array of historical information on public companies. For example, size, growth rates, and profitability data are readily available, both in print and online.

(c) USE OF THE INTERNET. The value of the Internet as an acquisition research tool cannot be overstated. In fact, the volume of information available is so great that *selectivity* has become a greater challenge than the accessibility of information. Virtually all of the sources described in the preceding section can be accessed via the Internet, as can other electronic databases, such as *Lexis-Nexis, Factiva,* and *Hoover's Online.* In addition, individual company Web sites generally provide company profiles and current, detailed product and/or service information. Also, some public companies participate in quarterly Webcasts with analysts that can be accessed by the public. These events provide excellent insights into a company's strategy as well as its recent performance. The Internet has evolved as a powerful research tool that can significantly facilitate intelligence gathering if used effectively.

(d) NETWORKING. Networking herein refers to the human contact aspect of intelligence gathering. The value of human intelligence cannot be overestimated. Research provides a solid base of understanding, but networking provides enhanced context and texture. Typical sources of human intelligence are trade shows, trade organizations, and industry intermediaries. Attendance at trade shows and participation in trade organizations provide real-time inputs into the intelligence-gathering process. Trade show attendance can be particularly valuable as a venue for observing new product introductions and for discerning changes in strategic direction by industry participants. Trade organization participation can be very helpful in establishing relationships with industry peers, facilitating contact when it is desirable.

Arguably, the most valuable sources of industry intelligence in the context of an acquisition are intermediaries. Intermediaries are a varied group but can be broken down into several key categories, namely business brokers, investment bankers, M&A attorneys, and industry consultants. All have the potential of providing insights that cannot be easily obtained from other intelligence sources. Invariably, they have their fingers on the pulse of the industry in which they operate; and very often they will have exclusive arrangements with their clients and may provide the only path to a potential acquisition. Each of these intermediaries is profiled next.

- *Brokers.* The term "broker" generally refers to business brokers, intermediaries who are active in the M&A arena in representing sellers or potential sellers. Their clients are frequently privately held companies or public companies wishing to divest of small to midsize business units. (Investment bankers, discussed next, generally fulfill this intermediary role in larger transactions involving the sale of a publicly traded company.) Brokers usually focus on discrete industries, or, if their business is more broad-based, they are organized along industry lines, with individuals or small groups focusing on specific segments of the broader market. Their industry focus enables them to be fully conversant in all aspects of the industry/market they cover. The best brokers understand the makeup and dynamics of their respective markets and are generally intimately familiar with their participants and, very often, their availability. Therein lies their networking value.

  As noted, brokers generally represent sellers, but they themselves try to remain networked with potential buyers, both strategic and financial, throughout the industry so that they are able to service their clients effectively. It should be understood that brokers have agendas. Because they are compensated on a commission/transaction basis, all things being equal, they have a vested interest in selling a business at the highest possible price. That said, serious acquirers should maintain periodic contact with all the major brokers in the industry being assessed for acquisitions.

- *Investment Bankers.* Investment bankers serve a role similar to that of brokers, but differ in a number of ways. Whereas brokers bring market expertise to a transaction, bankers generally bring financial expertise and capabilities. As noted, bankers generally play an intermediary role in larger transactions. Investment banking operations, more often than not, are part of a larger financial institution, usually a bank or brokerage house. Large financial institutions generally have other financial relationships with the client they represent and may be involved periodically with public and private placements of their securities. Bankers can be valuable from a networking perspective, but generally they are not as active as business brokers in the midmarket (transactions of less than $250 million), where the vast majority of transactions take place.

- *M&A Attorneys.* Attorneys active in the M&A arena frequently specialize in industry clusters (e.g., attorneys will generally not specialize in narrow industries, such as publishing, but very often will focus on broader clusters, such as communications, where issues such as intellectual property, technology, and distribution systems require specialized legal expertise). Although they do not engage in the actual selling activity, they can be valuable sources of potential or impending industry transactions. Acquisitive companies generally find M&A attorneys to be a very useful component of their networking efforts.

- *Industry Consultants.* Successful consultants who specialize in specific industries are constantly reinforcing their market knowledge. Their contact with clients causes them to continuously update their understanding of market trends and individual company intentions. Although confidentiality agreements and business ethics limit the amount of specific information they are able to share, they are still valuable sources of industry information and market trends, and occasionally are engaged by companies to represent them in the selling process.

(e) CONCLUSION.   Effective intelligence gathering is a multifaceted, cumulative, and ongoing process. Properly coordinated, research and networking efforts combine to yield a whole that is greater than the sum of its parts. Superior execution of the search process can provide the aspiring acquirer with a significant competitive advantage. Better market knowledge frequently enables the acquirer to be first in line with potential acquisitions, a position that ultimately can obviate competitive pressures.

2.5 CANDIDATE SCREENING

(a) BASIC CRITERIA.   Whereas the search process entails casting the net as wide as possible to identify the largest potential pool of relevant acquisition targets, the screening process is the first step in the effort to qualify the candidates identified. It is only a first step because the volume of information available at this point in the process is insufficient to fully qualify potential acquisition candidates. However, candidates can be screened based on broad criteria. Basic criteria such as those described in the sections that follow (and reflected in the acquisition mandate or charter) can be employed by the core acquisition team at this stage to begin the winnowing process.

(i) Availability.   The first determination in the screening process that the acquirer should attempt to make is whether the candidate company is in fact available for sale. Often it is very difficult and sometimes it is impossible to make this determination at this stage of the acquisition process. However, the unavailability of the target may be known based on information obtained in the research process or from the candidate's reaction to overtures made in the past. If there is concrete evidence that the property is unavailable, any further pursuit is a waste of effort and time, regardless of how attractive the property, and the company should be eliminated as a candidate for acquisition.

(ii) Strategic Fit.   Assuming that there is reason to believe that the property might be available for acquisition, the acquirer's most important consideration is the strategic fit of the candidate company. The acquirer should perform a detailed assessment of the assets and capabilities of the candidate company in light of the acquisition charter. This may require the input of line managers familiar with the company's products and services, and who are not on the core acquisition team.

The target's position in the market segment or segments it serves should be assessed as well. Acquirers frequently have stated preferences relative to a potential acquisition's market position and where it and its products are in their life cycles. For example, many acquirers will rule out targets that are not number one or number two in their market. Alternatively, some acquirers may find emerging companies with potential for significant expansion attractive targets. Brands and brand strength may also be an important consideration in the evaluation process, as might technology, intellectual property assets, or other unique capabilities.

The acquirer should also consider the applicability or desirability of acquiring *all* the assets and capabilities of the candidate. Frequently, a candidate will possess some assets or capabilities that are an excellent strategic fit, but others that are not. In such cases, the acquirer will have to determine whether the desired assets or capabilities alone can be acquired or, if not, whether an acquisition of the entire company makes strategic and financial sense. At a minimum, the screening process should clearly identify all operations that are extraneous to the strategic objectives of the acquirer.

(iii) Liabilities.   A company's assets and capabilities may be attractive, but the company may have "baggage" that offsets its appeal. Such baggage can take a number of forms and may be knowable at this point in the process. Typical examples of undesirable liabilities are actual or pending litigation and environmental exposures. The attorney on the team is best able to determine if there are such risks.

Although not a legal or accounting liability, issues associated with company culture may be cause for concern. This can be the case when there is an idiosyncratic owner or CEO. These issues may not be sufficiently crystallized to enable the team to make a definitive judgment on whether they are grounds to eliminate the company as a candidate. However, at a minimum, any concerns should be surfaced and cataloged for future consideration as more information becomes available.

(iv) Size.   At the extremes, size is a consideration for virtually all acquirers. Smaller acquisitions that can be folded into the acquiring company easily may be very attractive. However, the more complex its integration into the operation of the acquirer, the less desirable smaller acquisitions generally will be. At the other extreme, very large acquisitions may not be able to be funded or may be beyond the acquirer's ability or desire to digest.

As a general rule, the larger the acquisition, the greater the transaction risk (i.e., the risk that the acquisition price paid will not ultimately be justified). Premiums paid for anticipated synergies in large transactions are invariably large in absolute terms, and frequently quite material on a percentage basis. Synergies are discussed in detail in section 3.2, but suffice it to say here that large acquisitions have a poor record for producing the synergies projected and carry high transaction risk. In addition, they can present formidable integration challenges. If the acquisition charter has been thoughtfully crafted, general parameters on size will have been established and clearly inappropriate candidates can be screened out at this point in the process.

(v) Growth Characteristics. The historical growth pattern of the candidate is an important metric because it provides insight into the potential for future growth (effectively, "past as prologue") and because it provides a comparison to overall market growth (did the company underperform or outperform the market?). Although these measures are not absolute, they are suggestive of the business's health. They raise issues such as the maturity of product lines, the currency of technological capability, and the quality of management.

Company growth statistics are readily available for public companies. They are much more difficult to obtain for closely held businesses, but some of the sources identified in the section on candidate search will generally be helpful in this regard. At this stage in the process, the focus of the evaluation is not necessarily on precision; rather, it should be on establishing a preliminary view of where the business appears to be in its growth curve.

(vi) Profitability. Understandably, the profitability of an acquisition candidate is a critical issue for most acquirers. Over time, it is the ultimate measure of financial health. For publicly traded companies whose earnings per share (EPS) is tracked by analysts, significant dilution can be a show stopper, unless a compelling strategic argument can be made for acquisition. As with other financial metrics, profitability information is easily accessible for public companies. However, if the candidate company is privately held, it is generally extremely difficult to obtain such data. Because of its importance, to the degree that it can be determined, it should be part of the team's early assessment of the candidate company's relative attractiveness.

(vii) Potential Synergies and Efficiencies. Once a candidate has been identified, consideration of synergistic benefits should start immediately and should continue as long as the company remains in the sights of the acquirer. Buyers can expect to pay premiums for acquisition, especially in a competitive environment. It is the rule rather than the exception. Premiums assume the creation of a combined entity that will yield more value than the two organizations individually. That expectation establishes the relationship between acquisition price and synergies. Because of the fundamental impact of anticipated synergies, efforts to identify synergistic benefits should be part of the screening process. While it is unlikely that the acquirer can quantify these benefits

at this stage of the acquisition process (that generally will occur during the valuation phase), the team should identify such benefits on a qualitative basis.

(b) IDENTIFICATION. This screening process just described should dramatically reduce the field of candidates and result in the development of a short list of potential targets by the core acquisition team. That list, accompanied by an analysis and comparison of the targets, should provide the basis for a detailed acquisition discussion between senior management and the core team. That discussion is likely to initiate an iterative process, involving further research, analysis, and discussion, and should ultimately result in the prioritization of the list and direction to the core acquisition team to aggressively pursue the most attractive target company.

(c) CONTACT WITH THE TARGET COMPANY. Contact with the targeted company can be initiated in a number of ways. Clearly, if the company is represented by an intermediary, the intermediary will arrange for contact between the parties. In some cases there may be professional relationships between a member of the acquirer's management team and that of the target company. If such a relationship exists, it may be appropriate for the acquiring company to leverage that relationship to establish contact. In still other cases, a cold call from a member of the core team to a senior official at the target company may be an effective mechanism to initiate contact.

Once contact is made, it is a fairly straightforward proposition to determine whether there is any interest in continuing discussions. These discussions can result in a relatively rapid meeting among principals, or there may be a need for extended preliminary discussions to establish a comfort level on the part of the target's principals. The need for extensive discussion can result from a variety of factors. The need may be purely psychological, as in the case of a closely held company with a simple ownership structure, where the owners have a need to be courted. Or it could be the result of the need for extensive internal discussion in an organization with a more complex ownership structure and/or the requirement of the management to confer with its board of directors. In any event, the objective of making contact is to determine if the principals of the target company are open to the prospect of being acquired and willing to meet to discuss that possibility.

(d) CONFIDENTIALITY. If the principals are interested in pursuing discussions, the next step will be to execute a nondisclosure or confidentiality agreement (NDA) and schedule a face-to-face meeting. NDAs are agreements that:

- Protect the parties from misuse or misappropriation of confidential information
- Prevent premature disclosure of the transaction
- Establish rules for return of information if discussions are discontinued

The agreement may also include provisions for:

- Nonsolicitation of employees if the transaction falls apart
- A specific term for nondisclosure, nonsolicitation, or the return of proprietary information

Although the potential seller generally has disproportionate risk of disclosure, the acquirer also benefits from the execution of an NDA. An NDA also provides a psychological benefit to both parties because it enables them to have candid exchanges about sensitive issues.

(e) MEETING WITH THE PRINCIPALS OF THE TARGET COMPANY. Once the principals of the acquisition target have clearly expressed an interest in engaging in discussions about a potential transaction, a meeting of decision makers from both organizations should be arranged. Generally, this would include the principals, their financial advisors, and legal counsel. The acquirer's core team would minimally consist of the company's CEO and the assigned business and finance executives. The meeting should be used to:

- *Confirm the commitment of the owner to sell.* Until such confirmation is obtained, it generally makes no sense to invest any additional time and resources in the process.
- *Discuss how the acquisition process would unfold as well as estimate its duration.* More often than not, this is the first such transaction the prospective seller will have been involved in; the buyer will generally have had considerably more experience in this arena.
- *Discuss how value will be arrived at (as opposed to citing an actual value or purchase price) and other relevant aspects of the*

transaction. This may include a discussion of such things as the approach and methodology the acquiring company would employ to determine value (e.g., use of a discounted cash flow model), multiples for similar transactions recently experienced in the market, the form of the transaction (stock or assets), and how the transaction would be financed (cash, note, or stock).

- *Discuss the acquirer's need for information to begin the valuation process.* The volume of information that will be requested, if there is mutual agreement to proceed, will be fairly voluminous and highly proprietary. (A typical package of preliminary information is described in section 3.3(a).)

- *Confirm the acquirer's understanding of the financial dynamics of the target, specifically size, growth, and profitability.* There may be some reticence on the part of the target company to share precise details, but the acquirer should leave this meeting with an understanding of the order of magnitude of these metrics.

- *Discuss potential synergies that a business combination may yield.* This is an opportunity for the prospective acquirer to begin to validate its assumptions about synergies and efficiencies and identify any other such benefits that may not have been identified.

- *Obtain a preliminary understanding of the target company's culture.* Postacquisition integration of the target company will be a high priority of the acquirer. An early understanding of the target company's culture may identify potential impediments to integration that should be understood.

- *Discuss the ongoing role of owners, and possibly the existing management team, after the acquisition is consummated.* Frequently, these are important issues for both buyer and seller and are best addressed early in the acquisition process.

This initial meeting should not be seen as an opportunity to negotiate; rather, it should be used to take the measure of the prospective sellers, to confirm their commitment to the transaction, and to shape the sellers' expectations relative to price and process.

(f) QUALIFICATION. Once there has been a face-to-face meeting with the target company ownership and/or executive management, the acquirer will have had the opportunity to gather additional intelligence and confirm, modify, or contradict assumptions about the company's financial dynamics and fundamental attractiveness. Effectively, this is the second stage of the screening process. The acquirer will have had the benefit of further probing issues like strategic fit, size, growth, and profitability, but will also have had enough exposure and observation of the target's principals and team to make a preliminary read on their compatibility and their willingness to pursue further discussions and negotiations.

Clearly, if the principals are unwilling to proceed or if the acquirer's assumptions and expectations about the overall attractiveness of the target's business have not been met, the process would terminate. However, if the initial contact with the prospective acquisition substantially confirms the acquirer's assumptions and expectations, the next step would be for the acquirer to obtain internal agreement (among executive management and the board of directors, if appropriate). It is advisable that the core acquisition team documents this decision, the reasons for pursuing the opportunity, and any apparent risks associated with this course of action.

(g) MUTUAL AGREEMENT. Obviously, if a decision to terminate the acquisition effort was made, its principals would be notified of that decision. If the acquirer decides to continue in its efforts to pursue the target company, the parties would come to a mutual agreement to proceed. This would then lead to the next phase in the process, valuation and preliminary agreement on the terms of the transaction, the topic of Chapter 3.

ACQUISITION CHARTER

Note: The objective of this document is to provide clear direction to those involved in the acquisition process. It also ensures that internal data are leveraged in the search, identification process, and qualification of potential acquisition targets.

ACQUISITION CHARTER
XYZ CORPORATION
FEBRUARY 2007

The company is in the process of identifying and prioritizing acquisition candidates to support an acquisition program that is consistent with the company's strategy to substantially grow its presence in the market. The objectives, criteria, and process associated with this effort are outlined below.

TARGETING OBJECTIVES The objectives of targeting efforts are twofold:

1. Develop and actionable acquisition "Target List."
2. Create an expansive "Watch List" of companies that are of interest but are not immediate targets for acquisition.

PROFILE DATA To be included on the Target List, companies must fill a compelling strategic need and be accretive to earnings. In addition, to be included on the list, there must be a reasonable probability that the listed company is capable of being acquired (e.g., those companies that are known *not* to be available will not be included on the Target List).

Such companies that fulfill other strategic criteria, but are currently unavailable, would be captured on the Watch List. In addition, major competitors and significant emerging competitors will be included on the Watch List.

The data fields to be captured on both lists include:

- Company name and ticker symbol, if publicly traded
- Company location(s)
- Ownership form and owner name(s), if privately held
- Name of CEO, CFO, and Business Development executive (if applicable)
- Product/services descriptions
- Market segment(s) served
- Actual or estimated revenue for the most current fiscal year
- Estimated profitability
- Actual or estimated number of employees
- Comment/observations relative to recent developments of strategic interest (e.g., new product introductions, change in strategic direction, management changes, or any recent contact with senior executives).
- Date last updated

The Business Development Department will have responsibility for the maintenance of this information. By the very nature of acquisition prospecting, these lists will be dynamic and will change over time as candidates are added and deleted as circumstances dictate. The immediate objective is to establish a starting point in that process with initial lists of "targeted" and "watched" properties that are consistent with the company's growth strategy.

ACQUISITION CRITERIA Candidate companies that will be targeted for acquisition will be subject to these criteria:

- They will be among the market leaders in the segments of the markets in which they compete. This will generally mean that they are either number one or two in their market in terms of market share and reputation.
- They will generate revenue of $50 to 100 million.
- They will have demonstrated consistent growth at or above the rate of average market growth for the last three fiscal years.

- They will have delivered consistent earnings before interest, taxes, depreciation, and amortization (EBITDA) margins in excess of 15% for the last three fiscal years.
- They will generate postacquisition internal rate of return (IRR) of at least 17.5% and provide a payback of less than seven years.

CHAPTER 3

VALUATION AND PRELIMINARY AGREEMENT

3.1 INTRODUCTION

After the search and qualification effort has been completed, the next phase of the acquisition process involves the valuation of the target company and, assuming a continued desire to proceed with the transaction, the forging of an agreement on the basic terms of the transaction. The five specific steps in this phase of the process are:

1. Developing a valuation range for the target company
2. Determining acceptable terms of an agreement
3. Establishing internal agreement on terms and negotiating position
4. Negotiating the basic terms of the agreement with the seller
5. Documenting of terms of the agreement in the form of a letter of intent

These steps, preceded by a discussion of the valuation theory and practice and the treatment of synergies, are detailed hereafter.

3.2 VALUATION OVERVIEW

This overview of the valuation theory and practice is not intended to be an in-depth treatment of what can be a very complex and nuanced topic. It is an overview of the most important and relevant aspects of valuation, as they are applied to acquisitions. There is a vast amount of literature available on virtually every aspect of valuation.[1]

(a) **CONCEPTUAL FRAMEWORK.**   Application of valuation concepts can be complex and generally requires a high degree of expertise, experience, and professional judgment. However, conceptually, the valuation of an acquisition candidate is a fairly simple proposition. It entails establishing a range of possible purchase prices, based on the determination of both the *stand-alone fair market value* and the *investment value* of the target company. Whereas the stand-alone value is a baseline value of the company grounded in a calculation expected returns, *exclusive of synergies* resulting from the combination of the buyer and the seller, investment value is based on the expected returns *inclusive of the synergistic benefits* resulting from that combination. These two values establish the low end (stand-alone value) and the high end (investment value) of the valuation range a seller would accept and a buyer would pay for the target company. This range is based on the commonsense assumptions that a knowledgeable seller would sell for no less than stand-alone value and an informed buyer would be unwilling to pay more than investment value. (It therefore follows that, for a financial buyer or portfolio holding company with no synergistic assets, stand-alone value and investment value would theoretically be the same.)

Of course, a seller that is poorly advised or under duress may sell for less than stand-alone value. Similarly, buyers may pay more than investment value, usually as a result of overestimating the value of presumed synergies. Regardless, the concept of a valuation range bounded by stand-alone value and investment value is a very useful tool for those engaged in the acquisition process. The fact that prices outside that range are paid does not call into question the validity of this conceptual framework; rather, it generally reflects a poor understanding of the underlying financial dynamics of the transaction by either the buyer or the seller, or the proverbial "triumph of hope over good judgment" on the part of the buyer.

As noted, while this simple conceptual framework is absolutely valid and quite useful, its practical application is considerably more complex. This complexity stems from the fact that valuation is not a precise discipline and, in fact, consists of as much art as science. Even though historical information forms the bedrock for valuation analysis, the calculation of acquisition values is ultimately based on estimates, forecasts, and assumptions about *future performance*. Because valuations are rigorously modeled and neatly quantified, they tend to imply a degree of precision that may be misleading to those who are not familiar with the nature of the underlying analysis. The reality is that the practical application of valuation theory and methodology is a complex process that is as reliant on professional judgment as it is on financial and analytical skills. The discussion that follows is meant to illustrate the challenges and complexities associated with the valuation process.

(b) PUBLICLY TRADED ACQUISITION TARGETS. The most straightforward calculation of value, and the best point of departure for a discussion of valuation, is the stand-alone market value of a publicly traded company. Because there is an active market continually adjusting a public company's share price, a market-determined value can generally be ascribed to the target company with a high degree of confidence. In addition, a wealth of publicly available information and analysis that can be used to validate that value is easily accessible to the potential acquirer. As a result, more often than not, the floor on value of a publicly traded target can be readily determined.

While the determination of the low end of the range is relatively easy, the determination of investment value introduces a complicating new variable into the valuation process. As previously noted, the calculation of investment value includes the consideration of the synergies that will result from the business combination and integration of the acquired company into the acquiring company. And in addition to determining investment value, anticipated synergies play a pivotal role in establishing the price a potential acquirer will be willing to pay for the targeted business. It is therefore important to understand the nature of synergies and their impact on the valuation process and on negotiations on price.

(c) SYNERGY. The term "synergy" refers to financial returns that will result from a business combination that would not have been realized if the businesses had operated independently. Synergies predominantly take two forms: revenue or growth synergies and cost or operational synergies.

(i) Revenue Synergies. Revenue synergies result from market expansion (i.e., the ability of the combined company to reach more customers than the individual companies would operating on their own) and, in some cases, from increased pricing power. The former usually reflects the benefits of distribution leverage (e.g., cross-selling or using sales outlets not previously available to one of the transacting parties), while the latter reflects the ability of the new entity to leverage brand recognition (e.g., the use of the acquired company's superior brand to increase the price of the acquiring company's products). Revenue synergies such as these not only promote growth, they also enhance profitability and net cash flow. However, accurate quantification of these benefits is extremely difficult and can be quite speculative.

(ii) Cost Synergies. Operational efficiencies or cost synergies result from factors such as:

- Realization of greater economies of scale as a result of increased capacity utilization of plant and equipment
- Increased purchasing/bargaining power of the combined entity

- Elimination of redundant functions in the combined company
- Adoption of process improvements that have been developed by one of the parties to the transaction

All such synergies will generally yield increased profitability as well as increased net cash flow. However, even though operational synergies are relatively easy to identify and quantify, their realization is by no means assured and requires detailed planning and disciplined execution in the postacquisition phase of the transaction (see Chapter 6 for a detailed discussion of postacquisition integration).

(iii) Impact of Synergies on Purchase Price.   The introduction of synergies into the valuation analysis significantly increases the level of uncertainty, and risk, associated with acquisitions. This is because of the strong relationship between synergies and purchase price. Although an acquirer will be (and should be) reluctant to pay for all of the synergies associated with a combined entity, some portion of that value is almost invariably reflected in the purchase price. Therefore, for the acquisition to be considered successful, the returns generated by the acquisition must exceed the increment or "premium" paid above stand-alone value. However, the professional literature is replete with evidence that premiums paid frequently are not justified by the actual returns generated by the acquisition. This can usually be attributed to two factors: the overestimation of synergies and poorly executed integration of the acquired company. Because unrealized synergies are common, there is a direct relationship between the extent to which they are incorporated into the acquisition purchase price and the level of risk assumed by the acquirer.

(d) PRIVATELY HELD ACQUISITION TARGETS.   The challenges associated with establishing a valuation range for privately held companies are compounded by the lack of an established base or stand-alone market value for the targeted business. Even in cases where there have been recent sales of shares of a private company, it is unlikely that such sales are indicative of market value, whether stand-alone or investment. As a result, a valuation range will have to be established and a valuation model will have to be developed through detailed analysis and the application of one or more well-established valuation methodologies. Valuation approaches and methodologies that are used to do so are briefly described in the next sections, and more detailed discussion appears in Appendix 3A.

(e) VALUATION APPROACHES AND METHODOLOGIES.   Valuations are performed for a variety of reasons. In addition to acquisitions, they are performed for gift and estate purposes; for marital, partnership, and corporate dissolutions; for bankruptcy reorganizations; and for initial public offerings. Because of the differing objectives for each of these situations, the valuation methodology employed for each can differ, and it is important to match the approach used to the purpose of the valuation. There is general agreement among M&A professionals that the approaches most appropriate for the valuation of a business for acquisition purposes are the income approach, the asset-based approach, and the market approach. Each is briefly discussed in the next sections.

(i) Income Approach.   The income approach assumes that the value of the acquisition candidate is worth the future benefit of its net cash flow, discounted to present value, after reflecting investment risk. Net cash flow (also called free cash flow) is cash flow, including dividends, after all taxes and the funding of working capital and capital expenditures have been satisfied. Two variations on the income approach are commonly employed to value a business:

- *Discounted Cash Flow (DCF) Method.* When using the DCF method, net cash flow is converted to value with the application of a discount rate. The discount rate represents the total rate of return an investor expects to realize on the amount invested and is measured against similar investments of comparable risk. The discount rate is applied to a series of expected future net cash flow streams discounted back to a present value, and reflects the expected compounded growth rate of the cash flow stream.
- *Capitalization of Earnings Method.* When using the capitalization of earnings method, net cash flow is converted to value by the application of a capitalization rate. In contrast to the DCF method, which applies a rate to a stream of cash flows, the capitalization rate applies to a single-period net cash flow stream and is not influenced by an expected growth rate.

The DCF method is generally the preferred method in valuing acquisition targets. The capitalization of earnings method, in comparison, is a considerably more blunt instrument in that its result is built off a single year's performance. The DCF method allows for greater variability in net cash flow streams and therefore provides more flexibility in projecting future years' performance.

(ii) Asset-Based Approach.   The asset-based approach assumes that the buyer will not pay more for the purchase of the assets than it would pay for similar assets. Computationally, this approach calculates the current value of assets of the business, less the current value of its liabilities. The remainder is the current value of the company's equity. This approach can be applied to a company that is a viable operating entity (a going concern) and has material tangible assets, but is generally more appropriate for a company in liquidation. Assuming the targeted company is a going concern, the asset-based method should not be the primary approach, but can be more appropriately used in conjunction with the income approach.

(iii) Market Approach.   The market approach requires the search for companies that are comparable or similar to the acquisition candidate. Value is then determined by prices that have been paid for comparable properties in the same marketplace. The search criteria that the valuator uses are of paramount importance in locating similar companies. The more alike or similar the companies located, the more valid the data utilized. That data generally takes the form of multiples, most often of earnings before interest and taxes (EBIT) or earnings before interest, taxes, depreciation, and amortization (EBITDA) or revenue. For example, recent transactions involving like businesses in the same industry may have sold for seven to eight times EBITDA or 1.5 to 1.7 times revenue. These multiples are simply derived by dividing the selling price by the most recent year's revenue or income. The market approach is useful, but is extremely dependent on the true similarity (in size, breadth of products, nature of revenue streams, and financial performance) of the businesses being compared. Also, it is extremely important that the comparables are current. The passage of a relatively short period of time can make comparables stale, especially in industries that are highly reliant on technology.

The approaches just described are used in combination by most acquirers. Although methodologies differ based on the facts and circumstances peculiar to an individual transaction, as previously noted, there is a strong bias on the part of acquirers and their advisors toward the use of the DCF method as the primary valuation technique, with reliance on market multiples as a confirmatory tool.

3.3 VALUATION MODELING

(a) GENERAL.   The application of the principles, methods, and approaches described to create the valuation model begins with the accumulation of foundational information. In situations where the entity being valued is a publicly traded company, much of the information that can be used to create the model is available in the public domain. However, a good deal more proprietary information may be requested, if the anticipated transaction is a negotiated (friendly versus hostile) acquisition.

When the target is a privately held business, the availability of proprietary information is essential. A substantial amount of detailed information would be obtained from the target company. The volume and granularity of this information in this request, often characterized as a preliminary information request (to be distinguished from the comprehensive information request made in advance of conducting due diligence), must be sufficient to enable the acquirer to develop a valuation model that would reflect the stand-alone and investment value of the target company.

(b) PRELIMINARY INFORMATION REQUEST.   Typically, the acquiring company would request detailed financial, legal, tax, and other business information. The meeting with the principals of the target company, described in Chapter 2, should have alerted them to a forthcoming request for a substantial amount of such information. This information should include the items listed next, to the extent that they are available. The existence of certain of these items would be dependent largely on the size and sophistication of the target company. Additionally, the quality of the data will vary from company to company. For example, although audited financial statements are always preferable to unaudited statements, that preference may be academic in the case of smaller companies. The items requested should include:

- A complete set of historical financial statements for a minimum of the three prior years and year-to-date financial statements for the current year
- A description of key accounting policies for revenue, expense, and balance sheet accounts
- Budgets, with budget versus actual analysis for the last three years and year-to-date for the current year
- Tax returns for a minimum of the last three years
- Revenue breakdowns by major product line, by type of revenue (e.g., subscription, new versus renewal, long-term contract, discrete sales), and by customer category or concentration for the prior three years as well as year-to-date for the current year
- Profit by product line
- Expense breakdown, by direct and indirect cost and by functional cost, for the past three years and year-to-date for the current year
- Employee compensation by individual within each functional area, with a breakdown by salary, commission, bonuses, and benefits for prior three years and year-to-date for the current year
- Unusual or nonrecurring items impacting historical or future revenues and expenses (e.g., loss or gain of a major customer or customers, discontinuation of a product line, systems or infrastructure investment)
- A current organization chart and headcount for last three years
- A description of the target company's ownership structure (e.g., limited liability corporation (LLC), S corporation, C corporation), and individual ownership shareholdings and percent ownership

It is important that the ownership and management of the target company are sensitized to the need to be candid about the accuracy and completeness of the information being provided. It should be emphasized that there is a very high probability that any purposeful omissions or material inaccuracies would be uncovered during the due diligence process and that anything less than full disclosure would be counterproductive to efforts to consummate the transaction.

Before developing a valuation range, this information will enable the acquirer to confirm or modify its understanding of the dynamics of

the target company's business. Validation of the acquirer's understanding of the target's business model and financial dynamics is a critical
first step in the valuation process. An incomplete or inaccurate view
of the business will undermine the entire valuation process. Once the
acquirer's understanding has been established, it would usually then
build its model by executing these five steps:

1. Create normalized profit and loss (P&L) and cash flow statements for prior years
2. Create a base model establishing a stand-alone value for the
   target business
3. Create an investment value model for the business
4. Validate the value range that has been established through the
   use of multiples
5. Compare that value range with the acquirer's internal investment criteria

(c) **NORMALIZATION OF HISTORICAL RESULTS.**   The first step
in the modeling process would be the creation of normalized P&Ls
for at least the three complete prior years. If the financial statements
are audited, there may be little or no need to adjust these P&Ls. At
the other extreme, if the company is not audited and is run by an
owner/manager, the adjustments required to bring the statements into
conformity with generally accepted accounting principles (GAAP) can
be both numerous and material. Typical adjustments would relate to
revenue and expense recognition as well as adjustments to owner salary
and compensation to bring them into line with industry norms. Once
the P&Ls for these periods have been normalized, net cash flow (the
company's ability to convert income into excess cash) for each year
should be determined. This exercise will provide the acquirer with
a view of the fundamental growth and profitability characteristics of
the target and with the basis for creating a model for future growth,
earnings, and net cash flow. Exhibit 3.1 illustrates this normalization
process.

(d) **ESTABLISHING STAND-ALONE AND INVESTMENT VALUE.**
Because most acquisitions involve companies, business models, and
markets with which the acquirer has considerably more than passing
familiarity, the acquirer is generally able to develop a meaningful valuation model at this point in the process. As previously noted, although

$000's	2007	2006	2005
Revenue	$16,408	$13,895	$12,610
Adjustments	147	135	(515)
Normalized Revenue	**16,555**	**14,030**	**12,095**
Growth Rate	*18.0%*	*16%*	*—*
Expenses	13,944	12,186	10,408
Adjustments*	125	120	115
Normalized Expenses	**14,069**	**12,066**	**10,523**
Operating Income (before Income Taxes)	**2,486**	**1,964**	**1,572**
Depreciation and Amortization Addback	825	685	605
EBITDA	**3,311**	**2,649**	**2,177**
EBITDA Margin	*20%*	*18.9%*	*18%*
Free Cash Flow (FCF)	**1,093**	**874**	**718**

EXHIBIT 3.1 NORMALIZED P&L AND CASH FLOW

*Typical adjustments to revenue and expenses include those involving recognition policies to bring the P&L in conformity with GAAP and those involving excess compensation for owner/managers of closely held businesses.

there are a variety of valid valuation methods that can be used, individually or in combination (see Section 3.2(e)), most companies and valuation consultants utilize a DCF model for valuation of acquisitions. The base model will incorporate assumptions about the growth and the profitability of the acquisition target, exclusive of synergies, over an extended period of time (anywhere from 5 to 15 years). A second iteration of the model will reflect the impact of revenue and expense synergies. These two iterations will effectively provide a value range that would be the basis for ultimately determining a purchase price. This process is illustrated in Exhibits 3.2 and 3.3.

Exhibit 3.2 presents a simple model for purposes of illustration. It calculates the stand-alone enterprise value of the company using a five-year growth period, with an assumption of zero growth in the terminal year (year 6) and thereafter. Growth and profitability are projected based on assumptions about the potential of the business and the outlook for the market. Free cash flow (FCF) is then projected based on the assumed impact of tax and interest expense, capital expenditure needs, and changes in working capital needs on gross cash flow. FCF is then adjusted to reflect the present value (PV) of the FCF for each of the first five years of the projection. The PV of the FCF stream is

Assumptions:
- 10% discount rate for years 1 through 5
- 14% discount rate for terminal value
- 67% reduction of EBITDA to reflect income tax and interest expense, capital expenditures, and changes in working capital needs

$ 000's	2007 Actual	2008 Projected	2009 Projected	2010 Projected	2011 Projected	2012 Projected	Sum of PV	2013P Terminal
Revenue	$16,555	$19,866	$22,650	$24,950	$26,400	$27,460		$27,460
Growth %	18%	20%	14%	10%	6%	4%		0%
EBITDA	3,311	3,925	4,530	5,240	5,545	6,040		6,040
EBITDA Margin	20%	20%	21%	21%	21%	22%		22%
Adjustments*		2,650	3,020	3,490	3,695	4,025		4,025
Free Cash Flow (FCF)		1,325	1,510	1,750	1,850	2,015		2,015
Discount Factor (10%)		.909	.826	.751	.683	.621		
PV of FCF		1,205	1,247	1,314	1,264	1,251		
Sum of PV							6,281	
Terminal Period PV (14%)							14393	
Enterprise Value							20,674	

*Adjustments include taxes, interest, and capital expenditures, as well as changes in working capital.

Exhibit 3.2   Stand-alone Value (Zero Terminal Growth in Year 6, 2013)

calculated by simple addition. The terminal value is then calculated by applying a discount rate to the FCF (FCF/discount rate). The PV of the FCF stream is added to the terminal value to arrive at enterprise value, $20,674,000 in this example.

The model in Exhibit 3.3 employs the same methodology as that used in Exhibit 3.2, but also includes the effect of revenue and cost synergies and assumes a more favorable flow through of these benefits (40% versus 33% in model in Exhibit 3.2) to FCF.

The two models reflected in Exhibits 3.2 and 3.3 establish the outer limits of the valuation range. As indicated in the discussion of synergies and premiums, these extremes theoretically identify the minimum price a seller would accept and the maximum price a buyer would pay. In practice, the range of realistic executable price will generally fall somewhere within this range. Where it would fall depends on a number of variables, but price is strongly influenced by comparable

Assumptions:
- 10% discount rate for years 1 through 5
- 14% discount rate for terminal value
- 60% reduction of EBITDA to reflect income tax and interest expense, capital expenditures, and changes in working capital needs

$000's	2007 Actual	2008 Proj.	2009 Proj.	2010 Proj.	2011 Proj.	2012 Proj.	Sum of PV	Terminal 2013
Revenue	$ 16,555	19,866	22,650	24,950	26,400	27,460		27,460
EBITDA	$ 3,311	3,925	4,530	5,240	5,545	6,040		6,040
Revenue Synergies (net)	$ —	1,500	1,600	1,700	1,800	1,900		1,900
Cost Synergies (net)	$ —	1,000	1,050	1,100	1,150	1,200		1,200
Adjusted EBITDA		6,425	7,180	8,040	8,495	9,140		9,140
Adjustments*		3,855	4,308	4,824	5,097	5,484		5,484
Free Cash Flow (FCF)		2,570	2,872	3,216	3,398	3,656		3,656
Discount Factor (10%)		0.909	0.826	0.751	0.683	0.621		
PV of FCF		2,336	2,372	2,415	2,321	2,270		
Sum of PV's							11,715	
Terminal Period Value (14%)							26,114	
Enterprise Value							**37,829**	

*Adjustments include interest, taxes, capital expenditures, as well as changes in working capital

EXHIBIT 3.3 INVESTMENT VALUE (ZERO TERMINAL GROWTH IN YEAR 6, 2013)

61

recent transactions, the degree to which the buyer is willing to pay for synergies, and the desire of the seller to consummate the transaction. The influence of recent transactions (in the form of multiples of revenue and income) and the buyer's willingness to pay more than stand-alone value (in the form of payback on the investment) are discussed in the next two sections.

(e) VALIDATION OF VALUE BY USE OF MULTIPLES.   The values determined would generally be validated through the use of multiples. The model will provide potential values that can then be expressed in terms of multiples of revenue and income (usually EBITDA). For most industries, multiples of revenue and income for recent transactions can be determined through research and discussion with intermediaries (although the input from intermediaries should be viewed with healthy skepticism and validated independently). The search for multiples should focus on acquisitions that have the same characteristics as the one being considered: The more comparable the transaction, the more applicable the resulting multiple. (See section 3.2(e) for a discussion of the use of multiples.) If the company is acquisitive, it will generally compare the value range arrived at with recent acquisitions of similar companies.

Exhibit 3.4 illustrates the use of multiples as a validation tool. In this case, it identifies the multiples paid for four recent transactions in the same industry. They establish a reasonable range of revenue and EBITDA multiples that can be used to validate the range of potential

$000's	MULTIPLES	
ACQUISITION CANDIDATE	REVENUE	EBITDA
High Value ($32,000)	1.93	9.66
Mid Value ($28,500)	1.72	8.61
Low Value ($25,000)	1.51	7.55
Recent Transactions		
Able Co.	1.12	7.7
Bravo Co.	1.23	7.6
Charlie Co.	1.42	7.9
Delta Co.	1.76	8.9

EXHIBIT 3.4   COMPARISON OF RECENT MULTIPLES

	High Value	Middle Value	Low Value
Payback	9.7	8.5	7.6

EXHIBIT 3.5   COMPARISON TO INVESTMENT CRITERIA

prices a buyer might consider. While the use of multiples is an inexact process, recent transaction prices in this case suggest that the market has been at the low end of the range suggested for the target company (i.e., $25 to $32 million).

(f) COMPARING VALUATIONS TO INVESTMENT CRITERIA.   The final step in this process would generally consist of comparing the price range to internally developed investment criteria. The criteria used will generally be some combination of investment payback, internal rate of return, or return on invested capital. These criteria would be applied on a sensitivity basis, illustrating returns or payback at a variety of prices throughout the value range.

Exhibit 3.5 illustrates a comparison of payback benchmarks at the prices in the range being considered. In this illustration, simple payback (not affected by present value) has been used. Present value–based payback, internal rate of return, and other return calculations are also commonly used in concert with each other.

(g) USE OF A COMPREHENSIVE MODEL.   The process just discussed and illustrated in Exhibits 3.1 through 3.5 is intended to present the process and data in bite-size chunks, so that the dynamics of the approach can be more easily understood. In practice, the vast majority of acquiring companies and virtually all valuation practitioners use a comprehensive model that incorporates most of the data presented in the preceding exhibits. That model would generally be supported by detailed inputs and supporting schedules, but typically has a summary page such as that presented in Exhibit 3.6.

Buttressed by this information, the acquirer can begin to establish its position on price. It should be obvious that the soundness of that position is only as good as the assumptions that are embodied in the modeling process and the quality of the comparable information on multiples.

| | Discount Rate 10% Tax Rate 40% | Acquirco 15-Nov-06 | | | | | | | | Terminal Year |
	2005	2006	2007	2008	2009	2010	2011	2012	2013
Revenue	$ 12,095	$ 14,030	$ 16,555	$ 19,866	$ 22,650	$ 24,950	$ 26,400	$ 27,460	$ 27,460
Synergies	$ —	$ —	$ —	$ 1,500	$ 1,600	$ 1,700	$ 1,800	$ 1,900	$ 1,900
Total Revenue	**$ 12,095**	**$ 14,030**	**$ 16,555**	**$ 21,366**	**$ 24,250**	**$ 26,650**	**$ 28,200**	**$ 29,360**	**$ 29,360**
Expenses	$ 10,523	$ 12,066	$ 14,069	$ 16,862	$ 19,179	$ 20,912	$ 22,180	$ 22,877	$ 22,877
Synergies	$ —	$ —	$ —	$ (1,000)	$ (1,050)	$ (1,100)	$ (1,150)	$ (1,200)	$ (1,200)
Total Expenses	**$ 10,523**	**$ 12,066**	**$ 14,069**	**$ 15,862**	**$ 18,129**	**$ 19,812**	**$ 21,030**	**$ 21,677**	**$ 21,677**
Operating Income	**$ 1,572**	**$ 1,964**	**$ 2,486**	**$ 5,504**	**$ 6,121**	**$ 6,838**	**$ 7,170**	**$ 7,683**	**$ 7,683**
Depr. & Amort.	$ 605	$ 685	$ 825	$ 921	$ 1,059	$ 1,202	$ 1,325	$ 1,457	$ 1,457
EBITDA	**$ 2,177**	**$ 2,649**	**$ 3,311**	**$ 6,425**	**$ 7,180**	**$ 8,040**	**$ 8,495**	**$ 9,140**	**$ 9,140**
FCF	$ 718	$ 874	$ 1,093	$ 2,570	$ 2,872	$ 3,216	$ 3,398	$ 3,656	$ 3,656
Growth Rates									
Revenue		16%	18%	29%	13%	10%	6%	4%	0%
EBITDA		22%	25%	94%	12%	12%	6%	6%	0%

EXHIBIT 3.6 SUMMARY PAGE OF VALUATION MODEL

Price Sensitivity

Purchase Price	Payback	2005 Multiples	
		Revenue	EBITDA
$ 25,000	7.6 Years	1.51	7.55
$ 26,750	8.0 Years	1.62	8.08
$ 28,500	8.5 Years	1.72	8.61
$ 30,250	9.1 Years	1.83	9.14
$ 32,000	9.7 Years	1.93	9.66

←—Relevant Range

Recent Comparables

Company	Revenue	EBITDA
Able Co	1.12	7.7
Bravo Co	1.23	7.6
Charlie Co	1.42	7.9
Delta Co	1.76	8.9

EXHIBIT 3.6 (continued)

3.4 ACQUIRER'S INTERNAL APPROVAL TO PROCEED

Once the valuation model has been finalized, the preparation of a brief paper (sometimes referred to as a position paper) is recommended, describing the business, outlining key issues, explaining the strategic rationale for the proposed acquisition, summarizing the contents of the valuation model, and recommending a purchase price range. This paper would be used as a focal point for internal discussion and—whether as-presented or modified as a result of these discussions—as the basis for approval to proceed.

The approval process will vary based on a number of variables, such as the size and structure of the acquiring company and the size of the acquisition. Smaller acquisitions may be within the purview of the CEO, while larger transactions will generally require the approval of the board of directors. In any event, the documentation of the case to proceed (or not) should be a standard procedure in the decision-making process.

This is the point in the process where the position of the acquirer should be solidified. Assuming that there is agreement on the fundamental attractiveness of the target company, the acquirer must determine the basis upon which it will proceed. This obviously includes a decision on price, but would also include a position on other aspects of the transaction (such as a stock or asset purchase and how the transaction will be financed). Once a decision to proceed has been made, a ceiling on purchase price should be established and firm positions on other major terms of the prospective transaction should be agreed on, as should the approach or strategy best employed to gain closure with the candidate company.

It is strongly recommended that the discussion include consideration and analysis of a "walk-away" position (i.e., a price above which the company would walk away from the transaction) and the strategic implications of a decision to do so. The importance of establishing such a position at this juncture in the process cannot be overemphasized. The organization will be investing a significant amount of time and resources in pursuing the acquisition target, and there will be a tendency to continue to stretch the bounds of the terms agreed to internally, if a clear line of demarcation is not made. Although the attractiveness of the target may not change as the process continues, the wisdom of the investment will if the terms of a prudent walk-away position are exceeded.

Additionally, this is an appropriate point in the process to decide who from the acquiring company would be assigned to flesh out the due diligence team. An early alert to the prospective team members should be issued, and they should be briefed on the nature of their participation and the anticipated timing and duration of the due diligence process.

3.5 ESTABLISH A MUTUAL UNDERSTANDING OF BROAD TERMS OF THE TRANSACTION

Once the decision has been made to pursue the transaction on the basis of the terms agreed to internally, negotiations with the seller on those terms would proceed in earnest. This is usually a phase in the process requiring intense involvement of the acquiring company's CEO.

Generally, discussions with the principals would have been ongoing since the initial meeting, and a basic outline of the transaction is likely to have evolved since that meeting. Frequently, negotiations will have progressed to the point that there is tacit agreement on price or price range and other major aspects of the transaction. This is not to suggest that agreement would be automatic; often negotiations are protracted and iterative, requiring numerous discussions and meetings.

Although the nature and tone of negotiations will be peculiar to each transaction, there are a number of constants that should be adhered to:

- Negotiating in good faith
- Extensive use of and reliance on professional advisors
- Knowing if and when to terminate negotiations

More than any other type of transaction, the sale and purchase of a business requires the parties to negotiate in good faith. The parties should, therefore, be disposed to a high degree of disclosure. The seller will be compelled to do so in the face of the extensive discovery afforded the buyer in the form of due diligence and contractual commitments (representations and warranties) as well as being subject to potential state and federal sanctions if it makes material misrepresentations. The buyer is less constrained by these factors but must consider the practical aspects of transitioning the business to its control.

It is also important that both parties avail themselves of professional support and analysis. Valuation professionals, M&A attorneys, and brokers provide valuable inputs. When both parties to the transaction are well advised, the likelihood of closing a mutually acceptable deal is substantially enhanced.

While the valuation process has a large subjective component and price is a highly negotiable element of the transaction, a relatively narrow range of value is very likely to be established, and any expectation to arrive at a price substantially outside that range is generally unlikely. If expectations cannot be set or reset within that range for both buyer and seller, it is usually advisable to terminate discussions, at least for the immediate term.

Once agreement has been reached, at a minimum, this should include explicit concurrence on price, the form of the transaction (stock or assets), consideration given (cash, note, or acquiring company's stock), and the nature of the seller's relationship with the company postacquisition. It is absolutely necessary that there is agreement on these issues before the transaction proceeds to the due diligence stage. Absent such agreement, the potential for misunderstanding and for the transaction to unravel is dramatically increased.

3.6 DOCUMENTATION OF THE BROAD TERMS OF THE TRANSACTION

(a) GENERAL. The major terms of the agreement are often documented in the form of a letter of intent (LOI). The issuance of a LOI is an important, necessary step in the process in the vast majority of acquisitions. Some have argued that, because the LOI is a nonbinding document, it is of limited use. Although significant terms of an LOI are of a nonbinding nature, the letter serves as documentation and confirmation of the broad terms agreed to and sharply reduces the potential for future misunderstanding. It also will usually provide a time frame within which to complete the transaction on an exclusive basis.

(b) CONTENT OF LETTER OF INTENT. The form and content of an LOI can vary considerably from transaction to transaction. It is imperative that the attorneys involved in the transaction draft or review its content because, although most aspects of the LOI are nonbinding, some binding terms (such as confidentiality and nonpoaching of employees) may be included and can have future ramifications. Typically the LOI should include (but not necessarily be limited to) reference to these terms:

- *Purchase price.* The proposed price, subject to any potential adjustments that may have been agreed to
- *Clear indication of what is being purchased and the structure of the transaction.* Whether the transaction contemplates a sale of stock or assets, and if assets, a description of which assets, as well as any liabilities that may be assumed as part of the transaction
- *Form of consideration.* Whether consideration will take the form of cash, note, or purchaser's stock
- *Timing.* A clear indication of target date for the consummation of the transaction
- *Escrow.* An indication of any amounts to be held in escrow and the term of any such holdback
- *Consulting or employment agreements.* A clear indication of any ongoing role that the seller may play postacquisition
- *Access to books and records.* A clear understanding of the need for unencumbered access to the books and records of the company

The LOI should also note an expiration date, usually a week to 10 days from the time of issuance, to motivate rapid execution. For an illustration of a sample letter of intent, see Appendix 3B.

3.7   REQUEST FOR INFORMATION TO BE USED IN DUE DILIGENCE

A formal information request should accompany the LOI, and it should identify all those books and records that the acquisition candidate should make available for due diligence. Traditionally, the company being reviewed will choose a location (referred to as the data room), either on or off company premises, where the information will be housed and reviewed. However, technology is increasingly being utilized to create virtual data rooms to satisfy this requirement.

The acquirer should also ask that these data be indexed, usually using the information request as the basis for that indexing. An example of an information request document is illustrated in Appendix 3C. At this stage of the process, the acquirer should also discuss other important aspects of the due diligence review with the principals of the target company. This would include the need for presentations by key members of the target company's staff, the ability to interview managers and legal and accounting advisors, and the opportunity to tour the premises where business is conducted.

The steps just described provide a solid basis for proceeding with a productive due diligence. This process ensures that there is a mutual understanding of terms, process, deliverables, and timing. In addition, it ensures that there is internal agreement on the part of the acquirer on all the important aspects of the prospective transaction.

End Notes

1.   For a thorough treatment of valuation, these texts can be consulted: *Valuing a Business*, 4th ed. (McGraw-Hill, 2000, New York, NY) by Shannon Pratt et al. is arguably the most comprehensive treatment of valuation theory and practice; *Applied Mergers & Acquisitions* (Wiley, 2004, Hoboken, NJ) by Robert F. Bruner provides an exhaustive treatment of valuation, particularly of publicly traded companies; and *Valuation for M&A: Building Value in Private Companies* (Wiley, 2001, New York, NY) by Frank Evans and David Bishop focuses on issues and techniques particularly relevant to the valuation of closely held businesses.

A SURVEY OF VALUATION METHODOLOGY AND TECHNIQUES

VALUATION MODEL

The valuation modeling process requires thorough research of the acquisition candidate. When performing a valuation, the valuation analyst has the responsibility to compile relevant internal and external data about the company, its industry, and the effect of the current economy on its value. It is critical that the valuation analyst identify the risk components that materially impact value.

To complete a valuation, an analyst should include:

- The standard of value
- The operational analysis
- The financial analysis; the valuation approach
- The valuation methodology
- The analysis of discounts and premiums
- The estimate of value

The first step in a valuation engagement is the preparation of a *document request form*. This form will list all the relevant data to be compiled by management of the acquisition candidate. In addition to a review of the documents, the valuator analyst should interview the company's management and key employees. These interviews should be conducted on the company's premises to enable the analyst to gain a more thorough perception of such things as the strengths and weaknesses of the company, its location, the condition of the equipment, the size and condition of the facility, and the level of obsolete product lines.

STANDARD OF VALUE   Defining the standard of value is fundamental to correctly valuing the acquisition candidate. Choosing an incorrect standard of value can materially impact the valuation. Typically, the appropriate standard of value in an acquisition is either *fair market value* or *investment value*. *Fair market* is defined by the Internal Revenue Service in Revenue Ruling 59–60 as: "the price at which the property would change hands between a willing buyer and a willing seller when the former is not under any compulsion to buy and the latter is not under any compulsion to sell, and both parties have reasonable knowledge of the relevant facts."

Investment value is the specific value of the targeted company to the owner or future owner(s).

Both the fair market value and investment value standards consider the subject company to be a going concern. While market value assumes a *hypothetical buyer and seller,* investment value assumes *a specific buyer and seller.*

Other standards of value that might be considered include:

- *Fair value.* A statutory standard (see state law for applicability) that typically applies in dissenting shareholder cases. This standard usually applies to minority shareholders. Most courts do not recognize a discount for lack of marketability; a material difference between fair value and fair market value.
- *Intrinsic value.* A value that is interpreted between analysts. It is usually based on the investor's perception of true worth.
- *Liquidation value.* A value an owner can realize after the sale of all company assets less costs associated with the sale, including commissions, administrative, taxes, and professional fees.
- *Book value.* A generally accepted accounting principle, not a valuation standard. It represents the net of assets less liabilities.
- *Going-concern value.* Not considered a standard of value as discussed in the previous examples. A going-concern value assumes that the subject company is a financially functioning operating entity.

OPERATIONAL ANALYSIS   To determine the value of an acquisition candidate, the valuation analyst must have a thorough understanding of its organizational processes. To evaluate the potential risk factors of a company, the analyst should consider:

Company Operations
- Is the company divided into departments? (Ask for an organization chart.)
- Is decision making centralized or decentralized?
- What are the departmental responsibilities?
- What are the flow transaction processes?

Products and Services
- What are the company's products and services?
- What is the cost to purchase products and services?
- Does the targeted company lose money on any products and services? Which ones?

Territory Expansion
- What is the current sales territory?
- Has the targeted company prepared a demographic study of the sales territory?
- How far can the territory be expanded?

Industry Trends
- What is the current and future outlook for the products and services being sold by the targeted company?
- Is the targeted company current with industry trends? If not, why not?

Competition
- Where does the targeted company currently rank in terms of market share?
- Where did the targeted company rank five years ago?
- If the rank is different today, why?
- Does the targeted company keep up with the competition? If not, why not?

Relationship with Customers
- What is the customer profile?
- Who are the top five customers?
- What is the billing and collection history of the customer base?

Relationships with Vendors

- Who are the five largest vendors?
- What products are purchased from them?
- What are the payment terms and payment histories?

Policies and Procedures

- Does the company have written policy and procedure manuals?
- Is the company in compliance with the Department of Labor?
- Are the benefits of the targeted company equal to the acquiring company's benefits?
- If the benefits are more comprehensive, how will they impact the acquiring company's staff and operating budget?

Employee Relations

- Who are the key employees?
- What is the compensation history?
- What training programs are in place?
- What are the staff performance review policies?

Quality Control Process

- Who is in charge?
- What is the quality control process?
- Is it written?

FINANCIAL ANALYSIS   When performing a financial analysis, the valuator analyst should interview the acquisition candidate's management and key employees to discuss the company's financial status, including information that is and is not disclosed on the financial statements.

A thorough understanding of the balance sheet and income statement items will enable the valuation analyst to evaluate the targeted company's policies and procedures. These may include policies and issues related to cash investment, credit, bad debt, inventory valuing and pricing, inventory obsolescence, fixed assets/depreciation schedules, loan balances, contingent assets and liabilities, retirement plan accruals, nonrecurring income and expenses, legal fee invoices, tax provisions, contracts and agreements supporting notes payable, labor contracts, buy-sell agreements, information about prior sales of company stock, supplier agreements, customer agreements, and other significant agreements and contracts.

In addition to the these data, the valuator should also analyze corporate and partnership documents, related party agreements, sales and marketing data, capital and operating budgets, and sales forecasts.

When analyzing the targeted company's financial statements, ratio computations should be analyzed to compare the targeted company's significant ratios with those within the industry. In-depth analyses of financial ratios for a prior five-year period should be conducted. They will provide a valuator with a good trend analysis that can be used to evaluate strengths and weaknesses in the targeted company. Following are five examples of financial ratios that should be considered when valuing a business. (The ratio formulas are beyond the scope of this discussion.)

1. *Asset ratios.* To measure the efficiency of the targeted company's assets
   a. Accounts receivable turnover
   b. Inventory turnover
   c. Sales to net working capital
   d. Sales to fixed assets
   e. Sales to total assets

2. *Capital structure ratios.* To measure long-term solvency of the business
   a. Total debt to total assets
   b. Equity to total assets
   c. Long-term debt to total capital
   d. Fixed assets to total equity
   e. Debt to equity

3. *Income statement coverage ratios.* To measure the margin by which certain company obligations are being met
   a. Times interest earned
   b. Coverage of fixed charges

4. *Income statement profitability ratios.* To measure operating performance
   a. Gross profit to sales
   b. Operating profit to sales
   c. Pretax income to sales
   d. Net income to sales

5. *Return on investment ratios*

    a. Return on equity

    b. Return on total assets

VALUATION APPROACH   There are three approaches to determining the estimated value of a business:

1. Income approach

2. Asset-based approach

3. Market approach

    The approach that is most appropriate when valuing tangible and intangible assets directly corresponds to the type of asset being valued. The valuator can use one or a combination of the three approaches to assess value of the acquisition candidate.

Income Approach   The theory behind the income approach is that the value of the acquisition candidate is worth the future benefit of its revenue streams, discounted to present value, after reflecting investment risk and the time value of money. When evaluating the acquisition candidate, both dividends and net cash flow contribute to income inflows. This measurement is termed "economic income" and is converted to value with the application of either a discount rate or a capitalization rate. The discount rate represents the total rate of return an investor expects to realize on the amount invested. The total rate of return is measured against similar investments of comparable risk. Although the discount rate applies to a series of expected future income streams discounted back to a present value, the capitalization rate applies to a single-period income stream. The discount rate reflects the compounded expected growth rate while the capitalization rate is not influenced by the expectant growth rate.

Asset-Based (Cost) Approach   The asset-based (cost) theory suggests that the buyer will not pay more for the purchase of the asset than for what a similar asset could be purchased. Computationally, this approach equals the current value of assets less the current value of liabilities. The remainder equals the current value of the company's equity. This approach applies to both a company that is a viable operating entity (going concern) and to a company that is not considered a viable operating entity (liquidation basis). The asset-based approach usually applies to a control interest valuation. It is also an appropriate approach to use when a target company has material tangible assets. Assuming the targeted company is a going concern, the asset-based method should not be the primary approach. The income approach would be more appropriate.

Market Approach   The market theory suggests that, in valuing companies, the analyst should search for ones that are comparable or similar to the acquisition candidate. The search criteria that the valuator analyst uses are paramount in locating similar companies.

The market approach provides a minority interest market value. Using the market approach, the valuator must adjust the multiple computations from a minority interest value to a control interest value. The multiplier represents a relationship between the gross purchase price and either book value or a defined revenue stream.

VALUATION METHODOLOGY   A number of commonly used valuation methods can be used by the valuator analyst. The chosen methodology is dependent on the valuation approach(es) selected—for example, income, asset-based, or market (as previously discussed). These approaches provide specific methodologies for computing the value of an acquisition candidate. The most commonly used valuation methodologies are discussed hereafter.

Capitalization of Earnings   Capitalization of earnings (an income approach) is appropriate for valuing a profitable business when the investor's goal is to provide an annual return on investment in excess of reasonable owner's compensation. To utilize this method, future estimated earnings is calculated and converted to a value by dividing it by a capitalization rate. This method does not separate tangible and intangible assets and should not be used for businesses that are capital intensive.

Discounted Earnings Method   The discounted earnings method (DEM), another income approach, is also referred to as the discounted cash flow method. With this method, it is important to define the earnings that will be used to compute the company's value. Examples of earnings used in this method are cash flow from operations and after-tax cash flow. Using a discount rate instead of a capitalization rate, the theoretical assumption is that the total value of the business is determined by computing the present value of the projected future earnings plus the present value of the terminal value. When acquiring a company, the valuation analyst should be confident that the projected earnings are based on management's assumptions and represent reasonable future earnings.

Price/Earnings Ratio Method   Theoretically similar to the capitalization of earnings method, the price/earnings ratio method (an income and market approach) uses market comparisons to determine the multiple to be applied against after-tax earnings. The future estimated net income (after tax) is capitalized by a weighted average price/earnings ratio of comparable publicly traded companies. In using market comparisons, the difficulty is in finding publicly traded comparables that are similar to the targeted company. Usually this method is more appropriate when valuing larger and more diverse companies.

Dividend-Paying Capacity Method   The dividend-paying capacity method, another income and market approach, is appropriate for valuing large companies that pay dividends. Also an income approach because of its capitalization focus, it uses market comparisons in its methodology. The future estimated dividends to be paid, or that have the capacity to be paid, are capitalized by a five-year weighted average of dividend yields of five comparable companies. Usually this method is more appropriate when valuing larger and more diverse companies.

Net Asset Method   The net asset method (an asset-based [cost] approach) addresses the fair market value of each asset and liability at the date of valuation. The value of the equity equals the adjusted assets minus the adjusted liabilities. Typically, an acquiring company would use this method to purchase underperforming assets.

Excess Earnings (Return on Assets) Treasury Method   The treasury method (an income and asset-based [cost] approach) distinguishes between adjusted net tangible assets and intangible assets. The intangible value component is computed by capitalizing the earnings of a business that are in excess of those earnings related to a reasonable return on the fair market value of the company's net assets. The total value of the business is then determined by adding the tangible net adjusted assets, at fair market value, to the intangible value as computed above. This methodology utilizes industry averages or average returns on equity from comparable companies to determine a reasonable return when computing an appropriate capitalization rate.

Excess Earnings (Return on Assets) Reasonable Rate Method
Instead of using an industry rate of return as in the treasury method, a reasonable rate of return (another income and asset-based [cost] approach) is applied to the adjusted net assets, such as the cost of debt. The intangible value component is computed by capitalizing the earnings of a business that are in excess of those earnings related to a reasonable return on the fair market value of the company's net assets. The intangible value is then added to the fair market value of the adjusted net assets to determine the total value of the business.

Guideline Method   The guideline method (a market approach) compares the targeted company with public companies that are similar in nature. It is necessary, however, for the valuator to be confident that the public companies (otherwise known as the guideline companies) and the targeted company are similar in operations, product and service lines, and geographic location.

It is important for the valuator to use professional judgment when analyzing both qualitative and quantitative data. To properly compare the research data to the targeted company, the valuator should make adjustments to the financial statements of the public entities being used for comparison. The valuator must also refine the search criteria to make consistent and reliable comparisons, to select the appropriate ratio measurement, and to determine if further adjustments should be made for the premiums and discounts.

Examples of ratio measurements include:

- Price/earnings
- Price/pretax earnings
- Price/earnings before interest and taxes (EBIT)
- Price/earnings before interest, taxes, depreciation, and amortization (EBITDA)
- Price/book value

This chapter does not discuss in detail the steps to search out comparable guideline companies.

Direct Market Data Method   The direct market data method (a market approach) involves the use of actual industry sales transactions as a comparison with the acquisition candidate. It is sometimes difficult to validate comparable sales data because the comparative studies do not disclose the underlying reasons for the acquisition. Since transactions are often consummated because of acquired synergies, favorable purchase terms, and to achieve a greater market share, certain multiples, such as gross selling price to sales revenue, may not be appropriate measures of value. The valuator may need to adjust the direct market data used for a discount or premium.

Rule of Thumb and Formula Method   The rule of thumb and formula method (another market approach) is a derivative of the direct market data method. A multiplier or formula is developed from industrywide experiences in the marketplace. The multiplier or formula addresses the relationships between the sales price and an industry-specific operational unit of measurement.

The rule of thumb and formula method does not factor in risks that can materially impact value. These risk factors may include capital structure, stability of earnings, variances in market share, and management depth. This method does act, however, as a sanity check when comparing value estimates computed from other more sophisticated methodologies.

ANALYSIS OF DISCOUNTS AND PREMIUMS   When discussing discounts and premiums, it is necessary to focus on minority versus controlling interest and the lack of marketability of the acquisition candidate.

Discount for a Minority Interest   Minority interest discounts are relevant to the value of a company because a minority share of stock lacks the control features that the majority share possesses and consequently is sold at some discount from the worth of a share of a controlling interest. Conversely, when a majority block of stock is acquired, a premium is often applied because of the rights of the control owner. Control owner rights include the right to:

- Appoint management
- Determine management compensation prerequisites
- Set policy and change the course of business
- Acquire or liquidate assets
- Select people with whom to do business and award contracts

- Make acquisitions
- Liquidate, dissolve, sell out, or capitalize the company
- Sell or acquire treasury shares
- Register the company's stock for public offering
- Declare and pay dividends
- Change the articles of incorporation or bylaws[1]

Premiums   When a strategic buyer acquires a controlling interest in a targeted company, the price paid in excess of the minority share is called a control premium. A strategic buyer will often pay a premium because of synergies that can develop as a result of the acquisition of the candidate.

Discount for Lack of Marketability   When an owner of a publicly traded stock decides to sell a share, his or her broker is contacted and, within a short period of time, the value of the shares is converted into cash. When a shareholder of a privately held company decides to sell his or her shares of stock, however, the value of the ownership interest cannot be converted into cash as quickly, because privately held companies do not have access to a ready market. The difference between what an investor pays for similar publicly traded stocks and the price paid for privately owned stocks is known as the discount for lack of marketability.

In terms of discounts for lack of marketability for controlling interests, the general theory is that these discounts are typically lower than similar discounts for lack of marketability for minority interests.

For purposes of an acquisition, the price paid for a controlling interest in a privately held company may or may not be adjusted to reflect a discount to the transaction price. Ultimately, the valuator must analyze all the relevant facts and circumstances of the transaction and use professional judgment in determining the appropriate discounts.

ESTIMATE OF VALUE   When valuing an acquisition candidate, two types of assets should be valued: tangible assets and intangible assets. Tangible assets are real and personal property. They are reflected on the company's balance sheet at their cost. These need to be adjusted to fair market value at the date of valuation.

---

1.   Shannon P. Pratt, Robert F. Reilly, and Robert Schweihs, *Valuing Small Business and Professional Practices,* 2d ed. (Burr Ridge, IL: Irwin Professional Publishing, 1993), p. 526.

Intangible assets include such items as customer lists, employment contracts, licenses, trademarks, patents, copyrights, covenants not to compete, and goodwill. Intangible assets must be evaluated to determine their impact on the targeted company's earning capacity. The values of these intangible assets are, however, often difficult to determine.

Goodwill is an example of an intangible asset. The Internal Revenue Service in Revenue Ruling 59–60 Section 4.1(f) describes goodwill, with respect to earnings, in this way:

> In the final analysis, goodwill is based upon earnings capacity. The presence of goodwill and its value, therefore, rests upon the excess of net earnings over and above a fair return on the net tangible assets. While the element of goodwill may be based primarily on earnings, such factors as the prestige and renown of the business, the ownership of a trade or brand name, and a record of successful operations over a prolonged period in a particular locality also may furnish support for the inclusion of goodwill.

In evaluating the existence of goodwill, it is useful to ask three questions.

1. Can the purchaser reasonably expect continued excess earnings?
2. Does the business have a competitive advantage in its industry?
3. Will the business be continually supported by its existing customer base?

Another example of an intangible asset is the covenant not to compete. To preserve the targeted company's value, Internal Revenue Service Code Revenue Ruling 77–403 addresses three questions to consider when allocating value to a not-to-compete agreement. The three questions are:

1. Absent a covenant-not-to-compete, would the seller compete?
2. Does the seller have the ability to compete?
3. Does the seller have the feasibility to compete?

To determine the answers to these questions, it is important to assess the covenantor's (the seller's) ability to compete with respect to:

- Age, health, and educational background
- Geographic location of residence

- Financial capability
- Technical expertise
- Equipment and machinery
- Continued relationships with company employees, industry vendors, and professionals
- Legal capacity
- Ability to attract existing clients/customers
- Future interest in competing
- Business reputation
- Extent of consultation services performed
- Current occupation subsequent to sale
- Ownership interest in new companies
- Preasset sales report citing advantages and disadvantages of sale
- How values for not-to-compete agreement were determined
- When the not-to-compete agreement became part of the sale negotiations
- How the length of the covenant was determined
- How the total amount of the covenant was determined
- Appraisals of the business (prior to or as part of the purchase)

To identify the tangible and intangible assets of an acquisition candidate, the valuator analyst should interview the company owners and management. The analyst should also review legal documents and company minutes as well as analyze the company's financial statements for a minimum of five years, as applicable.

The most practical ways to determine the value of intangible assets are by capitalizing earnings, applying earnings multiples, or using the present value of discounted future earnings. When determining the capitalization rate, a number of risk factors can materially impact the final rate. These risk factors include external factors, internal factors, and investment factors.

Examples of external factors include expectations and existing conditions of the economy, the targeted company's industry, and its competition. Internal factors include the targeted company's stability of earnings, management depth, financial position, and the size of the business being valued. Investment factors include the amount of the investment into the business being valued, the associated risks of the investment, the expectation of capital invested, and the potential liquidity of the proposed investment.

SYNTHESIZING THE ESTIMATE OF VALUE: FINAL COMMENTS

The valuator analyst, in computing the estimated value of an acquisition candidate, must complete an in-depth due diligence process. The relevant information collected is then assessed to determine the selected valuation approach(es) and methodology(ies) to be utilized to determine the final estimated value of the acquisition company.

The professional judgment of the valuator analyst is fundamental to this process. The choices made by the analyst in constructing the valuation process affect the end product (i.e., the estimated value of the acquisition candidate). For example, when using the market data or guideline methods, the search criteria for comparable companies become the basis on which all later decisions are made. Comparable companies must be similar not only in industry, operations, and sales volumes, but geographic location as well.

Failure to undergo a thorough due diligence process can create a significant decrease in value, over time, in relation to the negotiated price paid to the seller. In one situation known by the author, an insurance agency and its client list was purchased. The valuator failed, however, to closely analyze the client list. It was later found that the acquiring company had purchased a list of clients primarily composed of elderly people who were unlikely to renew their policies because of their age. The future revenue streams of the client list were so significantly impacted that the acquisition price, in reality, was not justified.

In another scenario known by the author, a company purchased the customer list of an acquiree without realizing its economic dependence on only a few customers. Loss of just one client had a devastating financial effect on the acquiring company. Better examination of the client list by the valuator analyst would have avoided this situation.

Horror stories abound from acquiring companies whose valuation analyst completed an engagement without thoroughly understanding the risk factors, the marketplace, and the company operations. All applicable valuation procedures cited in the chapter should be followed to provide a sensible estimate of value.

ILLUSTRATION OF LETTER OF INTENT

[Date]

John A. Seller, President Company B [Address]

Re: *Purchase of Stock*

Dear Mr. Seller:

This letter sets forth our preliminary understanding with respect to the proposed purchase by Company A of all of the issued and outstanding shares of stock of Company B. For convenience, we will refer to Company B as the "Company," to you individually as the "Seller," and to Company A as the "Buyer."

1. *Purchase and Sale.* Buyer intends to purchase from Seller all of the issued and outstanding stock of the Company and related noncompetition rights for total consideration of $2 million. This consideration will be paid by delivery of $1 million in cash at the time of closing and by further delivery of a promissory note in the amount of $1 million, bearing interest at 8 percent per annum, amortized over 10 years, with a 5-year balloon.

2. *Security for Payment.* The $1 million promissory note will be secured by the following: (i) the unlimited personal liability of Buyer; (ii) a pledge of all the shares of stock of the Company;

and (iii) the guarantee of the Company and a security interest in all the furniture, fixtures, and equipment of the Company.

3. *Consulting and Noncompetition.* Seller will enter into a consulting and noncompetition agreement providing for services to be rendered on a part-time basis by the Seller to the Buyer after the closing date on a mutually agreed-upon schedule. The Seller will further agree not to compete with the business of the Company for a period of 5 years and within a radius of 250 miles of the current principal place of business of the Company.

4. *Exchange of Information.* The Buyer will immediately have the right to inspect, through its accountants and other agents, all of the books and records and assets of the Company. The Buyer agrees that all such information is confidential and proprietary to the Seller, and the Buyer will use such information only for the purpose of evaluating its proposed purchase of the Company. The Buyer may disclose such information to its lending bank and its agents, including its accountants and attorneys, but in all other respects, the information shall be held confidential. In the event the purchase does not occur as intended hereunder, all such information shall be returned to the Seller. None of such information shall be used in any manner that is competitive with or adverse to the Company or the Seller.

5. *Final Agreement.* Within 30 days after acceptance of this letter of intent, the Buyer will advise Seller if its inspection of the books and records pursuant to paragraph 4 (preceding) has been satisfactory. If so, the Buyer will promptly proceed to have its legal counsel draft a standard Stock Purchase Agreement, including customary representations and warranties on the part of the Seller and the Company for transactions of this type. Such agreement shall be subject in all respects to review and negotiation by the Seller and the Seller's legal counsel.

6. *Confidentiality of Transaction.* The existence of this letter of intent and the intention of the parties to engage in the transactions described herein are confidential and will not be disclosed to any third party except those parties essential to the investigation and negotiation procedures related hereto.

In particular, the Buyer will not disclose its intention to purchase the Company to any of the Company's employees, agents, customers or suppliers, except with the prior written consent of the Seller.

7. *Operations Prior to Closing.* Seller will not cause or permit the Company to make any distributions or payments (other than salaries at current levels) to or for the benefit of Seller. Seller shall cause Company to continue to operate its business, consistent with past practice, through the date of closing.

8. *Closing.* The closing for the transactions contemplated by this letter of intent shall occur within 90 days of the date of this letter of intent at a time and place designated by the Buyer.

9. *Exclusive Dealing.* The Seller agrees that, for so long as Buyer is proceeding in good faith to complete its due diligence and to negotiate in completing an agreement of purchase, the Seller shall not enter into substantive negotiations with any third party for the sale of the Company or any interest therein. The Seller may, however, terminate its obligations hereunder 30 days after acceptance if the Buyer has failed to advise the Seller by that time that it has satisfactorily completed its investigation under paragraph 4, and the Seller may further terminate 60 days hereafter if the parties have not by that date entered into a formal and enforceable Stock Purchase Agreement.

10. *Legal Effect.* This letter agreement represents an expression of intent of the parties only, except that the provisions of paragraphs 4 and 9 shall be enforceable in accordance with their terms. The parties intend to use this letter of intent as a basis for consummating a sale transaction, and both parties agree to use their best efforts to enter into a formal and binding contractual agreement as promptly as possible hereafter.

If you agree with the foregoing, please indicate your concurrence by signing and returning one copy of this letter of intent to the undersigned.

Very truly yours,
Buyer
Agreed to this _____ day of _____, 20___.

ILLUSTRATIVE INFORMATION REQUEST

XYZ SOFTWARE CO

Please provide the following information related to the due diligence review to be conducted from MM/DD/YR to MM/DD/YR. Label all documents clearly and provide an alphanumeric index that corresponds to the following listing.

GENERAL

1. All contracts and agreements (value exceeding $5,000) including agents, distributors, customers, and suppliers.

   a. Include all licenses or royalty arrangements.

2. Detail of business ownership.

   a. Shareholders and ownership amounts.
   b. Special severance agreements, management bonus plans, or other agreements.

3. Details of any borrowing arrangements.

   a. Restrictions/covenants.
   b. Details of any security interest in assets.

4. Copies of copyrights, patents, trademarks, or service marks.

   a. Include copies of all in-process applications or filings.

5. Standard forms of customer software license agreements.

    a. Copies of any special license agreements or maintenance/ service agreements.

6. Details of all insurance coverages.

FINANCIAL

1. Financial statements for last three years and current year to date.

2. Current budget or business operating plan for last year and this year with commentary, if any.

3. Tax returns.

4. Reconciliation to company financial statements.

5. Details of any audits or other tax disputes in progress.

6. Monthly company financial statements for last year and current year to date.

7. Bank statements and reconciliations for same periods.

8. Access to accounting system, records, and historical financial reports.

9. Current balance sheet and supporting records and reconciliations.

10. Current accounts receivable detail, records, and aging reports.

11. Access to customer transaction records and customer correspondence files.

12. Details of historical write-off experience.

13. Current inventory records.

14. Access to physical inventory.

15. Fixed asset records.

    a. Access to fixed assets.

    b. Documentation relating to building purchase (e.g., closing statements).

    c. Building mortgage and documentation of tax assessments.

    d. Building appraisal.

    e. Inventory of fixed assets, purchase amounts, purchase dates, and depreciated value.

HUMAN RESOURCES

1. Current organization chart with all personnel (including contractors and temporary and staff), job titles, and date of hire by company.

2. Copies of job descriptions, if available. Alternatively, describe roles/responsibilities of positions.
3. Salary, bonus, profit sharing, and merit increase information for all employees for the last three years and current year.
4. Sales compensation plans, if used (commission or bonus plans for sales performance).
5. Details of employee benefits and retirement plans.
6. Company policies on vacation, sickness, bereavement, work schedules, and performance reviews.
7. Quantify accrued leave time for employees (vacation and any other).
8. Identify any employee terminations for cause during last three years and current year.
9. List commonly observed company holidays.

LEGAL/REAL ESTATE

1. Any threatened, potential, or pending litigation.
2. Any communication regarding noncompliance with government laws or regulations.
3. Any documentation regarding compliance with government laws or regulations.

CUSTOMER INFORMATION, ORDER ENTRY, AND BILLING SYSTEMS

1. Customer information and order system description, documentation/user guides.

    a. Access to customer information/billing system to obtain detailed customer records (lists, transactions, reports).
    b. Identify and describe software used.

2. Indicate file format of the customer database. Describe structure of these files (fields, lengths, etc.). Describe options and formats available from this software.

    a. Total number of customer records.
    b. Aging of records (number of unique records for versions of product).
    c. Estimate percentage of customer records for which address information is current, and basis for estimate (e.g., feedback from customer mailings).

3. Same information as in 2 above for prospect database(s).
4. Complete list of all products, services, and combinations sold.
5. Indicate standard billing terms for individual customers, agents, distributors, resellers, and institutional customers. Provide explanation of all special contracts/agreements.
6. Is a maintenance service offered or any add-on for-fee or for-free service/support for customers? If yes, describe.
7. Describe how upgrades are processed.

SHIPPING/PRODUCTION

1. Describe shipping procedures and methods, including turnaround time.
2. Estimate what inventories will be on hand at settlement.
3. Provide estimates or feedback from distributors or sell-through of inventory.
4. Provide samples of packaging and products shipped.
5. Indicate product labeling requirements.
6. Provide the bill of materials (include costs) for each product or sku.
7. Indicate media used for each product (download, CD, DVD, diskettes).
8. Indicate total volume of units shipped annually for last three years.
9. Indicate mix of domestic and foreign shipments.
10. Indicate advertised delivery methods, fees, and delivery/shipment times.
11. Describe production procedures.

SALES AND MARKETING

1. Documentation of agreements with agents, resellers, and distributors (other than provided under A1).
   a. List of agents, resellers, and distributors.
   b. Pricing and discount policies with these sellers.
   c. Policies relative to Sales return and Allowances.
2. Monthly sales by product (unit and dollars).
3. Report of sales by channel (direct, agents, distributors, resellers) and end-user customers.

    a. Sales from top 10 channel customers (revenue and units).

    b. List of top 50 end-user customer organizations (revenue and units).

4. Analysis of sales by geographic region.

    a. Domestic sales and unit volume by state.

    b. International sales and unit volume by country.

5. Describe any unique pricing/discounting practices.

6. Copies of any recent market research or customer satisfaction studies.

7. Collateral materials.

    a. Provide a list of standard pricing and volume discounts.

    b. Provide a list of all site licenses and terms. Including sales history for the last three years.

    c. Provide samples of all product literature, ads, newsletters, faxable documents, price sheets, and so on.

    d. Provide complete set published product reviews.

    e. Describe how networks are sold and priced.

    f. Provide sample pieces and records of promotions mailings; include costs listed used, and sales results.

    g. Indicate ad commitments in place for current year.

    h. Indicate trade show schedule commitments for current year.

    i. Are ad agencies or public relations firms used? If so, identify and describe their roles and services provided.

8. Describe demo program, packaging/documentation, and any functional limitations.

    a. Volume of physically shipped demos last year.

    b. Volume of downloads from Web site last year.

BUSINESS PLANNING AND DEVELOPMENT

1. Describe all alliances, agreements, and ongoing initiatives with principal contacts.

    a. Current status.

    b. Objectives going forward.

2. Provide product plans and designs.

3. Provide marketing budget for last year and current year.

    a. Budget by category (ads, exhibits, channel promotions, direct mail, training/travel).

    b. Reviews in process.

    c. Agency projects.

PRODUCT/TECHNOLOGY

1. Source code documentation.

    a. Describe source code.

        i. An inventory of source code and executables, including third-party software dependencies.

        ii. A road map of source files.

        iii. File structure of the database.

        iv. File structure of other files such as output formats and connection files.

        v. Review documentation of the structure of the application.

        vi. Describe the coding conventions.

    b. Provide documentation of known bugs.

    c. Provide a fix log.

    d. Identify version-control software and procedures.

2. Source code itself.

    a. A list of product software configurations for each platform and product variant.

    b. What language is the program written in?

    c. Which compliers were used (specific versions)?

    d. Is the code based on a standard application framework?

    e. What other third-party tools were used?

        i. Are they provided with source code?

        ii. Do they have documentation?

        iii. What is the licensing consideration?

    f. How is the source code structured and layered?

    g. Are there discreet levels?

    h. Are calls to the database engine localized/encapsulated into a specific layer, or are they made directly throughout the program?

      i. Where is the source code archive?

      j. Is source code in escrow? If so, provide details.

3. Technical/user feedback.

      a. Provide technical help desk records for each product/platform (inquiry volume, and bug reports).

      b. Provide any written testing guidelines.

      c. Provide all FAQ/responses.

4. Product end-user documentation.

      a. Describe utilities and software used to produce documentation and online help files.

      b. Where is the archive of documentation files located?

MISCELLANEOUS OPERATIONS

1. What is the current volume of incoming phone calls, faxes, e-mails, and correspondence? Provide a breakdown of activity for Sales versus Tech Support versus Order Processing.

2. Describe internal network operating system(s).

3. Inventory software products used and license agreements/users:

      a. E-mail.

      b. Calendar scheduling.

      c. Word processing, database, and spreadsheet.

      d. Development and programming.

      e. All other business and productivity applications.

CHAPTER 4

PREPARING FOR AND EXECUTING DUE DILIGENCE

4.1 INTRODUCTION

Once preliminary agreement has been reached and a letter of intent (LOI) has been executed, the process proceeds to the due diligence phase. Due diligence refers to evaluative measures employed by an acquiring company to:

- Validate financial, legal, and business representations made by an acquisition candidate.

The author would like to thank Daniel T. May and Brian W. Meara, who wrote the version of this chapter that appeared in the last edition.

- Validate the acquirer's assumptions and expectations regarding the future performance of the business.
- Assess the quality of the target company's management, staff, technology, and operations.

For the vast majority of transactions, these evaluations are an indispensable component of the acquisition process. They will either confirm or modify the acquiring company's estimation of the acquisition candidate's value, and, ultimately, they will mitigate the risks associated with what is almost invariably a significant potential investment.

Due diligence, by definition, is ambitious in scope. Given the time constraints under which due diligence is generally conducted (typically, less than 10 days in duration), it is critically important that the process is properly staged, effectively organized, and efficiently conducted. Accordingly, this chapter discusses measures and procedures that enhance the efficiency and effectiveness of that process.

By far, the most common type of acquisition transaction is that of smaller, privately held businesses by midsize and large companies. This discussion, therefore, focuses on the process and procedures involving these types of transactions, although most of the concepts and procedures described are applicable to all types of acquisitions, regardless of the size of the acquiring company or the one to be acquired. The discussion is biased toward a disciplined, structured, and well-documented process. Acquiring companies that are small in size may choose to eschew some of the formalities, due to resource constraints or company culture, but the basic logic and sequencing of the steps in the process should be consistently applied.

The next several sections deal with the process associated with noncompetitive transactions (i.e., those involving a single potential buyer). That discussion is followed by a description in section 4.7 of the dynamics of auction sales (i.e., those that involve multiple potential buyers).

4.2 CREATION OF THE DUE DILIGENCE TEAM

(a) GENERAL. Even the largest organizations generally do not have a standing due diligence team. From a practical standpoint, the volume of acquisition activity over time is too uneven to justify dedicated staff in all areas where expertise is needed. In addition, needs change from one assignment to the next, further complicating any attempt to build a staff of dedicated professionals.

As discussed in Chapter 2, however, larger and more acquisitive companies may have a core team consisting of merger and acquisition (M&A) or business development professionals, peopled by staff (versus line) personnel with specific expertise in areas such as strategic planning, acquisition law, tax, and financial modeling. In these cases, business development and finance personnel generally drive the acquisition process, but they rely heavily on managers from various parts of their overall organization to supplement their efforts, once it becomes clear that the acquisition is likely to materialize. Accordingly, line managers from the departments responsible for technology, human resources, sales and marketing, and operations are enlisted as part of an acquisition team to supplement the finance and business development staff.

In smaller organizations, as previously noted, selected business and finance managers are generally assigned responsibility by the chief executive officer (CEO) for shepherding the acquisition process through to the due diligence stage and coordinating with external professionals as needed. Once an LOI has been signed, the process of expanding the team to include managers from other areas of the organization would proceed in much the same manner as just described.

(b) COMPOSITION OF THE DUE DILIGENCE TEAM. In either case, as it becomes clear that the acquisition is likely to be pursued, the individuals assigned to the due diligence team would be formally apprised of its imminence and that they will play an active role in the process. The team would generally be constituted along the lines indicated in the list that follows. For each functional area, if there is more than one reviewer involved, there should be a lead member for that function who will have responsibility for coordinating the review of that area and for reporting on the results of their review. In addition, the team members should be apprised of the confidential nature of the prospective transaction, and restrictions outlined in the governing confidentiality agreement (and the LOI, if applicable) should be reviewed.

- *Finance and Accounting.* The financial aspect of the review is clearly of great importance and, accordingly, is an area where substantial resources should be brought to bear. The number of finance professionals on the due diligence team from the acquiring company is largely dependent on the size and complexity of the company being reviewed and the volume of documents to be reviewed. It is also dependent on whether outside accounting firm assistance (discussed next) is enlisted or not.

- *Outside Accountants.* The decision to utilize an outside accounting firm may stem from a number of considerations. It may simply be a matter of a desire for increased staffpower and enhanced expertise (in an area such as taxation), or it may result from a desire to have third-party confirmation and the comfort this may provide executive management. If the financial statements of the prospective acquisition are not audited, serious consideration should be given to utilizing an independent firm.

- *Business Development.* As noted, the existence of a business development function is dependent on the size and appetite for acquisitions of the acquiring company. In those instances where the function exists, the acquisition process in general and the due diligence review in particular will usually benefit from the experience of the business development staff in managing the process.

- *Legal.* Whether inside or outside counsel or both are used, those staffing the legal arm of the team would have been involved early in the process, with the drafting of the confidentiality agreement and the LOI. Their continued participation in the process is critically important from a number of perspectives. They will provide the necessary expertise to review legal documents and assess legal issues of all sorts during the review. In addition, because they will also be intimately involved in the negotiation and drafting of the purchase agreement, their participation will provide a solid foundation for doing so. And finally, as described in section 2.3, they will provide valuable guidance throughout the process.

- *Human Resources.* Human resources staff involvement should take into consideration the need to cover the range of issues associated with both personnel management (i.e., hiring, evaluating, and terminating) and compensation plans and benefits management (i.e., pension, 401(k), and healthcare plans), and should be staffed accordingly.

- *Information Technology.* The technology function generally has two elements to deal with: purely operational technology (i.e., hardware, software, and connectivity) and product or product support technology (particularly in the case of software, communications, and entertainment businesses). Depending on the nature of the business being reviewed, this area can require a substantial commitment of resources.
- *Sales and Marketing.* Because the financial review would focus on historical performance, the focus of the sales and marketing review should generally be on the confirmation of cross-company synergies and the ability of the company to generate growth consistent with the projections in the valuation model. This should include an assessment of the quality of customer relationships.
- *Product Management.* Whether the function goes under the title of product management, product development, or something else, the reference here is to that department within the organization responsible for the development and management of products or services (in the case of a service business). The review of this area is often critical because the reviewer is charged with determining whether there is sufficient life in existing products, and a healthy enough pipeline of new products, to support the growth assumptions embedded in the valuation model.
- *Production/Operations.* The operational review would generally concentrate on facilities, fixed assets, real property leases, and production, with a strong bias toward identifying or confirming the existence of cross-company efficiencies. The individuals handling the operational review are also the most likely candidates to manage postacquisition integration. As a result, much of the attention of these reviewers will be focused on potential cost savings and preliminary plans for integration implementation.

(c) OTHER CONSIDERATIONS. In addition to the previous observations, it is important to note that there are other areas of review either that may be taking place offline or that should be considered, due to special circumstances. An example of the former is the work of the acquiring company's tax professionals or advisors. They would have been involved in early stages of the process to determine the tax and financial ramifications in structuring the acquisition, and would be involved in the post–due diligence stage to ensure optimal tax treatment going forward.

An example of special circumstances that might require additional outside assistance is one in which proprietary product information of the target company must be reviewed by an independent third party to ensure against potential litigation, in the event the transaction is *not* consummated. For example, this can be the case when a software company is being reviewed and the quality and documentation of source code are important due diligence issues that cannot be handled by the acquiring company, in the event that the acquisition effort is terminated.

At the time team member involvement is formalized, members should be provided with these documents to enable them to prepare their portion of the due diligence program and to prepare for the execution of the due diligence review:

- The internal approval document (position paper)
- The valuation model, including major assumptions, such as those regarding growth, synergies, and efficiencies, underlying the model
- Company and product information, such as promotional documents, that may be available
- A copy of the information request
- A preacquisition checklist such as the one found in Appendix 4A

The team members should then be assembled and thoroughly briefed on the contents of these documents and on the key issues associated with the acquisition. The confidential nature of internal analysis of the transaction should also be emphasized at this time. For obvious reasons, the acquirer would not want these documents falling into the hands of the principals of the target company.

4.3 DEVELOPMENT OF THE DUE DILIGENCE PROGRAM

(a) **GENERAL.** The due diligence program is the "playbook" used in the conducting of the review. It consists of a functional breakdown of procedures to be performed and questions to be answered, based on information requested by the acquiring company and supplied by the company being reviewed and interviews of the key managers of the target company by members of the due diligence team. An illustration of a section of a due diligence program appears in Exhibit 4.1.

A logical starting point for the development of a program is the information request. If thoughtfully assembled, the information request will be organized along functional lines and will identify key

---

Objective: To obtain and document an understanding of contractual, environmental, litigation, insurance, and intellectual property rights issues

1. Obtain and review all copies of facility leases and addenda thereto.
2. Determine existence of any environmental permits or environmental issues or violations.
3. Review all material contracts and agreements. Document major terms relative to:
   a. Agent agreements
   b. Distributor agreements
   c. Customer agreements
   d. Supplier agreements
   e. Licenses
   f. Royalty arrangements
   g. Other agreements
4. Obtain documentation of any outstanding or threatened litigation.
5. Review all documentation relative to intangible assets, indicating status of:
   a. Copyrights
   b. Patents
   c. Trademarks
   d. Service marks
6. Determine states in which the business should be qualified.
7. Review details of insurance coverage, specifically:
   a. Property coverage
   b. Other coverages and potential exposures

CONCLUSION: (Express conclusions relative to overall objectives and specific objectives associated with this section of the program)

Preacquisition follow-up
(Note any issues or items that must be addressed prior to closing.)

Postacquisition follow-up
(Note any items or issues that must be addressed after the close, such as integration issues.)

EXHIBIT 4.1 LEGAL SECTION OF ILLUSTRATIVE DUE DILIGENCE PROGRAM

documents to be provided that will suggest questions and procedures relevant to the area being reviewed. The information request, in conjunction with a comprehensive preacquisition checklist, would provide a solid basis for the creation of the due diligence program.

The program must be tailored to the industry and company being reviewed. The team members, therefore, should be assigned the development of the program and the transformation of the information request into a proactive, procedural document that will induce the team members to review the appropriate materials, ask the right questions, and focus on the issues of greatest importance.

A due diligence review is by no means the same as an audit. Constraints on time and resources limit the depth of the evaluations conducted. However, a due diligence review is analogous to an audit, and the types of procedures that should be reflected in the program are not unlike what one would find in an audit program. Also, an aspect of the review that is, arguably, as important as the program itself is the healthy skepticism one would employ when conducting an audit. Because of these similarities, inclusion of financial team members who have audit experience can be beneficial. They can also be of great assistance to other team members in creating and modifying the due diligence program and in coaching those team members who have not previously been involved in a due diligence review.

(b) KEY ASPECTS OF THE DUE DILIGENCE PROGRAM.   Although all programs are situation- and company-specific, there are key aspects of the program that should be included, regardless of the nature or size of the company being reviewed. It is important to remember that the overarching objective of due diligence is the mitigation of acquisition risk, that is, paying a price in excess of the acquisition's value to the buyer. Accordingly, the items that follow, to varying degrees, are reflective of that objective.

- *Review Objectives.* The program should contain clearly stated objectives, both for overall review and for each individual functional area. Overall objectives should focus on such things as the sustainability of projected growth and potential issues of impairment of value. Objectives for individual functional areas should focus on establishing, confirming, and documenting the reviewers' understanding of processes, policies, and procedures

The primary objectives for the due diligence review associated with the acquisition of XYZ Corporation are to:

- Identify items that would preclude proceeding with the acquisition.
- Identify items that would impair the valuation of the acquisition.
- Identify material issues and items that must be addressed prior to the acquisition.
- Identify material items and issues that must be addressed as part of the postacquisition integration process.

EXHIBIT 4.2 DUE DILIGENCE PROGRAM: OVERALL OBJECTIVES

for that area. The explicit inclusion of objectives serves as an important point of focus for the reviewer. See Exhibit 4.2 for examples of review objectives.

- *Breadth of Coverage.* All major functional areas within the organization being reviewed should be assigned and covered. Although the emphasis in due diligence is on areas of greatest potential exposure, the breadth of coverage should be sufficient to identify any significant problem areas in the business that may not have been previously known.
- *Focus of Coverage.* The inherent limitations of due diligence make it necessary to be selective about the areas that receive in-depth attention. Therefore, the initial focus of the review should be on areas of concern (or potential opportunity) that will have surfaced in the course of preliminary evaluation, analysis, and discussions. Naturally, the scope of the review should be expanded if additional issues emerge during the course of the review. Reference to the approval document (position paper) and input from those managing the process are important sources of information in determining the areas of exposure and of opportunity (i.e., revenue synergies and cost efficiencies).
- *Conclusions about Work Performed.* Reviewers should be made to express a general conclusion about the area of their responsibility. Accordingly, it is recommended that, at the end of each individual portion of the program, there is a "Conclusion" section requiring the reviewer to explicitly indicate (express an opinion and sign off) whether there were any issues that came to light that might impair the value of the target company (see

Exhibit 4.1 for an illustration). This mechanism establishes clear responsibility on the part of the reviewer and introduces a compelling element of individual accountability that, in turn, inspires a high level of professionalism.

- *Preclosing, Contract, and Postclosing Issues.* In the course of due diligence, numerous important issues arise that will require resolution. They may need to be addressed before the transaction is consummated; they may have a bearing on the terms of the purchase agreement; or they may require action after the close of the transaction. These issues encompass a broad range of possibilities, but would include such things as determining the impact and options associated with the nontransferability of a minor license agreement to contractual mitigation of potential sales returns to issues associated with postacquisition integration. The program should accommodate the need to efficiently capture and aggregate this type of information. See Exhibit 4.1 for an illustration.

4.4 PLANNING DUE DILIGENCE

Once the consolidated program has been developed, a meeting should be convened, under the direction of the lead members of the team, to thoroughly discuss the due diligence plan. This meeting should be used to accomplish these objectives:

- *Finalize the Program.* Before beginning the review, the due diligence program must be finalized. The individuals with primary responsibility for each functional area to be reviewed should submit their final version of their portion of the program to the individuals leading the due diligence review.
- *Clarify Roles.* The roles of the team members should be clearly understood. It is important that any questions about responsibilities and deliverables are answered *before* the review begins.
- *Resolve Issues of Overlap.* There is generally an overlap of interest in certain documents (e.g., contracts, licenses, leases) among various functional areas. For example, this commonly occurs between the legal reviewers and reviewers of other areas, such as human resources, sales, and real estate. The individual doing the legal review will look at many of the same documents as the individuals performing reviews of these other areas, but

from a different perspective. It is advisable to request multiple copies of such documents or, if this is problematic, to coordinate these efforts so that inefficiencies are minimized and proper coverage is assured. Additionally, those whose reviews overlap should communicate and cross-check their findings and conclusions.

- *Coordinate Access to Key Individuals.* Just as there are potential problems of access to documents, there are potential problems of access to key individuals, both within and outside the target company's organization. This is especially the case with smaller acquisitions, where there frequently are a small number of senior managers and decision makers. Optimizing access to key individuals can be assured if there is proper coordination and prioritization of the major issues that are to be addressed in the review.

- *Communicate Logistical Information.* This generally takes the form of a memo indicating the location and timetable for review as well as the responsibilities of the individual team members. This appears to be a relatively mundane matter, but it is a prudent measure that obviates the risk of misunderstandings when coordinating the efforts of a sizable group.

- *Communicate Responsibility and Timing of Report Submissions.* The review will result in a due diligence report, composed of the individual fieldwork and findings of team members. The individual responsible for the review of each of the functional areas should understand what is to be submitted and when it is due. In addition, it should be clear to all members of the team which team leader or leaders will have responsibility for compiling, synthesizing, and summarizing the team's findings. The deadline for individual submissions should be aggressive but reasonable. The longer the time between the time the fieldwork is done and reports are finalized, the greater the potential for information to be lost and memory to fade.

4.5 CONDUCTING DUE DILIGENCE

(a) COMPONENTS OF THE DUE DILIGENCE REVIEW. Typically, due diligence consists of management presentations, interviews with key employees, review of the data in the data room, follow-up questions about issues arising from presentations, interviews, and data review, and a physical tour of the facility where business is conducted. These elements of the review are discussed in detail next.

- *Management Presentations.* The acquirer should request that key individuals on the management team of the target company make presentations on their respective areas of responsibility. Presentations should focus on the dynamics of the business, its market, and underlying strategies and initiatives to build and grow the business. Presentations of this nature are beneficial to team members in refining their understanding of the company and its business before becoming immersed in more detailed fieldwork such as document review. They also potentially raise issues, heretofore not obvious, that reviewers may further explore in interviews and in question-and-answer sessions. Additionally, presentations provide an opportunity for the due diligence team members to assess the quality of the target company's management talent and their command of the information relating to the company's products, markets, and customers.

- *Interviews.* Key members of the target company's management team (generally those in charge of product/business development, sales and marketing, finance and technology) should also be interviewed, preferably by their functional counterpart on the review team. Interviews provide an opportunity for reviewers to delve more deeply into issues that may have been covered too superficially in management presentations and to explore areas outside the scope of those presentations. Provision should also be made to obtain access to key advisors, such as the company's outside accountants.

- *Data Review.* The major tool utilized in the data review process is the due diligence program. The program should provide a logical and efficient path for evaluating operations, validating representations, and assessing assumptions about future performance. It is extremely important that observations, analysis, and validation procedures are thoroughly documented. The program should be procedural and interrogatory in character and should induce the reviewer to document observations and evidentiary information.

- *Follow-up Discussions.* Presentations, interviews, and data review will provide insights and answers, but they will also generate additional questions requiring follow-up discussions with the management of the target company as well as requests for additional information. Meetings with managers should be scheduled periodically to have questions answered and outstanding issues resolved. For purposes of efficiency, it is generally preferable to group or collect questions relevant to a particular topic and discuss them all at one time, rather than to attempt to get answers to individual questions in real time. Some issues may require research or analysis that will have to be provided by the target company subsequent to the review period. A good rule of thumb is to ensure that all follow-up items are resolved within a week of the end of the review period so that the process is kept on track.

- *Tour of the Facility.* Touring the facility has a number of benefits. It provides context for the business. Rather than being an abstraction, the business takes on more meaning when one sees it in operation. It also provides those evaluating operations and technology with concrete information about their areas of review. This is particularly the case when the acquisition involves companies with manufacturing facilities, complex operations, and large inventories. In addition, a firsthand view of the operations often provides meaningful impressions of whether the business is well run or poorly run. Needless to say, such impressions should not be confused with validation; but as a supplement to the other elements of the review, they often support conclusions about the quality of the operation under evaluation.

In addition to these measures, the due diligence team may also choose to perform customer research to confirm the quality of the products and/or services that the target company provides. Such reviews would generally be conducted by independent third parties, with the cooperation of the target company.

(b) OTHER CONSIDERATIONS. In addition to the aspects of the process just described, these points should be considered:

- *Meet early and often* with team members. It is good practice to schedule a team meeting midday, the first day of the review, to get initial impressions of what has been seen and heard and whether any major issues have surfaced. At a minimum, the team should continue to meet daily at the end of each day to share information and impressions.

- *Schedule periodic discussions with management* of the target company. There should be a fluid flow of information between the principal(s) and the lead members of the due diligence team. This helps avoid bottlenecks and inefficiencies that can occur in what is a potentially chaotic environment.

- *Have the discipline to discontinue the process if "deal killers" surface* (i.e., issues that clearly and materially impair the value of the target company in the eyes of the acquisition team). It may be tempting to continue the review in the face of such deal killers for a variety of reasons. The efforts exerted and the expenses incurred to this point in the process have been significant, and expectations of a successful transaction have been raised within the acquiring company. However, efforts to that point have to be seen for what they are, sunk costs, and expectations should be dealt with sooner rather than later, before further expenditures of time and resources are incurred.

- *Be willing to expand the scope of the review* if necessary. If issues arise causing the need to extend the review, the acquirer should be prepared to do so. This point suggests that there should be sufficient time built into the process to enable the team to expand the scope of the review should circumstances dictate.

- *Ensure that postacquisition integration issues and opportunities are identified.* Efficiencies that have been assumed in valuation modeling should be validated and any additional opportunities should be identified.

4.6 REPORTING ON DUE DILIGENCE

(a) **GENERAL.**   The due diligence process should generate a report that contains particulars about the process and its findings. The findings will result in a recommendation to proceed, a recommendation to disengage, or a recommendation to renegotiate. The first two options are fairly straightforward. The third assumes that the acquisition is still attractive, but at a lower purchase price, due to a moderate level of impairment. It also assumes that a price adjustment is feasible, based on discussions with the target company's owners.

If properly conducted and documented, the report would be detailed and lengthy and, therefore, should be accompanied by a summary document. The full report, at a bare minimum, should contain everything needed to support the conclusions and recommendations contained therein. This would typically include a description of what was reviewed, copies and summaries of the most relevant documents, analyses of key data, and evaluations of each of the functional areas and the business as a whole.

(b) SUMMARY REPORT. The summary report should provide the reader with an overview of the process, its major findings, conclusions relative to the review's objectives, and a recommendation to proceed or disengage from the acquisition. The summary report should be directed at those who have approval authority for the transaction. An annotated outline recommending the form and content of the summary report follows.

- *Background and Introduction.* This section of the report should discuss the circumstances leading up to the acquisition and the agreement on terms under which to proceed with the transaction. Frequently, the ultimate decision makers are not close to the transaction, so it is advisable to provide context with basic background information.
- *Due Diligence Team.* This section should describe the makeup of the due diligence team and team member review responsibilities.
- *Due Diligence Objectives.* This section should articulate the primary objectives of the review and the areas of exposure that the review focused on.
- *Review Process.* This section should comment on the quality of the information supplied by the target company, the level of cooperation of management, and the relative effectiveness of the review.
- *Major Findings.* This section should indicate whether there were any issues that came to light that would preclude moving forward with the acquisition and should comment on the quality of the business and management.

- *Conclusions.* This section should contain a recommendation to proceed or to discontinue efforts to buy the business. If the recommendation is to proceed, major preclosing and postclosing items should be presented.

(c) FINAL APPROVAL DOCUMENT.   In addition to the due diligence report, those leading the acquisition process would generally draft a final report (sometimes referred to as a board paper, because it is the document sent to the board of directors for final approval in some organizations). This paper is an enhanced and updated version of the position paper, which was used to support the initial decision to pursue the acquisition. It would generally contain a discussion of these items:

- The business and its organization and management
- The strategy underlying the acquisition
- The market and competition
- The technology supporting the business
- The results of due diligence
- The postacquisition integration plan
- The financial dynamics of the acquisition
- The valuation analysis
- A recommendation to proceed (at either the original purchase price or a renegotiated price) or disengage

This report would be used to obtain final approval or, if circumstances indicate, to explain why efforts to acquire should be discontinued. Assuming the former, the process would advance to the negotiation of the purchase agreement (as described in Chapter 5).

4.7 VARIATION ON THE THEME: AUCTIONS

(a) GENERAL.   The process just outlined describes the steps involved in noncompetitive acquisition transactions (i.e., those in which there is only one potential buyer). These are arguably the most common types of transactions involving sales of closely held businesses. They originate in a variety of ways. A business broker representing the seller may approach a potential buyer; the acquirer may approach the owner of a business in its market that it finds strategically attractive; or a seller may make contact directly or indirectly with a potential acquirer with the intent to initiate a transaction. In these and other situations in which a sales transaction originates on a noncompetitive basis, the logic and sequencing of events described earlier are applicable.

In contrast, an auction, as the term implies, is a process that a company will put in motion that requires any interested potential buyers to bid on the business being sold. This is almost invariably done through a broker representing the seller's interest. This approach will be employed when owners believe that they can generate a better purchase price and sales terms by stimulating competitive offers. For this approach to make economic sense for the seller, the anticipated tax-effected price differential generated by competitive bids would have to exceed the commission paid to the broker. It is an approach that is most common in cases where large companies are divesting product lines or business units that are no longer in line with the strategic direction of the company (see Chapter 8 for a thorough discussion of divestitures). It is also employed, though less commonly, by other business owners who believe that there are numerous potential buyers of their enterprise.

(b) AUCTION PROCESS. Although the process leading up to due diligence in bid situations is substantially different from that described in the previous sections, the planning and conducting of due diligence is similar. Any difference in the due diligence process would relate to constraints that may be placed on the acquirer's review. These would generally take the form of a reduced time frame and limitations on the materials made available for the initial review. For example, once the prevailing bidder (the presumptive buyer) is determined, a second level of "confirmatory" due diligence typically will be conducted. These differences, described in more detail later, reflect the competitive nature of the bid process and the concomitant shift in leverage from the buyer to the seller.

The way in which the bidding process is handled can vary, but generally it includes these steps, and follows this sequence:

Initiation of the bidding process. Often there is an early indication of the availability of the business in the form of a "teaser," a document that provides minimal substantive information but is designed to test the interest of an identified pool of potential buyers.

Receipt of an offering document or prospectus. This document generally describes the business, its financial dynamics, and the reason why it would be attractive to potential buyers. It is sent to those who have expressed an interest in the company by responding to the teaser.

Development of a valuation model. The offering document is a selling tool, but will also generally contain enough financial information for those interested to develop a valuation model. Those companies interested in pursuing an acquisition would use that information to develop a model to establish a preliminary purchase price.

Issuance of an indication of interest (IOI) by interested prospective buyers. An IOI is a nonbinding document formally expressing a desire to pursue the transaction. Those prospective buyers who continue to be interested in pursuing the transaction would respond to the receipt of the offering document with an IOI, generally addressed to the broker representing the seller. The IOI would also indicate a purchase price (or price range) at which the buyer would be willing to consummate the acquisition, and other material terms of the transaction, all of which would be subject to due diligence. Often the seller will specify detailed information that must be contained in the IOI.

Selection of finalists in the bidding process and initial due diligence. The seller would respond to the bids with an indication of who would proceed to the initial due diligence phase of the process. Generally several parties will be permitted to do so. They would be given presentations by the management team of the property being divested and would gain access to the data room. Follow-up questions and additional information requests would also be entertained.

Final bids and selection of the buyer. Final bids would be submitted and the buyer would be selected. The bidders will sometimes be provided with the purchase agreement in advance of making their final bids and asked to mark up the contract as part of their submission. This is done to maximize the seller's leverage, since the extent of the markup would be considered in making the final selection. Once selected, the presumptive buyer would request exclusivity. If the seller believes that the transaction will move forward, exclusivity would generally be granted.

Confirmatory due diligence. The presumptive buyer would be granted access to whatever information it would reasonably request, to answer any outstanding questions and satisfy any existing concerns.

Once confirmatory due diligence by the presumptive buyer is completed, the process would then proceed to the negotiation of the purchase agreement in much the same manner as would be the case in a noncompetitive transaction.

ACQUISITION DUE DILIGENCE CHECKLIST

The objective of this checklist is to assist in developing a customized due diligence program. The checklist is exhaustive and is organized into three sections:

1. Business overview
2. Financial review
3. Acquisition candidate information

BUSINESS OVERVIEW

I. COMPANY BACKGROUND AND ORGANIZATION The team should normally begin by reviewing relevant memoranda including product and corporate literature, plan and marketing materials, annual reports, minutes of meetings of directors and committees of directors, minutes of stockholders' meetings, and so on.

    A. Obtain an understanding of management's vision, mission, and strategy for the business and its divisions, if applicable. This would include:

- The company's competitive advantage and any barriers to competition the company enjoys
- Its current three- to- five-year business plan, including assumptions regarding product mix, price increase, cost reductions, and so on
- Overall financial strategies, criteria, and goals

   ○ Corporate development activities (e.g., specific acquisitions targeted)

B. Ascertain significant external events and developments (e.g., political, economic, technological) that have recently had, or could have in the future, a major impact on the business. Identify possible constraints on growth.

C. Identify any agreements that may limit the ability of the company to compete in a line of business or in a geographic area.

D. Outline the history of the company including major transactions. Describe the terms of major transactions and their accounting treatment.

E. Obtain a summary of the principal product development, distribution, and research and development facilities of the company.

F. Review the corporate status, capitalization, and ownership of the company. Obtain and make available to counsel a:

   ○ Copy of the certificate of incorporation and bylaws
   ○ List of subsidiaries; certificates of incorporation and bylaws of subsidiaries
   ○ List of jurisdictions in which the company to be acquired and each subsidiary is qualified to do business
   ○ List of shareholders cross-checked against stock certificate book
   ○ List of the classes of stock and other equity and convertible debt securities, which indicates shares authorized and outstanding, voting and preemptive rights, dividend preferences and amounts in arrears, conversion features, and the like
   ○ Roster of major shareholders for all classes of stock: number of shares of each class held both direct and beneficially; the shareholders' status—minors, trustees, and so on; note any shareholder agreements with respect to the stock

   Note that matters involving identification of shareholders and characteristics of the company's capitalization may not be relevant in asset transactions.

II. REVIEW OF PROPOSED TRANSACTION

A. Summarize major provisions of the proposed transaction.

B. Determine whether there are any provisions in the proposed agreement that would negate the intended tax structure of the transaction. Review the other tax considerations involved in the transaction.

C. Obtain or prepare pro forma financial statements and other financial data demonstrating the effect of the proposed transaction. In reviewing pro forma data, consider the adequacy of future cash flows.

D. Inquire of legal counsel as to the effect of antitrust regulations on the proposed transaction. Specifically, consider the Sherman Act, the Clayton Act, and Hart-Scott-Rodino Anti-trust Improvements Act of 1976 (HSR Act). If a pretransaction filing is necessary under HSR Act, obtain and read a copy of the filing document.

III. MANAGEMENT

A. Officers, directors, and key employees:

- Obtain a listing of officers, directors, and key employees, including: name, age, position description, background, length of service, and business affiliations. Review existing employment contracts and outline major provisions. List indebtedness of directors, officers, or employees to or from the company.
- List of compensation paid to directors, officers, and key employees during the past three years. Include salary, bonus, profit sharing, stock options (note present stock ownership), insurance, and any other forms of compensation or fringe-type benefits (including nonmonetary perquisites) both current and deferred.

B. Depth, structure, and philosophy of management:

- Comment on the abilities and depth of management.
- Consider whether there are any indispensable or key managers.
- Compare the organization chart with the actual operating structure. Consider whether the real power is maintained by one or a few officers.

- ○ Determine the function and importance of the board of directors and its major committees.
- ○ Is management oriented toward production, marketing, manufacturing, finance, and so on?
- ○ Considering the industry, competition, and the current economic environment, does this emphasis appear proper?
- ○ If outside advisors are used on an ongoing basis, consider whether this indicates any weaknesses within the company's management structure.
- ○ Inquire into the company's conflict of interest and ethics policy and its policies with regard to "improper payments." Obtain or review a copy of any recent investigative reports.

IV. RELATED PARTY TRANSACTIONS

A. Schedule significant related party transactions. The schedule should indicate the relationship and business purpose of such transactions.

B. Note any family relationships among officers, directors, and key employees. Also note any relationships of officers, directors, and employees with business organizations with which the company has significant dealings.

V. LABOR FORCE

A. Review organization and general workforce issues, including:
- ○ Structure of the organization; headcount distribution by department
- ○ Key operations management
- ○ General workforce characteristics (e.g., composition, turnover, absenteeism, recent hires, restructurings during the last three years, etc.)
- ○ Union involvement (if any)
- ○ General employee relations issues
- ○ Compliance with federal and state employment regulations

B. Review employee compensation, including:
- ○ Salary scales
- ○ All retirement and welfare plan features and costs
- ○ Contract employee agreements

  - ○ Incentive plans; special perquisites
  - ○ Sales compensation
  - ○ Severance plans/termination agreements

VI. PRODUCT DEVELOPMENT AND PRODUCTION

A. Production workflow: flowchart the data collection, conversion, editorial process:

  - ○ Identify all processes required to create final form(s) of product.
  - ○ Provide headcount by activity.
  - ○ Describe all technology employed.
  - ○ Describe major systems development efforts in progress, their status, and projected completion dates.
  - ○ Describe any major systems development efforts planned for the next two years.

B. Product development:

  - ○ Flowchart the product development/enhancement process from development of feature set definition through product release. Describe ongoing support requirements, including: help desk, documentation training software/equipment upgrades.
  - ○ Describe (flowchart) any proprietary software development employed.
  - ○ Describe current development projects and their status and those planned for the next three years.
  - ○ Analyze by product the ongoing maintenance/operational expense including amortization of accumulated development costs.

VII. RESEARCH AND DEVELOPMENT

A. Describe the target's research and development effort. Include the extent to which facilities are committed to this endeavor and the number of employees.

B. Inquire whether the target's success is dependent on the development of new and unique products.

C. Obtain a list of significant copyrights/patents (and their expiration dates) developed as part of the research and development effort. Does the company utilize significant patents owned by competitors?

D. Evaluate the importance of research and development within the industry and its importance to the company.

E. Obtain list of major projects currently being worked on indicating the stage of completion, the expenditures made, and the expenditures needed to complete.

VIII. MARKETING

A. Set forth the definition of the market and niche therein, if appropriate, served. Discuss alternative definitions. Describe strategies adopted toward significant competitors. Profile "unwanted" customers, if they exist.

B. Products and product lines:

- ○ Obtain a description of the product lines or major products of the company. How do the company's products compare with those of its competitors in quality, accuracy, timeliness, customer support, price, and the like?
- ○ Consider recent product obsolescence: Obtain a schedule that provides the current percent of sales derived from products introduced within the past three to five years.
- ○ Obtain a list of the company's more significant brand names, trademarks, and so on.
- ○ Inquire whether after-sales service plays an important role.
- ○ Inquire whether products are sold on consignment.
- ○ Obtain a random selection of customers and determine customer satisfaction with the target's product(s).

C. Product markets:

- ○ Obtain a breakdown of sales by: distribution channel; product categories; new versus renewal or repeat purchase; subscription, advertising, single copy, and so on.
- ○ Obtain an analysis of any seasonal or cyclical sales patterns.
- ○ Inquire as to the demographic markets to which major products are sold.

- ○ Determine the size of the company's markets and the company's share in each market.
- ○ If the company depends on repeat sales, analyze renewal rates during the last five years.
- ○ Inquire as to the percent of sales made to governmental agencies and units.

D. Distribution: Inquire as to the methods of distribution used by the company. Are they direct to end users, through wholesalers, retailers, or others?

- ○ Inquire as to how the marketing and sales departments are organized. Is the organization based on product groups, customer classes, geographic regions, or some combination thereof?
- ○ Obtain a summary of sales made by the target separated into those made by its own sales organization, franchised dealers, agents, and the like.
- ○ Inquire as to how noncompany sales organizations are used, controlled, and directed.

F. Pricing regulations: Inquire whether the company is in compliance with the price discrimination provisions of any relevant regulations in jurisdictions where the target does business. In the United States, this would include the Robinson Patman Act. Discuss discount policies and other special terms given to selected customers during prior years.

IX. LEGAL AND REGULATORY MATTERS

A. Inquire of management and in-house legal counsel as to pending or threatened litigation, claims or assessments, and pending governmental investigations that could give rise to contingencies. Corroborate the information obtained by confirmation with outside legal counsel.

B. Obtain schedule of major legal actions including government injunctions, restraining orders, and the like threatened during the past three years.

C. Obtain schedule of internal and external legal costs during the past three years. Inquire as to significant fluctuations that do not appear reasonable based on the above investigation.
D. Inquire as to which regulatory agencies (federal, state, or local) have an impact on the company. Inquire as to the status of company/regulatory agency relationships. Review all reports filed with regulatory authorities for the past three years.
E. Determine if there are any present or prospective regulations that may adversely affect the company's operations.
F. Coordinate with legal the gathering of materials needed to be "scheduled" for contract purposes.

X. CONTRACTS

A. Review all major contracts in force not reviewed elsewhere.
B. Note whether contracts are assignable or transferable in the event of an transaction.
C. Note whether there are escalation, renegotiation, or redetermination clauses in any contracts.

XI. INSURANCE

A. Review the company's insurance program. The policies will likely include, but not necessarily be limited to, Errors and Omissions, General Liability/Umbrella, Workers' Compensation (where applicable), and Crime and Property/Business Interruption coverage.
B. Review major risks the company may face—product and property liability—and compare with existing coverage. Indicate the adequacy of coverage. Confirmation of major policies is necessary.
C. Obtain schedule of insurance costs over the past three years by type of coverage including brokerage commissions. Pay particular attention to any retrospective provisions of the company's policies.
D. Obtain schedule of major casualty losses over the past three years whether covered by insurance or not. Obtain listing of areas where the company is self-insured.

FINANCIAL REVIEW
I. GENERAL

A. Obtain these financial data for the last three years: balance sheets; statements of income and retained earnings; statements of cash flows.

B. Review the financial statements and notes, noting the type of audit report and whether there are any unusual or significant footnote disclosures.

C. Describe the accounting principles employed by the company and the methods of applying those principles. Consider whether they are consistent with other companies within the industry. Your description should generally be more detailed than the information contained in the footnotes to financial statements. It should highlight differences in accounting principles employed by the buyer and seller, particularly where accounting determinations may have an effect on the transaction price.

D. Determine whether there have been any changes in the application of accounting principles or methods that could make comparisons of historical financial statements more difficult. Highlight the effects on financial trends during the most recent three years caused by changes in accounting principles or methods.

E. If the company has engaged a public accounting firm, arrange to review its work papers, paying particular attention to memoranda on accounting issues and legal matters and evaluations of internal accounting controls.

F. Review the reports of outside specialists (e.g., actuaries, financial consultants, etc.) used by the company for their potential effect on financial matters.

G. In connection with your review of the company, you should gain an understanding of the significant elements of the company's system of internal accounting controls. You should identify the key controls by discussion, inquiry and observation.

II. CASH

A. Obtain summary of banking relationships and a schedule of monthly bank balances during the year. Note trends during the year. Describe the company's policy regarding the investment of idle balances.

B. Review bank account reconciliations and obtain explanations for unusual reconciling items or reconciling items that have not been resolved on a current basis.

C. Describe the company's banking arrangements. In particular, review any restrictions on cash balances, compensating balance agreements, and line of credit arrangements. Do banking arrangements appear adequate based on the company's cash requirements?

D. Inquire whether there were any unusual receipts, such as settling insurance claims or other recoveries. Review the company's cash management system (forecasting, budgeting, etc.) and the attendant controls.

E. Marketable securities. Obtain a schedule of marketable securities, separated into current and noncurrent categories, and list original cost, date purchased, interest rate, maturity date, current basis of recording, and current market value.

III. ACCOUNTS RECEIVABLE

A. Obtain a reconciliation of the detailed accounts receivable records to general ledger control accounts and obtain explanations of unusual reconciling items.

B. Describe the company's credit system. Indicate current credit policies and normal special trade terms (particularly deferred payment terms or agreements to accept returns of goods). Note changes during the past three years in standard credit terms. Compare with customary credit terms in the industry.

C. Obtain an accounts receivable aging as of the most recent date possible and for the same date in the prior year. Also obtain a schedule of significant individual account balances. Discuss with management any large or overdue accounts.

D. Obtain a summary of all accounts in dispute or in process of legal collection.

E. Review the adequacy of the allowance for doubtful accounts, giving consideration to the current accounts receivable aging, the actual write-off experience during the past three years, and receivables collected subsequent to the balance sheet date.

Inquire as to the methods used by the company to establish the allowance for doubtful accounts.

F. Obtain a schedule of the number of days sales in accounts receivable for each month-end during the past three years. If the company does not use the last in, first out (LIFO) basis to calculate days sales outstanding (DSO), consider the appropriateness of the methodology used in light of the sales cycle.

G. Inquire as to unusual increases or decreases in the accounts receivable balances during the periods under review.

H. Obtain a summary of accounts factored or hypothecated, the attendant costs, and whether the accounts were sold with or without recourse.

I. Inquire as to company's policy for obtaining proper sales cut-offs.

J. If the company charges interest on past due accounts, inquire as to compliance with the Truth-In-Lending Act

IV. MISCELLANEOUS RECEIVABLES

A. Obtain a summary of miscellaneous receivables that includes their terms and repayment dates. Special attention should be directed toward receivables from employees, affiliated companies, shareholders, directors, underwriters, and other related parties.

V. INVENTORIES

A. Obtain an inventory summary by major product lines (or major product) for the current and prior year. Such a summary should show separately raw materials, work in progress, and finished goods.

B. Obtain a recap of the latest physical inventory by major product line (or major product) that shows a comparison of physical inventory results with book amounts. Obtain a list of book-to-physical adjustments for the past three years and obtain explanations of significant book-to-physical adjustments.

C. Inquire whether inventory consigned is excluded from the latest inventory listing and whether all owned inventory, including the inventory stored off company premises (warehouses, consignees, processors, etc.) is included. Also inquire as to the pledged or hypothecated inventory.

D. Describe the company's policy for providing for obsolete and slow-moving inventory. Obtain a summary of obsolescence write-offs and provisions for slow-moving inventory for the past three years. Relate this step to discussions with marketing and production personnel.

E. Describe the company's method of inventory control. Note how production schedules are coordinated with inventory levels and sales requirements.

F. Review the company's cost system, paying particular attention to:

- Whether standards are based on sufficiently detailed method studies
- Whether standards are developed (and actual cost accumulated) in a manner that enables determination of variances
- How often standards are updated to approximate actual
- How often overhead rates are reviewed, and the types of costs included in overhead
- The percentage relationship among labor, material, and overhead
- Whether the cost system is used as an effective management control tool or whether it is used only for financial reporting purposes

G. Obtain a schedule of inventory turnover rates and gross profit percentages by product line (or major product) for the past three years. If possible, compare to similar businesses within Thomson and/or industry data.

H. Physically observe the general condition and quality of the inventory.

I. Ascertain whether inventories are stated at the lower of cost or market, and describe the methods used by the company in making these calculations. Particular attention should be paid to products or product lines with low gross profit rates.

J. Obtain a schedule of major differences between the book and tax basis of inventories.

K. If inventories are determined on the LIFO basis, obtain a schedule summarizing the individual layers as of the review date and changes during the past three years. Outline the effect of any liquidations. Discuss with tax department whether acquiree appears to be complying with Internal Revenue Service LIFO regulations relating to method of computing LIFO.

VI. PROPERTY, PLANT, AND EQUIPMENT

A. Obtain a summary of property, plant, and equipment and accumulated depreciation broken down into category totals (e.g., land, buildings, equipment, etc.) for the past three years. Show beginning balances, additions (or provisions), retirements, and ending balances. Inquire as to significant fluctuations.

B. Obtain a current listing of each major owned facility showing location, original cost, age, and current book value. The listing should also provide the method and rate of depreciation.

C. Inquire as to replacement values of owned facilities. Review recent tax assessments and insurance appraisals, if any (indicate dates and methods of appraisals).

D. Obtain a listing of leased facilities showing locations, annual rentals, expiration dates, renewal options, ownership, and age. Note the accounting treatment of each lease.

   o Review terms of significant leased facilities. Consider the effect of the renewal terms. For leases about to expire, consider what the new rentals will be by reviewing current rents for similar facilities. Consider the effects of new rental terms on future financial results.

E. Obtain a listing of all major owned equipment that provides location, original cost, age, current book value, and replacement value as well as the method and rate of depreciation.

F. Obtain a listing of all major leased equipment that provides location, annual rental, expiration date, renewal options, ownership, and age. For leases about to expire, consider the effects of new rental terms on future financial results. Note the accounting treatment of each significant group of leased equipment. Review company policy regarding capitalization of leases.

G. Review company policy regarding repairs versus capital expenditures for both facilities and equipment.

H. Review the cost of maintenance and repairs of major facilities and equipment for the past three years. Investigate significant fluctuations.

I. Inquire as to whether any plant or equipment has become obsolete and should either be written off or have its useful life shortened.

J. Physically inspect property, plant, and equipment for its general condition and age and note equipment that does not appear to be in use. Note any evidence of obsolescence, such as partial replacement of a group of machines, few purchases of equipment in recent years, technological changes, machines with substantial idle time, proposed purchases, and so on.

K. Review company's method of physically identifying specific fixed assets and review the latest inventory of fixed assets.

L. Review the company's depreciation methods and rates.

M. Review company controls over capital asset appropriations and dispositions.

N. Obtain a schedule providing the differences between the book and tax basis of property, plant, and equipment

O. Inquire as to costs expected to be incurred for existing plant and equipment to comply with governmental regulations (e.g., Environmental Protection Regulations and the Occupational Safety and Hazards Act).

VII. PREPAID EXPENSES, DEFERRED CHARGES, AND OTHER ASSETS

A. Obtain a schedule of major prepaid expenses, deferred charges, and other assets. Review the method and period of amortization or write-off. Inquire as to the appropriateness of these accounts and propriety of the write-off period.

B. If key-person life insurance is recorded, ascertain that the company is the owner and beneficiary of the policy and that the cash surrender value is properly recorded as an asset. Obtain listing of any borrowings against loan values of the policies.

C. Review the propriety of classification of prepaid expenses, deferred charges, and other assets as current or noncurrent assets.

VIII. LONG-TERM INVESTMENTS

  A. Obtain a schedule of long-term investments showing the name, percentage of ownership, original cost, basis at which stated, and current market value.

  B. Determine that the method of valuation (equity versus cost) is proper as well as the method of recording income thereon.

  C. Obtain a schedule of all advances to affiliates or unconsolidated subsidiaries. Review the underlying financial, tax, and/or operating factors that gave rise to the balances that exist.

  D. Determine whether the tax basis of investments is substantially different from the book basis.

  E. Obtain a schedule of dividend and interest income related to investments.

IX. INTANGIBLE ASSETS

  A. Obtain a schedule of intangible assets showing the book basis and amortization policy.

  B. Ascertain the reasonableness of continuing value.

X. CURRENT LIABILITIES (OTHER THAN INCOME TAXES)

  A. Obtain a schedule of major current liabilities by category (trade payables, notes payables, accrued liabilities, etc.). Determine that their status as current is proper.

  B. Obtain a reconciliation of detailed accounts payable records to general ledger control account and obtain explanations for unusual reconciling items and reconciling items that are not resolved on a current basis.

  C. Inquire as to normal trade terms of accounts payable and special trade terms. Obtain a summary of discounts taken or lost during the past three years. Review the trend in days payables outstanding (DPO) statistics.

  D. Ensure that trade payables, notes payable, and accrued liabilities include all material items:

     ○ Accrued salaries, wages, vacation pay, commissions and bonuses, and related payroll taxes

     ○ Amounts withheld from employees

- Unemployment and workers' compensation liabilities
- Customer advances or credit balances
- Dividends declared/unclaimed dividends
- Advances from officers, employees, and others
- Judgments, damages, and other claims
- Retrospective insurance adjustments for open policy years (may also indicate potential payments to the company)
- Interest payable
- Provision for warranties
- Accrued taxes, other than on income
- Reserves for adjustments on renegotiable government contracts
- Pension and profit-sharing plan obligations

E. Identify any accrued liabilities (at the closing date) that require actual payment in order to be deductible for income tax purposes (e.g., if accrued salaries are not paid within two and a half months after year-end, there is no tax deduction in the year accrued).

F. Inquire as to company's policy for obtaining proper receiving cutoffs. Obtain a listing of open or unmatched receiving reports at the beginning and end of period and inquire as to treatment.

G. Consider whether a search for unrecorded liabilities is necessary. If so, pay particular attention to accounting conventions whereby the last month's recurring payables (e.g., rents, property taxes, and utilities) are recorded in the subsequent accounting period.

H. Ascertain that the short-term portion of long-term debt is appropriately included in current liabilities.

I. Obtain schedules of notes payable for each quarter during the past three years, including security description, ending balance, interest rate, maturity date and other pertinent terms. Also, note minimum and maximum borrowings in each year. Read and abstract note agreements.

J. Briefly outline the company's short-term financing methods. Inquire as to any restrictive terms or other significant terms. Obtain agreements for significant borrowings. Inquire as to conditions that may result in the withdrawal of commitments for unused lines of credit.

XI. DEFERRED REVENUE

    A. Analyze the deferred revenue balance for the last three years, in light of the billing cycle and renewal trends for subscription products. Investigate any unusual variances.

    B. Develop an estimate of the cost to fulfill the obligations represented by deferred revenue.

XII. INCOME TAXES

    A. Review the general corporate information (e.g., state of incorporation, corporate status, and capitalization structure). Identify which jurisdictions and what returns the company should be filing.

    B. Determine the company's tax accounting methods (e.g., cash or accrual, FIFO or LIFO, etc.) and the tax elections in effect (e.g., Sub S corporation, deferred subscription revenue, etc.).

    C. Ascertain and schedule the type, amount, and year of expiration of available tax carryovers (e.g., net operating losses, net capital losses, foreign, general business, and corporate minimum tax credits, charitable contributions, etc.).

    D. Review federal, state, and local tax returns (income, property, sales and use, employment, excise, etc.) for the last three years. Note whether and where consolidated returns are filed. Determine whether all compliance requirements have been properly and timely met. Indicate which years are still open.

    E. Determine the status of federal, state, and local tax audits. Review any revenue agent reports issued in the last three years. Indicate on a separate schedule the nature and amount of any deficiencies identified. Describe the issue and status of any current disputes with the IRS or other tax authorities.

    F. Review the company's operations and underlying documents to determine whether there are any tax exposures that could affect the company as the buyer (e.g., improper expensing of capitalizable expenditures, overvaluation or other §6662 [substantial valuation misstatement provisions covering corporations] exposures; intermingling of business and personal expenses; etc.).

    G. Schedule major differences between book and tax income for the years under review, and determine whether any of the differences result from questionable tax accounting practices. Review classification of deferred tax debits and credits and determine whether they are current or noncurrent. Review Schedule M timing and permanent differences, and describe and analyze any significant tax cushion or unprovided-for tax risks.

H. Review the purchase agreement and other documents and summarize the tax effects of the proposed transaction. Additionally, consider:

- ○ Tax planning opportunities
- ○ Whether it is advisable for the company to obtain an advance tax ruling on the proposed transaction
- ○ The potential exposure to the target company with respect to joint and several liability for the selling group's federal taxes
- ○ Whether there is exposure for failure to file income tax returns in states where nexus exists
- ○ The company's exposure to sales and use taxes
- ○ The possibility of unusual compensation issues
- ○ Unusual or innovative tax planning techniques the company has employed in past years, and their continued viability

I. Obtain a summary of property taxes for the past three years. Inquire as to any significant increases noted, and inquire whether any significant increases in property taxes are expected.

XIII. LONG-TERM DEBT

A. Obtain a schedule of long-term debt, which includes security description, principal amount, interest rate, advance payment privileges or penalties, late payment penalties, renewal and conversion privileges, sinking fund requirements, and principal repayment terms.

B. Review indentures and describe major restrictive covenants such as on working capital, dividends, reorganizations, and the like. Ascertain whether debt is callable based on a general provision, such as a material adverse change. Inquire of legal counsel whether the company is in compliance with restrictive covenants. If the company has defaulted, determine whether such default has been cured and whether the applicable penalties were satisfied or waived.

C. Inquire of legal counsel whether the impending transaction would, if executed, constitute an event of default. Inquire whether the debt would become callable or otherwise subject to renegotiation.

D. Review the relative significance of short- and long-term debt in the company's current capital structure. Inquire as to unused lines of credit and planned future borrowing requirements, both short and long term.

XIV. CONTINGENT LIABILITIES

A. Inquire whether there are any contingent liabilities outstanding. Obtain a description of any major contingencies identified. Specifically, investigate:

- Threatened litigation pending tax matters
- Liabilities arising out of regulatory investigations, allegations based on liable or erroneous or omitted data, obligations relating to warranties and product defects
- Collectibility of receivables
- Agreements to repurchase receivables sold
- Debt guarantees on behalf of unconsolidated and/or unaffiliated entities
- Price redeterminations and terminations under government contracts

XV. COMMITMENTS

A. Obtain a summary of major outstanding commitments, for example:

- Commitments for fixed asset purchases
- Fixed quantity purchase commitments for paper and other raw materials or services (e.g., printing, mastering, keying, etc.)
- Advertising campaigns and promotional services
- Physical plant or building construction
- Forward foreign exchange transactions
- Long-term purchase and sales agreements, employment contracts

- Pension and profit-sharing and similar plans
- Postemployment retirement health and welfare benefits

XVI. LEASES, FRANCHISE, AND ROYALTY AGREEMENTS

A. Obtain a summary of leases (coordinate with work performed on Property, Plant and Equipment [PP&E]) where the company is either lessee or lessor. Summarize significant aspects of the agreements (e.g., terms, minimum rentals, contingent rental arrangements, cancellability, assignability, renewal or purchase options, and escalation clauses). Also, inquire as to sale and leaseback arrangements.

B. Inquire as to the assignability or transferability of lease agreements in the event of transaction. Also, inquire as to escalation or renegotiation clauses, as appropriate.

C. Obtain a summary of franchise and/or royalty agreements, and describe significant terms of such agreements. Relate royalty agreements to major products and list royalty payments/receipts in each of the last three years. If royalty or franchise agreements are significant to the ongoing business, inquire whether agreements are cancellable if the proposed transaction takes place.

XVII. CAPITAL STOCK

A. Obtain a summary of all stockholder equity accounts indicating legal title of security, par or stated value, shares authorized, shares outstanding, liquidating preferences, dividends in arrears, participating rights, dividend preferences, sinking fund requirements, conversion privileges, dividend rate, and whether dividends are cumulative.

B. Obtain a listing of major shareholders of each type of equity security.

C. Schedule activity in paid-in capital and retained earnings accounts for the past three years. Review adjustments for items that should have been reflected in the income statement.

D. Schedule transactions in treasury stock; identify the objectives and reasons for treasury stock transactions. Inquire as to what method of valuation is used (cost or constructive retirement).

E. Obtain a schedule of cash and stock dividends and stock splits for the past three years, and review the appropriateness of their accounting treatments. Confirm that all such transactions have been authorized by the board and documented in the board of director meeting minutes.

F. Inquire whether there are any restrictions on retained earnings.

G. Obtain a summary of activity during the past three years relating to stock options, the stock purchase plan, stock warrants, or any other rights to purchase stock. Read the pertinent plans and agreements and consider what the status of these plans, warrants, and rights will be at the transaction date.

XVIII. INCOME STATEMENT ACCOUNTS

A. Obtain explanations for significant fluctuations in the income statements for the last three years. Captions such as cost of goods sold and selling and general and administrative expenses should be supported by detailed analysis.

B. Identify nonrecurring, extraordinary, or unusual items included in profit and loss.

C. Obtain an analysis of product or product line profitability (i.e., sales, cost of sales and direct selling, general and administrative expenses). Analyze gross profit percentages. Compare sales trends of product lines.

D. Schedule sales to the company's largest customers, affiliated companies, and other related parties for the last three years. For affiliates and other related parties, inquire whether sales were made at arm's-length prices. For individual customers who represent a significant volume of sales, evaluate their current financial status.

  ○ Also, for individually significant customers, coordinate with those Thomson individuals reviewing marketing to identify how these customers are treated/handled differently, if at all, and what the current status of the company's relationship with these customers is.

E. Review major long-term contracts (including government contracts; determine the method of income recognition). Inquire as to methods used by the company to monitor the status of long-term contracts and whether work in process will be completed at a normal profit margin.

F. Identify the company's policy with regard to sales returns and allowances and what the applicable accounting policies are. Schedule sales returns and allowances by product line (or major product) and customer. If significant returns and allowances are noted for a particular product line, identify the underlying reason. Consider the implication on matters such as the timing of the recognition of sales, adequacy of reserves, company's quality control and research and development efforts, and so on.

G. Obtain an analysis and understanding of key financial and operating statistics for the last three years and projected three-year period. In addition to classic accounting and investment ratios, examine those statistics that are fundamental to business's economics, for example:

- o Market growth/share renewal rates
- o Price
- o Real versus inflationary growth
- o Shifts in product mix and profitability
- o Revenue per customer
- o Revenue per sales representative
- o Sales and marketing as a percentage of sales
- o Other functional costs as a percentage of sales lead time required to ramp-up to the next level of sales activity
- o Fixed versus variable costs (from an economic perspective)
- o Average compensation
- o Headcount distribution
- o Operating income per employee

H. Analyze "other income and expense" accounts. Identify separately recurring and nonrecurring items.

I. Estimate increases or decreases in major income or expense categories posttransaction. Consider, for example, the effect of including the acquired company's employees under the acquiring company's profit-sharing and pension plans; operating efficiencies due to the combination of similar departments or sale of duplicate facilities; and so on.

XIX. BUDGETED AND FORECASTED DATA

A. Obtain a description of the company's budgeting system, and discuss sources of budget input data and budgeting system controls. It is important to determine whether budget is a bottom-up budget created by operating units or a top-down budget produced by senior management.

B. Review prior years' budgets and compare budgeted to actual results.

C. Discuss with management the basis of key assumptions, particularly where assumptions differ from recent trends.

D. Identify the company's business cycle and sensitivity to general economic trends.

XX. SYSTEMS

A. Identify, flowchart, and describe all systems:

- Transaction sales support and customer information
- Order entry and fulfillment
- Product development and delivery
- Work flow and other infrastructure
- Communications

B. Evaluate the adequacy of the system of controls (e.g., segregation of duties, input, processing, access and documentation controls, physical security, and system development and modification procedures). Provide headcount by function.

C. Indicate whether such systems are company managed or service bureau based.

D. Identify disaster recovery/contingency plans in place for key systems.

E. Describe any system limitations affecting the current business, including those impacting new product development activities and the company's ability to offer all media formats.

F. Detail ongoing support requirements and operational costs. Describe current ongoing development efforts and their status. Also describe any development projects planned for the next three years.

ACQUISITION CANDIDATE INFORMATION

Note: Detailed listing of materials that should likely be reviewed, for use as a checklist or data room request.

I. CORPORATE

1. Articles of incorporation and bylaws.
2. List of subsidiaries; certificates of incorporation and bylaws of subsidiaries.
3. Minutes of meetings of directors and committees of directors, and minutes of stockholder's meetings.
4. List of shareholders cross-checked against stock certificate book.
5. List of the classes of stock and other equity and convertible debt securities that indicates shares authorized and outstanding, voting and preemptive rights, dividend preferences and amounts in arrears, conversion features, and so on.
6. For all classes of stock, obtain a roster of major shareholders: number of shares of each class held both direct and beneficially; the shareholders' status—minors, trustees, and so on; and note any shareholder agreements with respect to the stock.
7. List of jurisdictions in which the company and each subsidiary is qualified to do business.
8. Any agreements that may limit the ability of the company to compete in a line of business or with a person or in a geographic area.

II. GENERAL

1. Current three- to five-year business plan, including assumptions regarding product mix, price increase, cost reductions, and so on. Plan projections and budgets applicable to current year and any year subsequent. Provide working capital estimates and underlying assumptions for all plan periods.
2. Management's description of the overall financial strategies, criteria, and goals for the company.

3. List of corporate development activities (e.g., specific acquisitions targeted).
4. Outline the history of the company, including major transactions. Describe the terms of major transactions and their accounting treatment.
5. Provide details of any loans, liabilities, or commitments (other than trade payables) the buyer would be expected to assume.

III. FINANCIAL
A. CURRENT YEAR AND HISTORICAL RESULTS

1. Annual reports for the last three years, including report of independent accountants. Financial statements to include income statement, balance sheet, and cash flow.
2. Results for the prior three years compared to budgets, with management comments. Reconcile to audited financials if management results are on a different basis.
3. Impact of acquisitions and disposals on revenues and operating profit during the past three years.
4. Impact of changes in currency rates on revenues and operating profit reported for the last three years.
5. Provide details of any special write-offs, write-backs and/or nonrecurring items affecting results for prior years or expected this year.
6. Provide the last six monthly management reports. For the most recent month, compare the current year's performance to budget, and include management's discussion of results/outlook for the rest of the year.

B. REVENUE

1. Details of each product providing over 5% of revenues and/or operating profit in each of the prior three years.
2. Schedule price increases in each of the last three years and the respective impact on revenues and unit sales.
3. Breakdown of revenues by major publishing program, including an analysis of revenue sources (e.g., subscription, advertising, copy sales, licensing, usage-based fees, custom project or general consulting fees, hardware fees, or other major sources).

C. OPERATING EXPENSES

1. Amount of new product development expense and contribution to sales and operating income of new products launched in this year and each of the last three years.
2. Analysis of central and other overheads.

D. BALANCE SHEET ACCOUNTS

1. Provide a summary of banking relationships and schedule of monthly bank balances during the year. Describe the company's policy regarding the investment of idle balances.
2. Schedule marketable securities; separate into current and non-current categories, and list original cost, date purchased, interest rate, maturity date, current basis of recording, and current market value.
3. Analyze accounts receivable, include an aging, details of bad debt provision, and historical write-offs.
4. Analyze changes in working capital, and provide a narrative explanation of the factors affecting these accounts.
5. Provide a summary of property, plant, and equipment and accumulated depreciation broken down into category totals (e.g., land, buildings, equipment, etc.) for the current and past three years. Show beginning balances, additions (or provisions), retirements, and ending balances. Explain any unusual/one-time capital expenditures made in the current or any of the prior three years.
6. Provide details of all other material noncurrent assets (e.g., author advances, deferred production costs, etc.).
7. Analyze goodwill and intangibles; identify the original transactions, amortization, and write-offs to date. For internally developed intangibles, provide an analysis that supports the net realizable value.
8. Provide a detailed trail balance of all material items in accrued expenses.
9. Analyze deferred revenue, and provide details of revenue recognition of policies by major product.

E. OTHER ACCOUNTING MATTERS

1. Statement of accounting policies; address revenue recognition by product line.

2. Copies of auditors' internal control memorandums for the past three years.
3. Details of acquisitions made. Cost, allocation of cost to assets, write-off policy on assets/liabilities, any special provisions made against acquisition cost, performance compared to acquisition expectations.
4. Capitalization policies and, outside of fixed asset expenditures, what costs are capitalized and the write-off policy. Include detail of project costs capitalized in accordance with Statement of Financial Accounting Standards (SFAS): 86.
5. Analysis of revenues and operating profit by country.
6. Detail of unremitted earnings and cash flows by country.
7. Amount of foreign source income included in financial results.
8. Detailed description of accounting, commercial, and management systems.

IV. TECHNOLOGY
A. GENERAL

1. Complete description of computer facilities, hardware, and software.
2. Provide descriptions/flowcharts of all systems: transaction; sales support and customer information; order entry and fulfillment; product development and delivery; work flow and other infrastructure; communications; and so on.
3. Provide disaster recovery plan.
4. Provide strategy and plans for major technology upgrades and enhancements, including costs and timing thereof.
5. Discuss plans for future search engine/user interface enhancements.
6. Provide details of capital expenditures (for the past three years) for technology and amounts included in projections.

V. PRODUCTS
A. GENERAL

1. Provide a list of all publications, products, and services offered by the company.

2. Describe arrangements and costs associated with data collection. Discuss stability of data supply.
3. Describe production process from receipt of material through delivery to customers.
4. Describe the value-added to basic data received and commodity/proprietary nature of products.
5. Describe major product enhancements and new products in development.

VI. MARKETING AND SALES
A. GENERAL

1. Provide details on sales activities: direct mail, sales force, telemarketing, and so on, and the contribution from each source. Provide an analysis of the cost of each marketing activity over the last three years.
2. Provide details of sales representative agreements/arrangements; describe sales incentive compensation plans.
3. Provide details on major warehousing, distribution, marketing, production, and advertising arrangements.
4. Provide competitive analysis of the company's products, accuracy, timeliness, and service compared to those of competitors; statistical analysis to support market share claims.
5. Provide copies of any recent market research and customer satisfaction studies.
6. Provide customer information reports by product to validate new orders, payment rates, renewal rates, product migration patterns, and the like.
7. Provide details on trade names, trademarks, copyrights, service marks, patents, licenses, and royalty agreements and similar documents.

VII. LEGAL
A. GENERAL

1. List of all litigation, claims or assessments, and judicial, administrative, or regulatory proceedings pending or threatened, including date filed, relief sought, forum in which brought, and status of the matter. Also, list any potential exposure.

2. Any government or regulatory reports/correspondence concerning noncompliance with any laws or regulations (including IRS, Department of Justice [DOJ], Federal Trade Commission [FTC], Occupational Safety and Health Administration [OSHA], Environmental Protection Agency [EPA], Equal
   Employment Opportunity Commission [EEOC], National Labor
   Relations Board [NLRB], etc.).
3. Agreements that limit the ability of the company to compete in
   any line of business or with any person in any geographic area.
4. Details of actual or attempted infringement of trademarks, trade
   names, patents, or copyrights.
5. Contracts or options relating to the acquisition of any business.
6. Documents relating to unrecorded liabilities, including unfunded vested pension liabilities, unfunded retiree medical and
   other benefits, multiemployer pension plan liability, product liability, environmental matters, and other contingent liabilities.

B. REGULATORY MATTERS

1. Provide details of all material licenses, permits, orders, approvals, filings, reports, correspondence, and so on from or with
   federal regulatory agencies and foreign, state, or local agencies
   performing similar functions, including:

   o Environmental Protection Agency
   o Equal Employment Opportunity Commission
   o Internal Revenue Service
   o Other (Department of Justice, Federal Trade Commission,
     Occupational Safety and Health Administration, Department
     of Labor, Department of Commerce, National Labor Rela-
     tions Board, etc.)
   o Export/import matters

2. If applicable, provide copies of these public filings:

   o Annual reports on Form 10-K and annual shareholder reports
     filed during the last five years
   o Quarterly reports on Form 10-Q and shareholder reports, and
     any reports on Form 8-K filed during the last three years
   o Proxy statements for the last five years
   o Any recent prospectus or offering memoranda or circulars

C. MATERIAL AGREEMENTS

1. Standard forms of customer agreements; description of major deviations therefrom.
2. Agreements with distributors and sales representatives.
3. Material agreements with vendors and customers other than purchase or sales orders entered into in the ordinary course of business.
4. Contracts, franchises, licenses, concessions, leases, and commitments that involve an obligation on the part of the company to make payments in excess of $10,000 in any one year, and other material agreements.
5. Loan or other financing agreements, including bank loans, lines of credit, letters of credit, mortgages, indentures, and a list of any property pledged as collateral.
6. Joint venture agreements and partnership agreements.
7. Guarantees by the company or its stockholders of any obligation of others.
8. Contracts with any governmental entity.
9. Material [author] contracts and standard forms of such contracts.
10. Contracts with providers of data, and discussion of possible constraints on future data availability.

D. FACILITIES

1. All deeds, surveys, title insurance policies, title reports, and legal opinions with respect to title, zoning, and related matters on all real property owned by the company.
2. All leases and subleases of real property to which the company is a party.
3. Copies of any option agreements, earnest money agreements, or other agreements to which the company is a party and that involve the purchase or sale of real property.
4. All agreements for use, easements, restrictions, rights of way, construction, architectural services, and any other agreements or documents relating in any way to the ownership or leasing of real property by the company.
5. Environmental reports and studies.

    6. Details of computer facilities (use, age, replacement program, backup facilities).

E. TAXES

    1. A description of audits and other tax disputes in progress.
    2. A description of any tax elections in effect.
    3. Tax rulings and tax closing agreements with any taxing authority (foreign or domestic) applicable to the assets of the company.
    4. Liens for taxes on any assets of the company.
    5. Any assets that are treated as owned by any other person under the "safe harbor lease" provisions of Section 168(f)(8) of the Internal Revenue Code.
    6. What is the nature and amount of assets by state for possible application of the state, local bulk sale rules, and notification requirements?
    7. Federal/state/local/foreign/other tax returns for all open years.
    8. Details of any tax-sharing agreements.
    9. Provide a summary of property taxes for the past three years, by individual location.

VIII. INSURANCE

A. GENERAL

    1. General liability/umbrella, publisher's liability/errors and omissions, workers' compensation, crime and property/business interruption, and other insurance policies (other than employee benefit policies).
    2. Schedule insurance costs over the past three years by type of coverage including brokerage commissions.
    3. Schedule major casualty losses over the past three years, whether covered by insurance or not. List areas where the company is self-insured.

IX. HUMAN RESOURCES

A. GENERAL

    1. Provide copies of employee handbooks and HR policy manuals and summary benefit plan documents.

2. Complete documentation and understanding of employee benefit plans available to company employees (including pension plan) and costs (total, % of payroll, and per employee) thereof. Include billing schedules, premium amounts for employee and employer, and levels of coverage for each plan.

3. Provide complete schematic organization charts for the company. The charts should include full-time equivalents (FTEs) for all areas, names and titles for anyone with supervisory authority, and total headcount (FTEs) for employees who report to them. Note where part-time employees or "temps" are used on an ongoing basis.

B. MANAGEMENT

1. Identify all key management employees (include all director-level positions and above), including their position in the organization, their profile, and the likelihood that they will remain with the organization postacquisition.

2. Copies of all senior management's most recent performance reviews.

3. Details of the company management compensation and incentive plans. Include copy of actual plan(s).

4. Information describing any individual (nonsales) incentive or bonus plans in effect during most recent three calendar years, names of participants, % of salary for which they were eligible, % actually paid compared to eligible %.

5. Copies of all employment contracts.

6. Details of special compensation arrangements including any special arrangements regarding the sale of the company, stock options, grants, golden (or tin) parachute, and "poison pill" benefits.

7. Information concerning any cars, memberships, or other perquisites currently assigned to any current or prospective personnel or director (if over and above what is included in employee handbook or otherwise available to general employee population without specific authorization), including names of such personnel and details regarding arrangements.

8. Copies of all severance benefits plans covering management or employees.

9. Copy of relocation policy.
10. Copy of confidentiality/conflict of interest agreement.
11. Copy of travel and entertainment (T&E) policy and procedures.

C. SIGNIFICANT AGREEMENTS: NONMANAGEMENT

1. Identify all independent contractors performing key or routine work for the company; identify amounts spent over the last three years, estimates of amounts to be spent during the plan period, and FTEs assigned over the respective periods requested.
2. Set forth details of union or collective bargaining agreements in force now or during the last five years. Provide copies of any such agreements.

D. EMPLOYEES

1. Employee list by location, including name (last name, first name, middle initial), date of birth, date of hire, title and job description, department, annual salary, years and months with the company, and total compensation (base salary plus all other forms of compensation reported on the employee's form W-2) identified separately for each of the last three years and estimated for the current year. The list should be provided in two formats: one sort by last name, another sort by estimated current-year compensation in descending order. Highlight those employees hired during the previous 12 months.
2. Information describing any team or group incentive plans in effect during most recent three calendar years, including data regarding payout.
3. Terms of sales force compensation plans, including discussion of significant changes from the prior year or changes anticipated in projections.
4. Description of performance review system and copies of related reports.

E. DEMOGRAPHICS

1. Data regarding numbers of employees by age broken into these groupings: 15–19, 20–24, 25–29, 30–34, 35–39, 40–44, 45–49, 50–54, 55–59, 60–64, 65+).

2. Provide a list of hires currently in progress.
3. Provide job application and "new hire" material provided to new employees.
4. Copy of leave of absence policy as well as history for two years and current status.

F. ISSUES MANAGEMENT

1. Document process for handling employee complaints, concerns, grievances, investigations, and so on.
2. Provide details of pending employee litigation, including charges of wrongful discharge.
3. Copy of current Affirmative Action program, three most recent Equal Employment Opportunity (EEO)-1 reports, names and titles of personnel responsible for administering related programs, information regarding any settled or pending suits in this area.
4. Information regarding Reductions in Force (RIF) since January 1, 1992, or planned RIF, including numbers, titles of employees terminated, method of selecting employees, claims settled or pending, copies of documents or notices used in the process, savings resulting from the reductions. Include pre-/post-organization charts, noting changes.
5. Copies of any termination agreements entered subsequent during the last three years.
6. For severance plans, provide a summary of payments made in last 24 months.

G. SAFETY MATTERS

1. Copy of OSHA log for the last three years.
2. Copy of injury/illness prevention program and any other health/safety programs/forms.
3. Workers' compensation claims experience over the last two years.

H. DEVELOPMENT

1. Copy of any internal training programs provided to employees over the last three years.

2. Copy of any employee communications, such as newsletters, letters from the president, and the like.
3. Copy of results from any recent employee surveys, including documentation of follow-up to the surveys. Include information on the process used to design, administer, score, and give feedback on surveys.
4. What process (e.g., suggestion program) is in place to encourage and recognize employees who have ideas that would improve processes, work environment, and the like?

I. EMPLOYMENT COSTS

1. Headcount statistics by department for past three years and management projections for the next five years.
2. Reconciliation of growth in total company compensation during the last three years to headcount changes and average compensation (merit increases). Same for plan projections.
3. Information outlining salary compensation planning for the past three years, including overall target merit increase %, grades (including which jobs are in each grade), and salary ranges for each grade, merit increase matrix (if used), % spread from minimum to maximum, % spread between midpoints of ranges.
4. Data indicating overall percent of employees in each salary quartile, including number of employees currently at the maximum of or under the minimum of their respective salary range.
5. Provide total benefits costs (health and welfare plans as well as employer benefits taxes, e.g., FICA) as a percentage of total pay.

J. BENEFIT PLANS

1. Provide plan documents, summary plan descriptions (and trust agreements for funded plans) for each of these retirement plans:
   ○ Pension plan(s)
   ○ Profit-sharing and other qualified defined contribution plan(s)
   ○ 401(k) savings plans
   ○ Nonqualified supplemental executive retirement plan(s)
   ○ Healthcare, life insurance, and other welfare benefit plans covering current and/or future retirees
2. Provide plan documents and summary plan descriptions for each of these welfare benefit programs:

- ○ Comprehensive medical plan
- ○ Other medical plan(s)
- ○ Dental plan(s)
- ○ Life insurance: basic life, supplemental life, dependent life, business travel accident, accidental death and disability
- ○ Disability: short term and long term
- ○ Time off: sick pay/vacation/holidays
- ○ Severance

3. Provide trust agreements for any Voluntary Employee Beneficiary Association (501(c)(9)) or other trusts.

4. Provide plan documents and summary plan descriptions for each of these stock-based programs:

- ○ Stock purchase plan
- ○ Stock option plan
- ○ Employee stock ownership plan

5. For each of these plans:

- ○ Comprehensive medical plan
- ○ Other medical plans
- ○ Dental plan (if any)
- ○ Life insurance: indemnity, optional indemnity, business travel accident
- ○ Disability: short term and long term

the following information is needed:

- ○ Form 5500
- ○ Audit reports for last two years
- ○ Details of actual cost of programs for last two years
- ○ Details of expected cost of programs for current year
- ○ Copy of all insurance policies covering employees
- ○ Copy of latest (and prior) insurance renewals, if insured
- ○ Details of claims experience (for last three years, if possible)
- ○ Details of any rate guarantees, liability limits, and stop-loss provisions currently applicable
- ○ Current status of reserves of each plan
- ○ Information on current financing vehicle(s), including any trusts (and the amount of any trust assets)
- ○ Current premium rate information

○ Current Consolidated Omnibus Budget Reconciliation Act (COBRA) rate information (medical and dental plans only)

6. Provide health plan census (number of employees enrolled in indemnity plan, health maintenance organizations).

7. Provide census or health plan coverage status (number of employees in each of these categories): Individual; Employee + 1; and Family Coverage.

8. For posttermination benefits, provide copy of most recent Financial Accounting Standards 112 report or letter.

CONTRACT AND CLOSE

5.1 INTRODUCTION

Once due diligence has been completed and the parties have agreed to proceed, the contracting phase of the transaction begins. The contract takes the form of a purchase agreement and supporting documents (described in the next section). The purchase agreement can take two distinct forms, depending on whether the purchase is for the stock of the company being sold (a stock purchase agreement) or selected assets of the company (an asset purchase agreement). In either case, the agreement's purpose is to:

- Set forth the terms of the transaction.
- Set forth legal rights and obligations of the respective parties.
- Provide the buyer with a detailed description of the business being acquired and afford the buyer remedies, if and when such descriptions are materially inaccurate.
- Allocate risk between the buyer and the seller.

(a) AGREEMENT AND SUPPORTING DOCUMENTS. Typically, the initial agreement is drafted by the buyer's counsel, although the seller's counsel will draft the initial contract in a bid or auction situation (see section 4.7 for a discussion of the auction process). The major components of the purchase agreement are: property transfer and purchase price, representations and warranties, covenants, conditions, indemnification terms, and supporting schedules and exhibits. Additional supporting documents generally include a noncompete agreement and employment and/or consulting agreements. If the transaction involves the divestiture of a non-standalone business unit, the package will also usually include a transition services agreement, which would outline support services to be provided by the seller for a defined transition period, typically several months. In some instances, certain of these items, such as a noncompete provision, may be incorporated into the body of the agreement. The agreement and supporting documents are discussed in detail in sections 5.2 and 5.3. In addition, examples of a stock purchase agreement and an asset purchase agreement are illustrated in Appendices 5A and 5B, respectively.

(b) SIMULTANEOUS VERSUS DELAYED CLOSE. Many smaller transactions are signed and closed simultaneously. However, there will be a delay between signing and close for larger transactions as well as for certain smaller transactions.

Transactions for over $53 million (a number that is periodically adjusted upward) are subject to antitrust scrutiny by the U.S.

Department of Justice and the Federal Trade Commission. The Hart-Scott-Rodino Antitrust Improvements Act of 1976 (HSR Act) requires an assessment by these bodies of the noncompetitive impact of transactions that exceed this threshold. (The HSR Act is discussed in more detail in section 11.5.) Frequently, nonpublic transactions that fall below the HSR threshold may also be delayed because of the need for the buyer to finalize financing arrangements.

Large transactions involving publicly traded companies are invariably subject to delay between signing and closing due to the need to adhere to HSR requirements and to obtain shareholder, third-party, and/or governmental consents, which are typically required to consummate such a purchase and sale. (Regulatory requirements are discussed in section 11.2.) It should also be noted that cross-border transactions, whether they involve publicly traded or privately held businesses, may be subject to scrutiny by, and filing with, non-U.S. regulatory bodies, thereby delaying the closing of a deal after the signing occurs.

(c) CONTRACT NEGOTIATIONS. Negotiation of the purchase agreement is generally a lengthy process, typically taking anywhere from six to eight weeks for a moderate-size transaction. Large, complex transactions involving public companies generally require substantially greater negotiation periods and the involvement of a substantial cadre of experts and advisors. However, the vast majority of transactions are negotiated by a relatively small team of professionals.

Usually, negotiation will include three coequal participants on each side, specifically each party's merger and acquisition (M&A) attorney, a senior businessperson (an executive or principal who is intimately familiar with the business and is able to make informed decisions on contractual issues), and a senior finance professional (generally the chief financial officer). The expertise of specialists, in areas such as technology or intellectual property, may be drawn on periodically, but it is this core team that will be intimately involved in the negotiating process. This approach ensures that the full range of issues that will emerge can be addressed expeditiously, resulting in a relatively fluid process and requiring a minimal number of contract iterations, that is, markups and exchanges. (It is reasonable to assume that every iteration or exchange of the contract represents the passage of at least one week. Hence the desirability of resolving as many issues as possible with each markup of the draft contract.) In most cases, the attorneys on each side will drive the negotiation process. Even before involving business and financial team members, they generally will try to resolve or narrow the many issues involving legal language and traditional or common practices.

5.2 ELEMENTS OF THE AGREEMENT

As noted, the major elements of the agreement are property transfer and purchase price information, representations and warranties (R&Ws), covenants, conditions, indemnification terms, and supporting schedules and exhibits. Each of these elements is discussed in the next sections.

(a) PROPERTY TRANSFER AND PURCHASE PRICE INFORMA-TION.   This section of the agreement identifies the nature of the property being transferred (stock in a stock purchase agreement or assets and any relevant liabilities in an asset purchase agreement), the purchase price, the form of payment (cash and/or note and/or stock), any security arrangements, and any purchase price adjustments, such as working capital adjustments.

(b) REPRESENTATIONS AND WARRANTIES.

(i) Representations and Warranties Common to Buyer and Seller. Representations and warranties by both the buyer and the seller are made in the agreement. Both would typically represent and warrant:

- *The Organization's Good Standing.* That they are valid entities, are legally in good standing, and are duly constituted (as a corporation, partnership, etc.).
- *Its Organizational Authority.* That they have the requisite power and authority to execute the transaction.
- *No Violations of Obligations.* That in executing the transaction they are not in violation or conflict with any bylaws, agreements, articles of incorporation, or laws.
- *Compliance with Law.* That neither party is in violation of any law, regulation, or other governmental requirement.
- *Legal Proceedings.* That there are no undisclosed proceedings pending or threatened against either party.
- *Complete Disclosure.* That the agreement and its supporting documents do not contain any misrepresentations by either party.

(ii) Additional Buyer Representations and Warranties. In addition, the buyer would generally represent and warrant:

- *Litigation.* That there is no action or lawsuit that would preclude the buyer from consummating the transaction.
- *Financial Statements.* That the financial statements provided by the buyer to the seller are fairly presented in accordance with generally accepted accounting principles.
- *Financing.* That the buyer has the financial capability to execute the agreement.

(iii) Additional Seller Representations and Warranties. The seller's representations and warranties are considerably more extensive. They provide the buyer with a snapshot of the business at a point in time, typically on the date of the agreement and again on the date of the closing (if they are not simultaneous). This generally includes the items described herein as well as the general provisions just noted. Some of these items are relatively straightforward, and some typically require the negotiation of terms or language, or both. This is because they are meant to provide an accurate and fairly complete picture of the condition of business being sold (whereas the representations and warranties of the buyer are simply meant to provide confirmation of its ability to legally execute the transaction).

- *Financial Statements.* The seller's financial statement representation indicates that the statements fairly represent the results of operations and the financial condition of the entity being sold, which may not be the entity selling (if the sale is of a business unit or subsidiary) for the periods agreed to. In addition, the statements, disclosures, and audit opinions (if audited) would be included in the accompanying schedules.
- *Assets.* The seller represents that it holds title to the assets being sold and that they have been stated at market value (e.g., inventory at the lower of cost or market and receivables net of bad debt reserve).
- *Liabilities.* The seller represents that all liabilities have been presented and that contingent liabilities have been disclosed.
- *Operations since Financial Statements.* This representation indicates that the entity will be run in a manner that could not

intentionally or knowingly result in a material adverse change in the business.

- *Material Agreements.* This representation indicates that all material contracts and agreements to which the seller is a party have been disclosed to the buyer. In addition, agreements above a certain threshold generally would also be listed in the accompanying schedules.
- *Employees.* All employees and their compensation would be disclosed, as would any claims by employees or actions by labor unions that have a right to bargain on the employees' behalf. A listing of employees and their current compensation would also be provided in the accompanying schedules.
- *Environmental Issues.* This representation indicates that the company being sold is in compliance with environmental regulation and law, and/or discloses any violations thereto.
- *Taxes.* This representation indicates that the company being sold has prepared and filed all required tax returns and paid all taxes due.
- *Insurance.* This representation indicates that the company being sold carries adequate insurance to protect against liability and property loss or damage.

(c) COVENANTS. Covenants govern the relationship of the parties over a certain time period. Some covenants apply from the signing of the agreement until the closing date and provide assurance that the proper actions are taken to facilitate closing of the transaction and preserve the business pending the closing. Other covenants survive the closing for a certain length of time, such as covenants requiring cooperation of the parties with respect to postclosing transition of the business.

(d) CONDITIONS. Acquisition agreements frequently contain conditions that must be met in order for the party receiving the benefit (usually the buyer) to be legally obligated to consummate the transaction. An example would be the assignment of a major contract requiring vendor or customer approval from seller to buyer. If the party fails to satisfy a condition by the date of the closing, the other party has a right to terminate the agreement and walk away from the transaction.

(e) INDEMNIFICATION.   Indemnification requires the parties to pay damages in the event of a breach of their respective representations, warranties, and covenants. Indemnification provisions also serve to allocate specific postclosing risks associated with the transferred business. The term of most indemnification items is generally two or three years, except tax and environmental representations, which generally survive the statute of limitations, and corporate authority, ownership, and title, which survive indefinitely.

This element of the contract would also indicate the types of penalties or obligations that would be triggered upon the breach of a representation or warranty. In theory, remedy could include anything from a lawsuit for monetary damages to a rescission of the transaction, including a refund to the buyer of his or her entire purchase price. The latter is rarely practical even if justified by the circumstances. Therefore, the parties usually bargain for an indemnification provision, which provides that if either of them violates any material term of the agreement, that party will indemnify the other party for any loss, including any attorneys' fees or other expenses incurred in connection with the matter.

Indemnification provisions can be complicated—for example, setting forth procedures for assigning liability and allowing each of the parties to participate in the defense or settlement of a third-party claim that may be subject to indemnification. Of particular importance is the desirability of negotiating both a "basket" and a "ceiling" to the indemnification obligations. A basket, sometimes referred to as a cushion, is a minimum amount. The parties agree not to assert indemnification claims against one another unless the total amount of the net claims exceeds the basket amount. A basket of 1% or so of the total purchase price is not uncommon. What the parties agree to therefore is that a dispute over a smaller amount would be more expensive and more disruptive to their relationship than simply accepting the loss. A ceiling is, of course, a limitation to the amount of total indemnification. A seller can be expected to negotiate for a very low ceiling amount, for example, an amount equal to a deferred portion of the purchase price—perhaps as low as 10% of the total price. A buyer, however, is likely to feel that it should be able to recover everything paid for the business if the problems with it are serious enough. In theory, the buyer could have damages associated with a breach of the agreement in an amount in excess of the purchase price. However, few sellers will agree to indemnify the buyer for more than the amount they have received in the transaction.

(f) SCHEDULES TO THE AGREEMENT.   The schedules to the agreement are an important, integral element of the agreement. They specifically identify key aspects of the business being sold and disclose all exceptions to representations and warranties. In an asset (versus stock) purchase, they detail the specific assets and any liabilities being transferred. This level of specificity is important to both buyer and seller. It dramatically decreases the potential for postacquisition disagreement, since it is designed to leave little to the realm of interpretation. For example, for certain schedules there may be no items to list, yet a schedule with an indication that there are, in fact, no such items would often be included to remove any possibility of misunderstanding.

The schedules are generally prepared by the seller and reviewed by the buyer. As a practical matter, the seller should initiate the process of identifying the schedules that will be included and preparing or populating them with the relevant information as early in the process as possible. Because there are generally numerous schedules to be prepared and many contain a substantial amount of detailed information, if schedule preparation is left until late in the closing process, it is very likely to delay the close. Since much of the detail needed to create the schedules will have been provided in the data room, it is good practice to coordinate data room preparation with schedule preparation.

A listing and brief description of specific schedules that typically accompany the purchase agreement follows. The listing and description are included for illustrative purposes, since the actual schedules for any given agreement are peculiar to each transaction.

- *Real Property Leases.* The seller would provide detailed descriptions of all real estate leases in effect, which would be included in their entirety as exhibits to the agreement.
- *Transferred Equipment.* This might include such things as all equipment, furniture, PCs, peripherals, copy machines, fax machines, and any other equipment that is integral to the operation of the company being sold. Such information would include a description (e.g., model number), serial number, and asset or tax number, if applicable.

- *Software and Computer Programs.* Any customized software would be described in detail. All packaged software should be listed with the number of licenses being transferred.
- *Transferred Contracts.* All letter agreements, service agreements, consulting agreements, and contracts should be listed with contacting parties, execution dates, and appropriate identifiers (e.g., contract or project number).
- *Excluded Contracts.* To the extent that such contracts exist, they would be listed.
- *Web Sites.* All Web sites that will be transferred would be listed.
- *Financial Statements.* Statements for the periods and year-ends agreed to would be supplied. If these have been audited, this would include the full sets of financial statements, along with footnote disclosures and audit opinions.
- *Litigation.* Any and all legal actions initiated against the company being sold would be described. If none exists, the schedule would generally be included and would indicate that there are none.
- *Liens.* Similar to litigation items, they would be described or, if there are none, the schedule would so indicate.
- *Intellectual Property.* A list of all intellectual properties (such as trademarks, trade names, copyrights, and patents) being transferred would be listed. The listing would generally include these items to ensure that the properties are clearly and properly identified: description, status (registered or pending), application number, registration number, renewal date, file date, registration date, country, owner, and class.
- *Taxes.* Any exceptions to compliance with federal, state, and local tax statutes would be listed or, if there are none, the schedule would so indicate.
- *Business Employees.* All individuals employed by the company being sold would be identified by such indicators as name, title, department, annual pay rate, hire date, and location. Any bonus and commission plans would also be described, and individuals entitled to such compensation would be identified.
- *Environmental Matters.* A list of any environmental citations or claims by governmental bodies would be listed, and if there are none the schedule would so indicate.

5.3 SUPPORTING DOCUMENTS

Additional supporting documents generally include a noncompete agreement, and employment and/or consulting agreements. If the transaction involves the divestiture of a non-standalone business unit, the package will also usually include a transition services agreement. These contracts are discussed in the sections that follow. Because the noncompete agreement is so fundamental to the transaction, it is discussed in great detail.

(a) NONCOMPETE AGREEMENTS.

(i) General.   An important element in many acquisitions, particularly for smaller companies, is a noncompetition covenant. This is often combined with other restrictive agreements that prevent or limit the seller from competing with the acquired business for a defined period of time after the sale. Particularly in a closely held business, where the reputation and goodwill of the business being sold is closely intertwined with the individual or individuals who own and operate the business, it is essential that the sellers be prevented from engaging in a new business that competes with the company they have just sold. In the broadest sense, this means effectively prohibiting them from starting a new business or from indirectly using their experience and reputations by, for example, going to work for an existing competitor or by providing advice to a third-party competitor.

The term "noncompetition covenant" means that one party, the seller in the case of an acquisitive transaction, agrees with the other party, the buyer in this case, that the seller will not compete within a defined type of business activity, within a specified geographic area, for a specified period of time. All three elements must be clearly defined within the agreement, which is characterized as a noncompetition covenant. Although, in a general sense, a noncompetition covenant is a contract addressed to a particular issue, its treatment by the law is so specialized that it is usually referred to as a *noncompetition covenant* to distinguish it clearly from other types of contracts and agreements. Occasionally this covenant is contained within the terms of the basic acquisition documents. More commonly, it is a distinct, separate document signed at closing.

Noncompetition covenants are widely recognized throughout the commercial world. There are, however, widely differing standards and customs with respect to the negotiation and enforcement of such covenants. The discussion in this chapter is limited to the use of noncompetition covenants in the United States. Even within the United States, standards for legal enforcement vary widely from one state to another and even from one court to another, as discussed in more detail herein.

(ii) Legal Status. A noncompetition covenant is a limited restriction of trade. The laws of the United States, and the laws of England from which our common law is derived, have traditionally looked at any kind of restraint of trade with extreme suspicion. As a general proposition, restraints on trade are illegal and unenforceable; however, noncompetition covenants represent a limited exception to that general rule. There is a history of case law going back hundreds of years in which noncompetition covenants have been treated as a special category of agreements that would be unenforceable under most circumstances but that, subject to very special limitations, are permitted in connection with certain types of transactions, including sales of businesses.

The common law attitude of the courts has been carried into the statutory laws of many states. Colorado and California are two examples of states that have passed legislation that limits the enforceability of noncompetition covenants to a greater extent than would be the case under common law. Some states either prohibit or greatly limit the use of noncompetition covenants in connection with employment relationships, holding that it is unjust for an employer to require, as a condition of employment, that employees enter into a noncompetition covenant that limits their future employability. However, absent such statutes, most states will permit limited enforcement of employment-related noncompetition covenants. This author is not aware of any jurisdiction in the United States that has prohibited the use of noncompetition covenants in connection with the purchase and sale of a business. Accordingly, for purposes of this chapter, a noncompetition covenant properly drafted and administered is likely to be enforced in accordance with its terms.

The general requirement for enforceability of a noncompetition covenant, in view of the fact that it is a type of agreement that is disapproved of by common law, is that it must be reasonable in all three of its essential elements: type of activity affected, geographic area, and duration. With respect to each of these three categories, a court is supposed to consider whether the limitation imposed is reasonably required for the protection of the purchaser, whether it imposes an unnecessary hardship on the seller, and whether it adversely affects the public interest by imposing a greater restraint on trade than is absolutely necessary for the accomplishment of its purposes.

As a very general rule, a noncompetition covenant given in connection with the purchase or sale of a business that defines the prohibited activity as the same business as the company being purchased, limits the geographic scope to the area in which the acquired company currently operates (and perhaps areas in which it may logically expand), and continues in effect for five years or so is likely to be enforced.

There is considerable older case law to the effect that a noncompetition covenant that prohibits competitive activity, *even for a limited period of time,* throughout the entire world, or even throughout the entire United States, is unenforceable. However, with the rapid growth of e-commerce and other high-technology activities that are essentially worldwide in nature, we are seeing more noncompetition covenants with very broad geographic limits, including worldwide application, but with very narrow defined areas of competition and short durations. For example, a traditional noncompetition covenant might prohibit someone from producing and selling bricks for five years within a 50-mile radius of the city limits of a specified city. A high-tech limitation might prohibit someone from designing or operating a Web site relating to the sale of a particular product anyplace in the world, but the duration of the covenant might be for a year or less. Although there has not been much opportunity yet to test the enforceability of the more modern type of noncompetition covenant, most practicing attorneys believe that such covenants covering wide geographic areas are probably enforceable.

To complicate the legal issues, noncompetition covenants are often enforced through an injunction or similar court order. Such orders are within the equitable power of the court. Equitable remedies are subject to a special set of standards. For example, a party seeking an injunction must have "clean hands." A buyer who has engaged in some type of misconduct in dealing with a seller may be found to have unclean hands and therefore be denied the requested relief.

(iii) Enforcement.   Most noncompetition covenants provide that they may be enforced in two ways: by an award of monetary damages and by the equitable powers of the court. Neither remedy is exclusive. In most cases equitable enforcement is of primary importance. The reason is that a lawsuit for damages is likely to drag on for an extended period of time, but a violation of a noncompete covenant is likely to cause immediate and substantial harm. The normal judicial standard is that where an action threatens "immediate and irreparable injury for which monetary damages would be inadequate or difficult to ascertain," equitable relief will be permitted. This does not mean that subsequent monetary damages are excluded. It only means that the injured party may immediately ask for equitable relief and defer trying its damage case. Equitable relief means that a court has the right, using its injunctive powers, to enter an order prohibiting continued violation. An injunction is enforceable in a variety of ways, including court-imposed monetary damages and even imprisonment. Such court-ordered relief can often be obtained within a few days through a procedure known as a *temporary restraining order.* The party requiring such relief, usually the purchaser of a business, is likely to be required by the court to post a monetary bond as security for the order. If, ultimately at trial, the order is found to have been unjustified, the bond may be forfeited in whole or in part to the other party.

Although none of the foregoing replaces the ability of an injured party to obtain monetary damages, most noncompetition cases are resolved rather quickly through the entry or denial of a temporary restraining order. There is also an intermediate stage in which the moving party seeks a *preliminary injunction.* This also is handled on an expedited basis and is apt to be decided within a matter of a few weeks after the entry or denial of the original temporary restraining order. In many cases, the court's decision to either grant or deny a temporary injunction terminates the case.

The practical ramifications of this are substantial. A party who negotiates a noncompetition covenant wants to make every effort to improve its probability of success at a temporary restraining order or preliminary injunction stage. Therefore, crafting the noncompetition covenant for maximum likelihood of success in the event of litigation is important. A common technique, for example, is a provision that says that if the court finds the covenant to be overly broad, it may enforce part but not all of the covenant. Under such a provision, if the court decided that the geographic area was too broad, it could reduce the area. Unfortunately, courts will sometimes reject the ability to scale back an overly broad covenant and instead declare the whole provision unenforceable.

A number of peculiar characteristics result from the procedural setting of noncompetition disputes. For example, this author (and many other attorneys) will include in a noncompetition covenant a clause in which the seller admits that equitable enforcement is appropriate. We also often attempt to include a clause that provides that the seller waive or severely limit his or her right to receive a monetary bond as protection at the time temporary relief is granted. Such provisions are often the subject of intense negotiation, but the typical attitude of a seller is that the noncompetition is so essential to the value of the business that strict enforcement is absolutely required.

Another consequence of the procedural setting is that the case law relating to noncompetition covenants, as compared to other areas of the law, is confusing. Most legal principles are derived from decisions by appellate courts, which render their decisions after careful review of a full trial on the merits of a case by a trial judge and jury. Most noncompetition covenants never get to an appellate court decision because they are resolved in a speedy hearing before a judge (juries normally do not participate in equitable decisions). These decisions are usually unreported and therefore tend to lack the consistency and precision of standards that are found in most other areas of the law. Accordingly, there is something in the nature of a shooting-from-the-hip process involved in trying to enforce a noncompetition covenant. A litigant is never quite certain how a particular judge will respond to a specific set of circumstances in the absence of detailed appellate court guidance. The conclusion most sellers reach from this is to reinforce their commitment to have an ironclad noncompete agreement that is likely to be enforceable no matter what judge hears the case or what circumstances exist at the time it is decided.

(iv) Tax Aspects.   Prior to the passage of Internal Revenue Service Code Section 197, there was confusion and room for disputes with the Internal Revenue Service over the tax treatment of noncompetition covenants. Section 197 has, however, eliminated much of this uncertainty by classifying a noncompetition covenant as an amortizable

intangible. As a result, a buyer who pays for a noncompetition covenant acquires an intangible asset that will be amortized over 15 years for tax purposes. A seller who receives a noncompetition payment receives ordinary income. In effect, the noncompetition covenant is a kind of negative service payment; the seller is paid not to do something, and this is treated as ordinary income to the seller.

This tax treatment of noncompetition covenants is not particularly desirable for either party. A seller is taxed at the maximum rate, and a buyer receives tax deductions over 15 years. Given the choice, most parties would prefer to allocate consideration to an asset that will result in a capital gain to the seller (e.g., goodwill) or a shorter-term write-off to the buyer (e.g., tools or equipment).

As a result, there may be some tendency during the course of negotiations for parties to try to minimize the allocation of consideration to noncompetition covenants and to reallocate such amounts to other assets instead. Of course, the Internal Revenue Code requires that allocations be made based on the actual fair market value of assets, and any artificial reduction of the allocation to noncompetition covenants could result in a reallocation by the Internal Revenue Service (IRS).

Apart from this problem, however, the buyer must be sensitive to the fact that a very low allocation to a noncompetition covenant may adversely affect the enforceability of the covenant. When a buyer goes to court to enforce a noncompetition provision, he or she must argue that a violation of the covenant is likely to cause immediate and irreparable damage. If the allocation of purchase price to the noncompete is nominal, the buyer's credibility before the court suffers. Moreover, if a lawsuit over a noncompetition covenant proceeds to trial and an award of damages, the judge or jury who determines the amount of damages may be influenced by the consideration that was originally allocated to the noncompete agreement. In practice, most experts believe that enforceability should not be tied to the amount of the tax allocation, but this issue nonetheless presents some potential problems that both parties, but the buyer in particular, should approach with caution.

(v) Other Limitations.   A noncompetition covenant is a very specific and narrow restriction on the seller's future activities. There are, however, numerous other restrictions that may be imposed and that may be helpful to the buyer.

A few examples follow.

- *Confidentiality.* Most agreements with a seller will include provisions protecting the confidentiality of proprietary information acquired in the transaction. To the extent possible, such a provision should be as detailed and specific as possible, itemizing, for example, such matters as lists of names and addresses of customers, pricing lists both for suppliers and customers, internal procedures such as bidding and pricing procedures, and of course obvious matters such as proprietary technology and know-how. Such provisions are generally enforceable and may supplement a noncompetition covenant by effectively preventing a seller from using information that is central to his or her ability to compete effectively.
- *Nonenticement.* It is fairly standard to include a provision that prevents a seller from hiring any of the employees of the acquired business. While technically such clauses are referred to as nonenticement or nonsolicitation clauses, it is obviously not very effective to prevent someone from hiring existing employees if the provision can be circumvented by saying that the employee initiated the contact. Therefore, such provisions usually provide that the seller cannot employ any of the existing employees of the business for some period of time after closing even if the employee actively seeks employment from the seller.
- *Customer Solicitation.* A similar provision prevents the seller from doing business with any of the customers or clients of the acquired business. In practice, such a provision is not very different from a noncompetition clause and is likely to be subject to the same type of strict scrutiny from a court in determining whether it can be enforced. Nonetheless, most experts will include a nonsolicitation clause in the same agreement that provides for noncompetition on the theory that they have one additional basis for claims against the seller.
- *Noncriticism.* This clause provides that the seller will not disparage, derogate, or otherwise criticize the future conduct of the business by the buyer. It is not clear whether this adds very much to the general right of one party to sue another for defamation, but such clauses are sometimes included and are thought to discourage a seller from making critical comments about the

buyer that might injure the buyer's business or assist the seller or some other party in competing with the buyer.

(vi) Negotiation. Noncompetition covenants are frequently among the most fiercely negotiated provisions in an agreement. For all of the reasons noted herein, the buyer is likely to insist on tough and clearly enforceable provisions. A seller, however, will be concerned that the noncompetition covenant may overreach its reasonable goals and prevent him or her from engaging in legitimate future business activities that do not directly compete with or injure the buyer.

Because the buyer is seeking the utmost enforceability, a noncompetition covenant will almost always cover various types of indirect competition, such as providing consulting services or financial assistance to a competitive business. A frequent complaint from sellers is that their children or other close associates may want to enter into a similar (but not directly competitive) business at some time in the future and they do not want to be subject to equitable penalties or large monetary damages simply because they choose to make a loan or gift of money or provide advice to such persons. At the extreme, some sellers fail to understand that a noncompetition covenant is necessary for the protection of the buyer and goes to the very heart of protecting the value of the business being acquired.

(b) EMPLOYMENT/CONSULTING AGREEMENTS. Another important area of negotiation is the relationship of the parties after the closing. A buyer will almost always require a brief period of consulting or employment by the principal employees of the seller after closing. These persons are most familiar with the business and should be available at least to assist in the transition and to provide information to the buyer. In some cases, the buyer will insist on an employment agreement that extends for several years with one or more of the sellers. It is important that such arrangements are explicit about the terms of the employee or consulting relationship, particularly the responsibilities of the employee/consultant and the compensation to be paid. There should be a clear distinction between the consideration paid for the property being purchased and the compensation paid for the services provided.

(c) TRANSITION SERVICES AGREEMENT. Divestitures frequently involve the sale of a business unit that may not be an entirely stand-alone entity. It is commonly the case that the business unit being divested has been owned by the seller for an extended period, in some cases for decades, and that the operational support of the property, in areas such as accounting, human resource administration, and technology services, is very likely to have become intertwined with that of the parent. As a result, the unit may require interim operational support until the buyer can fill any operational gaps that may exist. From a seller's perspective, such services can be burdensome, yet from a buyer's perspective, they may be absolutely necessary. The common ground that is generally found will provide for payment of services at cost or market rates for a limited period of time, generally no more than several months.

ILLUSTRATION OF STOCK PURCHASE AGREEMENT

Article IV Representations and Warranties of Buyer
    4.1 Organization and Qualification of the Buyer
    4.2 Corporate Authority
    4.3 No Violation of Obligations
    4.4 Financial Statements
    4.5 Liabilities
    4.6 Compliance with Law
    4.7 Legal Proceedings
    4.8 Liens
    4.9 Securities Compliance
    4.10 Complete Disclosure
Article V Information and Confidentiality
    5.1 Provision of Information Relating to Company
    5.2 Confidentiality
    5.3 Provision of Information Relating to Buyer
    5.4 Contacts with Third Parties
Article VI Consulting and Noncompetition Agreements
    6.1 Consulting Agreement
    6.2 Noncompetition Covenant
Article VII Conditions to Closing
    7.1 Seller's Conditions
    7.2 Buyer's Conditions
Article VIII Closing
    8.1 Certificates
    8.2 Company's Legal Opinion
    8.3 Endorsement of Stock Certificates
    8.4 Resignation of Seller
    8.5 Election of New Officers and Directors
    8.6 Issuance of New Stock Certificate
    8.7 Purchase Price
    8.8 Security for Purchase Price
    8.9 Consulting Agreement
    8.10 Noncompetition Covenant
    8.11 Noncompetition Payment
    8.12 Other Acts
Article IX Termination
    9.1 Failure to Close
    9.2 Failure of Condition
    9.3 Termination by Agreement

ILLUSTRATION OF STOCK PURCHASE AGREEMENT

This Stock Purchase Agreement is made and entered into as of 200X, by and among Corporation A, a [Name of State] corporation (here-inafter referred to as "Buyer"), John A. Seller (hereinafter referred to as "Seller"), and Corporation B, a [Name of State] corporation (here-inafter called the "Company").

ARTICLE I PURCHASE AND SALE

Subject to the terms and conditions of the Agreement set forth below, Seller agrees to sell, and Buyer agrees to purchase, all of the issued and outstanding shares of stock of the Company.

ARTICLE II PURCHASE PRICE AND NONCOMPETITION PAYMENT

The total consideration for the shares of stock to be purchased and the noncompetition covenant of the Seller hereunder is the sum of $2 million, payable as follows:

2.1 CASH PAYMENT. At the time of Closing, the Buyer shall pay to the Seller the sum of $750,000 in certified funds, by wire transfer, or in other form satisfactory to the Seller, as a down payment on the stock of the Company.

2.2 NONCOMPETITION PAYMENT. At the time of Closing, the Buyer shall pay to the Seller the sum of $250,000, in the same manner as the payment made under Section 2.1, as consideration for the Seller's noncompetition covenant as provided for in Section 6.2.

2.3 PROMISSORY NOTE. The balance of the purchase price of $1 million for the stock will be paid by the Buyer to the Seller by delivery of a promissory note in the form attached hereto as Exhibit A (the "Promissory Note"). The Promissory Note shall provide for the payment of $1 million with interest at the rate of 8 percent per annum in equal monthly installments, amortizing principal and interest over a term of 10 years, with a balloon payment of all remaining principal and interest due 5 years after Closing.

2.4 SECURITY. As security for the payment of the deferred purchase price hereunder, the Buyer shall do the following:

1. Pledge to the Seller all of the stock purchased hereunder pursuant to the Pledge Agreement in the form attached hereto as Exhibit B (the "Pledge Agreement"); and
2. Cause the Company to guarantee the payment of the Promissory Note and to grant to the Seller a security interest in the furniture, fixtures, and equipment of the Company, which security interest shall be senior to all other encumbrances and liens on such assets. The security interest in favor of Seller shall be granted pursuant to a Security Agreement in the form attached hereto as Exhibit C (the "Company's Security Agreement").

ARTICLE III REPRESENTATIONS AND WARRANTIES OF THE SELLER AND THE COMPANY

The Seller and the Company jointly and severally represent and warrant to the Buyer as follows:

3.1 ORGANIZATION AND GOOD STANDING. The Company is a corporation duly organized, validly existing, and in good standing under the laws of the State of [Name of State]. The Company is not required, by the nature of its assets or business, to qualify as a foreign corporation in any other jurisdiction. The Company has full power to own all of its properties and to carry on its business as it is now being conducted.

3.2   CORPORATE AUTHORITY.   The Company has the authority, pursuant to its articles of incorporation and bylaws, and pursuant to such additional action as is necessary by its officers, directors, and shareholders, to execute this Agreement and to consummate the transactions provided for herein.

3.3   CAPITALIZATION OF THE COMPANY.   The Company has only one class of stock authorized by its articles of incorporation. The Seller owns 10,000 shares of the issued and outstanding shares of such stock. Such shares, all of which shall be transferred to the Buyer pursuant to this Agreement, represent all the issued and outstanding shares of stock of the Company. The Company has no stock options, warrants, or other rights to acquire stock outstanding. The shares of the Company's stock to be transferred by the Seller to the Buyer hereunder are free and clear of any liens, security interests, pledges, or other claims or rights on the part of any third party.

3.4   NO VIOLATION OF OBLIGATIONS.   The execution and delivery of this Agreement, and the consummation of the transactions provided for herein, will not violate any agreement or commitment made by the Company, or any requirement binding on the Company, including, without limitation, any lease, contract, loan agreement, promissory note, franchise agreement, court order, judgment, regulatory ruling, or arbitration award.

3.5   FINANCIAL STATEMENTS OF THE COMPANY.   The financial statements of the Company attached hereto as Schedule 3.5 (the "Financial Statements") fairly present the financial position of the Company as of the respective dates thereof and the results of the operations of the Company for the periods indicated. All of the Financial Statements have been prepared in accordance with generally accepted accounting principles applied on a basis consistent with that of preceding years, but those Financial Statements that are internal and unaudited have been prepared without certain year-end adjustments that are reflected in the audited statements. Neither the audited fiscal year-end Financial Statements nor the interim internal Financial Statements are, to the best knowledge of Seller, misleading in any material respect.

3.6   ASSETS.   The Company has good and marketable title to all of the Company's assets reflected on the Financial Statements and to certain other off-book assets (including previously expensed supplies and written-off inventory) shown on the attached Schedule 3.6 and collectively referred to as the "Company's Assets." Except as disclosed in the Financial Statements of the Company, the Company's Assets are not subject to any deed of trust, mortgage, security interest, or other liens or claims of any nature whatsoever. All of the Company's Assets are in satisfactory and operational condition, except as otherwise shown on Schedule 3.6. All inventory is shown on the Financial Statements at the lower of current fair market value or cost, and the accounts receivable (net of bad debt reserves) are collectible in full in the ordinary course of the Company's business.

3.7   LIABILITIES.   Except as shown on Schedule 3.7, the Company has no liabilities, liquidated, actual, or contingent, except as shown on the Financial Statements and except for liabilities which have arisen in the ordinary course of business from and after the date of the most recent Financial Statement. Any liabilities arising after the date of the Financial Statements have arisen in the ordinary course of business of the Company and are substantially similar as to kind and amount to those shown on the Financial Statements.

3.8   OPERATIONS SINCE THE FINANCIAL STATEMENTS.   Since the date of the most recent Financial Statement, there has not been and there will not be through the date of Closing:

1. Any change in the business, results of operations, assets, financial condition, or manner of conducting the business of the Company, which has or may be reasonably expected to have a material adverse effect on such business, results of operations, assets, or financial condition;

2. Any decrease in the net book value shown on the most recent balance sheet included within the Financial Statements;

3. Any damage, destruction, or loss (whether or not covered by insurance) which has or may reasonably be expected to have a material adverse effect upon any material asset or the business or operations of the Company;

4. Any declaration, setting aside, or payment of any dividend or other distribution in respect to the stock of the Company;

5. Any increase in the compensation payable or to become payable by the Company to any of its officers, directors, employees, or agents;

6. Any other distribution of any nature whatsoever to or for the benefit of the Seller;

7. Any issuance of shares of stock of the Company, or any grant of any option to purchase, or other rights to acquire, stock of the Company;

8. Any employment, bonus, or deferred compensation agreement entered into between the Company and any of its directors, officers, or other employees or consultants;

9. Any entering into, amendment, or termination by the Company of any material contract, franchise, permit, license, or other agreement;

10. Any indebtedness incurred by the Company, any commitment to borrow money, or any guarantee by the Company of any third-party obligation, or the imposition of any lien on the Company's assets or the grant of any encumbrance by the Company; or

11. Any amendment of the articles of incorporation or bylaws of the Company.

3.9 LEGAL PROCEEDINGS. There are no private or governmental proceedings pending, or to the knowledge of Seller threatened, against the Company, including, without limitation, any investigation, audit, lawsuit, threatened lawsuit, arbitration, or other legal proceedings of any nature whatsoever.

3.10 MATERIAL AGREEMENTS. The Company is not a party to any employment agreement, equipment lease, real property lease, agreement for purchase or sale, franchise agreement, joint venture agreement, or any other contract, agreement, or other obligation, whether or not in writing, except for agreements that individually represent obligations on the part of the Company of less than $5,000 and in the aggregate obligations of not more than $25,000, other than agreements that are terminable at will by the Company and except for those agreements that are listed on Schedule 3.10 attached hereto. Copies of all agreements listed on Schedule 3.10 have been provided to the Buyer. None of such agreements is in default, nor is the Company or the Seller aware of any claim or penalty against the Company, which has accrued or which will accrue as a result of the Closing hereunder or for any other reason under any of such agreements.

3.11 EMPLOYEES.   Attached hereto as Schedule 3.11 is a list of all the Company's employees and the rate of compensation of each. None of such employees is a party to any employment agreement or other contract with the Company, nor are any of such employees entitled to any fringe benefits or other compensation from the Company except as reflected on Schedule 3.11 or separately reflected in a copy of the Company's employment manual, a current copy of which has been delivered to the Buyer. None of the Company's employees is subject to any collective bargaining agreement or other union agreement, nor is the Company or the Seller aware of any effort to organize any of the workforce of the Company. No disputes or claims against the Company exist on behalf of any of its employees, including, but not limited to, claims of employment discrimination, violation of wage and hour laws, or claims relating to past unpaid compensation.

3.12 COMPLIANCE WITH LAW.   The Company is not in violation of any material law, regulation, rule, ordinance, or other governmental requirement relating to its properties or its business. Neither the Company nor the Seller has knowledge of any development, occurrence, or condition that would adversely affect any of the Company's properties or that might curtail or interfere with the present or future use of such properties for the purposes for which they are now used.

3.13 ENVIRONMENTAL COMPLIANCE.   The Company is in full compliance with all applicable federal, state, and local laws, rules, and regulations relating to environmental regulation and to the disposal of waste products (including, but not limited to, those products defined as hazardous wastes under applicable federal and state laws). The Company does not lease, own, or operate a facility on, and has not leased, owned, or operated a facility on, any land or real property subject to any environmental contamination, violation, or requirement for cleanup or any other environmental remediation.

3.14 TAX RETURNS.   The Company has timely and correctly prepared and filed all tax returns, including federal and state income tax returns and sales tax returns, and the Company has paid all taxes due pursuant to such tax returns as well as all other taxes, including real and personal property taxes for which the Company is liable, except for certain property taxes which are accrued but not yet due as shown on Schedule 3.14. The Company has not filed for and is not now subject to any extension of time with respect to the filing of any tax return. The Company has provided to the Buyer true and correct copies of all federal and state income tax returns filed by it for the past three fiscal years. The Company is not aware of any actual or threatened tax audit. The Financial Statements reflect an adequate reserve, as of the dates thereof, for income taxes then due for the present tax year. The Company maintains all required payroll trust accounts, and the Company has timely paid all employee and employer withholding taxes into such trust accounts.

3.15 INSURANCE.   The Company maintains adequate insurance with qualified insurance carriers with respect to liability and property loss or damage. A list of insurance policies showing coverage amounts, insurance carrier, and type of coverage is set forth on Schedule 3.15. Copies of all such policies have been provided to the Buyer.

3.16 COMPLETE DISCLOSURE.   This Agreement and the agreements and instruments attached hereto and to be delivered at the time of Closing do not contain any untrue statement of a material fact by the Seller or the Company. This Agreement and such related agreements and instruments do not omit to state any material fact necessary in order to make the statements made herein or therein by the Company or the Seller, in light of the circumstances under which they are made, not misleading.

ARTICLE IV REPRESENTATIONS AND WARRANTIES OF BUYER

The Buyer represents and warrants to the Company and to the Seller as follows:

4.1 ORGANIZATION AND QUALIFICATION OF THE BUYER.   The Buyer is a corporation duly organized, validly existing, and in good standing under the laws of the State of [Name of State]. The Buyer is not required, by the nature of its assets or business, to qualify as a foreign corporation in any other state. The Buyer has full power to own all of its properties and to carry on its business as it is now being conducted.

4.2 CORPORATE AUTHORITY. The Buyer has the authority, pursuant to its articles of incorporation and bylaws, and pursuant to such additional action as is necessary by its officers, directors, and shareholders, to execute this Agreement and to consummate the transactions provided for herein.

4.3 NO VIOLATION OF OBLIGATIONS. The execution and delivery of this Agreement, and the consummation of the transactions provided for herein, will not violate any agreement or commitment made by the Buyer, or any requirement binding on the Buyer, including, without limitation, any lease, contract, loan agreement, promissory note, franchise agreement, court order, judgment, regulatory ruling, or any arbitration award.

4.4 FINANCIAL STATEMENTS. The financial statements previously delivered by the Buyer to the Seller are true and correct in all material respects. Such financial statements have been prepared in accordance with generally accepted accounting principles applied on a basis consistent with that of preceding years. The Seller has not experienced, will not experience through the time of Closing, and does not expect to experience thereafter, any material adverse change in the nature of its operations or business. Without limiting the foregoing, the Buyer has the ability to honor all of its obligations undertaken pursuant to this Agreement, specifically including the obligation to pay all amounts due pursuant to the Promissory Note in accordance with the terms thereof.

4.5 LIABILITIES. The Buyer has no liabilities, liquidated, actual, or contingent, except as shown on the financial statements previously provided to the Seller and except for liabilities that have arisen in the ordinary course of Buyer's business from and after the date of the most recent financial statements so provided. Any liabilities arising after the date of such financial statements have arisen in the ordinary course of business of the Buyer and are similar as to kind and amount to the liabilities shown on such financial statements.

4.6 COMPLIANCE WITH LAW. The Buyer is not in violation of any material law, regulation, rule, ordinance, or other governmental requirement relating to its properties or its business. The Buyer has no knowledge of any development, occurrence, or condition that would adversely affect any of the Buyer's properties or that might curtail or interfere with the present or future use of such properties for the purposes for which they are now used.

4.7 LEGAL PROCEEDINGS.   There are no private or governmental proceedings pending, or to the knowledge of Buyer threatened, against the Buyer, including, without limitation, any investigation, audit, lawsuit, threatened lawsuit, arbitration, or other legal proceedings of any nature whatsoever.

4.8 LIENS.   Except as disclosed in the financial statements of the Buyer, the Buyer and the assets of the Buyer are not subject to any deed of trust, mortgage, security interest, or other lien or claim of any nature whatsoever.

4.9 SECURITIES COMPLIANCE.   The Buyer is a sophisticated purchaser who either is experienced in evaluating and acquiring businesses similar to the Company or has had adequate advice from persons who have such experience. Buyer acknowledges that it has been provided with all information about the Company requested by Buyer, that Buyer, itself or through its advisors, has the expertise necessary to evaluate such information, that Buyer has been afforded opportunities to conduct its own investigation and to request additional information, and that Buyer does not desire any further information or opportunity to investigate the Company. Buyer intends to hold all of the Company's stock for investment purposes and has no intent to resell or otherwise distribute any of such stock.

4.10 COMPLETE DISCLOSURE.   This Agreement and the agreements and instruments related hereto do not contain any untrue statement of a material fact by the Buyer. This Agreement and such related agreements and instruments do not omit to state any material fact necessary in order to make the statements made herein or therein, in light of the circumstances under which they are made, not misleading.

ARTICLE V INFORMATION AND CONFIDENTIALITY
5.1 PROVISION OF INFORMATION RELATING TO COMPANY.   Prior to the execution of this Agreement, the Seller and the Company have

made available to the Buyer information relating to the Company, including, without limitation, financial statements and records, depreciation schedules, lists of equipment, copies of contracts and agreements, and access to the properties, assets, and operations of the Company. To the best knowledge of the Company and the Seller, all such information is substantially correct and complete. From and after the date of this Agreement and continuing through Closing, the Company and the Seller will continue to make available to the Buyer all information required hereunder or otherwise reasonably requested by the Buyer with respect to the Company.

5.2 CONFIDENTIALITY.   The Buyer acknowledges that all information with respect to the Company made available prior to and subsequent to the date of this Agreement and through the date of Closing is confidential. The Buyer shall use such information only for the purpose of evaluating the proposed transactions hereunder. In the event the transactions provided for in this Agreement fail to close for any reason whatsoever, the Buyer will promptly return all such information to the Seller, including any extracts, copies, or analyses based thereon which were prepared by the Buyer. The Buyer will not use, nor will it permit any third party to use, any of such information in any manner which is competitive with or injurious to the Company.

5.3 PROVISION OF INFORMATION RELATING TO BUYER.   The Buyer has provided certain information to the Seller, including financial statements and other information relating to the ability of the Buyer to carry out its obligations hereunder. The Buyer represents and warrants that such information is complete and accurate, and the Seller agrees that all such information is to be treated as confidential and will be used only for the purpose of evaluating the Seller's decision to consummate the transactions provided for herein.

5.4 CONTACTS WITH THIRD PARTIES.   The existence of this Agreement and the transactions provided for herein are confidential. Public announcements shall be made only pursuant to mutual agreement of the parties hereto. Prior to the time of any such public announcement, the Buyer shall not disclose to any third party that it is contemplating the purchase of the Company, but the Seller agrees that it will at mutually agreeable times arrange for interviews by the Buyer, at which a representative of the Seller may be present, with key employees, suppliers, and customers of the Company. The Buyer agrees to conduct such interviews in such manner as to avoid any interference with the Company's relationships with such persons and subject to such reasonable constraints as are requested by the Seller.

ARTICLE VI CONSULTING AND NONCOMPETITION AGREEMENTS

At the time of Closing, the Seller, individually, will enter into the following agreements:

6.1 CONSULTING AGREEMENT.   A consulting agreement in the form attached hereto as Exhibit D (the "Consulting Agreement") providing for substantially full-time consulting services to be rendered by the Seller to the Buyer and the Company for a period of 60 days after Closing and for part-time services to be rendered thereafter on a schedule mutually agreeable to the Buyer and the Seller.

6.2 NONCOMPETITION COVENANT.   The Seller shall further enter into an agreement in the form attached hereto as Exhibit E (the "Noncompetition Covenant") whereby the Seller will agree not to compete with the business of the Company within a radius of 250 miles of the present principal place of business of the Company for a period of five years from and after the time of Closing.

ARTICLE VII CONDITIONS TO CLOSING

The obligations of the parties to close the transactions provided for herein are subject to the following conditions, as well as to any other conditions expressed or implied in this Agreement:

7.1 SELLER'S CONDITIONS.   The obligations of the Seller and the Company are subject to the following conditions:

1. All representations, warranties, covenants, and other agreements contained herein on the part of the Buyer will be true and correct at the time of Closing.
2. The Seller will be satisfied, at its sole discretion, with the financial ability of the Buyer to honor its obligations pursuant to the Promissory Note.

3. No lawsuit, governmental action, or other legal proceeding shall have been commenced which shall materially interfere with the ability of the parties to consummate the transactions provided for herein.

7.2 BUYER'S CONDITIONS.   The obligations of the Buyer to complete the transactions provided for herein are subject to the following conditions:

1. All representations, warranties, covenants, and other agreements contained herein on the part of the Seller and the Company will be true and correct at the time of Closing.
2. No lawsuit, governmental action, or other legal proceeding shall have been commenced that shall materially interfere with the ability of the parties to consummate the transactions provided for herein.
3. Buyer will have completed an investigation and examination of the Company, the results of which will be satisfactory to the Buyer in its sole discretion.
4. The book value of the Company will be not less than the amount shown on the most recent balance sheet included in the Financial Statements.
5. The Buyer will be reasonably satisfied as to the willingness of the key employees of the Company to continue working for the Company after the Closing hereunder.

ARTICLE VIII CLOSING

The Closing of all transactions provided for herein will occur at the offices of legal counsel for the Buyer at 10:00 A.M. on [date] (the "Closing"). The transactions at Closing, when effective, will be deemed to be effective as of the opening of business on the day of Closing, except as otherwise specifically provided at the time of Closing. All actions to be taken at Closing will be considered to be taken simultaneously, and no document, agreement, or instrument will be considered to be delivered until all items that are to be delivered at the Closing have been executed and delivered. At the Closing, the following actions will occur:

8.1 CERTIFICATES.   The Buyer, the Seller, and the Company will each, respectively, execute a certificate stating that all representations and warranties made by them respectively in this Agreement continue to be true as of the time of Closing.

8.2 COMPANY'S LEGAL OPINION.   The Seller will deliver to the Buyer an opinion of Seller's and Company's legal counsel, in form reasonably satisfactory to the Buyer, opining favorably as to the matters set forth in Sections 3.1, 3.2, 3.3, and, to the best of such counsel's knowledge, to the matters in Section 3.4 of this Agreement.

8.3 ENDORSEMENT OF STOCK CERTIFICATES.   The Seller will execute and deliver to the Buyer the stock certificate or certificates evidencing all ownership of all the stock of the Company that is now issued and outstanding, duly endorsed for transfer to the Buyer.

8.4 RESIGNATION OF SELLER.   The Seller shall resign as an officer, director, and all other positions with the Company.

8.5 ELECTION OF NEW OFFICERS AND DIRECTORS.   The Buyer will cause the Company to elect new officers and directors designated by the Buyer.

8.6 ISSUANCE OF NEW STOCK CERTIFICATE.   The new officers and directors designated by the Buyer will cause a new stock certificate, evidencing ownership of all the shares of the stock that it surrendered, to be issued to the Buyer.

8.7 PURCHASE PRICE.   The Buyer will pay the purchase price for the shares of stock purchased by delivery of $750,000 in cash or certified funds, by wire transfer, or in other form satisfactory to the Seller, and by execution and delivery of the Promissory Note.

8.8 SECURITY FOR PURCHASE PRICE.   As security for the payment of the deferred purchase price, the Buyer shall do the following:

1. The directors of the Company, designated by the Seller, will cause the Company to guarantee the Promissory Note, by delivery of a duly authorized written guarantee in form satisfactory to the Seller.
2. The Company will grant to the Seller a security interest in its furniture, fixtures, and equipment by executing and delivering

the Company's Security Agreement and a Uniform Commercial Code financing statement fully executed in form suitable for recording.

3. The Buyer will deliver to the Seller, endorsed in blank, the stock certificate or certificates evidencing ownership of all the stock purchased hereunder, and a fully executed Pledge Agreement.

8.9 CONSULTING AGREEMENT.   The Company, acting through the officers and directors appointed by the Buyer, shall execute the Consulting Agreement, and the Seller shall execute the Consulting Agreement.

8.10 NONCOMPETITION COVENANT.   The Buyer and the Company, acting through the officers and directors appointed by the Buyer, shall execute the Noncompetition Covenant, and the Seller shall execute the Noncompetition Covenant.

8.11 NONCOMPETITION PAYMENT.   The Buyer shall pay the Seller the sum of $250,000 in cash or certified funds, by wire transfer, or in other form satisfactory to the Seller, as consideration for the Seller's noncompetition covenant.

8.12 OTHER ACTS.   The parties will execute any other documents reasonably required to carry out the intent of this Agreement.

ARTICLE IX TERMINATION

This Agreement will terminate in accordance with the following provisions:

9.1 FAILURE TO CLOSE.   If the purchase and sale provided for herein fails to close by the date provided in Article VIII above, then this Agreement shall terminate, unless the parties have, by mutual agreement, extended the time for Closing in writing. Termination shall not release any party of any liability for damages arising out of the breach, if any, of this Agreement, except as provided below.

9.2 FAILURE OF CONDITION.   If this Agreement terminates by reason of the failure of any condition provided for herein to be satisfied at the time of Closing, and if the failure to satisfy such condition occurs without material fault on the part of either party hereto, then this Agreement shall terminate without liability on the part of either party hereto, except that the confidentiality provisions set forth in Sections 5.2 and 5.3 shall remain in effect.

9.3 TERMINATION BY AGREEMENT.   If the parties hereto agree to terminate this Agreement, such termination shall be effective without liability to either party hereto.

ARTICLE X MUTUAL INDEMNIFICATION

Each of the parties hereto agrees to indemnify and hold harmless each of the other parties against any loss resulting from a violation of this Agreement on the part of the indemnifying party. Such indemnification obligation shall include indemnification for any costs reasonably incurred by the indemnified party, including, without limitation, legal costs and reasonable attorney's fees. However, no right to indemnification shall arise hereunder unless the aggregate of all indemnified losses of any party hereto (net of any losses of the other party that are subject to indemnification) exceeds the sum of $25,000.

ARTICLE XI POSTCLOSING OPERATIONS

From and after the time of Closing, the Buyer agrees as follows:

11.1 RELEASE OF SELLER.   The Buyer and the Company will utilize their best efforts to cause the Seller to be released from any guarantees or any other contingent obligations that the Seller may have with respect to the liabilities of the Company. Without limiting the generality of the foregoing, the Company will advise all lenders, lessors, and suppliers, at the time of renewing any existing leases, loans, lines of credit, or other obligations, that the Seller is no longer responsible for the obligations of the Company.

11.2 OPERATIONS IN ORDINARY COURSE.   The Company shall continue to operate its business in the ordinary course, fulfilling all contracts and other obligations that have been properly disclosed hereunder and that are not yet completed as of the time of Closing. The Company will maintain in effect all insurance policies, or will establish substantially similar coverage, with respect to any liabilities of the Company for which the Seller may have personal responsibility.

11.3 REPORTS. For so long as any amount remains outstanding pursuant to the Promissory Note, the Company and the Buyer will cause copies of the Company's annual financial statements to be delivered to the Seller promptly after the preparation of such statements.

ARTICLE XII GENERAL PROVISIONS

The following general provisions shall apply to this Agreement:

12.1 SURVIVAL OF AGREEMENT. This Agreement, and all terms, warranties, and provisions hereof, will be true and correct as of the time of Closing and will survive the Closing for a period of three years.

12.2 NOTICES. All notices required or permitted hereunder or under any related agreement or instrument (unless such related agreement or instrument otherwise provides) will be deemed delivered when delivered personally or mailed, by certified mail, return receipt requested, or registered mail, to the respective party at the following addresses or to such other address as each respective party may in writing hereafter designate:

1. To Seller:
2. To Buyer:
3. To Company:

12.3 SUCCESSORS AND ASSIGNS. This Agreement will be binding upon the parties hereto and their respective successors, personal representatives, heirs, and assigns. However, no party hereto will have any right to assign any of its obligations pursuant to this Agreement, except with the prior written consent of all of the other parties.

12.4 MERGER. This Agreement and the exhibits and other documents, agreements, and instruments related hereto set forth the entire agreement of the parties with respect to the subject matter hereof and may not be amended or modified except in writing subscribed to by all such parties.

12.5 GOVERNING LAW. This Agreement is entered into in the State of [name of State], it will be performed within such state, and all issues arising hereunder shall be governed in all respects by the laws of such state.

12.6 OBLIGATIONS TO BROKERS.   No party hereto has incurred any obligation for the payment of any brokerage commission, finder's fee, or any other similar obligation relating to this Agreement or the consummation of the transactions provided for herein.

12.7 MODIFICATION OR SEVERANCE.   In the event that any provision of this Agreement is found by any court or other authority of competent jurisdiction to be illegal or unenforceable, such provision shall be severed or modified to the extent necessary to render it enforceable and as so severed or modified, this Agreement will remain in full force and effect.

12.8 CAPTIONS.   The captions in this Agreement are included for convenience only and shall not in any way affect the interpretation of any of the provisions hereof.

IN WITNESS WHEREOF, the parties have read and entered into
    this Agreement as of the date above written.
Buyer:
By:
Seller:
Company: By:
LIST OF EXHIBITS
Exhibit A   Promissory Note
Exhibit B   Pledge Agreement
Exhibit C   Company's Security Agreement
Exhibit D   Consulting Agreement
Exhibit E   Noncompetition Covenant

ILLUSTRATION OF ASSETS PURCHASE AGREEMENT

ILLUSTRATION OF ASSETS PURCHASE AGREEMENT

This Assets Purchase Agreement is made and entered into as of 200X, by and among Corporation A, a [Name of State] corporation (hereinafter referred to as "Buyer"), John A. Seller (hereinafter referred to as "Shareholder"), and Corporation B, a [Name of State] corporation (hereinafter called the "Seller").

ARTICLE I PURCHASE AND SALE OF ASSETS

Subject to the terms and conditions of this Agreement set forth below, Seller agrees to sell, and Buyer agrees to purchase, all of the assets of the Seller and to assume certain specified liabilities of the Seller. The "Assets" to be acquired hereunder are all of the assets of the Seller shown on the financial statements of the Seller as of the date of closing, all assets arising in the ordinary course of business from and after the date of such balance sheet, and any and all other assets, owned by the Seller, including its files and records, intangible information, trademarks and trade names, previously expensed tools and supplies, and all other assets now located at the principal place of business of the Seller, except for those assets which have previously been identified by the Buyer and Seller as being the property of the Shareholder, which are to be retained by the Shareholder at the time of closing, which excluded assets are referred to herein as the "Excluded Assets."

ARTICLE II PURCHASE PRICE AND NONCOMPETITION PAYMENT

The total consideration for the Assets and the noncompetition covenant of the Seller is the sum of $2 million, payable as set forth below, plus assumption of certain of Seller's liabilities as provided for in Article III below:

2.1 CASH PAYMENT.   At the time of Closing, the Buyer shall pay to the Seller the sum of $750,000 in certified funds, by wire transfer, or in other form satisfactory to the Seller.

2.2 NONCOMPETITION PAYMENT.   The Buyer shall further pay the sum of $250,000 to the Shareholder, individually, at Closing as consideration for the noncompetition covenant provided for in Section 7.2 later.

2.3 PROMISSORY NOTE.   The balance of the purchase price of $1 million will be paid by the Buyer to the Seller by delivery of a promissory note in the form attached hereto as Exhibit A (the "Promissory Note"). The Promissory Note shall provide for the payment of $1 million with interest at the rate of 8 percent per annum in equal monthly installments, amortizing principal and interest over a term of 10 years, with a balloon payment of all remaining principal and interest due 5 years after Closing.

2.4 SECURITY.   As security for the payment of the purchase price hereunder, the Buyer shall execute and deliver to the Seller a security agreement in the form attached hereto as Exhibit B (the "Security Agreement") providing to the Seller a senior security interest in all of the furniture, fixtures, and equipment purchased hereunder and a security interest subordinate only to the security interest of Buyer's lending bank in the accounts receivable, inventory, and other Assets acquired hereunder. The subordination agreement between the lending bank and the Seller shall be in the form of the subordination agreement attached hereto as Exhibit C (the "Subordination Agreement").

ARTICLE III ASSUMPTION OF LIABILITIES

Subject to the terms and conditions of this Agreement, the Buyer agrees, as further consideration for the Assets to be acquired hereunder, to assume and pay in the ordinary course of business after closing all of the liabilities of the Seller as shown on its most recent balance sheet included in the "Financial Statements" attached as Schedule 4.4 and all liabilities arising in the ordinary course of business from and after the date of such balance sheet, provided that such further liabilities shall be of similar kind and amount to those which have previously arisen in the ordinary course of the Seller's business.

ARTICLE IV REPRESENTATIONS AND WARRANTIES OF THE SHAREHOLDER AND THE SELLER

The Shareholder and the Seller jointly and severally represent and warrant to the Buyer as follows:

4.1   ORGANIZATION AND GOOD STANDING.   The Seller is a corporation duly organized, validly existing, and in good standing under the laws of the State of [Name of State]. The Seller is not required, by the nature of its assets or business, to qualify as a foreign corporation in any other jurisdiction. The Seller has full power to own all of its properties and to carry on its business as it is now being conducted.

4.2   CORPORATE AUTHORITY.   The Seller has the authority, pursuant to its articles of incorporation and bylaws, and pursuant to such additional action as is necessary by its officers, directors, and shareholders, to execute this Agreement and to consummate the transactions provided for herein. Without limiting the generality of the foregoing, the shareholders of the Seller will unanimously approve the transactions provided for herein prior to closing.

4.3   NO VIOLATION OF OBLIGATIONS.   The execution and delivery of this Agreement, and the consummation of the transactions provided for herein, will not violate any agreement or commitment made by the Seller or the Shareholder, or any requirement binding on the Seller or the Shareholder, respectively, including, without limitation, any lease, contract, loan agreement, promissory note, franchise agreement, court order, judgment, regulatory ruling, or arbitration award.

4.4   FINANCIAL STATEMENTS OF THE SELLER.   The financial statements of the Seller attached hereto as Schedule 4.4 (the "Financial Statements") fairly present the financial position of the Seller as of the respective dates thereof and the results of the operations of the

Seller for the periods indicated. All of the Financial Statements have been prepared in accordance with generally accepted accounting principles applied on a basis consistent with that of preceding years, but those Financial Statements that are internal and unaudited have been prepared without certain year-end adjustments that are reflected in the audited statements. Neither the audited fiscal year-end Financial Statements nor the interim internal Financial Statements are, to the best knowledge of Seller and the Shareholder, misleading in any material respect.

4.5   ASSETS.   The Seller has good and marketable title to all of the Assets. Except as disclosed in the Financial Statements of the Seller, the Assets are not subject to any deed of trust, mortgage, security interest, or other liens or claims of any nature whatsoever. All of the Assets are in satisfactory and operational condition, except as otherwise shown on Schedule 4.5. All inventory is shown on the Financial Statements at the lower of current fair market value or cost, and the accounts receivable shown thereon (net of bad debt reserves) are collectible in full in the ordinary course of business.

4.6   LIABILITIES.   Except as shown on Schedule 4.6, the Seller has no liabilities, liquidated, actual, or contingent, except as shown on the Financial Statements and except for liabilities that have arisen in the ordinary course of Seller's business from and after the date of the most recent Financial Statement. Any liabilities arising after the date of the most recent Financial Statement have arisen in the ordinary course of business of the Seller and are substantially similar as to kind and amount to those shown on the Financial Statements. Schedule 4.6 specifically sets forth all accrued benefits due to employees, including sick leave and vacation rights, whether or not such liabilities are reflected on the Financial Statements.

4.7   OPERATIONS SINCE THE FINANCIAL STATEMENTS.   Since the date of the most recent Financial Statement, there has not been and there will not be through the date of Closing:

1.   Any change in the business, results of operations, assets, financial condition, or manner of conducting the business of the Seller, which has or may be reasonably expected to have a

material adverse effect on such business, results of operations, assets, or financial condition;

2. Any decrease in the net book value of the Seller shown on the most recent balance sheet included within the Financial Statements;

3. Any damage, destruction, or loss (whether or not covered by insurance) that has or may reasonably be expected to have a material adverse effect upon any material asset or the business or operations of the Seller;

4. Any declaration, setting aside, or payment of any dividend or other distribution with respect to the stock of the Seller;

5. Any increase in the compensation payable or to become payable by the Seller to any of its officers, directors, employees, or agents;

6. Any other distributions by the Seller of any nature whatsoever to or for the benefit of the Shareholder;

7. Any issuance of shares of stock of the Seller, or any grant of any option to purchase, or other rights to acquire, stock of the Seller;

8. Any employment, bonus, or deferred compensation agreement entered into between the Seller and any of its directors, officers, or other employees or consultants;

9. Any entering into, amendment, or termination by the Seller of any material contract, franchise, permit, license, or other agreement; or

10. Any indebtedness incurred by the Seller to borrow money, any commitment to borrow money, or any guarantee by the Seller of any third-party obligations, or the imposition of any lien on the Seller's assets or the grant of any encumbrance by the Seller.

4.8 LEGAL PROCEEDINGS.   There are no private or governmental proceedings pending, or to the knowledge of the Shareholder or Seller threatened, against the Seller, including, without limitation, any investigation, audit, lawsuit, threatened lawsuit, arbitration, or other legal proceedings of any nature whatsoever.

4.9 MATERIAL AGREEMENTS.   The Seller is not a party to any employment agreement, equipment lease, real property lease, agreement for purchase or sale, franchise agreement, joint-venture agreement, or any other contract, agreement, or other obligation, whether or not in writing (other than agreements that individually represent obligations on the part of the Seller of less than $5,000 and in the aggregate obligations of not more than $25,000), except for agreements that are terminable within 30 days by the Seller and any assignee of the Seller and except those agreements that are listed on Schedule 4.9 attached hereto. Copies of all agreements listed on Schedule 4.9 have been provided to the Buyer. None of such agreements is in default, nor is the Seller or the Shareholder aware of any claim or penalty against the Seller that has accrued or that will accrue as a result of the Closing hereunder or for any other reason under any of such agreements.

4.10   EMPLOYEES.   Attached hereto as Schedule 4.10 is a list of all the Seller's employees and the rate of compensation of each. None of such employees is a party to any employment agreement or other contract with the Seller, nor are any of such employees entitled to any fringe benefits or other compensation from the Seller except as reflected on Schedule 4.10 or separately reflected in a copy of the Seller's employment manual, a current copy of which has been delivered to the Buyer. None of the Seller's employees is subject to any collective bargaining agreement or other union agreement, nor is the Seller or the Shareholder aware of any effort to organize any of the work force of the Seller. No disputes or claims against the Seller exist on behalf of any of its employees, including, but not limited to, claims of employment discrimination, violation of wage and hour laws, or claims relating to past unpaid compensation. The Shareholder and the Seller believe that substantially all of the Seller's employees will accept employment with the buyer on terms substantially similar to the terms under which they are employed by the Seller.

4.11   COMPLIANCE WITH LAW.   The Seller is not in violation of any material law, regulation, rule, ordinance, or other governmental requirement relating to its properties or its business. Neither the Seller nor the Shareholder has knowledge of any development, occurrence, or condition that would adversely affect any of the Seller's properties or that might curtail or interfere with the present or future use of such properties for the purposes for which they are now used.

4.12   ENVIRONMENTAL COMPLIANCE.   The Seller is in full compliance with all applicable federal, state, and local laws, rules, and regulations relating to environmental regulation and to the disposal of waste products (including, but not limited to, those products defined as hazardous wastes under applicable federal and state laws). The Seller does not lease, own, or operate a facility on, and has not leased, owned, or operated a facility on, any land or real property subject to any environmental contamination, violation, or requirement for cleanup or any other environmental remediation.

4.13   TAX RETURNS.   The Shareholder has timely and correctly prepared and filed all tax returns, including federal and state income tax returns and sales tax returns, and the Seller has paid all taxes due pursuant to such tax returns as well as all other taxes, including real and personal property taxes for which the Seller is liable, except for certain property taxes that are accrued but not yet due, as shown on Schedule 4.13. The Seller has not filed for and is not now subject to any extension of time with respect to the filing of any tax return. The Seller has provided to the Buyer true and correct copies of all federal and state income tax returns filed by it for the past three fiscal years. The Seller is not aware of any actual or threatened tax audit. The Financial Statements reflect an adequate reserve, as of the date thereof, for income taxes now due for the present tax year. The Seller maintains all required payroll trust accounts, and the Seller has timely paid all employee and employer withholding taxes into such trust accounts.

4.14   INSURANCE.   The Seller maintains adequate insurance with qualified insurance carriers with respect to liability and property loss or damage. A list of insurance policies showing coverage amounts, insurance carrier, and type of coverage is set forth on Schedule 4.14. Copies of all such policies have been provided to the Buyer.

4.15   COMPLETE DISCLOSURE.   This Agreement and the agreements and instruments attached hereto and to be delivered at the time of Closing do not contain any untrue statement of a material fact by the Shareholder or the Seller. This Agreement and such related agreements and instruments do not omit to state any material fact necessary in order to make the statements made herein or therein by the Seller or the Shareholder, in light of the circumstances under which they are made, not misleading.

ARTICLE V REPRESENTATIONS AND WARRANTIES OF THE BUYER

The Buyer represents and warrants to the Seller and to the Shareholder as follows:

5.1   ORGANIZATION AND QUALIFICATION OF THE BUYER.   The Buyer is a corporation duly organized, validly existing, and in good standing under the laws of the state of [Name of State]. The Buyer is not required, by the nature of its assets or business, to qualify as a foreign corporation in any other state. The Buyer has full power to own all of its properties and to carry on its business as it is now being conducted.

5.2   CORPORATE AUTHORITY.   The Buyer has the authority, pursuant to its articles of incorporation and bylaws, and pursuant to such additional action as is necessary by its officers, directors, and shareholders, to execute this Agreement and to consummate the transactions provided for herein.

5.3   NO VIOLATION OF OBLIGATIONS.   The execution and delivery of this Agreement, and the consummation of the transactions provided for herein, will not violate any agreement or commitment made by the Buyer, or any requirement binding on the Buyer, including, without limitation, any lease, contract, loan agreement, promissory note, franchise agreement, court order, judgment, regulatory ruling, or any arbitration award.

5.4   FINANCIAL STATEMENTS.   The financial statements previously delivered by the Buyer to the Seller are true and correct in all material respects. Such financial statements have been prepared in accordance with generally accepted accounting principles applied on a basis consistent with that of preceding years. The Buyer has not experienced, will not experience through the time of Closing, and does not expect to experience thereafter any material adverse change in the nature of its operations or business. Without limiting the foregoing, the Buyer has the ability to honor all of its obligations undertaken pursuant to this Agreement, specifically including the obligation to pay all amounts due pursuant to the Promissory Note in accordance with the terms thereof.

5.5   LIABILITIES.   The Buyer has no liabilities, liquidated, actual, or contingent, except as shown on the financial statements previously provided to the Seller and except for liabilities that have arisen in the ordinary course of Buyer's business from and after the date of the most recent financial statements so provided. Any liabilities arising after the date of such financial statements have arisen in the ordinary course of business of the Buyer and are similar as to kind and amount to those shown on such financial statements.

5.6   COMPLIANCE WITH LAW.   The Buyer is not in violation of any material law, regulation, rule, ordinance, or other governmental requirement relating to its properties or its business. The Buyer has no knowledge of any development, occurrence, or condition that would adversely affect any of the Buyer's properties or that might curtail or interfere with the present or future use of such properties for the purposes for which they are now used.

5.7   LEGAL PROCEEDINGS.   There are no private or governmental proceedings pending, or to the knowledge of Buyer threatened, against the Buyer, including, without limitation, any investigation, audit, lawsuit, threatened lawsuit, arbitration, or other legal proceedings of any nature whatsoever.

5.8   LIENS.   Except as disclosed in the financial statements of the Buyer, the Buyer and the assets of the Buyer are not subject to any deed of trust, mortgage, security interest, or other lien or claim of any nature whatsoever.

5.9   COMPLETE DISCLOSURE.   This Agreement and the agreements and instruments related hereto do not contain any untrue statement of a material fact by the Buyer. This Agreement and such related agreements and instruments do not omit to state any material fact necessary in order to make the statements made herein or therein, in light of the circumstances under which they are made, not misleading.

ARTICLE VI INFORMATION AND CONFIDENTIALITY

6.1   PROVISION OF INFORMATION RELATING TO SELLER.   Prior to the execution of this Agreement, the Shareholder and the Seller have made available to the Buyer information relating to the Seller, including, without limitation, financial statements and records, depreciation schedules, lists of equipment, copies of contracts and agreements, and access to the properties, assets, and operations of the Seller. To the best knowledge of the Seller and the Shareholder, all such information is substantially correct and complete. From and after the date of this Agreement and continuing through Closing, the Seller and the Shareholder will continue to make available to the Buyer all information required hereunder or otherwise reasonably requested by the Buyer with respect to the Seller.

6.2 CONFIDENTIALITY. The Buyer acknowledges that all information with respect to the Seller made available prior to and subsequent to the date of this Agreement and through the date of Closing is confidential. The Buyer shall use such information only for the purpose of evaluating the proposed transactions hereunder. In the event the transactions provided for in this Agreement fail to close for any reason whatsoever, the Buyer will promptly return all such information to the Shareholder, including any extracts, copies, or analyses based thereon which were prepared by the Buyer. The Buyer will not use, nor will it permit any third party to use, any of such information in any manner that is competitive with or injurious to the Seller.

6.3 PROVISION OF INFORMATION RELATING TO BUYER. The Buyer has provided certain information to the Shareholder, including financial statements and other information relating to the ability of the Buyer to carry out his obligations hereunder. The Buyer represents and warrants that such information is complete and accurate, and the Shareholder and the Seller agree that all such information is to be treated as confidential and will be used only for the purpose of evaluating their decision to consummate the transactions provided for herein.

6.4 CONTACTS WITH THIRD PARTIES. The existence of this Agreement and the transactions provided for herein are confidential. Public announcements relating to this Agreement shall be made only pursuant to mutual agreement of the parties hereto. Prior to the time of any such public announcement, the Buyer shall not disclose to any third party that it is contemplating the purchase of the Assets, but the Seller agrees that it will at mutually agreeable times arrange for interviews by the Buyer, at which a representative of the Seller may be present, with key employees, suppliers, and customers of the Seller. The Buyer agrees to conduct such interviews in such manner as to avoid any interference with the Seller's relationships with such persons and otherwise subject to such reasonable constraints as are requested by the Shareholder.

ARTICLE VII CONSULTING AND NONCOMPETITION AGREEMENTS

At the time of Closing, the Shareholder, individually, will enter into the following agreements:

7.1 CONSULTING AGREEMENT.   A consulting agreement in the form attached hereto as Exhibit D (the "Consulting Agreement") providing for substantially full-time consulting services to be rendered by the Shareholder to the Buyer for a period of 60 days after Closing and for part-time services to be rendered thereafter upon a schedule mutually agreeable to the Buyer and the Shareholder.

7.2   NONCOMPETITION COVENANT.   The Shareholder (as well as the Seller) shall further enter into an agreement in the form attached hereto as Exhibit E (the "Noncompetition Covenant") whereby they will agree not to compete with the purchased business within a radius of 250 miles of the present principal place of business of the Seller for a period of five years from and after the time of Closing. The sum of $250,000 shall be paid at closing by the Buyer to the Shareholder in consideration of this noncompetition covenant.

ARTICLE VIII CONDITIONS TO CLOSING

The obligations of the parties to close the transactions provided for herein are subject to the following conditions, as well as to any other conditions expressed or implied in this Agreement:

8.1   SHAREHOLDER'S AND SELLER'S CONDITIONS.   The obligations of the Shareholder and the Seller are subject to the following conditions:

1. All representations, warranties, covenants, and other agreements contained herein on the part of the Buyer will be true and correct at the time of Closing.
2. The Shareholder and the Seller will be reasonably satisfied with the financial ability of the Buyer to honor its obligations pursuant to the Promissory Note.

3. No lawsuit, governmental action, or other legal proceeding shall have been commenced that shall materially interfere with the ability of the parties to consummate the transactions provided for herein.

8.2   BUYER'S CONDITIONS.   The obligations of the Buyer to complete the transactions provided for herein are subject to the following conditions:

1. All representations, warranties, covenants, and other agreements contained herein on the part of the Shareholder and the Seller will be true and correct at the time of Closing.
2. No lawsuit, governmental action, or other legal proceeding shall have been commenced that shall materially interfere with the ability of the parties to consummate the transactions provided for herein.
3. Buyer will have completed an investigation and examination of the Seller, the results of which will be satisfactory to the Buyer in its sole discretion.
4. The book value of the Seller will be not less than the amount shown on the most recent balance sheet included in the Financial Statements.
5. The Buyer will be reasonably satisfied as to the willingness of the key employees of the Seller to continue working for the Buyer after the Closing hereunder.

ARTICLE IX CLOSING

The Closing of all transactions provided for herein will occur at the offices of legal counsel for the Buyer at 10:00 A.M. on [date] (the "Closing"). The transactions at Closing, when effective, will be deemed to be effective as of the opening of business on the day of Closing, except as otherwise specifically provided at the time of Closing. All actions to be taken at Closing will be considered to be taken simultaneously, and no document, agreement, or instrument will be considered to be delivered until all such items that are to be delivered at the Closing have been executed and delivered. At the Closing, the following actions will occur:

9.1   CERTIFICATES.   The Buyer, the Shareholder, and the Seller will each, respectively, execute a certificate stating that all representations and warranties made by them respectively in this Agreement continue to be true as of the time of Closing.

9.2   SELLER'S LEGAL OPINION.   The Shareholder will deliver to the Buyer an opinion of Shareholder's and Seller's legal counsel, in form reasonably satisfactory to the Buyer, opining favorably as to the matters set forth in Sections 4.1 and 4.2 and, to the best of such counsel's knowledge, to the matters in Section 4.3 of this Agreement.

9.3   ASSIGNMENT AND BILL OF SALE.   The Seller will execute and deliver to the Buyer an assignment and bill of sale, in form satisfactory to the Seller, transferring good and marketable title to all of the Assets to the Buyer free and clear of any liens or other adverse interests.

9.4   ASSIGNMENT OF INTANGIBLES AND CONTRACTS.   The Seller will execute such further assignments or other transfer documents as may be necessary to transfer all intangible assets to the Buyer, including consents from third parties to the extent necessary to provide valid contract assignments. The Shareholder will confirm his prior transfer to the Seller of all information necessary to Seller's business.

9.5   ASSUMPTION OF ASSUMED LIABILITIES.   The Buyer will execute an assumption of liabilities, in form satisfactory to the Seller and the Shareholder, assuming and agreeing to pay all of the Assumed Liabilities in the ordinary course of the Buyer's business from and after the time of closing.

9.6   PURCHASE PRICE.   The Buyer will pay the balance of the purchase price for the Assets by delivery of $750,000 in cash or certified funds, by wire transfer, or in other form satisfactory to the Seller, and by execution and delivery of the promissory note to the Seller.

9.7   SECURITY AGREEMENT.   The Buyer shall execute and deliver the Security Agreement and shall execute and deliver a customary Uniform Commercial Code financing statement fully executed in form suitable for recording.

9.8   NONCOMPETITION COVENANT.   The Seller and the Shareholder shall execute the Noncompetition Covenant.

9.9 NONCOMPETITION PAYMENT. The Buyer shall pay to the Shareholder the sum of $250,000 in cash or certified funds, by wire transfer, or in other form satisfactory to the Shareholder in consideration of the noncompetition covenant.

9.10 CORPORATE AUTHORIZATION. The Buyer shall provide such corporate authorization as the Seller and the Shareholder may reasonably request for the purpose of verifying the validity of all instruments and security documents delivered at the time of closing by the Buyer.

9.11 TAX ALLOCATIONS. The parties shall mutually agree to a schedule showing allocations of the purchase price to the various Assets, which allocations shall be consistent with Section 1060 of the Internal Revenue Code and the Regulations thereunder.

9.12 SUBORDINATION AGREEMENT. The parties shall execute the Subordination Agreement in form satisfactory to Buyer's lending bank, in accordance with Section 2.4.

9.13 CONSULTING AGREEMENT. The Shareholder and the Buyer shall execute the Consulting Agreement.

9.14 OTHER ACTS. The parties will execute any other documents reasonably required to carry out the intent of this Agreement.

ARTICLE X TERMINATION

This Agreement will terminate in accordance with the following provisions:

10.1 FAILURE TO CLOSE. If the purchase and sale provided for herein fails to close by the date provided in Article IX above, then this Agreement shall terminate, unless the parties have, by mutual agreement, extended the time for Closing in writing. Termination shall not release any party of any liability for damages arising out of the breach, if any, of this Agreement, except as provided below.

10.2 FAILURE OF CONDITION. If this Agreement terminates by reason of the failure of any condition provided for herein to be satisfied at the time of Closing, and if the failure to satisfy such condition occurs without material fault on the part of either party hereto, then this Agreement shall terminate without liability on the part of either party hereto, except that the confidentiality provisions set forth in Sections 6.2 and 6.3 shall remain in effect.

10.3   TERMINATION BY AGREEMENT.   If the parties hereto agree to terminate this Agreement, such termination shall be effective without liability to either party hereto.

ARTICLE XI MUTUAL INDEMNIFICATION

Each of the parties hereto agrees to indemnify and hold harmless each of the other parties against any loss resulting from a violation of this Agreement on the part of the indemnifying party. Such indemnification obligation shall include indemnification for any costs reasonably incurred by the indemnified party, including, without limitation, legal costs and reasonable attorney's fees. However, no right to indemnification shall arise hereunder unless the aggregate of all indemnified losses of any party hereto (net of any losses of the other party which are subject to indemnification) exceeds the sum of $25,000.

ARTICLE XII POSTCLOSING OPERATIONS

From and after the time of Closing, the Buyer agrees as follows:

12.1   RELEASE OF SHAREHOLDER.   The Buyer and the Seller will utilize their best efforts to cause the Shareholder to be released from any guarantees or any other contingent obligations which the Shareholder may have with respect to the liabilities of the Seller. Without limiting the generality of the foregoing, the Seller will advise all lenders, lessors, and suppliers, at the time of renewing any existing leases, loans, lines of credit, or other obligations that the Shareholder is no longer responsible for the obligations of the acquired business.

12.2   OPERATIONS IN ORDINARY COURSE.   The Buyer shall continue to operate the acquired business in the ordinary course, fulfilling all contracts and other obligations which have been properly disclosed hereunder and which are not yet completed as of the time of Closing. The Buyer will maintain in effect all insurance policies, or will establish substantially similar coverage, with respect to any liabilities of the Seller for which the Shareholder or the Seller may have responsibility.

12.3   REPORTS.   For so long as any amount remains outstanding pursuant to the Promissory Note, the Buyer will cause copies of its annual financial statements to be delivered to the Shareholder promptly after the preparation of such statements.

ARTICLE XIII GENERAL PROVISIONS

The following general provisions shall apply to this Agreement:

13.1   SURVIVAL OF AGREEMENT.   This Agreement, and all terms, warranties, and provisions hereof, will be true and correct as of the time of Closing and will survive the Closing for a period of three years.

13.2   NOTICES.   All notices required or permitted hereunder or under any related agreement or instrument (unless such related agreement or instrument otherwise provides) will be deemed delivered when delivered personally or mailed, by certified mail, return receipt requested, or registered mail, to the respective party at the following addresses or to such other address as each respective party may in writing hereafter designate:

1. To Shareholder:
2. To Buyer:
3. To Seller:

13.3   SUCCESSORS AND ASSIGNS.   This Agreement will be binding upon the parties hereto and their respective successors, personal representatives, heirs, and assigns. However, no party hereto will have any right to assign any of its obligations pursuant to this Agreement, except with the prior written consent of all of the other parties.

13.4   MERGER.   This Agreement and the exhibits and other documents, agreements, and instruments related hereto set forth the entire agreement of the parties with respect to the subject matter hereof and may not be amended or modified except in writing subscribed to by all such parties.

13.5   GOVERNING LAW.   This Agreement is entered into in the State of [name of State], it will be performed within such state, and all issues arising hereunder shall be governed in all respects by the laws of such state.

13.6 OBLIGATIONS TO BROKERS. No party hereto has incurred any obligation for the payment of any brokerage commission, finder's fee, or any other similar obligation relating to this Agreement or the consummation of the transactions provided for herein.

13.7 MODIFICATION OR SEVERANCE. In the event that any provision of this Agreement is found by any court or other authority of competent jurisdiction to be illegal or unenforceable, such provision shall be severed or modified to the extent necessary to render it enforceable and as so severed or modified, this Agreement will remain in full force and effect.

13.8 CAPTIONS. The captions in this Agreement are included for convenience only and shall not in any way affect the interpretation of any of the provisions hereof.

IN WITNESS WHEREOF, the parties have read and entered into this Agreement as of the date above written.
BUYER:
By:
SHAREHOLDER:
SELLER: By:

POSTACQUISITION INTEGRATION

6.1 GENERAL

Chronologically, the postacquisition integration process starts after the transaction has been finalized. However, if it is seen as a discrete activity beginning immediately after the close, it is extremely unlikely that it will be executed efficiently and effectively, and it is virtually guaranteed not to meet the operational objectives expected as well as

The author would like to thank Price Pritchett, who wrote the version of this chapter that appeared in the last edition.

the financial assumptions embedded in the valuation model used to gain approval for the transaction.

It has become an article of faith in acquisition lore that the lack of effective integration accounts for a large portion of acquisition failure (i.e., the inability of the investment to justify itself on financial terms). More often than not, these failures can be traced directly to poor integration execution, which in turn can be traced to poor integration planning.

(a) INTEGRATION AND SYNERGIES. Therefore, it is important that postacquisition integration is seen in the context of the entire acquisition process, beginning with the strategic rationale for the transaction. This can be best understood by visualizing the link between synergies and integration. To a great extent, integration can be seen as the process of extracting the value of synergies. As a result, integration issues should be identified as early as possible in the acquisition process, and preliminary integration planning should begin when synergies are identified and incorporated into the valuation of the target company. As the process progresses, the plan should be modified and adjusted based on the availability of better intelligence and on an improved understanding of the target company's business dynamics.

(b) OPERATIONAL INTEGRATION. It is also important to note that, in addition to synergy-related integration issues, there is a substantial volume of operational integration measures that routinely must be addressed in virtually all acquisitions. The vast majority of them relate to either connectivity and/or standardization. The typical areas of activity include e-mail standardization, Web site linkage and identification, letterhead and signage, accounting and reporting systems, and administrative policies and procedures. These are by no means trivial issues. However, many are either cost neutral or immaterial from an expense perspective, and those that do require material expenditures generally entail one-time (versus continuing) costs. This class of integration activity is clearly important, because inattention to it can have serious negative operational consequences. However, acquisitions regularly succeed or fail based on the acquirer's ability to execute on synergy-related integration measures. Accordingly, the focus of much of the discussion that follows is on those integration issues and activities that relate to the synergistic benefits the combination has been projected to provide.

(c) IMPORTANCE OF SPEED OF IMPLEMENTATION. The speed with which the integration plan is implemented is a critical issue. Merger and acquisition (M&A) literature frequently refers to the importance of making substantial progress in the first 100 days following the close. Insofar as integration benefits are concerned, opportunities deferred are generally opportunities lost. Delays in the integration process result in uncertainty, paralysis, employee disaffection, and loss of momentum, all conditions that can lead to the impairment of the value of the investment. Supported by clearly articulated objectives and continuous communication, crisp and thoughtful execution provides the antidote to value impairment.

6.2 PRE–DUE DILIGENCE PHASE

As early as the valuation phase of the process, assumptions regarding synergies are made and, at that time, initial thoughts about unlocking those synergies through effective integration should start. As the acquisition process approaches the due diligence phase, concrete steps related to integration planning should be initiated. This would include:

- The identification of a leader of the integration team
- The staffing of the team and the assignment of responsibilities
- The development of a preliminary view of integration steps based on synergistic assumptions that are baked into the valuation
- A preliminary evaluation of the target company's culture

(a) INTEGRATION LEADERSHIP. Acquisitive companies develop and adapt M&A best practices through trial and error and the thoughtful retrospective analysis of past transactions. One of the best practices that have emerged over time is the assignment of an integration leader or integration manager who has primary, dedicated responsibility for scoping, planning, and executing postacquisition integration. The rationale for assigning such responsibility is the realization of the extreme importance of the integration process in the successful execution of the transaction. If clear responsibility and authority are not assigned, the potential for missed opportunities increases substantially. Because integration spans many functions and processes, and interrelationships link many of these, the acquirer cannot afford a diffusion of responsibility (and authority)—a condition that is likely to lead to poor decisions and delay.

The challenges are such that the combination of skills required for managing an effective and efficient postacquisition integration process are extremely varied and often difficult to find embodied in the same individual. However, efforts to identify individuals with the optimal mix of skills should consider these points.

- *A comprehensive knowledge of the acquiring company.* Unquestionably, the manager chosen for this assignment must have a deep understanding of all aspects of the acquiring company's operations, its key personnel, and its culture. Effective management of the process would be virtually impossible to accomplish under the leadership of an overachieving junior manager or someone, no matter how talented, who comes from outside the organization. Accordingly, the integration leader must be a seasoned and knowledgeable insider and must possess strong general management skills.
- *A thorough understanding of the strategic thinking underlying the acquisition.* As noted, the key to successful integration is the effective and efficient translation of assumed synergies into actual value. It is extremely helpful if those synergies are understood within the context of the overarching strategic rationale for the acquisition. If the integration process represents "how" value will be realized and the synergies represent "what" the benefits are, the strategy represents the all-important "why."
- *Strong project management skills.* The assignment is extremely process-oriented and built around objectives, milestones, and concrete accomplishments. Clearly, a necessary (yet not sufficient) characteristic is an operational mentality. Pure theoreticians need not apply. Although conceptualization skills are certainly helpful, the position requires an individual with an action-oriented mentality.
- *The ability to adapt to change.* By its very nature, there are a host of unknowns to be dealt with in the integration process. Regardless of how well the manager and his or her team know their own operation, they invariably will have incomplete knowledge and understanding of the target company's processes,

capabilities, and personnel. As more information becomes available, the manager should be nimble enough to adjust course when the facts conflict with preconceptions. Rigid adherence to a plan that is based on faulty information can spell disaster.

- *Strong interpersonal skills.* Integration is as much about people as it is about process. The manager will be continually dealing with individuals who are experiencing a wide range of emotions: concern about continued employment, status, position, loss of responsibility, and fundamental changes in processes and interpersonal interactions, to name but a few. The need to optimize results in what can be a fragile environment places significant value on the integration leader's people management skills.

- *An understanding of the importance of cultural differences.* The manager should have an understanding of the nature of corporate cultures, their differences, and the fault lines that can result when divergent cultures are brought together under one roof. In the broadest sense, culture informs behavior. These behavioral characteristics translate into policies and procedures that are ingrained within the organization. More often than not, attempts to change policies and procedures without a full appreciation for their origins are analogous to a doctor treating symptoms rather than the disease. And, to take the analogy a step further, just as the symptoms will reappear if the root causes of disease are not treated, behavioral change will be short-lived (and often resisted) if there is no attention paid to the behavior's cultural underpinnings. Although dealing with cultural issues is much more art than science and, accordingly, does not lend itself to neat prescriptions, there is clearly a fundamental need to consider the linkage between culture and ingrained behaviors when attempting to implement change. The ability to do so is arguably one of the most important traits of the integration manager.

- *A best practices mentality.* No organization does everything right. Yet there is a strong tendency on the part of acquirers to assume that their practices, policies, and procedures are superior to those of the company being acquired. As a result, one of the benefits that are frequently not optimally leveraged is the adoption of the acquiree's superior processes by the acquirer. It is extremely desirable for the integration manager to approach change with this in mind, and remain sufficiently flexible to implement change on the basis of best practice, even in the face of resistance from colleagues.

(b) THE TEAM. The integration team will typically be made up of individuals who have other day-to-day responsibilities for operations within the acquiring company. In addition, they very often will be assigned additional due diligence responsibility that falls outside the scope of the integration process. In other words, they are not totally dedicated to the integration process. That said, the team should be staffed in a manner that ensures that all key aspects of the integration are covered. Once again, the frames of reference for determining what areas are "key" are primarily the synergies assumed in the acquirer's strategic justification for the acquisition and the valuation developed to support that justification.

(c) PRELIMINARY PLAN. In the pre–due diligence phase of the process, an outline of the integration plan should be created with the objective of designing procedures that will enable team members to:

- Identify operational integration issues.
- Validate the existence of assumed synergies.
- Assess the assumed value of those synergies.
- Determine the process by which they will be extracted.
- Determine the time frame in which they would be realized.

Such a plan represents a baseline document that will be modified and expanded as more information becomes available and the acquirer's understanding is enhanced.

(d) CULTURAL EVALUATION. One of the more significant potential impediments to successful integration is cultural dissonance. This can take a number of forms, depending on the nature of the organizations being combined, but there are some predictable types of combinations that are frequently encountered. For example, when smaller, closely held companies are acquired by larger, publicly traded companies, a common cause of conflict is the clash of the entrepreneurial, nonbureaucratic culture of the target with the highly structured, buttoned-down culture of the acquirer. If the acquirer assumes that it can just swallow up the target without consideration to clear cultural differences, it does so at the risk of compromising the value of the assets it has purchased. Even in situations where both companies are publicly traded and highly structured, significant differences in corporate values, ingrained procedures, and strategic approach often create wide intercompany gulfs that have to be bridged, if the acquirer is going to realize the value assumed in its purchase price. It is therefore extremely important that such cultural differences are identified and a plan to deal with them is crafted well in advance of the close of the transaction.

6.3 DUE DILIGENCE PHASE

Once due diligence is initiated, the integration planning process should be significantly ratcheted up. This is the phase of the integration process when "the rubber meets the road," that is, when preconceived notions are compared to actual conditions. Due diligence provides those involved in the integration process the opportunity to refine their view of synergistic benefits and validate the opportunities assumed in the valuation model as well as to confirm or modify their understanding of operational integration issues and the associated costs. By the time the due diligence review is completed, the acquirer's view of the realizability of synergies and the challenges of operational integration should be well formed. Based on that assessment, the integration plan should be refined and should contain a clear statement of objectives, time frames for implementation, and milestones to track progress. It is also at this point in the process that the acquirer should begin to formulate plans to communicate with various stakeholders affected by the transaction. This effort is generally executed through a formal communication plan.

The communication plan is an integral element of the integration effort. As the transaction approaches close, the integration manager, usually in conjunction with senior members of the acquirer's human resources department, should develop a communication plan that would be initiated as soon as the transaction closes. Contents of the plan will be specific to the individual transaction. However, there are a number of generalizations that can be made about its development. Some general guidelines in this regard follow.

- *Identify the stakeholders.* Stakeholders will invariably include employees, customers, and major vendors of both parties to the transaction. When two publicly traded companies are involved, shareholders and the investment community will generally also be considered key constituencies that should be communicated with.

- *Determine the message that is appropriate for each class of stakeholder.* The message to these stakeholders will vary. The message to the employee populations should be designed to alleviate anxiety (to the extent that is possible) and should be used to establish management's credibility. This requires balancing the delivery of an upbeat message with a candid view of the impact of the combination on future operations. Implications that there will not be change can have a deadly effect on employee relations, if such a message is followed by a wave of changes and terminations. Therefore, it is important that initial communications are consistent with the actions that follow.

The primary message to customers should be that continued superior customer service is of paramount importance. The benefits of the business combination to the customer base are certainly worth noting, but the organization should not lose sight of the fact that the most important assurance customers can receive is that the service and product quality that has made them customers in the first place will be maintained. The message to major vendors should be similar to that of customers (i.e., one of business as usual, unless there are compelling reasons for change that affects them).

Stockholders and the investment community as a whole are singularly interested in shareholder value. Accordingly, the message for these populations should focus on how the combination of the two entities will deliver increased value.

- *Determine how the message will be communicated for each class of stakeholder.* Employee populations should be communicated with via a range of vehicles. It is usually a very bad practice to simply issue a memo. Written communication should be reinforced by employee assemblies, smaller meetings for individual facilities or departments, follow-up meetings in small groups, and progress reports through e-mail or memo.

Insofar as customers are concerned, it is generally wise to segment the customer base and have senior sales executives meet with major customers, contact them and other large customers by phone, and follow up with customer letters to the entire customer base. Vendor communication, which is generally a lesser concern, should follow a similar pattern.

Stockholder and investment community communication is desirable when a publicly traded company makes a large acquisition, particularly if the acquisition is of another public company. Major acquisitions generally receive significant coverage in the financial press and also routinely require a substantial amount of communication with stockholders. Management should leverage the financial press through the use of Webcasts, press releases, and interviews, promoting the strategic rationale for the combination and the resulting enhancement of stockholder value.

- *Ensure that the communication process is proactive and ongoing and that it is linked to the integration process.* The message to certain stakeholders should be reinforced over time. This is particularly true of the employee population. Employees should be kept abreast of progress and made to feel they are part of the "solution," not simply observers of the process. Generally, there is no need for ongoing communication with customers and vendors, unless there are developments that directly impact them. Conversely, it is generally advisable to reinforce the organization's message to shareholders and the investment community, especially if anticipated successes are realized.

6.4 POST–CLOSE PHASE

Upon close, the communication plan and the integration plan should be launched immediately. Three aspects of implementation should be stressed. As noted throughout this chapter, there should be intense emphasis on speed of implementation. In addition, to the extent possible, key employees of the acquired company should be involved in the process. And, finally, there should be a strong emphasis on "early wins." The need for crisp decision making and speed of implementation cannot be overemphasized. Accomplishments inspire confidence and build momentum. More important, indecision and delay feed speculation and uncertainty, the enemies of integration success. The greater the extent to which the employees of the acquired company can feel as if they are participants, the greater their degree of buy-in to the objectives of the integration effort. Similarly, concrete evidence of early success provides validation.

The implementation phase of the process should be flexible enough to accommodate change in the face of new information, and it should make provision for periodic assessment of progress. Although the integration manager should be sufficiently empowered to drive the plan, it is critical that the plan include milestones and time frames and that progress against those benchmarks is reported on to senior executive management, ideally the chief executive officer. As the process unfolds, it is also important to communicate progress to the broader constituencies, most notably the employee population. Finally, for all acquirers, but particularly for the more acquisitive companies, it is extremely beneficial to conduct a lessons learned exercise to see what was done well, what was done poorly, and how those lessons can be used to improve future acquisition efforts.

6.5 OVERVIEW OF THE PROCESS

A summary view of the overall integration process is illustrated in Exhibit 6.1.

PRE–DUE DILIGENCE →	DUE DILIGENCE →	POST–CLOSE
Appoint integration leader	Refine view of operational integration issues	Implement communication plan
Assign team member responsibilities	Refine view of synergies and impact on integration	Implement integration plan and focus on early wins
Identify operational integration issues	Develop communication plan	Assess results and report to executive management
Identify potential synergies and develop preliminary view of related integration issues	Develop concrete integration plan with milestones and time frames	Communicate successes and reinforce integration objectives
Conduct preliminary assessment of target corporate culture		Conduct lessons learned exercise and document for future reference

EXHIBIT 6.1   INTEGRATION PROCESS OVERVIEW

6.6 AREAS OF FOCUS

The integration process is different for every transaction. However, there are some predictable patterns or issues that will emerge in most acquisitions. General guidance is provided in the sections that follow on areas of particular importance.

(a) HUMAN RESOURCES. Human resource (HR) issues generally cut across all areas of integration, both operational and synergistic, and across all functions within the organization. HR integration includes compensation and benefits standardization, reorganization, terminations, and alignment of titles and of personnel policies and procedures. Because these are issues that impact employment, compensation, and position and status within the newly combined organization, they are among the most important and sensitive aspects of the integration process. Accordingly, they should be the focus of activity and communication as early as possible in the process.

It is critical that issues and decisions related to reorganization and termination, and their consequences, have been thoroughly considered and thought through well in advance of the close and that the organization is positioned to take action immediately after the transaction has been consummated. Once action has been taken, it is important that it be comprehensive and that it is credibly communicated to the employee population. Few things can be as damaging as the widespread uncertainty around employment issues. Not only is it important to avoid a repeated string of terminations and reorganizations, and the announcements that accompany them, it is equally important to avoid *the fear* of them. A key aspect of the organization's communication efforts should be reassurance to the remaining employees and a focus on getting on with business.

One of the more difficult aspects of HR integration is the alignment of compensation plans when there is significant variation between those of the acquired company and the acquirer. In such situations, the organization must balance the desirability for standardization with the risk of losing key employees. This is particularly the case with sales personnel (discussed in more detail in section 6.6(e)). It is generally wise to make such adjustments over extended periods, rather than to submit to a desire for immediate uniformity.

(b) FACILITIES.   Facilities integration is a fairly straightforward process. Production facilities and office space consolidation are generally functions of strategic decisions made about capacities and volumes. If there is replication of capacity, decisions should be made based on such things as location, the cost of labor (both actual labor rates and potential ongoing costs associated with labor agreements), the cost of space, and the condition and caliber of equipment.

Facilities integration is generally driven by cost synergies that will have been quantified in the acquisition valuation model. It is not uncommon that the benefits of consolidation have been quantified but that the actual execution has not been thoroughly thought through (i.e., the financial analysis has been done, and done quite well, but those who will be tasked with the actual engineering of the consolidation have not been sufficiently engaged in planning and, therefore, are unprepared to execute). In such cases, the potential outcomes can be extremely counterproductive. At best, there will be delay (at a cost), and at worst, the process will be rushed and execution will be poor from both a financial and an employee relations perspective.

(c) INFORMATION TECHNOLOGY.   Information technology (IT) integration is mostly about connectivity, standardization, and security. Accordingly, it is primarily an operational (versus synergistic) undertaking. If there is a substantial difference in the IT infrastructures of the two combining companies, there may be significant efficiencies that can be realized, but such situations are extremely rare. More commonly, IT integration will focus on the standardization of such things as hardware and software, Web site linkage, and phone systems. The emphasis in the IT area should be on speed of execution to ensure that intercompany communication is expedited and the acquired company is made to feel part of this new organization.

(d) RESEARCH AND DEVELOPMENT AND PRODUCT DEVELOPMENT.   The marriage of research and product development capabilities between newly combined companies is among the most desirable and the most difficult objectives to accomplish. These are areas within organizations where it is significantly more common that homegrown approaches and individual cultures develop. Attempts at integrating these functions can be extremely frustrating, because the potential benefits are usually among the most significant, but the cultural impediments are among the most intractable. As a result, it is an area in which the speed plays second fiddle to effectiveness. This is an area where it is generally counterproductive to try to impose the acquirer's approaches and techniques on the acquired company. A thoughtful approach based on best practice has the most potential for success. Such a collaborative approach can work only over time and after the confidence of the acquired company's staff and management has been earned.

(e) SALES. Sales organizations are generally among the most independent elements of any organization. In most organizations, salespeople are detached from the organization and do not have a particularly acute sense of company loyalty. This stems from their personalities as well as from the fact that they are frequently out of the office interacting with clients and, therefore, less integrated into the fabric of the company that employs them. The result is a mentality that borders on that of an independent contractor. In some respects this makes integration of the sales organization easier, because the "hired gun" mentality makes the new organization just another constituency to deal with. The key issues for sales integration have more to do with product and compensation. As long as the business combination does not interfere with their ability to sell a superior product, and they are compensated in a manner that is substantially consistent with their preacquisition package, they will generally not represent a major integration challenge. However, the risks associated with alienating the sales organization of the acquired company are considerable. Replacement of strong producers is difficult, time-consuming, and costly. Therefore, the focus in the area of sales should be on retention, close management, and cultural conversion over time. It is generally a bad idea to burden salespeople with new administrative requirements, training that is not product-focused, or new policies and procedures that are not mission critical. That is not to say that salespeople should be given free rein; rather, the focus should be on control through strong sales management that tracks behavior and results.

(f) MARKETING. Marketing integration stands in contrast to sales integration. Marketing is grounded in culture and strategy and therefore does not lend itself to bifurcation. Approaches of the new entity to promotion and pricing have to be consistent. They represent messages to the marketplace, the universe of customers and prospective customers that are critical to the success of the business. This does not mean that promotional and pricing policies should be mindlessly superimposed on the acquired company, but it does mean that a best practices approach has to be agreed on and implemented rapidly so that a singular position can be presented to the market.

(g) ACCOUNTING AND REPORTING SYSTEMS.   Intense consideration well in advance of the close should be given to the integration of accounting and reporting systems. If the organization is fortunate, there may be a high degree of compatibility between the parties' systems. However, that is infrequently the case. Such incompatibility presents a significant challenge to the new entity. The absence of good data makes decision making difficult at best, and the absence of compatibility can be an enormous drain on the company's planning and reporting resources, which will be forced to spend more time on parsing and reconciling information than on planning and analysis. The prescription for the integration of accounting and reporting systems is detailed planning well in advance of the close; it frequently requires the involvement of consultants.

6.7 CONCLUSION

Postacquisition integration is a key to unlocking the value of most acquisitions. To be effective, it must be well planned and thoughtfully executed, preferably under the leadership of a strong manager who has been empowered and will be supported by the highest levels of executive management. It is also important to understand that integration is more art than science. Although process and disciplined implementation are extremely important, the single most important element in the equation is the human element. Even the most strategically convincing transactions for the best planned integrations will fail, if the employees who are relied on to make it work are not invested in its success.

GUIDELINES FOR MANAGERS AND EXECUTIVES

It is worth noting that, for both the parent company and the acquired firm, the greatest sins of postmerger management are sins of omission. In opting to do nothing in an effort to avoid doing wrong, critical mistakes are made. It is, in fact, a time for stepping forward to take charge. During the integration phase of an acquisition, there are opportunities to be seized and problems to be attacked aggressively.

It is all too common for senior management in the parent company to minimize the problems that emerge during the integration process. Parent company executives generally give themselves high marks for the way they have handled an acquisition. In strong contrast, people in the acquired firm commonly deliver scathing indictments of the way they have been treated.

The lists that follow contain recommendations that can mitigate the disruptive impact of an acquisition. They provide guidance from the perspective of both the acquiring and acquired companies.

GUIDELINES FOR MANAGERS AND EXECUTIVES IN THE ACQUIRING FIRM

Following are 25 key considerations for managers and executives in an acquiring firm.

1. *Don't promise that things will remain the same in either company.* Most people will not believe you anyway, and most

221

of those who do will later insist that you have lied or misrepresented your plans and intentions to them. Explain that there will be changes, but that extreme effort will be made to (a) consider the interests of each employee and (b) keep them as well informed as possible of forthcoming changes. Remember, if you acquire another organization and do not make some changes, the odds are 10 to 1 that you have failed to take advantage of outstanding opportunities to make various changes that would be constructive, are needed, and would be adapted to quite well by incumbents.

2. *Make few promises.* In addition to the admonitions offered in the preceding guideline, you should realize that promises of any type, as a general rule, will end up making life harder for you. In fact, even when you communicate something through innuendo, you can create expectations that will later prove to be a problem. Your hints will often be taken as hard data.

3. *Keep your promises.* When you do go on record making a commitment, be as good as your word. There is a tremendous need in the postmerger environment for you to instill confidence and concentrate on developing a high degree of credibility. Do everything you can to improve the trust level. Understand that paranoia, guardedness, and suspicions in target company employees are very natural reactions to the situation.

4. *Do talk in specifics whenever you can.* Try not to add to the ambiguity. Try to be structured in your approach. What seems obvious to you is often unfamiliar and complex to others. Explain things in clear, straightforward language—avoid in-house jargon—and do not be too sketchy or talk in too general terms. Always confirm your listeners' understanding.

5. *Be acutely aware of the impact of your comments.* People will be trying to read things into almost everything you say. An offhand remark or slip of the tongue and one of the best people in the target company could be alienated.

6. *Don't feed the rumor mill.* A casual remark or careless wording can crank up another rumor when you should be doing everything you can to short-circuit rumors, conjecture, and misinformation.

7. *Provide more communication than usual during and after the merger/acquisition.* Strive to overcome the information vacuum that typically develops. Maintain closer-than-usual contact because everyone becomes increasingly hungry for information.

8. *Be a problem solver.* If you do not have the answer that people in the acquired firm need, help them find it. Do not be responsible for giving them the runaround. Instead of being a buck-passer, fill the role of problem solver.

9. *Go the extra mile.* Be helpful. Look for opportunities to facilitate the merger process. Anticipate the needs, and the questions, of people in the other organization, and then take the initiative in meeting those needs. Get the idea across that you are on their side, or at least that you are both on the same side. This can help defuse adversarial relations.

10. *Listen with the third ear.* Pay attention to how something is said as well as the actual verbal content of the message. The "process" by which someone in the acquired firm communicates may provide you with better information than do the words themselves. Be alert to implied meanings and hidden agendas. Deal with the total message—that is, what is not said as well as what is, the nonverbal as well as the verbal, what is implied as well as what is actually verbalized.

11. *Be humble.* Go out of your way to avoid behaving in a manner that might be construed as arrogance, feelings of superiority, criticalness, abrasiveness, or the like. People in the acquired firm will be defensive. Do not threaten or intimidate, even accidentally, as there is enough anxiety out there already. Be respectful.

12. *Exercise your best public relations skills.* Make people in the acquired firm feel important. Help make them feel like they are a welcome part of the corporate family, not a stepchild or adopted second-class citizen. Show empathy and patience. Be personal and try to have a human touch. Try to get to know those in the acquired firm as people with names and certain jobs. Be encouraging, supportive, and generous with positive reinforcement. Show interest and concern. Do not ignore them

or be indifferent, as that represents just one more blow to the individual and organizational ego in the acquired firm.

13. *Be prompt.* Act expeditiously. Even if you make a concerted effort to be timely, the acquired firm is almost certain to feel that things are proceeding too sluggishly, that it is taking too long to make decisions and take action. Mergers and acquisitions mean that, in conducting business, things have to go through more channels. Decision making will be more blurred. Procedures will be changing and therefore more confusing. Do everything conceivable to tighten the response time.

14. *Provide a clear sense of direction.* Be purposeful. Any acquisition is more likely to be responsive to new leadership if there is straightforward communication regarding what the new leaders want done and how the acquired organization is expected to work toward those goals. Respect the fact that uncertainty at the top increases the resistance to change at the lower levels. The acquired workforce and management team are far more likely to rally and do battle for a new administration's goals if that leadership sounds the charge in an unambiguous fashion.

15. *Establish—and communicate—short-term goals and objectives.* Keep people in the acquired firm focused and future oriented. Make the targets specific, measurable, realistic, and yet challenging. Set definite timetables and deadlines. In the absence of goals that can provide a good sense of direction, the workforce often shifts into neutral and begins to drift or coast.

16. *Make changes quickly and decisively.* As Antony Jay wrote in *Management and Machiavelli,* you should do one of two things: Embrace the people and make them yours, or terminate them and get them out as quickly as possible. Get the surgery done with, then get on with business. Do not cut here, slice there, and after a while saw another limb off. Let the bleeding be done with so the healing can commence.

17. *Don't just assume anything.* The acquired company is not likely to follow the parent company rules, policies, and procedures without being told what they are. In fact, employees of the acquired company probably will have to be told a number of times before the message takes hold.

18. *Don't underestimate the amount of effort involved.* Guard against a common mistake in underestimating the time and planning required to appropriately manage the change process associated with mergers and acquisitions. Experience shows that small acquisitions often call for just as much attention as—and sometimes more hand-holding and getting-adjusted time than—large ones.

19. *Establish clear, well-defined reporting relationships and lines of authority.* Historically, the most unsuccessful mergers and acquisitions have suffered from unclear relationships and a tendency to change already vague, poorly defined reporting relationships several times in the first year.

20. *Don't relax once the merger/acquisition legalities have been consummated.* Now comes the critical period of making the deal work.

21. *Make a concerted effort to minimize corporate staff interference,* especially by middle-management personnel from the parent organization. Do not blitz the acquired firm with people who go in unannounced or unexplained.

22. *Recognize limitations of resources.* Demonstrate a high regard for the limits of all available resources when establishing goals and timetables for the acquired firm. Objectives should be challenging but not unrealistic. You should strive to engineer success experiences rather than structure goals that are likely to be an exercise in frustration and futility. It is critically important for your first few actions vis-à-vis the acquisition to be positive and successfully carried out. These first steps set the tone for the relationship and have far-reaching ramifications.

23. *Adopt best practices.* Be wary of replacing successful methods and procedures in the acquisition with new corporate rules from the parent company.

24. *Limit administrative demands.* Guard against overwhelming the acquired company with paperwork and new reporting requirements. Get people in the acquisition to help determine which existing reports and paperwork chores can be eliminated or perhaps allowed to remain in lieu of parent company requirements.

25. *Realize that you cannot keep everyone happy.* Unless parent company executives and managers play their parts right in the merger scenario, it is almost inconceivable that management in the acquired firm will handle things appropriately. As much as anything, the leadership in the target firm needs specific coaching regarding how the new owner expects them to perform in the postmerger setting. So much of the time, however, they do not get any guidelines that would give meaningful direction to their efforts to deal with the situation. So they play it by ear, make a multitude of mistakes, are condemned either overtly or covertly, and feel extremely victimized by the whole process.

GUIDELINES FOR MANAGERS AND EXECUTIVES IN THE ACQUIRED ORGANIZATION

Following are 16 key considerations for managers and executives of an acquired organization.

1. *Expect change.* Prepare for it. Instead of fighting or resisting, embrace it. Posture yourself as a change agent or as a facilitator at least. Certainly, do not let yourself be surprised by the changes you will see or that you are expected to implement. Look toward the future, rather than futilely grasping the past and the old way of doing things.
2. *Anticipate.* Demonstrate a new level of initiative and resourcefulness. Look for ways to contribute to the integration process. The organization, and particularly your people, need more from you now than they have in routine times.
3. *Stay goal-directed.* See that you operate with a sense of purpose, rather than moving into a holding pattern. Operate with clear-cut specific objectives, even if they have to be very short range. Establish interim goals relative to the merger process itself.
4. *Give subordinates more management direction.* Do not let your part of the organization fall victim to postmerger drift. Employ a more structured management style. Give marching orders to your employees in a thorough fashion, including clear objectives with definite timetables.

5. *Become a role model for a positive attitude toward the merger.* Guard against being an insurgent, one who implicitly legitimizes a negative attitude toward the merger.

    Look at it this way—if you did not leave, you decided to stay. Make the best of it. Subordinates will be very sensitive to your attitude, however subtle the signals are that you send out. In the end, negativism (whether yours or theirs) is almost certain to make your job as a manager more difficult from a morale and/or productivity standpoint. Bad-mouthing the merger has very little promise of benefiting you, and it can be hazardous to your career.

6. *Put more into your communication efforts.* Invite input from subordinates and listen better. Then read between the lines. Consider the need for more frequent meetings with subordinates to provide more opportunity for two-way communication.

7. *Demonstrate maximum openness and candor* (exercising prudence and the necessary discretion, of course). But do not feed the rumor mill with speculation, conjecture, or repetition of damaging hearsay.

8. *Guard against making extremist statements* or taking unnecessary stands vis-à-vis the merger. You may have to eat your words, swallow your pride, and end up with a lot of unnecessary heartburn. This is a quick way to lose stature and credibility in the organization.

9. *Make few promises,* even though people will be pressing you for hard-and-fast answers. Be wary of making commitments you may be unable to keep.

10. *Be sensitive to shifts in the power structure.* It is likely that the merger will result in changes in the way things get done or in the way decisions are made. Roll with the flow. Make the appropriate adjustments. Don't fight city hall.

11. *Motivate to the hilt.* Mergers destabilize and create dissonance in an organization. They serve as an unfreezing event, and this sort of organizational shake-up gets people's attention. It rattles their cages, making them introspect (i.e., evaluate) their performance or worth, and consider the need for behavior change. The time is right to push for new and better

behavior/performance. Capitalize on the motivating potential the merger creates. It is a tremendous opportunity to reenergize people and organizations that have grown complacent and perhaps a bit stale. There is another point to be made here: If you do not seize the opportunity and use the dissonance as a motivator, it inevitably will be a demotivator for many people.

12. *Expect slower response times.* Usually procedures are in a state of flux. Policies are changing. More people, and new people, are involved in the decision-making process. Often there is a lack of clarity regarding just exactly who should be included in problem-solving and decision-making activities. Keep in mind the fact that information flow has to cover greater distances and involve more people than before. Be patient.

13. *Make the acquisition a two-way street.* Get to know the other firm better. Learn how they do business. Make an effort to understand the parent company's values and management philosophy. Get a clear fix on their goals for your organization. In short, get on their wavelength.

14. *Remain a leader and decision maker.* Do not let preoccupation with playing it safe cause you to abdicate. Instead of letting all the confusion cause you to drift to the sidelines, wield your authority. You probably need to manage more, not less. And because mergers typically do slow response times, be sure you put forth more effort to be timely, decisive, and expeditious. Do not contribute to the slippage or loss of organization momentum.

15. *Show some ownership of organization problems.* Do not just project blame elsewhere and expect higher management (in your company or the new parent firm) to assume all the responsibility for correcting things. Instead of being a critic and finger-pointer, strive to be part of the solution.

16. *Help minimize surprises.* It is the unanticipated event that generates the most personal stress for people. Be a therapeutic agent during these difficult times, instead of doing things that would add to the anxiety, trauma, and mistrust.

FINANCING

7.1 INTRODUCTION

It makes no sense for an acquirer to buy a company if the purchase price and terms stretch the resources of the acquirer so far that its existing business, as well as the acquired business, is jeopardized. Thus, the decision of how much to pay is often determined by the question: How much can the acquirer afford to pay?

7.2 BUSINESS PLANS AND THEIR USES

An important aspect of most business acquisitions is financing the new enterprise, including providing adequate money for both the purchase and working capital needed to make the new business succeed. Abstract discussions about what a business is worth are often less important than the reality of the amount of purchase price the buyer can finance. The starting point for any useful analysis of how to finance a business, as well as a very good guide to what the business is really worth, is therefore a comprehensive business plan for the proposed business.

The business plan should be a great deal more than a description of the existing enterprise. Often a buyer intends to do new and different things with the operation compared with the way it has been run in the past. Such changes might include, for example, reducing costs, providing additional capital to expand the business, integrating the acquired concern with the buyer's existing organization (often with synergisms that reduce costs or provide for additional markets), and adding new products or lines of business. Frequently a purchaser will determine that the sellers have been distributing far too large a proportion of the profits from the company, such as excessive salaries and fringe benefits for the owners. Such distributions may have tax benefits, such as having personal benefits become deductible business expenses, or they may simply represent an effort by the sellers to maximize their own compensation without regard to what the fair market value of their services may be. In any event, a buyer examining a possible purchase should immediately consider how to cut costs, increase volume, improve profit margins, eliminate deadwood, and otherwise enhance the profitability of the acquisition candidate.

To provide some discipline for this thought process and to demonstrate the validity of the process to a third-party lender or investor, a buyer should consider preparing a business plan for the target company. A business plan should include a detailed description of the existing operations and actions that the buyer intends to take to improve operations. To the extent that a buyer does not want to acquire particular existing segments of the target company, the buyer may decide to spin off, or sell, these parts of the business and thus reduce the amount of financing needed for the acquisition.

(a) IMPORTANCE OF PROJECTIONS. Although a written explanation of anticipated operations is important, the heart of most business plans is the operating projections. Projections usually fall into three distinct categories: profit and loss projections, balance sheet projections, and cash flow projections. The projected statement of operations will probably be derived from the existing financial statements of the target company with the types of modifications previously outlined. The projections should demonstrate cost savings, revenue growth, and areas of synergism with the acquiring company. These projections should also typically take into account normal anticipated future market developments, such as the effect of inflation on both the revenues and the costs of the operation.

Using the existing balance sheet of the company as a starting point, and taking into account any changes in the capital structure that will result from the purchase transaction, the purchaser can project balance sheets by month, quarter, or year into the future based on projected profits and losses. Balance sheets are particularly important to an asset-based lender who will look to specific assets, such as accounts receivable, as collateral for its loans.

(b) CASH FLOW PROJECTIONS. Finally, and often most important, the buyer should prepare a cash flow projection. This often takes the form of a so-called earnings before interest, taxes, depreciation, and amortization (EBITDA) projection. An accurate EBITDA projection gives the buyer and the buyer's financial sources a sound basis on which to determine how much money is expected to be available to service debt, make necessary capital expenditures, and provide for growth of the business and eventual distributions of profits to the owners. The EBITDA projections are likely to be the set of numbers that a potential venture capitalist or lender will focus on and ask the most questions about. The credibility of these projections is therefore usually central to the financing of the entire transaction.

(c) BUSINESS PLAN AS VALIDATION OF THE ACQUISITION RATIONALE. Although the preceding discussion focuses primarily on how a business plan is used by investors and lenders, it should be readily apparent that the business plan should be of equal importance to the buyer who is trying to put the deal together. If the buyer's business plan shows a shortfall in the form of an inability to service the necessary financing or to provide for necessary growth, then the entire transaction may be ill advised; it may need to be restructured; the price may have to be renegotiated; or the entire project may have to be abandoned. The business plan, therefore, should be used as a sanity check for the buyer as well as a sales tool for the buyer to use with lenders and investors.

7.3 FINANCING RESOURCES

(a) USE OF INTERNAL ASSETS.   The easiest way to buy an acquisition candidate is to use the existing resources of the acquirer. If the fortunate acquirer has significant cash reserves or unencumbered assets that it can mortgage to secure future payments, then the acquisition is easy. If the acquisition candidate has stock, preferably publicly traded stock with an established market value, it may be able to trade its own stock for the seller's company or assets. This is even better, leaving the acquirer's cash and assets free for other purposes, although it does dilute the interests of the acquirer's existing shareholders. Acquisitions carried out completely with the internal resources of the acquirer are, however, not the general rule.

(b) LEVERAGED TRANSACTIONS.   Many acquisitions are leveraged in whole or in part. The hard assets of the acquisition candidate are appraised, the financial statements are recast showing a restructured company with assets at fair market value instead of book value, an EBITDA projection is prepared showing ability to service debt, and the transaction is financed with a bank, insurance company, or other institutional lender. In the go-go acquisition days of the 1970s and 1980s, we sometimes saw 100% leveraged transactions, often with management borrowing against the company's assets to buy stock from the outside shareholders. The subsequent collapse of many such leveraged buyouts (LBOs) has reduced the rate of such transactions in the current economy. However, the combination of a partially leveraged acquisition with some new capital being invested by the buyer is still the most common way of completing an acquisition.

There are various levels and types of debt financing. The simplest form of financing is borrowing as much as possible of the purchase price, encumbering all of the acquisition candidate's assets, and probably also encumbering all or some of the acquirer's assets with one mortgage. Note that borrowing against the acquisition candidate's assets almost certainly means paying off the candidate's existing debt because the new lender will want a senior encumbrance on all the assets.

After this simple scenario, there are many complex approaches. For example, a single lender might lend against the real property and equipment and other hard assets, and another lender or the same lender, under a separate loan agreement, might provide a revolving line of credit with receivables and inventory pledged as collateral. When arranging for such multilevel financing, it is useful to distinguish between acquisition financing (usually a term loan) and operating capital (usually a revolving line of credit). A line of credit is more or less permanent financing that funds ongoing operations and that should not require any outside collateral or guarantees. Acquisition debt is usually limited to a fixed payoff period and frequently requires additional collateral or guarantees until it is paid off.

Another lender, often referred to as a mezzanine lender, could make a further loan secured by a junior lien on the assets. Mezzanine financing is expensive, because it carries greater risk, which is customarily rewarded by providing stock warrants or other equity kickers to the lender as well as higher interest rates.

(c) SELLER FINANCING. Another feature of many acquisitions is some amount of *carryback* by the seller. In a wholly leveraged transaction, the buyer may mortgage the assets of the acquisition candidate to finance a down payment and then persuade the seller to carry back a note for the balance of the purchase price. The seller's lien rights in such a case would be subordinate to those of the lender. This degree of cooperation from sellers is a little unusual these days. However, if the acquirer invests a significant amount in the acquisition, then it may be able to combine its own investment with the proceeds of a senior loan to make a very substantial down payment. In such cases, the seller may be persuaded to carry back a promissory note secured by a junior security interest in the assets that are being sold and probably further collateralized by a security interest in some or all of the assets of the acquirer. In these circumstances, projections of future cash flow become critical. Both the lenders and the seller must be convinced that there will be sufficient cash flow to satisfy all of their needs, with enough left to satisfy the operational requirements of the acquired business.

(d) EQUITY AND DEBT FINANCING. If the business plan and projections are consistent with the objectives of the buyer and seller, and if they justify a price that is acceptable to both the buyer and the seller, then the structure of a deal and a basis for negotiation of financing become feasible. The buyer can think of the financing as being an inverted pyramid. At the bottom, sometimes the smallest portion of the total financing, there is equity, usually provided by the buyer or a group of investors working with the buyer. Above that base, there is frequently (although not always) a layer of intermediate subordinated debt, which may have some equity-type features. Finally, the bulk of the financing for many acquisitions, particularly working capital for future operations, may be in the form of conventional debt from a bank or other institutional lender.

(i) Allocation of Risk.   Next we discuss the principal characteristics of these three layers of financing. The equity represents ownership of the entire enterprise and is totally at risk if the enterprise fails. The equity holders typically receive no return until all of the debt has either been repaid or so fully secured that the lenders are willing to permit distributions to the equity holders. The subordinated debt represents debt that is to be repaid prior to any distributions to the equity holders, but it is junior to the rights of the senior lenders, including being secured by liens on assets that are junior to the security rights of senior debt. Because the subordinated debt is less secure than senior debt, it typically receives a higher-interest return and often has quasi-equity features, such as warrants or a right to convert into equity at some point in the future. Finally, the senior debt is conventional debt of the type any operating business might have. It is secured by a first lien on tangible assets or current assets, such as accounts receivable and inventory, and bears a market rate of interest (perhaps a point or two over prime, depending on the degree of risk the lender incurs).

The distinctions among the various types of financing are not as clear as the lines on the pyramid might suggest. There may be several categories of financing within each of the three principal types, and the most senior portions of one layer may overlap with the most junior portions of the next layer up. For example, some equity owners may hold preferred stock or other rights to preferential distributions and preferential rights upon liquidation, giving them seniority over more junior equity holders. In contrast, some of the subordinated debt holders may be subordinated to all of the debt above them (including other classes of subordinated debt), and may have rights very much like those of equity holders to participate in the future profits of the business or to convert their debt into a conventional form of equity. Even the most senior debt for a new business may have some mezzanine or quasi-equity features, such as the right to bonus interest payable out of future profits or increases in the fair market value of the enterprise. However, despite some blurring of the lines, the categories are of considerable conceptual value and are often important for tax and other legal purposes. For example, if debt is true debt, the interest is probably deductible for tax purposes, whereas dividends or other profit distributions on equity are not deductible. If a particular right is truly equity, it is almost certainly junior to the rights of any unsecured general creditor in the event of bankruptcy or other insolvency of the enterprise.

(ii) Importance of Equity. Obviously, the willingness of lenders to provide financing to the buyer is almost always contingent on the buyer proving that there is a satisfactory commitment of equity available. Thus, in practice, a buyer who is shopping for loan financing must be prepared to demonstrate that it already has or can readily obtain commitments for equity investments. In reality, however, what the investors can reasonably expect to receive from the business depends on what first must be given to the lenders to satisfy their needs. Thus, any analysis of the relative rights and benefits available in any particular transaction will probably start with an analysis of what collateral, interest, and other characteristics will attach to the debt. Thus, the most useful way to analyze the total structure and effect of the three-tiered financial structure is probably to start with the rights of the senior debt.

Incidentally, although there often are multiple layers of financing, it is also possible for an acquisition to be accomplished with only one or two layers. A buyer can make the entire purchase with its existing funds or by issuing stock, thus making it a 100% equity deal. More likely, if the purchaser is reasonably well financed, it will provide all the equity necessary for the transaction and will obtain operating capital with a conventional secured loan, thus resulting in a combination of equity and senior debt but with no intermediate subordinated debt in the transaction. However, for purposes of this discussion, we will continue to assume the use of at least three levels of financing, with the likelihood that there will be some subcategories within each of the three major components.

(iii) Shopping for Debt. For most senior debt, financing will be competitive and fairly generic. A buyer may wish to shop two or three banks or other institutional lenders but is likely to find that each of them

will make substantially similar offers, although relatively minor differences between two loan proposals are usually worth looking for. If a lender is interested in providing the financing, it will usually provide a commitment letter outlining the interest rate, total facility availability, required collateral, and other principal terms and conditions. A commitment letter is by no means a real "commitment." It is a letter of intent indicating the interest of the lender in making the deal on the terms specified; it can almost always be withdrawn or modified without penalty to the lender. In practice, however, most lenders will not issue a commitment letter unless they are confident they can proceed on the terms proposed.

If the buyer accepts the commitment letter, it is usually required to pay a fee to the lender at that point to cover the lender's time and expense in proceeding with due diligence and formal documentation of the loan. There may be an additional fee in the form of interest points on the total amount of the facility at the time the formal loan documents are executed.

(iv) ***Lender Leverage.*** Typical terms of a bank loan agreement are complex, onerous, and to a very large extent nonnegotiable. The buyer will be required to make numerous representations and warranties about both itself and the target business. The original advance of loaned funds, and any subsequent advances, will be tied to the satisfaction of various continuing conditions, and the loan agreement will contain detailed provisions about collateral and other security rights, probably including personal guarantees by the buyer's principals for smaller transactions. Of particular interest to any accountant working on a loan transaction will be a series of negative and affirmative covenants in the loan document. These covenants will cover a variety of topics, but the most important ones address financial issues. A negative covenant might, for example, be the absence of any litigation or other contingency in excess of a specified dollar amount. An affirmative covenant might be a requirement to maintain a certain level of net book value in the acquired business or a specified level of cash flow sufficient to service the debt and provide for other necessary items, such as projected capital expenditures. Minimum net earnings and net book value affirmative covenants are likely to be set forth either by month or by quarter, perhaps taking into account seasonality and other variations, but generally requiring a steady improvement in the financial condition

of the borrower. The unwary buyer may well be trapped here by its own business plan projections. If the lender approves the loan, the approval is probably based on acceptance of the projections that the buyer previously provided to the lender, and the lender's covenants are likely to be based on these book value, earnings, and cash flow projections. Although a lender will typically allow some deviations from projected numbers, a material failure to meet goals may trigger a default, with a right on the part of the lender to call the loan. Thus, the buyer's confidence in the business plan on which it has based the request for financing will be tested. Many business plans include several different projections, typically an expected case, a downside case, and an optimistic case. Usually the borrower will want to make sure that the financial covenants in the loan documents relate to the lowest case, not one of the higher ones.

Another area of concern for the buyer's accounting personnel is bank loan requirements for periodic reports to the lender. These may simply ask for annual audited and monthly internal financial statements, but they also often require more difficult and frequent reports, such as weekly or even daily accounts receivable reports. The accountant often must certify the accuracy of this information, and an error may expose the certifying officer to personal liability.

(v) Guarantees. Another area of individual concern in smaller transactions is that a senior secured lender may require personal guarantees from the buyer's principals. These are frequently joint and several guarantees of the entire principal amount of the debt, although many lenders are willing to accept limited guarantees subject to a cap for each of the individual guarantors. The lender's theory in this regard is that none of the guarantors has sufficient net worth to pay the entire amount of the debt, but each of them should have a guarantee exposure large enough to severely threaten their personal net worth as a means of keeping them focused and devoted to the success of the new business.

(vi) Subordination. Subordinated debt is available from a variety of sources. Many banks and other conventional lenders have a division or an affiliate that specializes in mezzanine financing.

Another common source of subordinated debt is the parties themselves. Some of the investors may feel that at least some of their investment ought to be secured (even if junior to the bank conventional financing) to give them an advantage over other investors and over general unsecured creditors in the event of insolvency. The senior lender may—although it will not necessarily—be relatively indifferent to the company's mix of equity and subordinated debt. From a senior lender's point of view, all other financing is subordinate to the senior lender, and therefore, in theory at least, equity and subordinated debt are equal. In practice, most banks and other senior lenders have a strong preference for a balance sheet that reflects equity rather than subordinated debt, and therefore this distinction may be more important to lenders than it seems it should be.

Another source of subordinated debt is the seller. Particularly if the seller is receiving a premium price or a price that is to some degree a contingent or earnout amount, it would be normal for the seller to take some of the consideration in the form of a long-term note. The senior lender will almost certainly require that any indebtedness to the seller be subordinate to the rights of the senior lender; therefore, if the seller wants to see the deal completed, it will probably have to agree that its debt will be subordinated.

The concept of subordination runs through any discussion on financing. Some subordination rights exist as a matter of law. Equity is almost always subordinate to debt; unsecured debt is subordinate to secured debt. There are, however, exceptions to these general rules. For example, in a bankruptcy proceeding, recent collateral rights granted to owners or other insiders are likely to be classified as preferences that may be set aside and disregarded by the bankruptcy court. Subject to these qualifications, the general proposition is that the law and the recorded security rights of the parties determine subordination to a substantial degree.

Aside from the question of priorities that exist by law, parties can enter into contractual subordination agreements. Most lending banks have a standard subordination agreement that they will try to require the borrower and all of the borrower's other lenders to sign. The basic concept of subordination certainly implies that the subordinated lender can be paid, in the event of liquidation, only if and to the extent that there is anything left after payment of the senior creditor. However, a bank subordination agreement is likely to go much further than this. It typically requires that no payments be made to any subordinated lender so long as any amount is still due to the senior lender. It may also contain other restrictions, such as a waiver by the subordinated lender of any rights it might otherwise have as a matter of law to foreclose on assets, commence legal proceedings to enforce its rights, and so on. These types of subordination agreement provisions are generally subject to modification through negotiations. A reasonable accommodation on priority of payments, for example, is an agreement by the senior lender that junior lenders may be paid periodic installments of interest as long as all payments are current to the senior lender and there are no defaults under the senior loan agreement. Arrangements permitting repayment of the principal amount of any subordinated debt are likely to require greater concessions to the senior lender. For example, a significant increase in the book value of the borrower might be a condition to repay any principal due on subordinated debt. The issues surrounding subordination agreements are often a principal subject of negotiation in the course of the financing.

(vii) Forms and Types of Equity.   Like debt, equity comes in many forms and types. The first equity in most deals comes from the buyer, which we tend to refer to as a single individual, but which is likely to be a company or group of individuals. These are the people whose money is at highest risk. They may in turn obtain additional equity subscriptions from friends and colleagues or from professional venture capital sources. Although venture capitalists can usually take care of themselves, a buyer who is in the business of raising money should emphatically be aware of the severe limitations placed on money raising by federal and state securities laws. Violations of these laws can be a criminal offense and, at a minimum, are likely to provide the investors with a civil right of rescission, meaning that if they become dissatisfied with the transaction they can, for an extended period after they make their initial investment, demand that the promoter of the deal rescind the transaction and personally refund to them the full amount of their investment. Thus, compliance with all applicable securities laws, although time-consuming and burdensome, is absolutely necessary for a buyer who is going outside its own resources to find risk capital support.

The ultimate source of equity financing is the general public. Financing through a public stock offering, often referred to as an initial public offering (IPO), is not usually used for funding an initial purchase price. It is, however, a way of raising additional operating capital as well as providing an exit strategy for the initial investors in the project (i.e., a means for them to liquidate their investment after the new company has become successful). Public stock offerings are a complex topic, and only a few issues need to be mentioned here. If a public offering is intended at some point in the foreseeable future, strict compliance with applicable legal and accounting standards is essential. When the company goes public, it must file a registration statement including historical audited financial statements and full disclosure of any significant legal issues. A clean accounting and legal history is therefore very important.

(viii) Public Offerings.   Another issue to understand when using a public offering as an exit strategy is that registration of stock does not usually provide immediate liquidity to the existing investors. Registrations apply to stock, not to companies. The stock that is likely to be registered in an IPO is previously unissued stock belonging to the corporation. Most underwriters are reluctant to allow existing investors to register any of their stock as part of the IPO, because this has the appearance of a bailout by the owners, which is detrimental to the perception of the company in the public market. Therefore, the stock owned by the existing investors is usually not registered; in any event, it is probably what is considered to be affiliate stock under the securities laws. Both because it is unregistered and because it is owned by affiliates, the insiders' stock can be sold only in accordance with Rule 144, which requires an extended holding period and limits the volume of shares that can be sold in any particular period. In addition, the underwriters will probably not only forbid the registration of existing outstanding stock but will also require that such stock be held in escrow or otherwise be made subject to restrictions on transfer so that it cannot be sold for a period of a year or two after the public offering. Therefore, although a public registration offers the potential for long-term liquidity, it does not usually provide an immediate exit event to the original investors.

Finally, it is worth noting that the requirements of the Securities and Exchange Commission and Nasdaq or a recognized stock exchange impose considerable new burdens on the company and potential legal liabilities on its officers, directors, and existing shareholders. Thus, the advantage of a public offering—primarily long-term liquidity and the availability of substantial new equity—should be weighed carefully against the expense and risk of securities compliance matters.

CHAPTER 8

SALES AND DIVESTITURES

8.1 INTRODUCTION

There are two general types of sales of an enterprise: the sale of an entire business and the sale, or divestiture, of a segment of a business, such as a subsidiary, business unit, or product line. The dynamics associated with each of these two categories of sales transactions are quite different. Accordingly, each is discussed separately herein. Section 8.2 addresses issues relevant to the sale of an entire business, and section 8.3 discusses those associated with divestitures.

8.2 SALE OF AN ENTIRE BUSINESS

The sale of a business may be *initiated* in a variety of ways. The owners (in the case of a closely held business) or the managers and board of directors (in the case of a publicly traded company) may seek to be acquired, or they may be approached by an interested potential buyer or its representative. In addition, the sales *process* associated with public company sales or mergers is considerably different from that of private company transactions. Also, the dynamics of sales of private companies that are unsolicited can be quite different from those that are initiated by the seller. The factors affecting these various public and private transactions are discussed in the sections that follow.

(a) ACQUISITIONS OR MERGERS OF PUBLIC COMPANIES. Public company transactions fall into two distinct categories: "hostile" takeovers and "friendly" acquisitions or mergers. Hostile takeovers represent an extremely small percentage of public transactions and involve attempts of the buyer to acquire a company despite the resistance of the target's management and board. Hostile takeovers entail a process by which the management and the board of the target company are bypassed and a tender offer is made directly to the shareholders of the company. Because a detailed discussion of hostile takeovers is beyond the scope of this discussion, suffice it to say that successful takeovers are rare in occurrence and present substantial challenges to the buyer (or "raider"), when they do occur.

Potential friendly transactions involving the acquisition of a publicly traded company or the merger of two public companies are much more common, but those that are consummated represent a small percentage of those that are initially contemplated. This is because they generally entail considerable discussion even before there is preliminary agreement to proceed with negotiations; they require long and complex negotiations before the deal is presented for stockholder approval; and they involve compliance with extensive administrative and regulatory requirements to finalize the transaction.

Throughout the sales process, the potential for a deal to unravel is significant. The time and resources of the target company, as well as that of the potential acquirer, required to execute a satisfactory transaction are quite substantial. As a result, many potential transactions die an early death, and those that are initially pursued frequently are abandoned. The 11-step sequence that follows illustrates the presales process and some of the challenges and difficulties associated with the full execution of such transactions.

1. *Initial Contact.* Initial contact generally originates with an overture from the potential acquirer. The prospective buyer's expression of interest will generally be accompanied by a view of the strategic benefit of the transaction to the target company and its stockholders. Appropriately, the argument for the combination will be made on its strategic merits; quantification of those benefits will largely be left to future discussions and negotiations. After these preliminary discussions have taken place, whether the combination is deemed to warrant further consideration will be left to the discretion of the target company. If the target company decides to pursue discussions, its chief executive officer (CEO) almost invariably would take the lead in discussions and, ultimately, negotiations. Typically, the circle of executives brought into the process at this stage would be small, in an effort to minimize publicity and the associated distraction that usually accompanies it.

2. *Nondisclosure Agreement.* If the overture is taken seriously, the parties will execute a nondisclosure agreement (NDA) that requires that discussions of the potential transaction and any proprietary information exchanged to be kept confidential. This is a particularly important document from the perspective of the target company. In the course of discussions and negotiations, a substantial amount of proprietary information will be requested by the prospective buyer, and the target will

want concrete, binding assurances that this information will be safeguarded.

3. *Agreement to Pursue Discussions.* The parties will also agree on the terms under which they will proceed. This would generally include a time frame, or exclusivity period, within which a mutually acceptable definitive agreement would be drafted or discussions terminated. As the process proceeds, it will become increasingly more consumptive of time, resources, and management attention. Accordingly, the more quickly the parties can come to a decision on aggressive pursuit of a deal, whether affirmative or negative, the greater the assurance that resources will not be misspent.

4. *Engagement of Advisors.* Once an agreement to proceed with discussions has been executed, the target company would engage a host of legal, business, and financial advisors to assist in the evaluation of the transaction and in the administrative process that naturally follows. This is a point in the process where activity begins to ramp up substantially and when the circle of internal staff is expanded.

5. *Letter of Intent.* Once agreement on the basic aspects of the prospective transaction has been negotiated, the target company can expect to receive a letter of intent (LOI) formalizing the basic terms agreed to. The LOI is a nonbinding document from a legal perspective, but it provides the benefit of a clear articulation of the terms contemplated. It is also a document that is subject to negotiation, and it is common for the target company to participate in its drafting, either through markups or direct participation.

6. *Due Diligence.* The target company will have agreed to allow the potential buyer to perform formal due diligence. Clearly, preliminary diligence will have been performed by the prospective buyer through analysis of publicly available information and the inputs of a wide variety of financial advisors and industry experts. Formal diligence will entail the creation by the target company of a secure data room (whether actual or virtual) to house substantial amounts of proprietary information as well as the development of procedures associated with controlling

access to the data and company personnel, answering questions, and responding to requests for additional information.

7. *Negotiation of a Definitive Agreement.* Assuming a positive outcome from the due diligence process, terms of the transaction would be documented in a definitive agreement that will require the two sides to consummate the transaction, generally subject to the approval of the target's board and its shareholders. This will usually result in a protracted and iterative process. It is also a process that involves a wide range of individuals, typically including the CEO and the senior members of his or her executive staff as well as numerous experts and advisors. Generally the board would also be involved in key decisions to ensure its support.

8. *Affirmative Vote of the Board.* If negotiations of a definitive agreement are successful, the agreement would then be put before the target's board for an affirmative vote. As noted, the board will have been involved in the negotiating process. In fact, the process would almost certainly not have progressed to this stage if there were any question about the affirmation of the board. Also at this time, the prospective transaction is revealed to shareholders, the public, and the appropriate regulatory authorities.

9. *Regulatory Filings.* The parties would then be required to adhere to the requirements of the Hart-Scott-Rodino (HSR) Act to ensure that the transaction does not create a monopolistic entity. (The HSR Act is discussed in detail in Section 8.3(c).) The size of a public transaction will undoubtedly trigger an HSR filing with the Federal Trade Commission (FTC) and the Department of Justice (DOJ). If these agencies determine that the transaction is anticompetitive, it may be blocked or the parties may be required to divest of certain properties to remedy that condition. If the filing results in the former, the negotiations between the parties would clearly be terminated. In the latter case, the parties must determine whether compliance is desirable. If not, the transaction would be abandoned.

10. *Shareholder Approval.* Assuming that the requirements of the HSR Act are met, the target company would then seek shareholder approval. The shareholder approval process required of the target company is burdensome and time-consuming. It calls for the development of a prospectus, a document designed to provide detailed information about the transaction, and a proxy statement that requests support of its execution. The development of these documents, their distribution, and the administration of the shareholder vote can be expected to take several months.

11. *Close.* Once shareholder approval is received, the transaction can proceed to close.

(b) ACQUISITIONS OF PRIVATELY HELD BUSINESSES. The dynamics involving the acquisition of privately held companies can vary considerably depending on whether the transaction is passive (the approach by the suitor is unsolicited) or active (the target company has made its desire to sell known to potential buyers). When the approach is passive, the target company is essentially in a reactive mode and must simply determine whether it wants to sell and, if so, at what price and under what conditions.

However, when a company has adopted an active posture, putting the company up for sale will generally be preceded by a process of preparing the business for the transaction. This can affect owner behavior leading up to the point when the business is put on the market as well as the manner in which the business is marketed.

In either case, the seller should enlist a team of specialists to assist in the process. This would include, at a minimum, a merger and acquisition (M&A) attorney, a tax advisor, and a valuation professional. In addition, a financial advisor with M&A experience and a broker, especially in the case where the owner is "shopping" the business, can provide valuable expertise.

(i) *Unsolicited Sales.* As noted, unsolicited sales by their very nature put the prospective seller in a reactive mode. Through the use of advisors, the seller should determine a reasonable range of values for the company, the preferred structuring of the transaction, and any non-negotiable aspects of the transaction. Armed with this information and the support of a qualified advisor (particularly a knowledgeable and experienced M&A attorney), the seller can confidently enter negotiations. The major considerations associated with shaping the transaction are elaborated next.

- *Price.* The seller should engage a qualified professional to establish a reasonable range of values for the enterprise being sold. In the case of an unsolicited transaction, it is very likely that the seller will not have a good sense of what the value of the enterprise is. A qualified valuator or appraiser is able to provide a reasonable range of values that can be used as a starting point for establishing the seller's position on sales price. That view of value can be further influenced by other factors, such as the nature of the buyer, the form of the transaction (whether a purchase of stock or assets), and the nature of the consideration paid by the buyer (cash, the buyer's stock, or debt).
- *Nature of the Buyer.* The buyer's position in the market can have a significant impact on the sale price that is eventually negotiated. With professional assistance, the seller can usually establish a reasonable and supportable standalone value of the business (see section 3.3(d) for a more complete discussion of business valuations). It is considerably more difficult to determine what type of premium above standalone value a competitor may be willing to pay. That said, the seller and its advisors should put themselves in the shoes of the suitor and value any synergies that may be apparent. Certain of those synergies will generally be revealed in discussions and negotiations, and the seller's team should be attuned to such revelations.
- *Form of the Sale.* The sale can take the form of either a stock sale or an asset sale. Although the benefits and disadvantages of each are discussed in detail in Chapter 9, it is invariably more beneficial to the seller to obtain treatment of the transaction as a sale of stock rather than a sale of assets. However, the converse is true for the buyer. This is usually a major point of negotiation, and the seller must decide fairly early in the process whether the requirement of an asset sale is a deal breaker or whether it is negotiable, and what the "price" of acquiescence is.
- *Consideration.* Consideration can take the form of cash, stock, or debt or some combination thereof. The benefits of a cash transaction are apparent. It leaves no doubt about the value of

the consideration given. However, if the buyer's stock will, in part or in total, constitute consideration for the transaction, the seller must determine whether and to what extent this would require a premium to be paid by the buyer. Similarly, the use of debt to fund the transaction may result in the desire for a step-up in purchase price, depending on how such debt is secured.

- *Role of the Seller.* In some instances, the role that the seller(s) will play in the management of the company postacquisition is a factor in negotiations. This is clearly a situation-specific consideration and is directly related to the preferences of the seller and the perceived needs of the buyer. Although it can be a significant point of negotiation, it is important that any financial arrangement is subject to an agreement separate from the purchase agreement and that any associated compensation is treated as salary (or consulting fees, in the case of a consulting arrangement) and kept separate from the purchase price.

- *Impact on Employees.* Frequently, sellers will have concerns about the impact of a sale on employees, particularly those who have been long-standing members of the seller's organization. This can be a significant point of contention in those situations where it is clear that the buyer will be consolidating the operations of the two businesses. Although there are potential remedies available to address such concerns, they generally will have a price tag associated with them, and who will absorb that cost is open to negotiation.

Once these and any other core issues are considered, the seller has put itself in a strong position to negotiate the terms of the transaction. Successful negotiations would lead to a preliminary, nonbinding agreement, generally in the form of an LOI, and the process would proceed to due diligence, and the negotiation of a binding, formal purchase agreement.

(ii) Preparing a Business for Sale.   When a sale of a closely held business is contemplated by its owner(s), the selling process will frequently be preceded by efforts to prepare (or package) the business for sale. This is because owner-managed businesses frequently are not subject to the same financial and operational rigor as a public company. For example, the entity and the personal assets and activities of

the owner(s) may become comingled or record keeping may not meet the standards desirable for the sales process.

To remedy such conditions, if they exist, a prudent seller will address such issues with the assistance of a financial advisor or business broker, or both. Depending on the extent of the work to be done, this effort may require anywhere from six months to two years to implement. The areas of focus would logically be those that could be expected to be subject to particular scrutiny in due diligence. This would generally include, but not necessarily be limited to, these areas:

- *Formalization of Accounting Policies.* This would include the documentation of policies governing such areas of revenue recognition, when items are expensed and when they are capitalized. Focus would be on conformity with generally accepted accounting principles (GAAP) as well as on consistency of application in areas where there are legitimate accounting treatment options.
- *A Review of Assets and Liability Accounts.* This would entail a fairly exhaustive analysis of potential impediments to a sale or items that could negatively impact value. It would include an analysis of asset values and the appropriateness of reserves as well as documentation of ownership, legal transferability, and registration (e.g., intangibles). It would also include a review of all material liabilities as well as tax returns and the resolution of any open issues with creditors or taxing authorities.
- *Contract Review.* This would include the review and possible modification of major contracts. Key areas include assignability, existence of key personnel employee contracts (and, if so, their terms), and any financing arrangements and major terms and covenants. All material contracts should be assessed in terms of their potential for raising buyer concerns and/or impairing the value of the enterprise. To the greatest extent possible, such issues should be resolved well in advance of putting the business up for sale.
- *Shareholder Issues.* A review and assessment of shareholder positions and dispositions toward a transaction and any impact on a potential transaction should be conducted. A positive, or at least neutral, position of all shareholders toward a sale of the business is extremely desirable. Common potential problem

areas include ownership positions held by estranged spouses, ex-spouses, and shareholder/partners and promises of sweat equity made to key employees. Potential buyers will clearly be reluctant to proceed with a transaction that has the potential for litigation by dissident shareholders or quasi-shareholders. These types of situations should be resolved before the sale process is put in motion. If resolution is not possible, the seller should assess the impact on the salability of the business.

- *Owner Compensation Issues.* Owner compensation (both salary and benefits) is commonly overstated in owner-managed businesses. Compensation should be normalized to reflect market rates. This will have a beneficial impact on the company's profit and loss (P&L) statement. Although a buyer will normalize expenses as part of its analysis, the ability to present a "clean" P&L has significant psychological benefits. In this regard, the stronger the impression of potential buyers that the business is professionally operated and managed, the higher the level of confidence in representations made by ownership.

- *Litigation.* Identification of actual or potential exposures and development of strategies to minimize any impediments to sale or any impairment of value should be initiated well in advance of putting the business on the market. If efforts to resolve suits and address claims are not successful, the seller, with the assistance of a qualified attorney, should lay out the details of the matter and the strength of the owners' position.

Once the business has been prepared for sale, the seller would put the business on the market, often with the assistance of a business broker. The value added by the broker can be quite substantial and is detailed in section 2.3(d).

8.3 DIVESTITURES

Companies occasionally decide to divest or dispose of elements of their businesses. The business units being divested may be individual products, product lines, or subsidiaries. In virtually all cases, two rationales underlie this decision: Business units are disposed of either for strategic considerations or out of financial necessity. In all cases, though, the objective of the divestiture *process* is to optimize the proceeds from the sale while minimizing management distraction and disruption to the core, or remaining, business.

This discussion is focused on the rationales, issues, and dynamics of the divestiture process and describes a structured approach to managing that process. It is organized into these sections:

- Divestiture rationales
- Predivestiture issues and considerations
- Divestiture planning
- Preparation for the transaction
- Execution of the transaction

(a) STRATEGIC DIVESTITURES. Most often, the underlying cause for divestiture is best described as "strategic" (i.e., the unit being sold no longer supports the strategic objectives of the overall business). As markets evolve, businesses adjust, and part of that adjustment process is the pruning of those elements of the business's portfolio that are no longer compatible with its current strategy.

That lack of compatibility may become apparent to management as the result of a disciplined process of evaluation or as a result of the continuous underperformance of the products or business units in question, or simply as a result of the recognition of their reduced relevance to the overall business. Some companies take a rigorous approach to refining their portfolios and will acknowledge a unit's lack of strategic fit fairly quickly. Those that do not employ a proactive approach may be slower to recognize that a divestiture is in order and are prone to react only when continued unsatisfactory performance draws management's attention to the problem business unit.

In any event, it eventually becomes clear to management that the business unit is not a candidate for continued investment and that, over time, a downward spiral of deteriorating performance, underinvestment, and further deterioration is a very real risk. Although there are situations where it may be advisable to milk a nonstrategic property for some period of time, management will generally conclude that the optimal alternative is to divest the property or properties in question.

(b) FINANCIAL DIVESTITURES. Although relatively infrequent, divestitures are also made for financial reasons, specifically, to generate cash. It is axiomatic that sustained unprofitability will ultimately result in cash flow problems. This condition will frequently cause the company in question to consider the divestiture of some portion of its portfolio. Predictably, it is the most valuable assets of the company that will command the most interest in the marketplace. As a result, financial divestitures generally involve the most attractive elements of the company's portfolio, and they are often made under duress.

Such transactions are almost always counterstrategic and are driven by necessity. More often than not, they not only delay the inevitable deterioration of the overall business, but they contribute to it. As the most valuable assets are stripped away, the core business is inevitably weakened and financial performance deteriorates further, frequently resulting in the business's death spiral. Despite this pattern, financial divestitures still occur when troubled businesses have no other alternatives to generating much-needed cash.

The discussion that follows focuses primarily on strategic divestitures, although many of the considerations and practices described, particularly those associated with planning, preparing for, and executing the transaction, apply to financial divestitures as well.

(c) PREDIVESTITURE ISSUES AND CONSIDERATIONS. There are important issues and considerations commonly encountered when divestitures are contemplated. These include:

- A tendency to delay the transaction
- The temptation to underresource the transaction
- The complications associated with disentangling the property to be divested from the core business
- The potential loss or disaffection of key employees of the property being divested
- The potential impact of the Hart-Scott-Rodino Antitrust Improvement Act

These items, discussed in detail in the next sections, all represent conditions that may increase the risks associated with the execution of a divestiture transaction. Those heightened risks increase the potential for either a suboptimal transaction (one in which materially less than full value is realized for the properties being sold) or a broken transaction (one which a sale is not consummated).

(i) Delay.   The decision to divest can be a difficult one for management to make for a variety of reasons. Despite an apparent lack of strategic fit, management may believe that it can reverse the negative trends in the business, even in the face of compelling evidence to the contrary. This attitude stems from the fact that, for many managers, divestiture is an unnatural act and the decision to sell may be seen as an admission of failure on their part. Additional resistance may come from some quarters within the management team because the prospective sale represents the diminution of their authority and responsibility.

Alternatively, the need to divest may be recognized, but the decision may be deferred for a number of reasons. Management may believe that the timing is poor due to a depressed market for the properties to be sold, it may be unwilling to commit limited resources to the management of the disposal process, or it may simply find it easier to procrastinate than to act.

Whatever the rationale, one thing is virtually certain: Failure to act will only increase the risk of further deterioration of the business unit and the erosion of its value in the marketplace. Accordingly, once it is recognized that a property falls outside the strategic focus of the core business, a decision regarding its disposition should be forthcoming as soon as reasonably possible.

(ii) Undercommitment of Resources.   The underresourcing of the divestiture effort, once the decision to sell has been made, is a common pitfall associated with divestiture transactions, and generally stems less from a conscious effort to withhold support than from the psychological dynamics surrounding the divestiture process.

Unlike acquisitions, which have a certain cache that causes executives and managers to want to be associated and involved, divestitures are transactions that have little in the way of inherent appeal. Whereas acquisitions are associated with success and growth, divestitures are more likely to be associated with failed strategy and a weakened business that has no future with the parent company. Accordingly, involvement with a successful acquisition is perceived to be a valuable professional experience, while association with a divestiture is likely to go largely unnoticed, unless it is perceived to have been poorly executed. This imbalance between risk and reward makes it under-standable why disposals rarely generate enthusiasm and a desire for involvement among members of a company's management team.

In addition, senior executive management will frequently adopt an out-of-sight, out-of-mind mentality once the decision to divest has been made. This is the function of a need and desire to focus on issues associated with running and building *the business that exists,* but it frequently results in a blind spot relative to the business being sold. Ironically, it is not uncommon that, once the decision to sell has been made, the divestiture process frequently falls off the corporate radar—just when all the work remains to be done.

It is necessary to understand these attitudes and perceptions because they can result in a lack of commitment of the resources neces-sary to properly execute the transaction. And, absent that commitment, the organization runs a substantially increased risk of suboptimizing the value of the property being sold.

(iii) Infrastructure Integration.   When the unit being divested is a standalone business with its own infrastructure, financial representa-tion of the entity's historical performance and condition is relatively straightforward. Comprehensive historical financial statements for the business will exist, and a self-sufficient enterprise, with the entire nec-essary infrastructure, can be presented for sale.

However, it is more commonly the case that the products or business unit being divested have been owned by the seller for an extended period, in some cases for decades, and that the operational support of the property is very likely to have become intertwined with that of the parent. As a result, from both a financial reporting and operational perspective, the unit may be difficult to present as a true standalone operation.

In situations where infrastructure and other aspects of operations are supported by shared services, the seller must decide how to best present the unit being divested and how to disentangle it in a manner that optimizes its value. This generally requires a considerable amount of thought, planning, and management effort.

Disentangling will usually have two related but distinct aspects: financial and operational. The financial statements of the property being divested will contain a variety of expense allocations from the parent company that reflect the expenditure of real resources but that cannot be presented on a dedicated basis. Typically, this will include expenses associated with such things as facilities (e.g., rent), accounting, technology, and human resource support.

As a result, a meaningful representation of the property being divested will often require the presentation of pro forma statements and possibly a carve-out audit (i.e., independent validation of the financial statements to be presented to potential buyers). Absent such a presentation, potential buyers may be unable or unwilling to determine a value for the business. If they are willing and able to do so, it is quite likely that the cost assumptions they will make will dampen projected margins and ultimately the valuation they arrive at.

The integration of the properties being divested into the core business also creates operational challenges. This type of condition may limit the sale of the properties to a buyer that has sufficient infrastructure to fill whatever operational gaps that result when separating the two entities. Even in cases where the buyer has the operational capability to do so, the seller may have to be prepared to provide transition services for the business being sold to fill these gaps for some interim period.

To the extent that they exist, these issues have to be anticipated and addressed by the seller. They can have a significant impact on the timing of the transaction, they can entail material expense, and they can limit the pool of potential buyers.

(iv) Personnel Issues. Once news of the divestiture becomes known by the management and employees of the properties being sold, the seeds of uncertainty will have been sown and the potential for loss and/or disaffection of key employees will be heightened. For these reasons, *it is imperative that the discussions of the potential sale are kept confidential during the planning and preparation stages of the process.* The circle of those who know about the impending sale should be kept as small as possible and be expanded only on a need-to-know basis.

The major issues associated with employee uncertainty and discontent relate to the ongoing management of the business during the sales period and the reliance on key personnel to present the business to potential buyers in the best possible light. Mishandling the announcement of the prospective sale and the inattentive treatment of employees during the sales period is guaranteed to negatively impact employee productivity and morale, increase the potential for alienation and loss of key personnel, and ultimately impair the value and marketability of the properties being sold.

These risks can be mitigated by the development and deployment of a retention plan for key employees (see "Retention Plan," section 8.3(d)(ii)) and a thoughtfully planned and executed internal announcement of the prospective transaction (see "Development of a Communication Plan," section 8.3(d)(v)).

(v) Hart-Scott-Rodino Act.　The Hart-Scott-Rodino (HSR) Antitrust Improvement Act of 1976 established a premerger program requiring those engaged in "large" M&As to notify the FTC and DOJ of the impending transaction. The parties to such a transaction must submit a notification and report form with information about their businesses and wait a specified period of time before consummating the transaction. The objective of the act is to inhibit transactions that result in monopolistic entities.

Despite the act's reference to "large" M&As, the threshold established by the HSR Act is quite low and, as a result, affects a significant number of transactions. Although these thresholds may be adjusted upward periodically, they generally apply to transactions in which one of the parties has $100 million or more in annual net sales or total assets and the other has $10 million or more, and the size of the transaction is in excess of $53 million. That said, the actual application of the act can be complex, so legal guidance should be sought to ensure compliance if a transaction involving amounts in this order of magnitude (or greater) is contemplated.

If a transaction does meet the criteria for the HSR Act, a number of factors should be taken into consideration. The first is whether there are indications that the resulting combination may be anticompetitive and, if so, whether the acquisition is still worth pursuing. If so, the acquirer must recognize that this could entail the disposal of certain properties to ameliorate that situation.

Assuming that the transaction will not result in an anticompetitive combination, there are additional factors to be considered. These include:

- *An Impact on the Timing of the Consummation of the Transaction.* The filing cannot be made to the FTC and the DOJ until a purchase agreement has been signed and, once signed, the waiting period is 30 days, unless a request for early termination is granted. There is no guarantee that early termination will be granted and, in fact, if one of these bodies requests additional information, it can be extended. Therefore, the planning for the transaction should accommodate a delay in closing the deal after the contract has been executed.

- *Judicious Characterization of the Market Position of the Business Being Sold.* Parties to the transaction should be aware of the potential for undue complications if the information submitted with the notification and report form (or any additional information requested) in any way suggests that the resulting combination would have an anticompetitive effect on a market. Accordingly, sales hyperbole should be avoided by the seller, and any internal communications of the buyer should steer clear of characterizations that diminish the position of competitors as a result of the transaction.
- *Recognition That There Is a Material Cost for Filing.* The cost of filing varies, depending on the size of the transaction. Although the fee is not substantial enough to influence the decision whether to proceed with the transaction, the seller should recognize that the expense associated with filing is not insignificant.

(vi) Conclusion. All of these predivestiture issues and considerations underline the need for crisp decision making, strong commitment to the transaction, detailed planning, and effective execution. Arguably, the most important aspects of the divestiture process are the planning and preparation leading up to the execution of the transaction. Although forward planning will not ensure a successful transaction, the lack of it dramatically increases the likelihood of an unnecessarily protracted process and an unfavorable outcome.

(d) DIVESTITURE PLANNING. As noted, proper planning of the divestiture reduces the risks of an undesirable outcome (i.e., a sale at a price that does not reflect the value of the property or, in the extreme, the inability to execute a sale at all). The next steps listed, discussed in the sections that follow, outline a planning process that significantly mitigates such risks.

- Development of an approval document
- Development of a retention plan for key personnel

- Creation of the divestiture team
- Development of an execution plan for the divestiture
- Development of a communication plan

(i) Approval Document.   Generally, the decision to dispose of a property will have to go through an approval process of some sort. The nature of the approval process will be dependent on the size of the property being disposed of and the size and structure of the company doing the disposing. Small divestitures may be within the purview of the company's CEO, but more material disposals typically require the approval of corporate headquarters (if the CEO reports into another layer of management, such as officers of a holding company) and/or the approval of the company's board of directors. However, even in cases where approval is within the purview of the CEO, it is advisable to document the rationale and impact of the divestiture.

Accordingly, the first tangible output of the planning process should be a brief paper (in many organizations referred to as a position paper) that contains all of the descriptive and analytical information needed for those with approval authority to make an informed decision.

The approval document would usually include:

- The rationale for the proposed divestiture
- A description of the property and products being recommended for disposal
- A discussion of the recent performance of the business
- An indication of the potential market for the property
- An anticipated range of sales prices, transaction costs, and proceeds (and accounting and tax gains or losses, if deemed relevant to the approval process)
- A description of any measures, such as an audit or creation of pro forma financials, necessary to properly present the business for sale
- A description of the process that will be employed to execute the transaction and an estimate of the timing and duration of the sales process

This document should focus discussion on all the relevant issues, and, assuming approval, it would trigger the divestiture process. The discussion should include consideration and analysis of a walkaway position (i.e., a price below which the property would be pulled from the market) and its implications. In the absence of such a discussion, it is implied that the transaction will occur at any price.

(ii) Retention Plan. Invariably, there are key employees who are critical to the ongoing performance of the business being divested. They are generally management and sales personnel. The loss or demotivation of these individuals would have a serious negative impact on the near-term performance of the business, which in turn would impact the ability of the parent to sell the business at a price that reflects its true market value. These individuals are also those who would be involved in presenting the business to potential buyers. Clearly, it is in the best interest of the seller to have them available and prepared to deliver a positive message.

It is important that these individuals are identified as early as possible in the process and that a plan is formulated to reward them for staying with the property being sold for at least as long as it takes to execute a transaction. With regard to the sales personnel, it may also be desirable to tie their performance to bonus payments that will reward them especially well for their efforts during the period between the announcement of the transaction and its consummation.

The plan should be developed and executed immediately after the approval to proceed with the transaction is forthcoming so that the key managers can be informed of the intent to sell and be brought into the planning process. Human resources would generally coordinate the development of the plan, which ultimately would be approved by the CEO.

(iii) Creation of the Divestiture Team. An important element of the planning process is the creation of the team that will help formalize the divestiture plan, drive the divestiture process, and ensure that it stays on track. The team leader would generally be assigned by the company CEO and the team would generally be constituted along these lines:

- *Finance and Accounting.* Finance and accounting personnel play a major role in any divestiture transaction. Arguably, the senior member of the finance team should be the overall divestiture team leader. Regardless, finance and accounting personnel will have responsibility for drafting the financial statements and supporting data, creation of the data room, management of the due diligence process, and liaison with outside accountants and brokers, if these resources are engaged.

- *Legal.* Whether inside or outside counsel or both are used, those staffing the legal arm of the team should be involved throughout the process, from drafting confidentiality agreements for possible buyers to the negotiation of the sales contract with the eventual buyer. It is particularly important that legal counsel keeps abreast of developments as the transaction unfolds, so that he or she has the background and context needed to help negotiate the terms of the final contracts.

- *Line Management.* It is advisable to have a senior line manager from the parent company as well as the key managers of the property being divested involved in the divestiture process as early as possible. Participation of the former is meant to ensure that the business is properly positioned for sale. The latter group is needed to develop and deliver presentations to potential buyers; but, more important, they are critical to the sales process insofar as they are an integral part of what is being sold. To the potential buyers, they are "the face" of the business. It should also be noted that these are usually the selfsame individuals who are offered retention agreements, so their involvement in the process is generally subject to discussion and execution of those agreements.

- *Human Resources (HR).* Because of the sensitive nature of the personnel issues involved, HR staff should play a prominent role in the process, particularly in communicating with the employees of the business being put up for sale. Senior members of the HR staff are the logical candidates for developing and managing the execution of the retention and communications plans. They also should be positioned to monitor and report on the morale and the productivity of the employees of the business being sold.

- *Broker.* In a transaction of any substantial size, it is almost always advisable to engage a broker. (See section 2.3(d) for a detailed discussion of the role of brokers in sales transactions.) As noted, dual objectives are being served in a divestiture transaction: to optimize the sales price and to minimize management distraction and business disruption. An effective broker, with strong market knowledge, good industry contacts, and expertise in the management of auction sales, can relieve the seller's management team of much of the administrative and sales burden generated by the transaction as well as assist in the effort to realize an optimal price for the business.

- *Outside Accountants.* The need for outside accountants in the divestiture process is generally directly related to the degree of complexity associated with the transaction. As previously noted, many divestitures involve properties that have been integrated into the fabric of the core or parent business. To the extent that this is the case, it is desirable to have the assistance of an outside firm in disentangling the business from its core, from a financial reporting perspective. In addition, an accounting firm's assistance will accelerate the transaction and provide independence of representation and expertise in presentation.
- *Other Resources.* The need for other types of support should be identified and assessed on as-needed basis. Although this will be peculiar to each transaction, it will usually include functions such as systems and technology and facilities management. The team should decide what additional involvement is critical to the execution of the transaction and request assistance as needed.

(iv) Development of the Divestiture Plan. Once the members of the team have been notified of their participation, the divestiture plan should be formulated and documented, along with timelines for each of its major elements. The plan should address these items:

- *Assignment of Responsibilities.* The responsibilities of team members should be assigned. The HR team member(s) would normally be assigned responsibility for the communications plan, which is discussed in section 8.3(d)(v). If the use of outside resources has been approved, their roles should be discussed and the process of identifying, vetting, and contacting candidate firms should be initiated by the appropriate members of the team.
- *Sales Process.* A number of techniques can be used to generate interest in the properties being offered for sale. In general, though, the seller would indicate to potential buyers, usually through a broker, that the property is available for sale. Those

interested would then respond and would be sent a detailed prospectus (alternatively referred to as an information memorandum or offering document) after signing a standard confidentiality agreement. Based on information contained in that document, interested prospective buyers would make an initial nonbinding bid for the property, subject to due diligence. Once due diligence is conducted by all interested parties, the seller would accept the best credible bid and proceed to contract and close. There are a number of minor variations on this approach. Those with approval authority may have stipulated how the process should be managed, or there may have been some latitude afforded the divestiture team. In any event, the specifics of the process would be discussed, finalized, and documented.

- *Timing.* The team should lay out a timeline for the events leading up to the transaction and for the execution of the transaction itself. Once again, the steps and timeline are largely dependent on the size and complexity of the transaction. Timing is also affected by such things as the need for accounting assistance for carve-out audits and/or the creation of pro forma financial statements or the desire to utilize a broker to assist in the sales process. It is reasonable to assume that the length of time needed for a transaction—from initial approval to close—is between four and six months in most cases. A detailed schedule is provided in Appendix 8A for illustrative purposes.

(v) Development of a Communication Plan.   A communication plan should be developed early in the divestiture process and is usually the first element of the execution phase of the process. It should have both internal and external components. The internal component should address employees of both the core company and the business being divested and the external component should address customers, suppliers, and, if appropriate, the investment community.

If practicable, the internal communications should consist of both live and written announcements. It is generally advisable for senior management (generally the CEO) to plan to meet with the two groups of employees separately, since there will be substantially different messages conveyed to each. Depending on the size of the employee population and where they are physically located, the live announcement may be only to senior managers, who in turn would then meet with subordinates to deliver the message. Written announcements to both employee populations should then be distributed. These announcements should be circulated soon after the meetings occur to ensure that the message delivered is clear and that the potential for any misunderstanding is minimized.

The external communications should be directed primarily at customers, with assurances that service levels will be maintained and that their satisfaction is of foremost importance. For key customers, consideration should be given to planning on personal contact, by phone and/or in person, by senior members of the staff. Although it is usually a lesser concern, the plan should include announcements to major suppliers and contractors. Also, it may be desirable to plan on the distribution of a press release to inform the investment community of the planned divestiture and its rationale.

(e) PREPARING FOR THE TRANSACTION. Parallel with, or immediately on the heels of, the planning process, preparatory steps should be initiated to ensure that the actual implementation of the transaction will proceed smoothly, once the announcement of the planned sale has been made. This includes these activities, listed and described in detail in the sections that follow:

- Selection and engagement of a broker
- Selection and engagement of an accounting firm
- Development of management presentations
- Development of an offering document (prospectus)
- Identification of potential buyers
- Preparation of the data room

(i) Engagement of Broker. If a broker will be used to assist in the sales process, one should be chosen as early as reasonable in the planning process, since a broker's involvement will require negotiation and ramp-up time. A broker who is familiar with the industry, the property being sold, and its products, and who has relationships with companies in the market is ideal. These qualities significantly reduce ramp-up time and assist in the identification of potential buyers and in the creation of a market for the property. The vetting and selection, as well as the subsequent negotiation with and management of, the broker will generally fall within the purview of the senior financial manager on the divestiture team.

(ii) Engagement of Accounting Firm.   As discussed previously, there may be a need to employ the services of an accounting firm to assist in the preparation of dedicated financial statements for the business being sold. Because this can involve substantial lead time, it is desirable to identify and engage a firm as early as reasonably possible, so work on this phase of the transaction can be under way well in advance of initiating the sales process. The selection and management of an assisting accounting firm logically would fall to the senior financial manager on the team.

(iii) Development of Management Presentations.   The senior managers of the business being sold will be expected to make presentations to potential buyers as part of due diligence. These presentations should focus on the dynamics of the business, its market, and expectations for profitable future growth. It should not be difficult to motivate the presenters, since these presentations are an opportunity to make an impression on their prospective new owner. Any risk lies in the possibility that those making the presentations believe it is in their best interest to deliver a message that is not consistent with that of the seller. Accordingly, these presentations should be in conformity with the message conveyed in the offering document (described in the next section), which will have been circulated to the pool of potential buyers. Consistency can be ensured by close involvement by the seller's management in the development and presentation process.

(iv) Development of an Offering Document.   Preparation of the offering document (or information memorandum or prospectus) also requires substantial lead time. A benefit of using a broker is that the broker can dedicate resources to this activity, an area in which an accomplished broker will have considerable expertise and, as a result, accelerate the drafting process. The offering document should focus on:

- *Investment Considerations.* This section would highlight those strategic qualities that would generate enthusiasm among potential buyers.
- *Industry Overview.* The industry overview should contain a description of industry dynamics and a discussion of how the property or properties being sold is/are positioned to exploit those dynamics.
- *A Description of the Business Being Sold.* This section would present a detailed description of the business, its products, its

targeted audiences, and its historical financial performance.

- *Organizational Structure.* This section should include an overview of the organization, including headcount by function.
- *Management Discussion and Analysis (MD&A).* The MD&A should include a discussion of measures taken to position the business for future profitable growth.

(v) Identification of Potential Buyers. Potential buyers should be identified during this preparation stage of the process. This is an area in which brokers can add significant value. Not only can they help identify candidates, very often they are in regular communication with companies in the market and have a sense of their predisposition to buy. They can also identify buyers who might not be on the radar of the selling company, such as venture capital firms or companies on the periphery of the market. Regardless of whether a broker is used, a comprehensive list of potential buyers, including the identification of the appropriate contact person, should be created and the method of contact should be confirmed.

(vi) Preparation of a Data Room. In advance of due diligence, a data room must be set up. The data room will contain all of the documents to be made available to potential buyers for their due diligence reviews. The information collected for this purpose is fairly voluminous and varies based on the nature of the business being sold. The information request in Appendix 3C provides a good overview of the quantity and the nature of the information typically provided. Because a significant portion of the information provided is financial statement related, the preparation and management of the data room is generally handled by finance personnel.

(f) EXECUTION OF THE TRANSACTION. The execution phase of the process is essentially the roll-out of the planning and preparation just described. This includes:

- The announcement of the prospective sale
- Solicitation of initial bids
- Management of due diligence
- Finalization of the bidding process
- Contract negotiation and close

(i) Announcement of the Prospective Sale. The announcement is essentially the execution of the internal and external elements based on the communication plan. Generally, meetings with key personnel of both the core company and the business being sold would have occurred immediately in advance of the broader announcement.

The primary objective of the internal component of the communication plan is to minimize disruption of the business being sold. From a practical standpoint, management should realize that it is very likely that there will be a period of distraction, accompanied by an initial drop in productivity. The goal of management should be to minimize the duration of such a period and the extent of any loss of productivity. The key to accomplishing that objective is to anticipate concerns and not to get caught in a reactive, flat-footed stance. An effective proactive technique that can be used is to develop and distribute a package of information that addresses the obvious potential concerns of this employee population (*What does this mean to me? Will I lose my job? What happens to my benefits?*). It is also advisable to make HR representatives available to answer questions during the period immediately following the announcement and to provide a mechanism to receive and respond to employee questions (perhaps via e-mail).

Concerns among the employee population of the core business are usually less of a consideration. However, in both written and personal communications to this constituency, it is advisable to assure employees that management remains committed to the core business and that no other major changes will be forthcoming.

Customer communications may be delivered in writing or personally (i.e., over the phone or by personal visit). Depending on the nature of the business and products, it may be wise to identify key customers or customers of both businesses to receive special attention. All inquiries to staff should be funneled to senior staff. To ensure consistency of message, management may also want to provide senior staff of both businesses with a script to refer to in the event customers or other interested parties of consequence inquire about the prospective transaction. The focus of all customer communication should be on the continued commitment of the company to both businesses and assurances that the highest level of service will be maintained.

(ii) Solicitation of Initial Bids. The seller, usually through its broker, will solicit bids for the business from a pool of potential buyers.

Although there are different techniques that can be used to solicit buyers (see section 4.7 for a description of a typical auction process), whatever method is used will ultimately result in a limited number of buyers that will proceed to the due diligence phase of the process.

(iii) Managing Due Diligence.   Typically, due diligence consists of management presentations, interviews with key employees, document review, and a physical tour of the facility where business is conducted. These elements of the review are described in detail in section 4.5. A seller will want to maintain as much control over the due diligence process as possible and will generally have significant leverage to do so in auction sale, because of the existence of multiple suitors. This enables the seller to dictate when due diligence will take place and how much time will be allotted to each bidder (usually two to four days, including management presentations). It may also enable the seller to be selective in determining the level of detail in the information made available in the data room. However, the seller will want to be reasonably forthcoming to avoid potential problems in the finalization of the transaction. As a general rule, the greater the confidence of the buyer in the representations substantiated in due diligence, the easier it should be to negotiate the final agreement.

(iv) Finalization of the Bid Process.   After the buyer has completed its due diligence, bids would be finalized and the team would generally report back to the decision-making individual (e.g., the CEO) or body (e.g., the board of directors) with their recommendation of the preferred buyer. More often than not, this is a straightforward decision based on price. However, there may be other factors (such as creditworthiness) that influence the selection. Once the final selection has been made, the seller would communicate the results to the buyer as well as the other bidders.

(v) Contract Negotiations and Close.   Very quickly after the selection of the buyer has been made, contract negotiations should be initiated. In auction sales, traditionally the seller's attorney will draft the initial sales contract for the buyer's attorney to review and mark up. (For an example of asset and stock transactions, see Appendices 5A and 5B.) It is common practice that both parties, buyer and seller, assign an attorney and a businessperson to the negotiation process.

Many of the preliminary discussions will revolve around legal issues that generally can be addressed by the attorneys. However, eventually there will be business issues that will require someone more knowledgeable about the product and market issues to be involved. That point person, logically the team leader throughout the process, will have the other members of the team to draw on if their input is needed. It is not uncommon for the contract to go through several iterations as points are negotiated. It is reasonable to expect that each iteration will add a week to the duration of negotiations. As a result, contract negotiations can be expected to last between one and two months.

In addition to the basic contract, other agreements may be necessary to close the transaction. These may include consulting or employment agreements and transition services agreements in situations where aspects of operational support for the business being sold continue to reside with the seller.

Contract execution and close frequently occur simultaneously. However, under certain circumstances (e.g., compliance with the HSR Act, see section 11.6), there may be a gap between the date the purchase agreement is executed and when the transaction is closed.

ILLUSTRATIVE DIVESTITURE TIMELINE

	Month 1	Month 2	Month 3	Month 4	Month 5	Month 6
Planning						
Develop Approval Document	|>|					
Develop Retention Plan	|>|					
Assemble Divestiture Team	|>>|					
Develop Execution Plan	|>>>|					
Develop Communication Plan	|>>>|					
Preparation						
Select and Engage Broker		|>>>>>>>>>>>>>>>>>>>>>>>>>>>>>|				
Select and Engage Accounting Firm		|>>>>>>>>>>>|				
Create Offering Document		|>>>>|				
Develop Management Presentations		|>>>>|				
Identify Potential Buyers		|>>|				
Prepare Data Room		|>>>>|				
Execution						
Announce Intent to Sell		|>|				
Solicit Bids		|>>>|				
Manage Due Diligence			|>>>>|			
Accept Final Bid			|>>|			
Negotiate Contract				|>>>>>>>>>>>|		
Comply with HSR Act Requirements					|>>>>>>>>>|	
Close Transaction						|>|

The timeline is presented to illustrate the timing and the relative duration of the steps involved in the divestiture process.

It assumes the use of a broker to assist in the transaction and an accounting firm to assist in the development and presentation of financial statements. Additionally, it assumes the need for an HSR Act filing.

FEDERAL INCOME TAXATION OF ACQUISITIONS

The author would like to thank Greg A. Dickey, who wrote the version of this chapter that appeared in the last edition.

9.1 GENERAL

(a) OVERVIEW.   This chapter discusses U.S. federal income tax considerations related to corporate acquisitions, based on the Internal Revenue Code (IRC) of 1986 and subsequent significant changes.

Tax considerations often influence the structure of acquisitions, but they are secondary in importance to overriding business, legal, and economic considerations. However, even if compelling business, legal, or economic considerations are present, it is important to quantify the tax cost or tax savings of possible alternative structures. Major questions about the tax aspects of an acquisition include:

- Is the transaction taxable or nontaxable?
- In transactions that are taxable, how much of any realized gain or loss will be ordinary and how much will be capital gain or loss?
- To what extent will tax attributes, such as net operating loss and tax credit carryforwards, be usable against future taxable income?

The Code defines gross income as "all income from whatever source derived." The Internal Revenue Service (IRS) and the tax courts generally start with this definition in considering the taxability of all transactions, including acquisitions. Acquisitions are taxable, nontaxable, or partially taxable. The taxability of a transaction is dependent on whether the transaction, or part of the transaction, meets the conditions of one or more of the specific tax-free exceptions permitted by the Code. Failing to qualify for an exemption results in the transaction being taxable.

(b) ORDINARY VERSUS CAPITAL GAIN OR LOSS. Generally, the sale of stock creates capital gain or loss. The exception to this is *small business stock,* which may generate ordinary losses under a specific set of rules. The gain or loss resulting from the disposition of all business and nonbusiness assets is generally capital in nature. There are exemptions for ordinary income assets, such as inventory, certain works created through personal effort, accounts receivable, and recapture assets (e.g., depreciable personal and real property).

(c) NONTAXABLE TRANSACTIONS. In a tax-free transaction involving corporations, the seller (the acquired corporation or, if relevant, its shareholders) generally recognizes no gain or loss. The buyer (the acquiring corporation) carries over the seller's tax basis, holding period, and other tax attributes subject to certain limitations. The tax deferral achieved in a tax-free acquisition can result in significant cash savings for the seller. Additionally, retained and usable tax attributes, such as net operating loss and tax credit carryforwards, may benefit the buyer in the future.

(d) IRS POWERS. The structure of a merger or acquisition will determine the tax ramifications for both parties to the transaction. However, the IRS and the courts have the capability of denying taxpayers anticipated tax benefits, even in carefully structured transactions. The IRS has broad powers to reallocate income, deductions, and credits among the parties. Judicial concepts such as *substance versus form sham transaction* and *no business purpose* are powerful weapons used by the IRS and the courts in unexpectedly reshaping a transaction for tax purposes, much to the disappointment and financial loss of the taxpayers. The IRC has integrated these concepts to apply to acquisitions as well as all other transactions. These judicial and statutory danger zones warrant careful consideration during analysis of potential transaction structures. *Substance versus form* is particularly difficult in the area of corporate acquisitions. In that area, there are often choices of form that have similar, at times identical, economic consequences. Clearly, in these situations, the tax planner must exercise additional care in documenting the intended form.

(e) BUYER-SELLER CONFLICT. Generally, the buyer and seller will be in conflict over tax considerations. This conflict stems from the general concept that what is advantageous for one is usually not so for the other. For example, one of the most common buyer-seller conflicts in corporate acquisitions is the buyer's desire to acquire assets and the seller's preference to sell stock. However, there are times when the tax goals of the parties provide the tax planner with an opportunity to obtain tax benefits for both. A transaction structured in a way that enables both parties to derive tax advantages may be subject to close IRS scrutiny. The tax planner must be ready to demonstrate that a transaction's form is consistent with the transaction's economic substance.

(f) NOTE OF CAUTION.   Note that these topics involve complex considerations, many of which are not apparent to other than a highly qualified tax specialist. It is important that a tax specialist be consulted regarding the tax aspects of any merger or acquisition.

9.2 TAXABLE ACQUISITIONS
(a) GENERAL.   Taxable acquisitions occur in two forms:

1. A purchase of stock
2. A purchase of assets

Considerations in deciding whether to complete an acquisition as a purchase of stock or a purchase of assets will be briefly discussed in this section.

Acquisitions of stock are generally easier to carry out than acquisitions of assets. Asset acquisitions involve such complications as asset title transfers and creditor notifications. The acquisition of assets can also trigger transfer taxes (such as sales taxes). Further, there are times that only a sale of stock can preserve nonassignable rights such as licenses, leases, trademarks, or other favorable contractual arrangements.

Consideration of unknown or contingent liabilities also affects the stock-versus-asset purchase decision. The seller may wish to pass risk of these possible liabilities on to the acquirer through the sale of stock. However, the acquirer may prefer to limit any exposure and be unwilling to accept responsibility for the unknown by purchasing assets. Having the seller indemnify the acquirer of stock for any undisclosed liabilities will sometimes allow a stock sale when other factors also favor a stock sale. In addition, usage of a contingent asset trust arrangement may allow for a stock sale. Other considerations may also determine the form of the transaction. Minority shareholders and undesirable assets that the buyer does not wish to purchase may require an asset acquisition instead of a stock acquisition.

General tax factors to consider when deciding the form of an acquisition transaction include these. Generally, only the seller recognizes taxable gain. The sale of stock results in only a single tax, generally at capital gain tax rates. The sale of assets normally results in two taxes. The first tax is at the corporate level upon the sale or distribution of appreciated assets. The second tax is at the shareholder level upon the distribution of the proceeds from sale of the asset or the liquidation of the corporation. These two taxes result in double taxation and significantly reduce the after-tax proceeds to the shareholder.

The tax basis of the assets acquired is a primary concern of an acquirer. In a purchase of stock, the historical tax bases of the underlying assets are carried over and are not stepped up to reflect the purchase price of the stock. This situation will not allow the acquirer to benefit from increased depreciation or amortization expenses of *inside basis* commensurate with the purchase price. The acquirer can obtain stepped-up inside basis equal to purchase price only through a liquidation of the corporation or an election made pursuant to IRC Section 338. Each of these actions generally results in additional corporate level tax.

(b) STRUCTURES OF TAXABLE ASSET ACQUISITIONS. Asset acquisitions can follow two patterns:

1. A selling corporation may sell its assets directly to a purchaser and distribute the proceeds and any unsold assets to its shareholders in complete liquidation.
2. A corporation may distribute its assets in complete liquidation to its shareholders after which the shareholders sell the assets.

The order of liquidation should be structured dependent on tax and nontax issues. Nontax issues include dealing with minority shareholders and potential title transfer problems.

(c) CORPORATE LIQUIDATIONS. The tax treatment of a direct sale of assets or a distribution in complete liquidation has similar effects to a selling or distributing corporation. IRC Section 336 provides that a corporation must recognize gain or loss on the distribution of property in complete liquidation. The gain or loss must be computed as if such property were sold at fair market value. A sale of the assets or distribution to shareholders of a business is a sale or distribution of each separate tangible and intangible asset in that business. This is true even though the buyer may view the transaction as the sale of a single going concern. It is necessary to identify the value and tax basis of each asset to compute a selling or distributing corporation's gain or loss and to establish the acquirer's tax basis in the acquired assets.

There is an exception to the general rule that gain is recognized by a corporation and its shareholders upon the complete liquidation of the corporation. Sections 337 and 332 of the IRC provide that a complete liquidation to an 80% corporate shareholder (an 80% distributee) does not result in gain or loss to the corporation or the shareholder. The corporate shareholder receives assets with carryover tax basis. Any *built-in* gain or loss attributable to the assets is deferred until the shareholder sells the assets. Therefore, a tax-planning opportunity exists for closely held corporations. If a single corporate shareholder has or can acquire the stock necessary to hold 80% of a selling corporation, there is an opportunity to avoid the double taxation caused by corporate liquidation. In such an instance, a corporation could be liquidated tax-free. The 80% distributee could then sell the assets, recognizing tax only at the shareholder level. This rule does not apply to partial liquidations.

(d) ALLOCATION OF PURCHASE PRICE IN ASSET ACQUISITIONS. Section 1001(b) of the IRC provides that the "amount received from the sale or other disposition of property shall be the sum of any money received plus the fair market value of the property other than money received." Also included in the amount received by a seller are any liabilities of the seller or liabilities associated with the transferred property that are assumed by the buyer. The amount received (sales or purchase price) is allocated to each asset. An acquirer of assets will usually wish to maximize purchase price to depreciable and amortizable assets so as to maximize future tax deductions. Conversely, a seller of assets will often wish to minimize the allocation to the same assets to reduce the tax effect of recapture items and will therefore prefer to allocate the purchase price to intangible assets such as goodwill. Before the Omnibus Budget Reconciliation Act of 1993 (1993

Act), the allocation of purchase price to intangible items was particularly detrimental to acquirers because amounts allocated to intangible assets, such as goodwill or going-concern value, were not amortizable for tax purposes. The 1993 Act reduced this conflict through its provision allowing acquirers to amortize these intangibles for tax purposes over 15 years. It is important to note that IRC Section 1060 requires that purchase price allocation be based on fair market value. However, fair market can be subjective, which leads to negotiation of fair market value amounts.

Section 1060 of the IRC requires that the purchase price of assets be allocated by the acquirer and seller using the *residual* method. The residual method allocates the purchase price first to the tangible and intangible assets, other than goodwill or going-concern value (up to their fair market values), with any premiums being allocated to goodwill or going-concern value. The IRC has devised four classes of assets for allocation purposes. Class I assets are basically cash items, such as cash, demand deposits, and similar accounts in banks or other depository institutions. Class II assets are highly liquid, cashlike assets, such as certificates of deposit, U.S. government securities, readily marketable stock or securities, and foreign currency. Class III assets are those assets being purchased other than Classes I, II, and IV assets. Intangible assets that are goodwill in nature are Class IV assets.

Exhibit 9.1 illustrates the application of the residual method of allocation of purchase price for tax purposes in an acquisition.

(e) GAIN OR LOSS OF THE SELLER IN ASSET ACQUISITIONS.

(i) Determining Amount and Character of Gain or Loss. After allocating the sales price to the individual assets, the seller's gain or loss is determined by subtracting each asset's tax basis from its allocated portion of the purchase price. The tax basis of each asset is the seller's original cost less the seller's allowed or allowable depreciation benefits. The resulting amount is the seller's adjusted tax basis.

A seller's gain or loss will either be ordinary gain or loss or capital gain or loss. Sellers generally prefer to have all income characterized as capital gains (taxed at preferred rates) and losses taxed as ordinary losses, which have higher tax benefits because of the higher tax rates on ordinary income. Determining the character of a gain or loss involves many factors. The most important factors are the nature

Assume that Company A acquires the business of Company B in an asset purchase for $5 million. The asset classes of the acquired assets consist of:

Fair Market			Purchase Price
Tax Basis		Value	Allocation
Cash (Class I asset)	$100,000	$100,000	$100,000
Equipment (Class III asset)	$2,000,000	1,900,000	1,900,000
Goodwill (Class IV asset)	None	Not directly determinable	3,000,000

EXHIBIT 9.1   RESIDUAL METHOD OF ALLOCATION OF PURCHASE PRICE FOR TAX PURPOSES

and use of the asset sold. Generally, if the asset sold is a capital asset as defined in IRC Section 1221, the seller will receive long-term capital gain tax treatment. Note that assets as defined in IRC Section 1231 must be held more than one year and used in the trade or business of the seller to qualify for favorable long-term capital gain tax rates.

(ii) Recapture.   Assets subject to an allowance for depreciation or depletion are subject to the recapture provisions under IRC Sections 1245 and 1250. These provisions override all other sections, including IRC Sections 1231 and 453, resulting in ordinary income to the extent of prior tax depreciation deductions. See Exhibit 9.2 for an illustration.

The gain computed in Exhibit 9.2 would result in federal income tax totaling $14,695, based on ordinary income of $38,780 taxed at 25% and the capital gain of $25,000 taxed at 20% for a noncorporate taxpayer.

(iii) Effect on Shareholders of Complete Liquidation after Sale of Assets by a Corporation.   After a corporation's assets are acquired by another, the shareholders must decide what to do with the sales proceeds. If the shareholders have common investment goals, they may decide to continue to operate a new venture in the continuing corporation. In that event, the corporation reinvests its sales proceeds and continues to exist as an ongoing entity. Note that some state legal provisions related to the continuity of doing business could apply. There

Assume that Company A purchased new equipment for $100,000. The equipment has a seven-year modified accelerated cost recovery system (MACRS) life and is depreciated for tax purposes using the double declining balance method. After two years, Company A has claimed depreciation deductions totaling $38,780. At the beginning of the third year, Company B purchases the equipment from Company A as part of the acquisition of a business. The equipment receives a $125,000 allocation of the purchase price. The table illustrates the computation of Company A's taxable gain attributable to the sale of the equipment:

Net proceeds received	$125,000
Adjusted basis	
Cost	100,000
Depreciation allowed	(38,780)
	61,220
Gain	$ 63,780
Character of gain	
Ordinary income (equal to prior depreciation)	$ 38,780
Capital gain	25,000
	$ 63,780

EXHIBIT 9.2 GAIN ON SALE OF EQUIPMENT

could also be complications in using tax attributes, such as net operating loss and tax credit carryforwards, from the old trade or business against income earned in a new trade or business. These tax attribute issues are discussed later in the chapter.

Sometimes shareholders want the cash that has accumulated in the corporation, in which case the cash is simply distributed to the shareholders in the complete liquidation of the corporation. The complete liquidation of a corporation can result in two levels of tax. The sale of assets by the corporation triggers the corporate level tax on gain, which was discussed earlier. The subsequent distribution of assets by the corporation to its shareholders causes the second level of tax. Generally, the distribution of assets from a corporation to its shareholders constitutes a dividend. The dividends create ordinary income to shareholders to the extent of accumulated corporate earnings and profits. However, special rules apply to the process of complete liquidation that permit capital gain treatment of liquidating distributions.

The intent to cease doing business and liquidate all remaining corporate assets causes the corporation to enter the *status of liquidation* as explained by IRC Section 1.332-2(c). The status of liquidation does not require a written plan of liquidation or that a corporation dissolve and end its legal existence. If factors suggest the intention to liquidate, the liquidation provisions apply. Provisions under IRC Section 331 allow for complete liquidation to constitute a sale of stock, providing capital gain treatment to the shareholders.

The fair market value of the assets received is the full payment for the surrender of stock. Under IRC Section 1001, shareholder gain or loss is equal to the difference between the net fair market value of the property received (fair market value of the assets received less any liabilities assumed by the shareholder) and the shareholder's basis of the stock surrendered. The basis of noncash assets received by a shareholder is equal to the fair market value on the date of distribution, under IRC Section 334(a).

If a shareholder has acquired shares at different times and for different amounts, each group of shares will require a separate gain or loss computation. The allocation of the liquidating distribution is based on the number of shares within each group. This individual group treatment can cause situations in which one group has capital gain while another group may have a capital loss. This is covered in IRC Section 1.331-1(e) and Revenue Rule 68–348, 68-2 C.B. 141.

A shareholder who receives all liquidating distributions in a single year reports the total gain or loss in the year of receipt. However, it is possible for a liquidation of a corporation to take several years. The recognition of gain or loss in this situation requires the use of the cost recovery method for recognition of gain or loss, as explained by Revenue Rule 68–348, 68-2 C.B. 141. This method allows the first proceeds received to reduce the shareholder's basis of the stock held. After the shareholder's stock basis is zero, all subsequent receipts represent taxable gain. Liquidations that cause a loss to the shareholder require that no loss be recognized until the final distribution.

(f) TAXABLE STOCK ACQUISITIONS.   The tax aspects of a stock acquisition are relatively straightforward in comparison with those related to asset acquisitions. If an acquirer purchases stock, the acquirer receives stock with a tax basis equal to the amount paid for the stock. The selling corporate shareholders recognize gain or loss determined by deducting their tax basis in the stock from the amount they receive. The acquired corporation did not participate in the sale transaction and generally will not recognize gain or loss related to the acquisition. The acquired corporation continues to exist and continues to hold assets with their historical tax basis and with tax attributes unchanged. The utility of the tax attributes will likely be limited due to the application of IRC Section 382, to be discussed in section 9.5(d).

After an acquisition, the acquired corporation may be liquidated. The effect of a poststock acquisition liquidation, barring the exception to 80% corporate shareholders as previously discussed, is that the acquiring shareholders will hold the asset directly with a stepped-up basis. Since these shareholders owned the corporation at the time of the liquidation, they bear the burden of the tax triggered upon liquidation. The practical application of this strategy for noncorporate and non–80% corporate shareholders is limited due to the obvious high tax cost.

9.3 IRC SECTION 338

(a) GENERAL.   Generally, the assets held by a corporation acquired in a stock acquisition retain their historic tax basis. The historical tax basis of the acquired corporation's assets may be stepped up by elective or deemed application of IRC Section 338 or an election under IRC Section 338(h)(10).

(b) REGULAR SECTION 338 ELECTION.   Section 338 of the IRC allows a corporation acquiring at least 80% of the stock of another corporation during a 12-month period (a *qualified stock purchase*) to elect to treat the stock acquisition as an asset acquisition. If a corporate acquirer elects under regular IRC Section 338, the acquired corporation is deemed to have sold all of its assets, subject to its liabilities, to a newly formed corporation. The acquired corporation is then deemed to have liquidated. The sale and liquidation have taken place after the purchase of the stock. Therefore, from the selling shareholder's perspective, this is a stock sale. The acquirer receives the step-up in tax basis in the assets acquired that is generally associated with an asset purchase.

The primary distinction between an asset sale and a deemed asset sale under IRC Section 338 is that the selling shareholders do not bear the burden for the tax triggered by the sale of the assets. This is due to the fact that the deemed sale occurs after the selling shareholders have transferred their stock.

If the acquired corporation was not a member of a controlled group prior to the acquisition, the deemed sale of the assets takes place in the final return of the acquired corporation. The final return of the acquired corporation will have a tax year that closes on the acquisition date. If the acquired corporation was a member of a controlled group prior to the acquisition, the acquired corporation will need to file two tax returns. The first tax return is for inclusion with the affiliated group, with a tax year ending on the date of acquisition. The other will be a special *one-day* tax return, which will include the gain on the sale and no other transactions.

The result of these rules is that the gain on the deemed sale is taxed to the acquired corporation. There is no shelter for this tax other than by tax attributes of the acquired corporation.

The results of a regular IRC Section 338 election are generally unwanted. The additional tax to the acquired corporation is generally a high price to pay for a step-up in underlying asset tax basis, unless the acquired corporation has adequate tax attributes to shelter the gain.

Section 338 of the IRC provides a special rule that deems a regular Section 338 election to have been made. This deemed election could have serious negative tax effects. The regular IRC Section 338 election is deemed to have been made if the acquiring corporation acquires any assets of the acquired corporation within the *consistency period*. The consistency period starts one year before the first purchase of stock constituting a qualified stock purchase and ends one year after the qualified stock purchase has been accomplished [IRC Section 338(h)(4)]. Note that there are some exceptions for acquisition of assets in the ordinary course of business and other circumstances.

Final regulations were issued February 12, 2001, T.D. 8940, regarding the allocation of the purchase price in a deemed 338 transaction and in an actual Section 1060 asset allocation transaction.

(c) SECTION 338(H)(10) ELECTION.   The election available under IRC Section 338(h)(10) is similar to a regular IRC Section 338 election. The IRC Section 338(h)(10) election provides special benefits for acquisitions of corporations out of affiliated groups. Unlike a regular IRC Section 338 election, the deemed sale takes place while the acquired corporation is still a member of the affiliated group, followed by the distribution of the sale proceeds in liquidation of the acquired corporation. These events allow for two advantages over a regular IRC Section 338 election.

The first advantage relates to the gain associated with the deemed sale of assets. As this gain is deemed to occur while the acquired corporation is still a member of the affiliated group, it is reported on the affiliated group's consolidated tax return. This allows the gain to be sheltered by the combined tax attributes of the affiliated group.

The second advantage relates to the liquidation treatment of the sales proceeds under an IRC Section 338(h)(10) election. This liquidating distribution is governed by IRC Sections 332 and 337. The parent corporation would qualify as an 80% distributee, as explained earlier, making the liquidation tax free.

The overall result of an IRC Section 338(h)(10) election is that a single level of tax is imposed to the acquired corporation's old consolidated group. This tax may be sheltered by the consolidated tax attributes of the affiliated group. Note that this gain is not generally larger than the gain the consolidated group would have recognized on sale of the acquired corporation's stock. The acquiring corporation receives a corporation holding assets with a tax basis stepped up to the purchase price of the stock.

9.4 TAX-FREE MERGERS AND ACQUISITIONS

(a) GENERAL CONCEPTS AND REQUIREMENTS.   Section 368(a)(1) of the IRC defines and describes forms of corporate reorganizations for which U.S. federal taxation does not occur. Each form of corporate reorganization has specific requirements, several of which are common to most forms of tax-free reorganization. Some of the reorganizations have well-known variances, such as *forward* and *reverse* triangular mergers under IRC Sections 368(a)(2)(D) and (E).

Reorganizations that involve the transfer of assets generally require that *substantially all* of the assets of the seller be transferred to the acquirer. By transferring specified minimum percentages of assets, transactions can fall within defined safe harbors for qualifying as substantially all of the assets. However, the type of assets transferred (e.g., operating assets or investment assets) is also important in determining whether substantially all of the assets of the seller have been transferred to the buyer.

Reorganizations involving exchanges of stock require that the acquirer gains *control* over the seller. Control is generally defined as acquiring 80% or more of the voting and nonvoting stock [IRC Section 368(c)(1)].

Another concept that is common to most forms of reorganizations is the doctrine of *continuity of interest.* To satisfy the doctrine of continuity of interest, the sellers must maintain specified minimum proprietary interests in the business after the reorganization is completed. Determining whether the continuity of interest requirement is met can be complex. Regulation Section 1.368-1(d) of the IRC provides guidance on the application of this doctrine. In theory, a tax-free reorganization involves only a structural change in a business without changing ownership. The doctrine of continuity of interest is a test for determining whether the transaction is only a structural change, or whether the purported reorganization is in reality a winding-up of the business affairs of the entity, which may be treated as a taxable liquidation.

Final regulations facilitate acquisitions by removing some of the more burdensome aspects of the continuity of interest and business enterprise doctrines and harmonizing the continuity requirements with modern corporate-group structure and the widespread stock ownership of publicly traded corporations.

The continuity of interest requirement is a judicially developed doctrine designed to prevent transactions that resemble sales from qualifying as corporate reorganizations with nonrecognition of gains and losses. As the doctrine originally developed in Supreme Court cases, there was no requirement that sales by former shareholders of the acquired corporation of a sufficient amount of stock in the acquiring corporation would disqualify the transaction from reorganization treatment. However, courts have reached different results on the issue of whether reorganizations are jeopardized by subsequent sales of stock of the acquiring corporation. Under the final regulations, postreorganization sales by former shareholders of the acquired corporation are generally disregarded.

At the same time, the continuity of interest requirement helps former shareholders, particularly minority shareholders, in the acquired corporation from having tax-free treatment of the transaction held hostage to unilateral disqualifying sales of stock in the acquiring corporation by majority or former major shareholders of the acquired corporation.

Continuity of interest in the target, however, is not preserved when the target is acquired for consideration other than stock in the issuing corporation.

Continuity of interest also fails when the issuing corporation redeems stock used as consideration in acquiring the target. The final regulations provide that acquisition of target stock by a party related to the issuing corporation for consideration other than stock of the issuing corporation will cause continuity of interest to fail.

The continuity of business enterprise doctrine is designed to ensure that tax-free reorganizations are essentially readjustments to continuing interests in businesses. Generally, the acquiring corporation must continue to conduct the business of the acquired corporation or use the assets of the acquired corporation in a business. The final regulations make clear that for purposes of this requirement, the assets and the businesses of a qualified group of corporations will be considered as assets and businesses of the issuing corporation so that the acquiring corporation need not directly conduct the business of the acquired corporation or use its assets in the conduct of the acquiring corporation's business.

Prereorganization redemption by a target can be a problem in the context of an acquisition attempting to qualify as a tax-free reorganization because the cashing out of the target shareholder can cause the transaction to more closely resemble a sale than a reorganization and can be a way of making an end run around the continuity-of-interest requirements. The temporary and proposed regulations provide objective criteria for determining if a prereorganization redemption fails the continuity-of-interest requirement. Continuity-of-interest requirements will not be met if the target issues a promissory note to redeem 70% of its stock, the issuing corporation assumes the note as part of the merger, and the remaining target shareholders receive only stock in the issuing corporation.

Statutory provisions under IRC Sections 269 and 482 also provide broad powers to the IRS to restructure a purported tax-free transaction into a taxable event that conforms to the underlying economic reality of such a transaction. These provisions are discussed in detail in section 9.5(c).

In some reorganizations, a buyer and seller are permitted to exchange, in addition to stock, limited amounts of other property that, although taxable to the extent of such other property, will not cause the transaction to fail as a reorganization. This property, which is partially taxable in an otherwise tax-free exchange, is called *boot*.

The courts and the IRS can utilize a variety of judicial doctrines and statutory provisions that enable them to restructure an attempted tax-free transaction into a taxable event if they believe such is appropriate. For example, *form over substance, sham transaction,* and *no business purpose* are three separate (although related) doctrines that look to the underlying economic reality of a transaction in determining tax consequences. Additionally, under the *step transaction doctrine,* a series of legally separate transactions, completed pursuant to a common plan or goal, can be collapsed into a single transaction and taxed accordingly by the IRS.

It is not uncommon for the IRS to apply the step-transaction doctrine. Recently the IRS ruled on a transaction in which a parent corporation distributed the stock of its wholly owned subsidiary to its shareholders. This distribution was followed by the exchange of the stock for an unrelated company's stock pursuant to a merger of the subsidiary into the company. At the time of the parent's distribution of the subsidiary's stock, there had been no negotiations regarding the subsidiary's acquisition by the company, and the only action taken by the parent with respect to the transaction was that the parent's directors had authorized the distribution of the subsidiary's stock to its shareholders. The shareholders then voted on the merger with the company after the distribution and were free to vote their stock for or against the merger.

The IRS ruling in this situation involved application of the step-transaction doctrine. The purpose of this doctrine is to collapse a series of transactions into a single taxable transaction. The IRS determined that the stock distribution was valid under IRC Section 355 because the shareholders of the subsidiary were given the opportunity to vote on the acquisition and because there were no negotiations between the parent corporation and the acquiring company prior to the stock distribution.

In a prior ruling, the IRS did not apply the step-transaction doctrine and gave the distribution tax-free treatment under IRC Section 355. In that ruling, the IRS relied on the fact that the shareholders had authorized the merger after the distribution.

In each of these rulings, it was significant that no negotiations had gone on prior to the stock distribution to the shareholders. The important thing to note is that the IRS is not reluctant to apply the step-transaction doctrine to disallow tax-free treatment of a series of transactions. The form and the substance must be consistent to receive favorable treatment.

Proposed regulations under Section 355(e) were issued on December 29, 2000, and should be reviewed for applicability in connection with mergers and acquisitions. Among other things, the regulations address the "reasonably certain" standards for acquisitions that occur within six months of reorganization.

Therefore, judicial doctrines, statutes, and also technical requirements must be considered by the tax planner in structuring any acquisition to be tax free.

Private Letter Ruling 200025001 explores the aggregate versus entity approach if a corporation is a partner in a partnership regarding the five-year test of the trade or business requirement of Section 355.

A Tax Court case [*Honbarrier v. Commissioner*, 115 T.C. No.23 (September 29, 2000)] held that a transaction was not a qualified type A merger because the acquiring corporation was not in the same business as the target corporation as of the date of the merger. The acquiring corporation discontinued its activities in the target's business area three years before the merger.

In Notice 2000-16, the IRS announced that "midco" transactions, structured with an intermediary corporation to provide the seller with stock sale treatment while treating the purchaser as acquiring assets, will be treated as a corporate *tax shelter* transaction.

(b) TYPES OF TAX-FREE REORGANIZATIONS

(i) Type A Reorganization–Statutory Mergers.   A *Type A* reorganization is defined as a statutory merger or consolidation meeting the conditions of IRC Section 368(a)(1)(A). A statutory merger occurs if an acquired corporation releases all of its assets and liabilities to an acquiring corporation in return for some of the acquiring corporation's stock. After the transaction is completed, only the acquiring corporation survives. A *consolidation* occurs if the two companies release all of their assets to a new corporation in return for stock of the new corporation. Upon completion of this transaction, only the new corporation remains.

Type A reorganizations do not have any statutory limitations on the consideration that an acquiring corporation can issue to the acquired corporation for its assets and liabilities. The acquiring corporation is free to issue any type of common or preferred stock as well as securities. While a Type A reorganization is very flexible, it must meet the *continuity-of-interest* requirement. Thus, the shareholders of the acquired corporation must receive enough stock in the acquiring corporation so that they have a continuing financial interest in the remaining corporation. Furthermore, a Type A reorganization is subject to all state laws that may have narrower definitions of acceptable consideration to be given up by the acquiring corporation.

In cases where it may be disadvantageous for the acquiring corporation to merge with the acquired corporation, the assets of the acquired corporation can be placed into a newly formed subsidiary of the acquiring corporation in a nontaxable IRC Section 351 exchange. Normally the step-transaction doctrine would be applicable, combining the two steps, and tax-free Type A reorganization treatment would not apply because all the assets are not in one corporation. Section 368(a)(2)(C) of the IRC has allowed this since the 1954 code. This technique is referred to as a *transfer to a subsidiary,* or a *drop down.*

Regulations 1.368–2(b) (1) were issued May 14, 2000, providing that nonrecognition treatment under Section 368(a)(1)(A) would not be allowed if one of the parties to the transaction is a disregarded entity.

(ii) Type B Reorganizations. A *Type B* reorganization is defined as the acquisition of the stock of one corporation by another. After the transaction, the acquired corporation is a subsidiary of the acquiring corporation. There are two requirements that must be met to have a successful Type B reorganization:

1. A *stock-for-stock* condition requires that the acquiring corporation must acquire the acquired corporation stock by exchanging only voting stock of the acquiring corporation.
2. Immediately following the exchange, the acquiring corporation must be in control of the acquired corporation.

Control is defined under IRC Section 368(c) as the acquirer receiving 80% or more of the stock of the acquired corporation (all stock, voting and nonvoting). For example, if Company A exchanges 1 share of voting stock for every 10 shares of Company B's voting stock and acquires all of Company B's voting stock, then a successful Type B reorganization has occurred. If Company B's shareholders have the *option* of taking $50 in cash or one voting share of Company A's stock, the Type B reorganization cannot be successful, even if 90% of Company B's shareholders accept stock. This is because stock must be exchanged solely for stock; the cash option is fatal to the Type B reorganization.

(A) Creeping Control

It is permissible under the regulations to have a *creeping Type B* reorganization. It is so called because the requisite *control* occurs as a result of several transactions. There are three requirements for a successful creeping Type B reorganization:

1. There must be an overall plan to gain control of the acquired corporation, and each acquisition transaction must be part of the overall plan.
2. This overall plan must cover only a short period of time, generally 12 months or less.
3. The acquisition must be made solely for voting stock.

Prior cash purchases are acceptable if they are a separate transaction that is not part of the overall plan.

(iii) Type C Reorganizations.   A *Type C* reorganization is defined as a transfer of *substantially all* of the assets of an acquired corporation solely for voting stock of the acquiring corporation. The acquired corporation, generally, must liquidate as part of this type of transaction unless waived by the IRS. There is a similarity between Type A and Type C reorganizations—Type C reorganizations are referred to as *practical Type A reorganizations.* One benefit of a Type C reorganization is that the acquiring corporation's shareholders need not approve the acquisition. The acquired corporation's shareholders generally must approve the sale of the assets and the liquidation.

Substantially all of the assets is not defined in the code. Revenue Procedure 77-37, 1977-2 C.B. 568, has set forth governing guidelines that the acquiring corporation must acquire at least 70% of the gross assets and 90% of the net assets of the acquired corporation. Furthermore, it is required that the assets critical to the continuation of the acquired corporation's business must be transferred.

Type C reorganizations have a *solely for voting stock* requirement. Liabilities, in this context, receive special treatment. Assumption of the acquired corporation's liabilities or taking property of the acquired corporation that is subject to a liability is not fatal to a Type C reorganization. When voting stock and assumed liabilities are transferred, the assumed liabilities have no effect on the transaction. In transactions that include other forms of *boot,* the assumed liabilities are considered as boot.

A minimal amount of boot is acceptable in a Type C reorganization. Boot is limited to 20% of the total consideration given. Therefore, to have a successful Type C reorganization, 80% or more of the fair market value of the assets must be received solely for voting stock. Liabilities assumed are not considered in this equation unless other property (boot) is also given. If the liabilities exceed 20% of the value of the assets, only voting stock can be used because these liabilities are ignored if no other boot is transferred. See Exhibit 9.3 for an illustration.

While it is not possible under a Type C reorganization to have a dropping down of the assets to a controlled subsidiary, it is acceptable to have a controlled subsidiary act as the acquiring corporation. If the transaction is structured that way, the acquiring subsidiary may use the voting stock of its parent corporation as considered for the acquisition,

> Assume that Company B transfers all of its assets, which have a fair market value of $1 million, to Company A in exchange for Company A's voting stock. Company A assumes $350,000 of Company B's liabilities. Even though the liabilities make up 35% of the consideration, the transaction is a valid Type C reorganization, as long as no other boot is given.

EXHIBIT 9.3 BOOT IN A TYPE C REORGANIZATION

instead of its own voting stock. It is not permissible to use both the parent corporation's voting stock and an acquiring subsidiary's voting as consideration in a Type C reorganization.

A private letter ruling permitted an acquisition by a holding company via a subsidiary to be treated as a tax-free Type C reorganization. The holding company directed its wholly owned subsidiary to acquire the target company by merger. The shareholders of the target received voting stock of the holding company's parent. This was viewed as an acquisition by the holding company of substantially all the assets of the target solely in exchange for the parent's voting stock and the assumption by the holding company of liabilities associated with the transferred assets. This acquisition was followed by a transfer of the assets and liabilities by the holding company to the subsidiary. The acquisition constituted a reorganization under IRC Section 368(a)(1)(C). No gain or loss was recognized by the parties to the transaction, and the holding period of each target asset received by the holding company included the holding period during which the asset was held by the target. The basis of each asset in the hands of the holding company equaled the basis of the asset in the hands of the target immediately before the exchange.

In addition, the basis of the parent stock received by the shareholders of the target equaled the basis of the target stock surrendered. The holding period of the stock received included the holding period of the target stock surrendered. The basis of each target asset transferred by the holding company to the subsidiary equaled the basis in the hands of the holding company immediately before the transfer. The basis of the stock in the subsidiary in the hands of the holding company equaled the basis of the stock immediately before the acquisition, increased by the basis of the target assets transferred to the subsidiary and decreased by the target liabilities assumed by the subsidiary. The subsidiary also succeeded to and took into account the earnings and profits of the target as of the date of the transfer.

The IRS has issued regulations reversing its long-standing position that the acquisition of a partially controlled subsidiary's assets does not qualify as a Type C reorganization. In summary, a partially controlled subsidiary's assets can now be acquired in a Type C organization. See IRC Section 368(a)(1)(C).

(iv) Type D Reorganizations.   There are two kinds of *Type D* reorganizations: acquisitive and divisive.

(A) Acquisitive Type D Reorganizations

A corporation transfers substantially all of its assets to another corporation in exchange for voting stock of the other corporation. The first corporation must receive enough stock to have control after the exchange. Control in all tax-free reorganizations is set at 80% of the voting stock and 80% of the total number of shares of all other classes of stock. The rest of the first corporation's stock and any other remaining assets are distributed to the other corporation's shareholders. After the transaction, the shareholders of the first corporation become the controlling shareholders of the other. A transaction may meet the requirements for both the Type C and Type D reorganizations, in which case it is considered *Type D*. See Exhibit 9.4 for illustration.

(B) Divisive Type D Reorganization

In a divisive Type D reorganization, before the transaction, there is one corporation, and after the transaction, there are two corporations. One of the most well-known divisive Type D reorganizations was the breakup of AT&T. Various circumstances lead to divisive Type D reorganizations, including federal mandates to avoid monopolies, as seen

---

Assume that Company A wishes to control Company B, with Company B being the survivor. Thus, a Type D reorganization is suitable. There are 1,000 shares of Company B voting stock issued and outstanding. Company A transfers all of its assets in exchange for 950 shares of Company B voting stock. Company A then dissolves by issuing Company B stock in exchange for Company A voting stock. Therefore, Company B survives with Company A's stockholders owning the controlling interest of Company B as a result of a Type D reorganization.

EXHIBIT 9.4 TYPE D REORGANIZATION

in the case of AT&T, the need to settle shareholder squabbles, and decisions to separate risky business sectors.

There are two steps to a Type D divisive reorganization. The first is to transfer assets of a going-concern business to a corporation in exchange for control of that corporation. The second step is the transfer of all the stock and securities of the controlled corporation to the shareholders of the corporation that transferred the assets. How the controlled corporation's stock is divided is key in determining whether the resulting transaction is a spin-off, split-off, or a split-up, techniques described next.

Spin-offs. A spin-off is similar to a normal dividend distribution, although a spin-off is tax-free. The controlled corporation's stock is distributed to the controlling corporation's shareholders. The result is that the shareholders own stock in both corporations. A spin-off provides the shareholders with continuing interests in the businesses of both the controlling and controlled corporations through separate stockholdings in each.

Split-offs. A split-off is useful if the shareholders wish to have a continuing interest in only one of the lines of business. In the case of a split-off, only some of the original corporation's shareholders retain the stock in the original corporation. Other shareholders relinquish their stock in the original corporation for stock in the newly formed corporation. The end result is that some shareholders own one corporation while another set of shareholders own the new corporation. This is an effective device if animosity exists between groups of shareholders.

Split-ups. A split-up is similar to a split-off except that the original corporation liquidates, with two new corporations being formed. The original corporation transfers some of its assets to a new corporation in exchange for all that corporation's stock, and the rest of its assets are transferred to another new corporation in exchange for all that other corporation's stock. The original corporation then liquidates, distributing the stock of the two new corporations to its shareholders.

All Type D reorganizations are required to meet the additional conditions of IRC Sections 354, 355, and 356. This area of law is the one in which tax planners will have their most difficult task in effecting a successful tax-free Type D reorganization. Section 354(a)(1) of the IRC provides that, in general, no gain or loss is recognized if stock or securities in a corporation, a party to a reorganization, are, in pursuance of the plan of reorganization, exchanged solely for stock or securities in such corporation or in another corporation that is a party to the reorganization.

Some exceptions are made regarding securities. These exceptions are intended to protect against a bailout of earnings and profits at the capital gain tax rate. Section 354(b) of the IRC provides that substantially all of the assets of the transferor must be transferred to qualify under IRC Section 354. Also required is the transfer of all stock, securities, and other property to the transferor's shareholders.

Section 355 of the IRC deals with the distribution of stock and securities. Stock is not required to be exchanged or otherwise redeemed from the shareholders. This section permits the transfer of less than substantially all of a corporation's assets in an exchange for stock or securities of the transferee. It is not required that distribution of stock be pro rata to all of the shareholders. Section 355 of the IRC includes provisions to protect against the bailout of earnings and profits at the capital gain rate. One of the more common requirements is that the transferor's business must have been engaged in an active trade or business for the previous five years.

Section 356 of the IRC provides some flexibility regarding the receipt of boot in a Type D reorganization. The general rule is that if boot is received, in an exchange that is governed by IRC Sections 354 or 355, gain is to be recognized to the extent of the boot. Boot includes cash and other property. Section 356 of the IRC determines whether the gain is capital or ordinary. In addition, it determines whether the exchange has the effect of a dividend.

To summarize, a successful Type D reorganization must meet four requirements:

1. The original corporation must distribute, to its shareholders, stock of a new subsidiary that results in control of that subsidiary.
2. Property distributed by the original corporation must consist solely of stock and securities of the new subsidiary.
3. After the distribution has occurred, both companies must be actively engaged in business.
4. The distribution must not be a tax-avoidance device used to bail out earnings and profits in either the original corporation or the new subsidiary.

(v) Hybrid Reorganizations: Triangular Mergers and Reverse Triangular Mergers. *Triangular merger* is a term used to describe a reorganization in which a parent company's subsidiary is acquiring or being acquired by another corporation.

(A) Triangular Merger

There are three requirements of a triangular merger.

1. The parent corporation must have a controlled subsidiary (80% owned) and must receive substantially all of the assets of the acquired corporation in the merger. As discussed previously, *substantially* means 90% of the fair market value of the net assets and 70% of the fair market value of the gross assets.
2. The transaction between the subsidiary and the acquired corporation must satisfy all the requirements of a Type A reorganization.
3. No stock of the subsidiary can be used in the transaction. See Exhibit 9.5 for illustration.

(B) Reverse Triangular Merger

The *reverse triangular merger* is a variation of the triangular merger. The acquired corporation is the surviving subsidiary instead of the subsidiary of the acquirer. The parent corporation's voting stock is transferred to the acquired corporation in exchange for the acquired corporation's stock, which must retain substantially all of its assets and property. The acquired corporation must acquire substantially all

---

Assume that Company A owns all of the stock of Company B. Company A wishes to acquire Company C. Company C transfers all of its assets to Company B in exchange for 100 shares of Company A stock. Company C's assets have a value of $100,000, all of which have been transferred to Company B. Company C dissolves and transfers its stock in Company A to its shareholders. This transaction qualifies as a valid triangular merger because Company B received more than 90% of the fair market value of the net assets as well as more than 70% of the fair market value of the gross assets of Company C. The second requirement is met because, if Company B had been merged directly into Company A, the merger would have qualified as a Type A reorganization. Finally, the only stock transferred to Company C was Company A stock.

Exhibit 9.5 Triangular Merger

of the assets and property of the acquiring corporation's subsidiary, and the acquiring corporation must obtain control (80% ownership).

(C) Continuity Requirement in a Reverse Acquisition

When a smaller group acquires a larger group for stock, it is considered a *reverse acquisition*. In a reverse acquisition, the smaller group is deemed terminated and the larger group continues as if it had acquired the small group. In a ruling, the IRS said that this rule applies only if the common parent ceases to exist. This ruling explained that the rule does not apply if the common parent ceases to be the common parent, but remains in existence as a subsidiary in the original group of corporations. This ruling appears to be at odds with the literal requirements of the IRC section.

For acquisitions and mergers prior to this ruling, continuation of the common parent had been considered crucial to continuation of the group. Termination of the group has major consequences because gain deferral, loss offsets, and other single-entity treatments generally end with a group's termination. The regulations technically restructure the members to avoid termination. As a rule, a group remains in existence for a tax year if the common parent maintains its status and at least one subsidiary affiliated with it at the end of the prior year remains affiliated with it at the beginning of the current year.

This is an example of revenue rulings that disregard the literal regulations. Prior revenue rulings have required continuity, in conformity with the regulations. This ruling appears to remove the continuity requirement in a reverse acquisition.

(D) Taking a Corporation Private Qualified as a Reverse Acquisition in Technical Advice Memorandum 9806003

To prevent trafficking in loss corporations, the consolidated return regulations provide a complex scheme of isolating losses of acquired companies in separate return limitation years to prevent their being used to shield income and gains of acquiring companies. In a complex corporate-going-private transaction, use of tax attributes, like net operating losses, is a key consideration, and using them effectively can depend on whether the acquired corporations survive as an affiliated group. In Technical Advice Memorandum (TAM) 9806003, the IRS ruled that the acquired corporate group survived in a reverse acquisition.

A reverse acquisition occurs when a corporation acquires a new affiliate (or purchases substantially all of its assets) for more than 50% of its own stock so that the shareholders of the so-called acquired corporation end up owning more than 50% of the so-called acquiring corporation. After a reverse acquisition, net operating losses, capital loss carryovers, unused foreign tax credits, and investment credits of the acquiring corporation and its affiliated group are treated as having been incurred in a separate return limitation year. Therefore, they can be used to offset the income of the resulting group only to the extent that it is attributable to the acquiring corporation.

The management of a corporation that was the parent of a consolidated group wanted to take the corporation private. A foreign corporation through a foreign subsidiary owned some parent stock and the remainder was publicly traded on Nasdaq. Holdings Corporation was formed to be the new parent for certain U.S. subsidiaries of the foreign corporation, including the parent. The foreign corporation and a group of investors, including management, each owned 50% of voting power of Holdings, but the foreign corporation owned 60% of the value.

In a complicated transaction, Holdings acquired the parent stock from the foreign subsidiary for a note. Later the foreign subsidiary acquired Holdings stock in return for a capital contribution. The parent then paid a previously declared dividend to Holdings and Holdings paid off the note. Subsequently, Holdings contributed its parent stock to an acquisition vehicle that merged into the parent, and the parent became a wholly owned subsidiary of Holdings, which in turn was a subsidiary of the foreign subsidiary.

The taxpayer consistently reported the transaction as a reverse acquisition, taking the position that the parent-affiliated group continued in existence with Holdings as the common parent. It argued that the proper time for testing whether the transaction satisfies the requirements of a reverse acquisition is immediately after Holdings paid off the note and before the transfer by the foreign subsidiary of the stock in Holdings.

The examining agent took the position that Holdings' acquisition of parent stock did not qualify as a reverse acquisition because Holdings did not acquire the stock of the parent in exchange for its stock, as required by the regulations, but rather by purchase. The agent also contended the subsequent transfer of Holdings' stock to other subsidiaries in the foreign corporations group violated the requirements for reverse acquisitions.

Noting that there is no requirement in the consolidated return regulations on how long the shareholders in the acquired corporation must hold on to their stock of the acquiring corporation, the IRS ruled in the technical advice that the transfer of the stock in the acquiring corporation to another subsidiary of the ultimate parent cannot cause an otherwise qualifying transaction to fail to qualify as a reverse acquisition. The transfer of cash by Holdings to the foreign subsidiary in exchange for parent stock was transitory in nature, and the transaction was in substance a transfer of parent stock by the foreign subsidiary for stock in Holdings.

9.5   TAX LOSSES AND TAX CREDIT CARRYOVERS OF ACQUIRED CORPORATIONS

(a)   GENERAL.   At one time, an important motive for many corporate acquisitions or mergers was the availability of tax loss or tax credit carryovers in the acquired corporation that could be used to offset taxable income of the acquiring corporation. *Loss corporations* were often advertised for sale in business magazines and newspapers. The price for a loss corporation often was based on a discounted value of the future tax reductions expected from utilization of the net operating loss or tax credit carryovers. However, a series of tax reforms enacted by Congress, including IRC Sections 269, 382, 383, 384, and 482, have greatly restricted the ability to offset an acquirer's taxable income by the tax loss or tax credit carryovers of an acquired corporation.

As a general rule, unused net operating losses may be carried back by the corporation that incurred the losses to each of the two taxable years preceding the taxable year of such loss [IRC Section 172(b)(A)]. Thereafter, any excess net operating loss may be carried forward to each of the 20 taxable years following the taxable year of such loss [IRC Section 172(b)(1)(B)].

Sections 381, 382, 383, and 384 of the IRC are the statutory provisions that apply to and govern the carryover and realization of tax benefits related to the carryover of tax losses as well as tax credits in mergers and acquisitions. Each of these is discussed in the sections that follow.

(b) IRC SECTION 381. Section 381 of the IRC generally provides that a corporation acquiring the assets of another corporation in a nontaxable reorganization or from the liquidation of a subsidiary shall succeed to and take into account, as of the close of the date of distribution or transfer, that other corporation's net operating loss carryovers, earnings, profits, and capital loss carryovers.

Section 381(b) of the IRC provides three operating rules for the carryover of tax attributes.

1. In any type of reorganization, except an F reorganization, the taxable year of the transferor ends on the date of the transfer, thus triggering the requirement of filing a tax return for the short taxable year ending on the date of the transfer.
2. The date of distribution or transfer is the date when the transaction is completed. If the transferor corporation retains some assets, the date of distribution is the date on which substantially all the assets were transferred to the acquiring corporation.
3. The acquiring corporation may not carry back a net operating loss or a net capital loss from a taxable year ending after the date of transfer to preacquisition years of the transferor corporation. See Exhibit 9.6 for an illustration.

Section 381 of the IRC provides that many tax attributes in a reorganization may be transferred. However, IRC Sections 269, 382, 383, and 482 set limitations on the benefits available from such tax attributes.

(c) IRC SECTIONS 269 AND 482. Sections 269 and 482 of the IRC can be best described as *antitax avoidance* provisions. They provide

---

On December 31, 1997, Company B merges into Company A in a Type A nontaxable merger. A loss incurred by Company A in 1998 may not be carried back to offset the income of Company B prior to the merger. The loss may be carried back only to offset taxable income of Company A for years prior to the merger.

EXHIBIT 9.6 IRC SECTION 381 CARRYBACK OF NET OPERATING LOSS

the IRS with substantial power to construe transactions in accordance with their substance rather than form.

Section 482 of the IRC allows the IRS to reallocate (but not to disallow) income, deductions, credits, or other allowances between or among related taxpayers. Section 269 of the IRC generally disallows the benefit of any deductions, credit, or other allowance obtained by acquiring property or control of a corporation for the principal purpose of avoiding tax. It should be noted that for IRC Section 269, control is defined as ownership of 50% or more. Section 269 of the IRC requires taxpayers to show that the choice of the most favorable tax route was motivated by substantial business reasons in addition to the opportunity to obtain the particular tax benefits inherent in the method selected. Several business-purpose criteria are set forth by IRC Section 269:

- Are the acquiring parties aware of the tax benefits at the time of transfer?
- Will the acquired corporation have a continuing business after the acquisition, not just a shell?
- Is the acquisition of control or assets necessary or useful to the acquiring corporation's activities?
- What are the results of a comparison of the economic benefit of the acquisition with the tax benefit of the acquisition?
- Could the challenged benefit be used by the taxpayer even if the acquisition did not occur?
- Was the type of transaction the most economically feasible way to reach the desired objective?

Section 269 of the IRC may overlap with IRC Sections 381 and 383. Sections 382 and 383 of the IRC do not limit the authority present in IRC Section 269, but the limitations of IRC Sections 382 and 383 can be relevant evidence in determining whether the principal purpose of an acquisition is the evasion or avoidance of income tax (IRC Reg. Section 1.269–7).

(d) IRC SECTION 382.

(i) General. Section 382 of the IRC was established to address perceived abuses from the acquisition of loss corporations. It imposes limitations on the use of net operating loss carryforwards and certain unrealized losses if an *ownership change* has occurred. This requires

careful evaluation whenever there have been substantial changes in the stock ownership of a loss corporation.

Under IRC Section 382, an ownership change occurs if the percentage of the stock owned by the loss corporation, owned by one or more 5% stockholders, has increased by more than 50% over the lowest percentage of such stock that was owned by those parties at any time during any three-year period. All transactions during the testing period, whether related to each other or not, are considered in determining whether an ownership change has occurred, including increases from multiple acquisitions, even if the percentage ownership between the first and last days of the testing period is the same or has decreased. The attribution rules of IRC Section 318 apply to the determination of ownership changes. All ownership changes of less than 5% stockholders are aggregated into a single shareholder unit referred to as the *public*. Any stock sales by the public to a 5% shareholder are included in the measurement of ownership change, whereas sales of stock by the public to other shareholders in the public group are not included in the measurement of ownership change. Public shareholders must be segregated if they receive loss corporation stock as a result of an equity structure shift or nontaxable exchanges of stock for property.

The testing period required by IRC Section 382 is a three-year period ending on the day following any ownership change. A loss corporation does not need to include in the measurement of ownership change any transactions that occurred on or before the date of the most recent ownership change in determining if another ownership change has occurred. The testing period does not begin until the corporation becomes a loss corporation—any ownership changes prior to the corporation becoming a loss corporation are not considered. See Exhibit 9.7 for an illustration.

Exhibit 9.7 illustrates a relatively simple IRC Section 382 three-year ownership change test. Exhibit 9.8 illustrates how the test is applied to slightly more complicated circumstances.

(ii) IRC Section 382 Limitation. The IRC Section 382 limitation is imposed after an ownership change has occurred. The calculation of this limitation is based on two factors: (1) the value of the loss corporation and (2) the long-term tax-exempt rate. The long-term tax-exempt rate is the highest of the federal long-term rates determined under IRC Section 1274(d), which states:

Shareholders A and B each own 40% of the stock of Company Z. The other 20% is owned equally by 100 other shareholders. Company C becomes a loss corporation in 1994. No shares have been traded prior to September 19, 1996. On September 19, 1996, Shareholder C purchases A's stock and, on April 16, 1998, purchases B's stock. As of April 16, 1998, there has been an ownership change because C's ownership has changed from zero to 80% during the testing period. The table computes the ownership changes at September 19, 1996, and April 16, 1998.

	Prior to 9/19/94	9/19/96	4/16/98
Stockholder A	40%	40%	0%
Stockholder B	40%	0%	0%
Stockholder C	0%	40%	80%
Price (less than 5% shareholders)	20%	20%	20%
Cumulative Owner-ship Change	Base	40%	80%

EXHIBIT 9.7   TEST FOR OWNERSHIP CHANGE UNDER CODE SECTION 382

The federal long-term rate shall be the rate determined by the Secretary based on the average market yield (during a 1-month period selected by the Secretary and ending in the calendar month in which the determination is made) on outstanding marketable obligations of the United States with remaining periods to maturity of over 9 years.

The maximum annual amount of net operating loss that an acquiring corporation can use to offset taxable income after an ownership change date is an amount equal to the value of the loss corporation immediately before the ownership change multiplied by the long-term tax-exempt rate. Exhibit 9.9 illustrates the computation of a Section 382 limitation.

Section 382(b)(2) of the IRC provides that if the amount of net operating loss that may be used in any postownership change year exceeds taxable income for that year, the excess loss permitted by the limitation may be carried forward to the next year and into the future until expiration of the net operating loss carryforward. In Exhibit 9.9, if Company A had only $50,000 of taxable income in 1999, there would be $10,000 ($60,000 less $50,000) of unused IRC Section 382

Company Z is a loss corporation with 200 shares of common stock outstanding. Shareholder A owns 100 shares, and Shareholders B and C each own 50 shares. On March 16, 1996, A sells 60 shares of stock to B, which causes B's ownership to increase by 30%, from 25% (50 shares/200 shares) to 5% (110 shares/200 shares). As a result of that transaction, A's ownership percentage is reduced to 20% (40 shares/200 shares). On November 10, 1997, A purchases all 50 shares of C's stock, causing A's ownership to increase to 45% (90 shares/200 shares), an increase of 25% in comparison with A's lowest ownership percentage during the testing period, which was 40% after A sold 60 shares to B on March 16, 1996. This increase is a 25% increase in ownership for the three-year ownership change test. Therefore, even though A and B have increased their aggregate ownership percentage by only 25% when compared with the ownership percentages at the beginning of the testing period, an ownership change has occurred because the total of their separate increases from the lowest point of each of their ownership percentages during the testing period equals 55%. The table computes the ownership changes.

	Prior to 3/16/96	3/16/96	Ownership Change	11/10/97	Ownership Change
Shareholder A	50%	20%	0%	45%	25%
Shareholder B	25%	55%	30%	55%	30%
Shareholder C	25%	25%	0%	0%	0%
Cumulative Ownership Change	Base		30%		55%

EXHIBIT 9.8 TEST FOR OWNERSHIP CHANGE UNDER CODE SECTION 382

limitation that is carried forward to 2000, making the IRC Section 382 limitation for 2000 equal to $70,000, comprising the $60,000 applicable to 2000 and the $10,000 carried forward from the prior year. If Company A has no taxable income in 1999, the limitation for 2000 would be $180,000, comprising $60,000 applicable to 2000 and $120,000 carried forward from 1999. The limitation and amounts available for utilization are computed in this cumulative manner until the net operating loss carryforwards expire. Expiration dates continue to be based on the 20-year carryforward period from the dates the losses were incurred. Unless a net operating loss carryforward can be utilized at a rate sufficient to enable its complete utilization within 20 years from

Assume that on December 31, 1998, there is an ownership change under IRC Section 382 with respect to Company A, when the long-term tax-exempt rate is 6%. The value of Company A's stock is $1 million and Company A has a net operating loss carryforward of $500,000. The IRC Section 382 limitation is $60,000 ($1 million × 6%). Accordingly, Company A's net operating loss carryforward may be utilized against future taxable income at a rate of $60,000 per year.

EXHIBIT 9.9   IRC SECTION 382 LIMITATION

the date the losses were incurred by the acquired company, some or all of the net operating loss carryforwards will expire. The proportion of an acquired company's value at date of acquisition to its net operating loss carryforward has become an important ratio that will determine the extent to which net operating losses of an acquired company can be utilized subsequent to the acquisition.

(e) IRC SECTION 383.   Section 383 of the IRC was implemented to provide limitations on utilization of *preownership change carryforwards* of unused general business credits, unused minimum tax credits, net capital loss carryovers, and unused foreign tax credits. The amount of any credit carryovers that may be used in a postchange year (as defined by IRC Section 382) is determined by converting the credits into the tax liability that the credits would offset. This tax liability is then converted to a taxable income amount. This taxable income is then limited to the IRC Section 382 limitation for such year.

The ordering provisions of IRC Section 383 provide that the five IRC Section 382 limitations will be used in the listed order:

1. Net capital loss carryovers
2. Net operating loss (NOL) carryovers
3. Foreign tax credits
4. General business credits
5. Minimum tax credits

(f) IRC SECTION 384.   Section 384 of the IRC was implemented to limit the use of a corporation's losses in situations in which the loss corporation does not undergo an ownership change. This can occur in an IRC Section 332 liquidation or a Type A, Type C, or Type D reorganization. Section 384 of the IRC prohibits the offset of any preacquisition loss against any recognized built-in gains in the gain corporation. Section 384(b) of the IRC provides an exception to this general rule. It states

Subsection (a) shall not apply to the preacquisition loss of any corporation if such corporation and the gain corporation were members of the same controlled group at all times during the 5-year period ending on the acquisition date.

The definition of a controlled group is set forth in IRC Section 1563(a) with the exception that 80% is changed to 50% when dealing with IRC Section 384. It is clear that current tax laws significantly limit the availability of tax losses and tax credit carryovers to acquiring corporations. Careful planning and strategy will allow some carryovers to the acquiring corporation.

9.6 MISCELLANEOUS TAX CONSIDERATIONS

(a) INSTALLMENT METHOD OF REPORTING GAIN NOT AVAILABLE TO ACCRUAL METHOD TAXPAYERS.
Effective for sales and other dispositions occurring after December 16, 1999, the Tax Relief Extension Act of 1999 provides that the installment method does not apply to income from an installment sale if the income would, without regard to the installment sales rules, be reported under an accrual method of accounting.

This provision of the law has had a dramatic tax effect on accrual method business entities that enter into transactions to sell their assets under an installment method. The seller is unable to recognize gain over the period of time that the sale proceeds are received.

The law, however, does provide for several exceptions. The prohibition on use of the installment method by accrual method taxpayers does not apply to (1) dispositions of property used or produced in the trade or business of farming, or (2) dispositions of residential time-shares or residential lots (if the lots are not to be improved by the taxpayer or a related person) if the taxpayer elects to pay to the Internal Revenue Service interest on the deferred taxes that are attributable to the deferred gain.

This legislation affects many accrual-method taxpayers. There are planning opportunities that taxpayers can use to mitigate or eliminate the tax effect of this potentially devastating provision. In 2000, P.L. 106–573, Section 2(b) amended Section 453 by removing Section 453(a)(2), which had prohibited accrual-method taxpayers from using the installment method. This change is effective with respect to transactions that occurred after December 17, 1999. Before this change of law, taxpayers considered taking the position that contingent purchase transactions were best reported as *open transactions.*

Wells Fargo & Co. et al. v. Commissioner, No. 99–3307 (8th Cir., Aug. 29, 2000), held that officers' salaries of the acquired corporation and legal and investigatory expenses incurred prior to the acquisition were deductible expenses under Section 162.

(b) EXPENSES OF TAXABLE ACQUISITIONS. A corporation will generally incur numerous costs in acquiring target company stock or assets in a taxable transaction and in obtaining financing for the acquisition, including legal and accounting fees, investment banking fees, and other fees and costs. Whether the costs incurred by the purchaser are deductible, amortizable, or added to the base of an asset generally depends on (1) the nature of the costs and the type of asset to which they relate and (2) whether the transaction is structured for tax purposes as an asset or stock purchase.

Costs incurred that are allocable to obtaining debt financing for the acquisition are generally not deductible but are amortizable over the life of the debt obligation to which the costs relate. Such expenses would include legal fees incurred in drafting and negotiating debt terms, commitment fees, and other closing costs.

Costs incurred that are allocable to obtaining equity financing for the acquisition are neither deductible nor amortizable. Such expenses include commissions, registration fees, costs of preparing offering materials, and costs of negotiating the deal and drafting documents.

The costs that are attributable to acquisition of assets or stock are generally not deductible but are added to the basis of the assets or stock so acquired. Such costs include costs of negotiating and drafting acquisition-related documents, investigating and due diligence costs associated with the purchased assets or stock, investment banking fees, and costs of closing the acquisition. It may be possible that investigatory and due diligence costs should be amortizable under Section 195 or immediately deductible if one can determine that the acquisition produces no significant future benefits for the purchaser.

(c) SMALL BUSINESS STOCK. Effective for sales after August 5, 1997, taxpayers other than estates, trusts, subchapter S corporations, and partnerships (i.e., individuals) may elect to defer recognition of capital gain realized from the sale of qualified small business stock held for more than six months if other small business stock is purchased by the individual during the 60-day period beginning on the date of sale. Gain is recognized only to the extent that the amount realized on the sale exceeds the cost of the replacement small business stock purchased during the 60-day period, as reduced by the portion of such cost, if any, previously taken into account. To the extent that capital gain is not recognized, that amount will be applied to reduce the basis of the replacement small business stock. The basis adjustment is applied to the replacement stock in the order in which such stock is acquired. For purposes of the rollover provision, the replacement stock must meet the active business requirement for the six-month period following its purchase. Except for purposes of determining whether the active business test six-month holding period is met, the holding period of the stock purchased will include the holding period of the stock sold.

The term *qualified small business stock* means stock of a domestic C corporation with gross assets of $50 million or less, if the stock was acquired after August 10, 1993, at the original issuance in exchange for cash or property (other than stock) or as compensation for services, and held for five years or more.

The *active business* requirement is that at least 80% of the corporation's tangible and intangible assets must be used in the active conduct of a qualified trade or business. Disqualified businesses include those providing health, legal, accounting, engineering, architectural, or consulting services and those engaged in farming, banking, investing, or motel or restaurant operations.

For individual investors with investments in qualified small business stock, the possibility to defer gain recognition offers significant tax-planning opportunities.

CHAPTER 10

PURCHASE ACCOUNTING

10.1 GENERAL PRINCIPLES OF PURCHASE ACCOUNTING

Purchase accounting is now governed by Financial Accounting Standards Board (FASB) Statement 141, *Business Combinations,* and FASB Statement 142, *Goodwill and Other Intangible Assets.* These statements supersede Accounting Principles Board (APB) Opinion 16, *Business Combinations,* and Opinion 17, *Intangible Assets.* Many requirements of Opinions 16 and 17 are carried forward, but there are some significant differences under the new rules.

Both Statement 141 and Opinion 16 identify the acquiring company as the one that distributes cash or other assets or incurs liabilities. Issuers of equity interests to effect the combination are generally the acquirers, but both pronouncements recognize that a smaller company may issue the equity interests and may assume the name of the acquired entity. This is referred to as a *reverse acquisition,* and the acquirer is really the larger company. In such cases, relative voting rights after the combination must be considered in identifying the acquirer.

In identifying the acquiring entity, Statement 141 adds to the consideration of existing voting rights the existence of any unusual or special voting arrangements and options, warrants, or convertible securities. These were not addressed as a consideration in Opinion 16. Statement 141 also addresses the existence of large minority interests where there are no other significant voting interests, ability to appoint the governing body, and the composition of senior management of the combined entity. These are concepts that have been considered as indicative of parent-subsidiary relationships in the FASB's Consolidations Project. Statement 141 also notes that, in an exchange of equity securities, the acquiring entity would normally be the entity that pays a premium over the market value of the other company's equity securities.

The general principles of the purchase method under both pronouncements are similar to the general principles of accounting for acquisitions of assets and issuances of stock.

- The total cost of the acquisition is determined.
- The cost is allocated to identifiable assets acquired and liabilities assumed, including deferred taxes, in accordance with their respective fair values.
- If the total acquisition cost exceeds the fair value of net identifiable assets, the excess is allocated to goodwill. Under Statement 141, significantly more emphasis is placed on identifying and allocating cost to identifiable intangible assets. Identifiable assets are amortized over useful lives under Opinion 16. Statement 142 indicates that certain identifiable assets could have indefinite lives, and amortization for those would not be required.
- Any excess of the total fair value of net identifiable assets over total cost is first applied as a pro rata reduction of long-term assets. Under Opinion 16, any remaining excess is recorded as a deferred credit in the balance sheet and amortized. Under Statement 141, any remaining excess is recognized in income immediately as an extraordinary gain.
- Goodwill is amortized over a period not exceeding 40 years under Opinion 16; under Statement 141, goodwill is not amortized but is subject to impairment testing for write-down or write-off, if necessary. This would also apply to identifiable intangible assets that are not being amortized.

- Prior periods are not restated; however, certain supplemental disclosures may be required.

Determining the cost of an acquisition and allocating the purchase price to assets acquired and liabilities assumed requires the application of specialized acquisition accounting concepts and procedures, which are discussed throughout this chapter.

10.2 DETERMINING THE COST OF AN ACQUISITION

(a) GENERAL.   The general approach to determining the cost of a purchase acquisition follows three general principles for accounting for acquisitions of assets:

1. An asset acquired in exchange for cash or other assets is recorded at cost (i.e., at the amount of cash disbursed or the fair value of other assets distributed).
2. An asset acquired by incurring liabilities is recorded at cost (i.e., at the present value of the amounts to be paid).
3. An asset acquired by issuing shares of stock of the acquiring corporation is recorded at the fair value of the asset (i.e., shares of stock issued are recorded at the fair value of the consideration received for stock). In cases where stock has a quoted price, one would, in fact, look first to the value of the stock for valuing the stock issued and assets received.

(b) STOCK ISSUED IN PAYMENT OF PURCHASE PRICE.   Many acquisitions are paid for by exchanging cash or incurring liabilities for the net assets or stock of another company. Alternatively, equity securities of an acquiring company are often issued in exchange for the assets or stock of an acquired company. The fair value of net assets acquired in exchange for stock that has determinable value is usually measured by the value of the stock at the date of acquisition. However, market prices for a reasonable period of time before and after the date an acquisition is agreed to and announced should be considered in establishing the value to be assigned to the securities to avoid volatility of stock prices unduly affecting accounting for the acquisition. If restricted securities are issued, an appraisal of value by qualified professionals, such as investment bankers, may be necessary to establish value.

If the fair value of stock is not readily determinable, other indicators of value should be used, such as an estimate of the value of the assets received, including an estimate of goodwill.

Emerging Issues Task Force (EITF) Issue 95-19, *Determination of the Measurement Date for the Market Price of Securities Issued in a Purchase Business Combination,* considered conflicting guidance in paragraphs 74 and 93 of Opinion 16 with respect to the valuation of securities that are issued as consideration in a purchase-method acquisition. Paragraph 74 says, "[T]he market price for a reasonable period before and after the date the terms of the acquisition are agreed to and announced should be considered in determining the fair value of securities issued." The guidance of paragraph 93 would value securities as of the date of the acquisition, which is defined as "the date assets are received and other assets are given or securities are issued."

The EITF indicated that the guidance of paragraph 74 should be used. The "reasonable period of time" should be very short, such as a few days before and after an acquisition is agreed to and announced. Thus, the measurement date for the value of securities issued is not affected by the need for shareholder or regulatory approval.

EITF 95-19 also indicates that the measurement date for a hostile tender offer occurs when the proposed transaction is announced and enough shares have been tendered to make the offer binding. If a proposed hostile tender offer becomes nonhostile, the market price at that time would be used based on the acquiree's agreement to the purchase price.

EITF 95-19 also provides that a new measurement date for marketable equity securities occurs if a purchase price is changed. Changes in a purchase price can result from further negotiations or changes in the market price of the equity securities that could cause a change in the security's exchange ratio or a change to a cash portion of a purchase price.

Some preferred share issues are similar to debt securities, while others are similar to common shares, with many gradations in between. Fair value of nonvoting, nonconvertible preferred shares that lack characteristics of common shares may be determined by comparing specified dividend and redemption terms with those of comparable securities and by assessing market factors. Thus, the cost of issuing senior equity securities may be determined in practice on the same basis as for debt securities.

(c) DIRECT COSTS OF ACQUISITIONS OTHER THAN PURCHASE PRICE. *Acquisition cost* includes all direct costs related to an acquisition, such as finders' and directly related professional fees (e.g., legal, accounting, and appraisal fees) and incremental costs that were directly caused by and related to the acquisition. The fixed costs of an internal acquisitions department or of the officers and employees who work on acquisitions should not be included in acquisition cost, because they are not incremental. Costs of registering and issuing equity securities are a reduction of the otherwise determinable fair value of the securities.

(d) PREMIUM OR DISCOUNT. Purchase accounting requires recognition of the time value of money in computing total acquisition cost as well as in determining the fair market values of assets acquired and liabilities assumed. Premium or discount on a debt security that is issued or assumed should be imputed to adjust the liability to present value based on current market interest or yield rates if the stated interest or yield rates vary significantly from current market rates. Assigning fair value to individual assets and liabilities (generally receivables or payables) may require discounting to present value or assigning a premium allocation. After an acquisition, interest expense or income should be recorded by amortization of the premium or discount using the interest method.

(e) ASSETS EXCHANGED. Assets given to a seller as consideration should be included in the total acquisition cost at fair value. Any deferred taxes related to assets given up should be removed from the balance sheet and accounted for as a reduction of the total acquisition cost.

(f) CONTINGENT CONSIDERATION. Consideration that is contingent on future earnings of an acquiree should be added to the acquisition cost when amounts are determinable beyond a reasonable doubt. Acquisition cost should be increased and the additional cost should be allocated to net assets acquired in accordance with the purchase method. This often results in an adjustment to long-term assets or goodwill. The additional cost should be depreciated or amortized prospectively over the remaining useful lives of the assets to which the additional cost was assigned.

If stock has been given in consideration for an acquisition with a contingency requiring the issuance of additional shares or payment of cash dependent on future security prices, issuance of additional shares does not result in an adjustment of acquisition cost. The recorded amount of shares previously issued is reduced by an amount equal to the fair value of the additional consideration (cash, stock, or other) paid upon resolution of the contingency.

Interest and dividends paid to an escrow agent on contingently issuable debt or equity securities should not be accounted for as interest or dividends. Upon resolution of the contingency, if payment of the escrowed funds by the agent to the seller is required, the amounts should be recorded as additional acquisition costs if the contingency was based on earnings. If the contingency was based on security prices, the accounting is the same as for contingently issuable securities—the value of securities previously issued is reduced and there is no change to total acquisition cost.

In EITF Issue 97-8, *Accounting for Contingent Consideration Issued in a Purchase Business Combination,* the EITF addressed accounting for contingent consideration based on earnings or a guaranteed value of securities that is embedded in a security or in a separate financial instrument (which may trade in financial markets). The EITF determined that if the seller has the right to transfer the security or instrument and if it is publicly traded or indexed to a security that is publicly traded, the security or instrument should be recorded as part of the purchase price at fair value at the date of acquisition (using the basis for determining value discussed in EITF 95-19 [Section 6.2(b)]). There is no later adjustment to the purchase price based on changes in value of the security or financial instrument.

If the security or instrument is not publicly traded or indexed to a security that is publicly traded (the contingent consideration), the contingent consideration is not recorded at the acquisition date and when the contingency is resolved, the purchase price is adjusted. EITF Issue 96-13, *Accounting for Derivative Financial Instruments Indexed to, and Potentially Settled in, a Company's Own Stock,* and EITF Issue 86-28, *Accounting Implications of Indexed Debt Instruments,* provide applicable subsequent accounting guidance for indexed securities or instruments.

EITF Issue 97-15, *Accounting for Contingency Arrangements Based on Security Prices in a Purchase Business Combination,* addresses situations where the acquirer agrees to pay cash or another form of consideration to the seller if securities issued as part of the purchase price do not have a specified value at a specified future date. These situations include a "below-market guarantee," where an acquirer agrees to issue additional consideration if the securities issued do not have, at a future date, a specified value that is less than the value at the date the securities were issued.

If a below-market guarantee is given, the purchase price should be recorded based on the fair value of the consideration unconditionally given at the date of the acquisition. For example, say an acquisition is consummated with the acquirer issuing 100,000 shares with a value of $22 per share, for a total purchase price of $2.2 million. The acquirer gives a below-market guarantee at a specified future date of $18 per share, or $1.8 million. When the future date arrives, the market price of the stock is $15 per share, for a total value of $1.5 million. The acquirer must provide additional consideration of $300,000, which could be cash, additional shares of stock, or some other form of consideration. This does not result in a change in the purchase price. The value of the initial consideration given is reduced by the amount of the additional consideration.

Some contingency arrangements that are based on security prices do not guarantee a minimum value of total consideration. Instead, they require additional consideration if the value of the shares issued at the acquisition date is less than a "target" value at a specified future date. The target value is the lowest amount at which additional consideration would not have to be issued. The amount of additional consideration is limited and, therefore, the total value of all consideration is not known at the acquisition date. In this instance, the purchase price should be recorded at an amount equal to the maximum number of shares that could be issued, multiplied by the fair value per share at the acquisition date if that amount is limited, but no greater than the target value. Said another way, the purchase price should be recorded at an amount equal to the lower of either the target value or the maximum number of shares that could be issued, multiplied by the market price per share at the date of acquisition. The conveyance of additional consideration would not result in a change in the purchase price recorded at the date of acquisition.

EITF Issue 95-8, *Accounting for Contingent Consideration Paid to the Shareholders of an Acquired Enterprise in a Purchase Business*

Combination, addresses situations in which contingencies are based on earnings or other performance measures where selling shareholders have positions that can affect the financial results of the acquiree after the acquisition. This could be as employees, officers, directors, consultants, or contractors. Issue 95-8 indicates criteria that should be used to determine whether the resolution of the contingency should be accounted for as an adjustment of the purchase price or as a compensation expense of the future period. These factors include:

- Is the contingent consideration forfeited if the employment terminates (which would indicate that the contingent consideration is compensation)?
- Does the length of time of requirements coincide with the contingent payment period?
- Is the employee compensation, excluding the contingent payments, reasonable in relation to that of comparable employees?
- Do the selling shareholders who become employees receive greater amounts of contingent payments than shareholders who do not become employees?
- Do the selling shareholders who become employees own substantially all, or only a minor amount, of the stock of the acquiree, and do all shareholders receive the same amount of contingent consideration on a per-share basis?
- Identify the reasons for the contingent consideration arrangement (e.g., if the initial purchase price is at the low end of a range established in a valuation study or if the contingent consideration formula is consistent with prior profit-sharing or bonus arrangements).
- Are there indications from the formula used to compute the contingent consideration?
- Identify the terms of other arrangements with the selling shareholders, including noncompete agreements, executory contracts, consulting contracts, and leases.

(g) PREACQUISITION CONTINGENCIES. The effect of the assumption of a contingency, whether or not there was an identifiable adjustment to the purchase price, should result in an allocation to a liability assumed. Certain resolutions of contingencies after the acquisition can result in adjustments to acquisition costs. See section 10.4(c).

If appreciated (fair value is higher than carrying value) non-monetary assets are given up as part of a purchase price, the acquirer would record a gain. This is necessary to achieve the Opinion 16 driving principle that assets given up should be included in the purchase price at fair value. When the author first encountered this in practice, he consulted with the FASB staff and confirmed that this is correct. While gain recognition is not specifically addressed in Opinion 16, the FASB staff indicated that the requirement to include the assets in the purchase price at fair value (which is then allocated to the net assets acquired) requires the gain recognition.

An issue relating to operating assets being exchanged for other operating assets is addressed in EITF Issue 98-3, *Determining Whether a Transaction Is an Exchange of Similar Productive Assets or a Business Combination.* The situation deals with the interplay of Opinion 16 and APB Opinion 29, *Accounting for Nonmonetary Transactions.* Opinion 29 indicates that it does not apply to business combinations. The opinion addresses the issues of when a transaction would be considered an exchange of similar productive assets that would be accounted for at historical cost under Opinion 29, and when it would be considered a business combination to be accounted for at fair value under Opinion 16.

The EITF members indicate that the answer lies in whether the assets exchanged are "businesses." Some EITF members suggested that work be done on what characteristics indicate that the operating assets exchanged are a business, in which case accounting should be done under Opinion 16. Other EITF members indicated that they believe that even if similar businesses are exchanged, the accounting could be done under Opinion 29 at historical cost. They indicated that they believe the EITF should work on what characteristics indicate that groups of assets are similar. The Securities and Exchange Commission (SEC) observer to the EITF has indicated that the SEC staff believes that Opinion 16 should be used for exchanges of businesses, even if the businesses are similar.

(h) STOCK OPTION EXCHANGES.   Options to purchase an acquiree's stocks that are exchanged for options to purchase the acquirer's stock should be considered part of the purchase price according to current practice and SEC guidance. The amount to be included in the purchase price is the fair value of the options of the acquirer that were exchanged, determined by using the Black-Scholes formula or another option valuation model.

In an exposure draft issued on March 31, 1999, *Accounting for Certain Transactions Involving Stock Compensation,* the FASB has proposed that only vested options should be included in the purchase price. Nonvested options would not be included in the purchase price.

For nonvested options, the FASB would require a new measurement date if the exchange of options resulted in more than a de minimus increase in fair value. Compensation cost would be recognized by the acquirer to the extent that costs were not recognized by the acquiree for nonvested options. If there is a new measurement date, additional compensation cost would be recognized to the extent that the intrinsic value of the acquirer's options exceeds the intrinsic value of the acquiree's options immediately before the exchange.

In EITF Issue 85-45, *Business Combinations of Stock Options and Awards,* the EITF indicated that if a target company settles stock options voluntarily, at the direction of the acquirer or as part of the plan of acquisition, the acquiree should account for the settlement as compensation expense under APB Opinion 25, *Accounting for Stock Issues to Employees.*

10.3 RECORDING ASSETS ACQUIRED AND LIABILITIES ASSUMED

(a) GENERAL.   In purchase accounting, total acquisition cost is allocated to assets acquired and liabilities assumed on the basis of their respective fair values. If total acquisition cost exceeds the fair values of identifiable net assets, the excess is allocated to goodwill. If the fair values of identifiable net assets and liabilities exceed acquisition cost, referred to as *negative goodwill,* the deficiency is applied as a pro rata reduction of the assigned costs of long-term assets, except for long-term investments in marketable securities. If the deficiency results in the elimination of long-term assets, any remaining negative goodwill is recorded as a deferred credit and amortized over a period not to exceed 40 years. FASB Statement 109, *Accounting for Income Taxes,* issued in 1992, provides requirements and procedures for establishing deferred taxes as part of an allocation of total acquisition cost in both goodwill and negative goodwill situations.

In a less-than-100% acquisition, adjustments to carrying value of identifiable net assets are made only for the proportionate share acquired. The portion of the acquired company attributable to the remaining minority interest continues to be accounted for on a historical basis.

(b) APPRAISALS.   Independent appraisals are often the primary way of determining estimated fair values to be used in assigning costs, especially for significant acquisitions. In the absence of evidence of better estimates, the appraised values are often used as the fair values.

In some formal appraisals, an amount may be assigned to goodwill. Goodwill can be attributed to many attributes of a going concern, including the existence of a customer base or market share, an assembled and trained workforce, high barriers to entry of competition, or other intangibles of value. The appraiser may estimate the fair value of appraised goodwill based on guidelines, including percentages of goodwill to total acquisition cost that was determined in recent comparable acquisitions.

If the total of the appraised values of identifiable assets varies significantly from total acquisition cost, there should be an identifiable reason. For example, the acquisition cost of a highly profitable business may include a higher-than-normal amount of goodwill. Conversely, the acquisition cost of an operation that has been experiencing losses or an operation that a seller must, for some reason, sell under distress conditions may be less than the fair values of the individual assets, resulting in negative goodwill.

In some cases, the appraised values of individual assets must be adjusted to reflect additional information that is more indicative of fair value, such as a subsequent sale of one or more of the acquired assets at an amount differing from the appraised value.

(c) GUIDELINES FOR ALLOCATING ACQUISITION COST TO INDIVIDUAL ASSETS AND LIABILITIES

(i) General.   The guidelines of paragraph 87 of Opinion 16 for allocating acquisition cost to assets acquired and liabilities assumed are presented next, along with comments about implementing the guidelines in practice.

(ii) Marketable Securities. Marketable securities should be recorded at current net realizable values.

(iii) Receivables. Receivables should be recorded at present values of amounts to be received determined at appropriate current interest rates, less allowances for uncollectibility and collection costs, if necessary.

In practice, acquired trade accounts receivable expected to be collected within normal collection cycles for a particular industry are not discounted to present value. However, if a receivable is expected to remain outstanding for a length of time that results in a significant discount factor, the discount should be reflected in the acquisition accounting. Notes receivable with interest rates that vary significantly from current market rates for similar notes should be adjusted for imputed discount or premium.

Adjustment for discount or premium results in an increase or decrease to interest income from the date of acquisition to the date of collection based on the present value of the amount to be collected using market interest rates as of the date of acquisition.

(iv) Inventories. Finished goods and merchandise should be recorded at estimated selling prices less the sum of: (a) costs of disposal, and (b) a reasonable profit allowance for the selling effort of the acquiring corporation. Work in progress should be recorded at estimated selling prices of finished goods less the sum of: (a) costs to complete, (b) costs of disposal, and (c) a reasonable profit allowance for the completing and selling effort of the acquiring corporation based on profit for similar finished goods. Raw materials should be recorded at current replacement costs.

Special aspects of purchase accounting for inventories are discussed in section 10.4(a).

(v) Plant and Equipment. Plant and equipment to be used should be recorded at current replacement costs for similar capacity, unless the expected future use of the asset indicates a lower value to the acquirer. Plant and equipment to be sold or held for later sale should be recorded at current net realizable value. Plant and equipment to be used temporarily should be recorded at current net realizable value, recognizing future depreciation for the expected period of use.

If the total fair value of identifiable net assets exceeds the total acquisition cost, the difference is applied as a proportionate reduction of the values assigned to long-term assets, including fixed assets. None of the excess is allocated to long-term marketable securities or to other long-term assets that have effective cash equivalency with easy conversion. This allocation interacts with computing deferred taxes related to long-term assets as described in section 10.5(b)(iii) and illustrated in Exhibit 10.5.

The reference to allocation to plant and equipment to be sold being recorded "at current net realizable value," which appears in paragraph 88(d) of Opinion 16, was amended to read "at fair value less cost to sell."

(vi) Intangible Assets.　　Intangible assets that can be identified and named, including contracts, patents, franchises, customer and supplier lists, and favorable leases, should be recorded at appraised values.

Identifiable intangible assets should be valued before amounts are allocated to goodwill. In addition to those mentioned previously, identifiable intangible assets include customer lists, technology rights, patents and trademarks, computer programs, and software.

If a purchase agreement includes a covenant that a seller will not compete with an acquirer for a specified period of time, a portion of the purchase price should be assigned to the covenant as an identifiable intangible that is amortized over the period of the covenant.

FASB Interpretation 4, *Applicability of FASB Statement No. 2 to Business Combinations Accounted for by the Purchase Method,* requires allocation of part of acquisition cost to assets resulting from research and development activities including:

- Assets acquired in the combination that result from research and development (R&D) activities of the acquired enterprise (such as patents, blueprints, formulas, and designs for new products)
- Assets acquired to be used in R&D activities of the combined enterprise (such as materials, supplies, equipment, and specific research projects in process).

If a substantial portion of the acquisition cost is allocable to R&D projects in progress, such amount should be charged to R&D expense in the income statement of the acquirer for the period in which the acquisition occurs. See section 6.4(f).

Paragraph 39 of Statement 141 emphasizes that an intangible asset should be recognized as an asset apart from goodwill if it arises from contractual or other legal rights (regardless of whether those rights are transferable or separable from the acquired entity or from other rights and obligations), or not arising from contractual or other legal rights, as an asset apart from goodwill only if it is separable (capable of being separated or divided from the acquired entity and sold, transferred, licensed, rented, or exchanged, regardless of whether there is intent to do so). An intangible asset that cannot be sold, transferred, licensed, rented, or exchanged individually is considered separable if it can be sold, transferred, licensed, rented, or exchanged in combination with a related contract, asset, or liability. An assembled workforce is not considered to be an intangible asset apart from goodwill. Appendix A of Statement 141 provides additional guidance about recognition of acquired intangible assets apart from goodwill, including an illustrative list of intangible assets.

(vii) Other Assets. Other assets, including land, natural resources, and nonmarketable securities, should be recorded at appraised values.

(viii) Accounts and Notes Payable. Accounts and notes payable, long-term debt, and other claims payable should be recorded at present values of amounts to be paid determined at appropriate current interest rates. The possible need to impute premium or discount to adjust stated interest rates to current market rates should be considered.

Considerations for accounts and notes payable are similar to those discussed in section 10.3(c)(iii) for receivables. Adjustment for premium or discount, if necessary, would be recognized as adjustments of postacquisition interest expense.

(ix) Accrued Liabilities. Liabilities and accruals, such as accruals for pension cost, warranties, vacation pay, and deferred compensation, should be recorded at present values of amounts to be paid determined at appropriate current interest rates.

(A) PENSION COSTS

Purchase agreements sometimes obligate an acquirer to provide retirement benefits for employees of an acquired company. Pension plans and related fund assets may be transferred intact to provide continuation of the existing plan or the employees may be included in a pension plan maintained by the acquirer. A purchase agreement may require adjustments to the purchase price for future benefits to be provided for preacquisition service. A seller may be required to make a payment to an acquirer or to a pension fund of an amount equal to any excess of vested benefits over pension fund assets as of the acquisition date. The acquirer should include a liability in the acquired balance sheet for the present value of the excess of the projected benefit obligation over pension fund assets, to the extent the seller does not eliminate such an excess. The same notion applies to other postretirement benefits, which are discussed in paragraphs 86 through 88 of FASB Statement 106, *Employers' Accounting for Postretirement Benefits Other than Pensions.*

(B) VACATION PAY AND COMPENSATED ABSENCES

Purchase agreements sometimes provide for a reduction of the purchase price for earned compensated absences, such as vested vacation pay to be paid after the acquisition date. FASB Statement 43, *Accounting for Compensated Absences,* provides accounting standards for accounting for compensated absences. Vacation pay and other compensated absences must be recorded as balance sheet liabilities if employees have earned vested right to such payments. Any earned compensated absences should be included as liabilities in the balance sheet at the acquisition date.

(x) Other Liabilities.   Other liabilities and commitments, including unfavorable leases, contracts, and plant closing expense incident to the acquisition, should be recorded at present values of amounts to be paid determined at appropriate current interest rates.

EITF Issue 95-3, *Recognition of Liabilities in Connection with a Purchase Business Combination,* addresses the types of direct, integration, or exit costs that should be accrued as liabilities in a purchase business combination accounted for under Opinion 16 and when to recognize those costs. The EITF reached consensus that the costs of a plan to (1) exit any activity of an acquired company, (2) terminate involuntarily employees of an acquired company, and/or (3) relocate employees of an acquired company should be recognized as liabilities assumed in a purchase business combination and included in the allocation of the acquisition cost in accordance with Opinion 16 if specified conditions are met.

(A) Costs to Exit an Activity of an Acquired Company

A plan to exit an activity of an acquired company exists if all of these five conditions are met:

1. As of the consummation date of the acquisition, management having the appropriate level of authority begins to assess and formulate a plan to exit an activity of the acquired company.

2. As soon as possible after the consummation date, management having the appropriate level of authority completes the assessment of which activities of the acquired company to exit, and approves and commits the combined company to the plan. Although the time required will vary with the circumstances, the finalization of the plan cannot occur beyond one year from the consummation date of the acquisition.

3. The plan specifically identifies all significant actions to be taken to complete the plan and activities of the acquired company that will not be continued, including the method of disposition and location of those activities, and the plan's expected date of completion.

4. Actions required by the plan will begin as soon as possible after the plan is finalized and the period of time to complete the plan indicates that significant changes to the plan are not likely.

5. A cost resulting from a plan to exit an activity of an acquired company should be recognized as a liability assumed as of the consummation date of the acquisition only if the cost is not associated with or is not incurred to generate revenues of the combined entity after the consummation date, and it meets either of these criteria:

    a. The cost has no future economic benefit to the combined company, is incremental to other costs incurred by either the acquired company or the acquiring company in the conduct of activities prior to the consummation date, and will be incurred as a direct result of the plan to exit an activity of the acquired company. The notion of incremental cost does not contemplate a diminished future economic benefit to be derived from the cost but, rather, the absence of the cost in either company's activities immediately prior to the consummation date.

b. The cost represents an amount to be incurred by the combined company under a contractual obligation of the acquired company that existed prior to the consummation date and will either continue after the plan is completed with no economic benefit to the combined company or be a penalty incurred by the combined company to cancel the contractual obligation.

The preceding criteria are essentially the same as the criteria in EITF 94-3 for the recognition of a liability for costs, other than employee termination benefits, that are directly associated with a plan to exit an activity.

(B) INVOLUNTARY EMPLOYEE TERMINATION BENEFITS AND RELOCATION COSTS

A cost resulting from a plan to involuntarily terminate or relocate employees of an acquired company should be recognized as a liability assumed as of the consummation date of the purchase business combination and included in the allocation of the acquisition cost if all of these four criteria are met:

1. As of the acquisition's consummation date, management having the appropriate level of authority begins to assess and formulate a plan to involuntarily terminate (relocate) employees of the acquired company.
2. As soon as possible after the consummation date, management having the appropriate level of authority completes the assessment of which employees of the acquired company will be involuntarily terminated (relocated), approves and commits the combined company to the plan of termination (relocation), and communicates the termination (relocation) arrangement to the employees of the acquired company. The communication of the termination (relocation) arrangement should include sufficient detail to enable employees of the acquired company to determine the type and amount of benefits they will receive if they are terminated (relocated). Although the time required will vary with the circumstances, the finalization of the termination (relocation) plan and the communication of the termination (relocation) arrangement cannot occur beyond one year from the acquisition's consummation date.

3. The termination (relocation) plan specifically identifies the number of employees of the acquired company to be terminated (relocated), their job classifications or functions, and their locations.

4. Actions required by the termination (relocation) plan will begin as soon as possible after the plan is finalized, and the period of time to complete the plan indicates that significant changes to the plan are not likely.

Costs related to activities or employees of the acquired company that do not meet the conditions described are indirect and general expenses related to the acquisition as discussed in paragraph 76 of Opinion 16. Indirect and general expenses are deducted as incurred in determining net income. With respect to exit plans and involuntary employee termination and relocation plans, initial or revised plan actions that result from events occurring after the consummation date do not result in an element of cost of the acquired company. The costs described previously are not recorded as part of the purchased entity and should be either expensed or capitalized when incurred based on the nature of the expenditure and the capitalization policy of the combined company.

Costs related to activities or employees of the acquiring company are not considered in the purchase price allocation, because the cost of the acquisition is not allocated to the assets and liabilities of the acquiring company, as discussed in FASB Technical Bulletin 85-5, *Issues Relating to Accounting for Business Combinations.*

When the ultimate amount of an expended cost is less than the amount recorded as a liability assumed in a purchase business combination, the excess should reduce the cost of the acquired company. The amount of a cost exceeding the amount recorded as a liability assumed in a purchase business combination should result in an additional element of cost of the acquired company if an adjustment to an original estimate is determined within one year of the acquisition date and thereafter should be included in the determination of net income in the period in which the adjustment is determined. Costs related to plans to exit activities and to involuntarily terminate or relocate employees that are recorded as part of the purchased entity under this issue are not preacquisition contingencies accounted for under FASB Statement 38, *Accounting for Preacquisition Contingencies of Purchased Enterprises.*

(C) DISCLOSURE

The combined company should disclose the next information, in addition to the disclosures required by Opinion 16. The information should be disclosed only if the acquired company's activities that will not be continued are significant to the combined company's revenues or operating results or if the costs recognized under the consensus as of the consummation date are material to the combined company. Notes to the financial statements of the combined company for the period in which a purchase business combination occurs should disclose:

- If the acquiring company has not finalized a plan to exit an activity or involuntarily terminate (relocate) employees of the acquired company as of the balance sheet date, a description of unresolved issues, the types of additional liabilities that may result in an adjustment to the allocation of the acquisition cost for the business combination, and how any adjustments will be reported
- A description of the type and amount of liabilities assumed and included in the acquisition cost allocation for costs to exit an activity of the acquired company or to involuntarily terminate (relocate) employees of the acquired company
- A description of the major actions composing the plan to exit an activity or involuntarily terminate (relocate) employees of an acquired company; activities of the acquired company that will not be continued, including the method of disposition; and the anticipated date of completion and a description of the employee group(s) to be terminated (relocated)

Notes to the combined company's financial statements for all periods presented subsequent to the acquisition date in which a purchase business combination occurred, through and including the period in which all actions under a plan to exit an activity or involuntarily terminate (relocate) employees of the acquired company have been fully executed, should disclose:

- A description of the type and amount of exit costs, involuntary employee termination costs, and relocation costs paid and charged against the liability
- The amount of any adjustment(s) to the liability account and whether the corresponding entry was an adjustment of the

acquired company's cost or included in the determination of net income for the period

EITF Issue 95-14, *Recognition of Liabilities in Anticipation of a Business Combination,* addressed the timing of recognition of liabilities, using the guidance in EITF Issue 94-3, *Liability Recognition for Certain Employee Termination Benefits and Other Costs to Exit an Activity (Including Certain Costs Incurred in a Restructuring),* for a plan to exit certain activities, to terminate certain employees, or both, if the plan will be implemented only if a business combination that an acquirer has agreed to is consummated, it is probable that the business combination will be consummated, and consummation is dependent only on the passage of time and completion of the closing documents.

The EITF determined that, in applying the guidance of EITF 94-3 to plans that will be implemented only if a business combination is consummated, the commitment date (for the costs of an exit plan) and the recognition date (for the costs of involuntary termination benefits) cannot occur prior to the consummation date of the business combination. In EITF Issue 96-5, the EITF reached the same conclusion for recognition at the date of business combination (rather than when consummation is determined to be probable) for termination benefits under a preexisting plan or contractual relationship and the effects on assumptions used in estimating obligations that result in curtailment losses for pension benefits, other postretirement benefits, and postemployment health benefits.

10.4 PURCHASE ACCOUNTING IN SPECIAL AREAS
(a) INVENTORIES

(i) Allocation of Acquisition Cost Including Seller's Profit.   The guidelines for recording acquired inventories are similar to the guidelines for other assets in that they are intended to result in assigning the amount an acquirer theoretically would have had to pay to acquire the assets individually in their current state. For inventory, the amount paid would be expected to include compensating a manufacturer for the profit earned for manufacturing work performed on work in process and finished goods inventories. Therefore, cost allocable to inventories is often higher than the acquiree's book value because of equivalent or higher replacement costs for raw materials combined with the addition

of a profit factor attributable to manufacturing work performed by the seller.

Allocating cost to inventory, as discussed, often results in a lower reported gross profit percentage in the income statement of an acquirer for the period following the acquisition because inventories sold in that period bear a higher-than-normal cost. The lower profit reflects that the earning process performed by an acquirer with respect to acquired finished goods and work in process does not include a profit factor for the manufacturing effort of the acquiree prior to the acquisition. This effect is illustrated in Exhibit 10.1.

(ii) Inventory Purchased in Separate Contract. The author has seen a few acquisitions that were structured so that inventory was acquired in a specific contract separate from the purchase agreement and for a separate and distinct payment for an amount equal to the book value of the inventories in the financial statements of the seller, or some other negotiated amount that was less than the amount that would be allocated based on the procedures described in section 10.4(a)(i). The result was that the one-time lower gross profit percentage described in that section did not occur. The specific circumstances of any such transactions must be evaluated to determine if there is some very unusual reason that makes it appropriate to account for the inventory acquisition separately from the acquisition of the other assets. However, if an acquisition has been broken into pieces only to avoid a higher allocation of purchase price to inventory, the author believes that the separate transactions should be *collapsed* into one, with an allocation of total acquisition cost to all the assets, including inventory, as required by Opinion 16, despite the specific price documented for inventory in a separate contract.

(iii) Last-in, First-Out Inventory. A business combination may be accounted for by:

- The purchase method but be tax-free
- The pooling-of-interests method but be taxable

In these situations, differences in the value assigned for accounting and tax purposes to last in, first out (LIFO) inventories can result.

In a purchase-method acquisition, an acquirer is required to revalue the inventories to fair value at acquisition date, and the entire

An acquired manufacturing company normally sells at a 40% markup, 15% of which is considered to relate to manufacturing and 25% to selling activities. The estimated sales amount to be realized from the sale of inventory is $2 million, 75% of which is related to finished goods and 25% to work in process. The cost to complete the work in process is estimated at $50,000, and the work in process is 50 percent completed with respect to manufacturing operations. Costs of disposal are immaterial and are ignored. The following table indicates the manufacturing and selling profits that would normally be reported.

	FINISHED GOODS	WORK IN PROCESS
Cost (when completed)	$1,071,429	$ 357,143
Profit factors		
Manufacturing (15%)	160,713	53,571
Selling (25%)	267,858	89,286
Selling price	$1,500,000	$5000,000

Following is a computation of the amounts to be assigned to the acquired inventories using the purchase method.

Finished goods	
Estimated selling price	$1,500,000
Minus normal selling profit	(267,858)
Amount to be allocated	$1,232,142
Work in process	
Estimated selling price	$500,000
Minus normal selling profit	(89,286)
Minus manufacturing profit on 50% of work in process	(26,786)
Cost to complete	(50,000)
Amount to be allocated	$333,928

The following computes the amounts that would be reported in the income statement of the acquirer in the period after the acquisition for the sale of the acquired inventory.

	TOTAL	FINISHED GOODS	WORK IN PROCESS
Sales	$2,000,000	$1,500,000	$500,000
Cost of sales			
Allocated amounts	1,566,070	1,232,142	333,928
Completion costs	50,000		50,000
	1,616,070	1,232,142	383,928
Gross profit	$ 383,930	$ 267,858	$116,072
Gross profit percentage	19.2%		

EXHIBIT 10.1 ILLUSTRATION OF REDUCED GROSS PROFIT PERCENTAGE IN PERIOD FOLLOWING AN ACQUISITION

The gross profit of 19.2% in the period following the acquisition is unusully low for this business. The next table computes the normal income statement effect of the sale of this inventory if a purchase price allocation had been made:

Sales	$2,000,000
Cost of sales ($2,000,000/1.40)	1,428,571
Gross profit	$ 571,429
Gross profit percentage	28.6%

Exhibit 10.1   (*continued*)

inventory is treated as a single LIFO layer acquired in the year of acquisition. If the transaction has been a tax-free exchange, the previous LIFO inventory layers and values may be carried forward for tax purposes. This would ordinarily cause the book LIFO inventory balance to be higher than the tax LIFO inventory. If a taxable transaction is accounted for as a pooling of interests, the reverse would ordinarily occur—the tax LIFO inventory amount would be higher than the book LIFO inventory amount.

The resulting differences between book and tax LIFO values and layers are carried forward from the date of acquisition. If inventory levels increase thereafter, book and tax cost of sales will generally be the same because the costs of current-year purchases or production will be the basis for cost of sales for both tax and accounting purposes.

Different values allocated to fixed assets for tax and accounting purposes can cause significant differences in depreciation charges allocated to production costs. These different depreciation amounts will cause different accounting and tax cost of sales and incremental LIFO inventory layer in periods after the acquisition. These differences, however, may exist where first-in, first-out (FIFO) inventories, as well as LIFO inventories, are present.

(b) LEASES.

(i) Unfavorable Leases.   Consistent with the principle that liabilities assumed should be recorded at fair value, if a lease assumed in a purchase bears a rental rate higher or lower than the current market rate for a similar lease, an intangible asset has been acquired or an intangible liability has been assumed. Accordingly, the difference between rentals

required by the assumed lease and current market rental rates, discounted to present value, should be included as an asset acquired or liability assumed in the acquired balance sheet. These are referred to as *unfavorable lease obligations*. Exhibit 10.2 illustrates computations related to an unfavorable lease assumed in an acquisition.

An acquirer assumes a lease on a 10,000-square-foot office building with an annual rental rate of $15 per square foot. Due to a decline in real estate values, similar properties can be rented at an average of $10 per square foot. The remaining term of the lease is two years, and rents are payable at the beginning of each month. A discount rate of 8 percent is appropriate.

MONTH	RENT PAYMENT	MARKET VALUE RENT	UNFAVORABLE LEASE OBLIGATION		
			TOTAL	INTEREST	PRINCIPLE
1	$12,500	$8,333	$ 4,167	$ 614	$ 3,553
2	12,500	8,333	4,167	591	3,576
3	12,500	8,333	4,167	567	3,600
4	12,500	8,333	4,167	543	3,624
5	12,500	8,333	4,167	519	3,648
6	12,500	8,333	4,167	494	3,673
7	12,500	8,333	4,167	470	3,697
8	12,500	8,333	4,167	445	3,772
9	12,500	8,333	4,167	420	3,747
10	12,500	8,333	4,167	395	3,772
11	12,500	8,333	4,167	370	3,797
12	12,500	8,333	4,167	345	3,822
13	12,500	8,333	4,167	319	3,848
14	12,500	8,333	4,167	294	3,873
15	12,500	8,333	4,167	268	3,899
16	12,500	8,333	4,167	242	3,925
17	12,500	8,333	4,167	216	3,951
18	12,500	8,333	4,167	189	3,978
19	12,500	8,333	4,167	163	4,004
20	12,500	8,333	4,167	136	4,031
21	12,500	8,333	4,167	109	4,058
22	12,500	8,333	4,167	82	4,085
23	12,500	8,333	4,167	55	4,112
24	12,500	8,333	4,167	28	4,139
			$100,008	$7,874	$92,134

EXHIBIT 10.2   COMPUTATION OF AN UNFAVORABLE LEASE OBLIGATION

As a result of the computations in Exhibit 10.2, the acquirer would record a liability at the acquisition date of $92,135, equal to the present value of the unfavorable-portion lease commitment. As each payment of $12,500 is made, rent expense would be charged for $8,333, interest expense would be charged for the corresponding amount in the *interest* column, and the unfavorable lease liability would be charged by the corresponding amount in the principle column.

If an acquirer is required to assume a lease for an asset or facility that is of no use, the present value of the entire lease may be established as a liability assumed. If only part of a leased facility or asset is of use to an acquirer, an unfavorable lease obligation should be established for the present value of the portion of future rent obligations attributable to the part of the facility or asset that is of no use.

(ii) Favorable Leases.   If future rent on an assumed lease is below the market rate, the acquirer should record an asset, sometimes referred to as a *favorable lease,* equal to the present value of the difference between the required rental rate and the market rate at the date of acquisition. That amount should be amortized to rent expense ratably over the remaining term of the lease. As in the case of an unfavorable lease, this allocation is made to result in accounting for the lease on equal footing with leases in the current market.

(iii) Lease Classification.   A lease assumed in an acquisition that was classified as an operating lease by the seller in accordance with FASB Statement 13, *Accounting for Leases,* should be accounted for as an operating lease by an acquirer if no changes are made to the terms of the lease. If the lease is modified, the amended lease is considered to be a new lease and should be accounted for based on the criteria of Statement 13. A lease reclassification does not eliminate the requirement to establish an asset or liability for an unfavorable or favorable lease commitment.

(iv) Assumption of a Leveraged Lease as Lessor.   A leveraged lease involves financing provided by a long-term creditor that is nonrecourse to the general credit of the lessor. The creditor may have recourse only to the leased property and rentals on it. These transactions provide the lessor with *significant leverage.*

If an acquirer assumes a leveraged lease, the lease retains its classification. The acquirer should assign a net amount to the investment in the leveraged lease based on remaining cash flows adjusted for estimated future tax effects. The net investment should be divided into these components:

- Net rentals receivable
- Estimated residual value
- Unearned income, including a discount to adjust the other components to present value

Thereafter, leveraged lease accounting, as described in Statement 13, should be used. This accounting is discussed and illustrated in FASB Interpretation 21, *Accounting for Leases in a Business Combination.*

(c) PREACQUISITION CONTINGENCIES.   Accounting principles for preacquisition contingencies are provided in FASB Statement 38, *Accounting for Preacquisition Contingencies of Purchased Enterprises.* A preacquisition contingency is:

> *(a) contingency of an enterprise that is acquired in a business combination accounted for by the purchase method and that is in existence before the consummation of the combination. A preacquisition contingency can be a contingent asset, a contingent liability, or a contingent impairment of an asset.* [FASB Statement 38, paragraph 4]

An assumed preacquisition contingency should be established as a liability in an amount equal to fair value. Fair value can be determined by the cost of resolution of a contingency during the *allocation* period or, if applicable, the amount that the parties agreed to in negotiation as an adjustment of the purchase price as a result of the existence of the contingency.

The allocation period for finalizing the amount to assign to a preacquisition contingency extends from the date of acquisition to when an acquirer is no longer waiting for information that it has arranged to obtain and that is known to be available or obtainable. The allocation period should usually not exceed one year from the date of the acquisition. Until the allocation period ends, the purchase price allocation should be adjusted for the effects of additional information about contingencies. After the allocation period, any changes in the estimated fair values of contingencies should be included in determining net income for the period in which the change is determined.

If the fair value of a contingency cannot be determined during the allocation period, the contingency should be assigned an amount determined in accordance with these two criteria:

1. Information available prior to the end of the *allocation period* indicates that it is probable that an asset existed, a liability had been incurred, or an asset had been impaired at the consummation of the business combination. It is implicit in this condition that it must be probable that one or more future events will occur confirming the existence of the asset, liability, or impairment.

2. The amount of the asset or liability can be reasonably estimated (from FASB Statement 38, paragraph 5).

If this approach of paragraph 5 of Statement 38 is used in valuing the contingency, the determination should be made in accordance with FASB Statement 5, *Accounting for Contingencies,* and the related FASB Interpretation 14, *Reasonable Estimation of the Amount of a Loss.*

(d) **FOREIGN CURRENCY TRANSLATION.**　In a purchase-method acquisition of a foreign operation, assets acquired and liabilities assumed are adjusted to fair values in foreign currency at the date of acquisition and translated at the foreign currency exchange rate on the date of acquisition. Any difference between the total cost of the acquisition in dollars and the translated net assets is accounted for as goodwill or negative goodwill. Future balance sheets are translated by converting the fair values at acquisition date into dollars using the exchange rate at the balance sheet date. Any differences caused by changes in exchange rates after the acquisition are accounted for in accordance with FASB Statement 52, *Foreign Currency Translation.*

(e) **MINORITY INTERESTS.**　If a minority interest exists after an acquisition, the adjustments of assets acquired and liabilities assumed to fair value under the purchase method are made only to the extent of an acquirer's proportionate share of the acquired company. The assets and liabilities prior to the acquisition and related future accounting effects remain on a historical basis to the extent of the percentage of minority interest outstanding.

Exhibit 10.3 illustrates the computation of acquisition adjustments if a minority interest remains outstanding. The illustration does not take into account complexities that might exist as a result of

Company A purchases 75% of the stock of Company B for $7.5 million cash. The historical carrying value of Company B's assets and liabilities follows. Following is Company A's accounting for the acquisition in its consolidated financial statements.

	HISTORICAL COMPANY B AMOUNTS	FAIR MARKET VALUE	EXCESS FAIR MARKET VALUE	CONSOLIDATION ENTRIES	AMOUNTS INCLUDED IN FINANCIAL STATEMENTS
Current assets	$ 3,000,000	$ 3,500,000	$ 500,000	$ 375,000*	$ 3,375,000
Fixed assets	7,000,000	9,000,000	2,000,000	1,500,000*	8,500,000
Goodwill				1,500,000*	1,500,000
	$10,000,000	$12,500,000	$2,500,000	$3,375,000	$13,375,000
Current liabilities	$2,000,000	$ 2,000,000	$	$	$ 2,000,000
Long-term debt	2,500,000	2,500,000			2,500,000
Stockholders' equity	5,500,000	8,000,000	2,500,000	2,000,000*	7,500,000
Minority interest				1,375,000*	1,375,000
	$10,000,000	$12,500,000	$2,500,000	$3,375,000	$13,375,000

Notes to "Consolidation Entries":
*Excess fair market value allocations:

	EXCESS FAIR MARKET VALUE	ACQUIRER'S PERCENTAGE INTEREST	ACQUIRER'S SHARE OF EXCESS
Current assets	$ 500,000	75%	$ 375,000
Fixed assets	2,000,000	75%	1,500,000
*Computation of goodwill:			$ 7,500,000
Purhase price			
For value of net assets		8,000,000	
Percentage interest acquired		× 75%	6,000,000
Goodwill			$ 1,500,000
*Computation of adjustment to equity:			
Company A investment in Company B			$ 7,500,000
Company B historical equity amount			5,500,000
			$ 2,000,000
*Minority interest: Company B historical equity			$ 5,500,000
Minority interest percentage			× 25%
			$ 1,375,000

EXHIBIT 10.3 PURCHASE ACCOUNTING WITH A MINORITY INTEREST

deferred taxes, in order to focus more directly on the procedure of making purchase accounting adjustments for only the acquirer's interest.

If an acquirer purchases some or all of a minority interest after initial application of the purchase accounting method, sometimes referred to as an *incremental* acquisition, a separate determination of fair values of identifiable assets and liabilities is made at the time of each separate purchase. Those fair values are used in assigning the cost of the partial interest acquired in each purchase, including separate goodwill determinations for each incremental purchase.

(f) PURCHASED IN-PROCESS R&D COSTS.   FASB Interpretation 4, *Applicability of FASB Statement No. 2 to Business Combinations Accounted for by the Purchase Method,* requires that a portion of a purchase price be allocated to the cost of tangible and intangible assets resulting from or to be used in R&D activities. Assets resulting from R&D could include patents received or applied for, blueprints, formulas, and specifications or designs for new products or processes. Assets to be used in R&D may include materials and supplies, equipment and facilities, and specific research projects in process. The allocation should be determined from the amount paid by the acquirer and not from the original cost to the acquiree.

The amount of a purchase price allocated to assets to be used in R&D should be charged to expense at the date of consummation of the business combination unless the assets have alternative future uses in R&D or otherwise as described in paragraphs 11(a) and 11(c) of FASB Statement 2, *Accounting for Research and Development Cost,* in which case the amount should be capitalized.

The assignment of part of the purchase price to R&D, which is then written off because it has no alternative future use (often referred to as "in-process R&D"), can be viewed as giving rise to a book-tax difference at the moment of allocation and prior to the write-off. This assumes that the R&D does not have tax basis. EITF Issue 96-7, *Accounting for Deferred Taxes on In-Process Research and Development Activities Acquired in a Purchase Business Combination,* indicates that the write-off of the in-process R&D occurs prior to the determination of deferred taxes. Therefore, there are no deferred taxes established for the difference, and the charge to expense is on a gross basis, without a tax benefit.

In 1986, the EITF considered Issue 86-14, *Purchased Research and Development Projects in a Business Combination.* The issue focused on "incomplete" (usually referred to as "in-process") R&D projects acquired in a purchase-method acquisition, considering as to whether a portion of the purchase price should be allocated to these projects and whether they should be capitalized or written off immediately. FASB Interpretation 4 covers these questions, requiring an allocation of part of the purchase price to in-process projects that have value and, if there is no alternative future use, requiring an immediate write-off. While the EITF acknowledged this, they questioned the rationale for this accounting and recommended that the FASB reconsider Interpretation 4, which could lead to a reconsideration of Statement 2. The issue was raised in July 1986, and in 1987 the FASB indicated that it did not favor reconsidering Interpretation 4 or Statement 2.

It is interesting to note that in 1999, as part of the current Business Combinations project, the FASB decided to do away with the immediate write-off of in-process R&D. This decision was then reversed by the FASB on the basis that this issue would have to be considered in connection with a comprehensive reconsideration of R&D costs.

(g) ACCOUNTING FOR ACQUIRED ASSETS THAT ARE TO BE DISPOSED OF. Assets to be disposed of should be valued in the purchase price allocation at fair value less cost to sell. Fair value should be the amount that the acquirer expects to realize in the sale of the asset. The amount realized in the subsequent sale of an asset is perhaps the most compelling evidence to be considered in the purchase price allocation for nonfinancial assets.

The author was a consultant in a particularly fascinating situation in which an acquirer had arranged a bulk sale of inventory of an acquiree to a third party for $2 million, concurrent with the closing of the acquisition, to obtain a portion of the funds used to pay for an acquisition. The inventory had a cost to the acquiree of $2.8 million, which would have been adjusted in the purchase accounting allocation to $3.2 million to add a manufacturing profit in accordance with the procedures described in section 6.4(a)(i). Two opposing views were expressed about how this situation should be accounted for:

1. The cost assigned to the inventory should be $2 million based on the view that the most compelling evidence of value is the price received in the sale of the inventory, concurrent with

the acquisition. The result would be no gain or loss in the postacquisition income statement.

2. The cost assigned to the inventory should be $3.2 million, in accordance with normal purchase accounting allocation procedures, resulting in a pretax loss of $1.2 million in the postacquisition income statement.

The author's client (the acquirer) believed that the first approach was correct. After extensive debate, the author and the acquirer were unable to resolve this issue with the acquirer's auditing firm, some of whose partners were adamant that the proper accounting was the second approach, in which case the acquirer would have to report a $2 million loss in the postacquisition income statement. The author prepared a description of the transaction, which was presented as a technical inquiry to the FASB staff. After some discussion, the FASB staff supported the first approach, saying that the proper application of Opinion 16 is to view a price obtained in a sale of an asset after an acquisition, and in this case, concurrent with the acquisition, as the compelling amount to be used in allocating acquisition cost.

EITF Issue 87-11, *Allocation of Purchase Price to Assets to Be Sold,* addresses allocation of purchase price to assets constituting a segment or a portion of a segment of a business that will be sold by the acquirer. The purchase price allocated should consider net cash flows from operations from the date of acquisition to the date of sale (the "holding period"), interest on incremental debt incurred during the holding period to finance the assets and the operation of the line of business or a portion of a line of business, and proceeds from the sale. EITF 87-11 also says that differences between the carrying amount of an operation to be disposed of and the sales proceeds realized should result in a reallocation of the purchase price unless there are specific identifiable events during the holding period that change the fair value of the subsidiary. Losses from such events should be recognized when probable, as defined in FASB Statement 5, *Accounting for Contingencies,* and gains should be recognized when realized.

The SEC indicated that the acquirer must be able to demonstrate that the operation to be sold had been identified at the acquisition date and that there was reasonable expectation of sale within one year at the acquisition date. The SEC indicated that the accounting described in EITF 87-11 is required in the circumstances contemplated. Also, the

SEC has stated that these disclosures must be provided for reporting periods in which the accounting of EITF 87-11 is applied:

- Descriptions of the operations held for sale and the method used to assign amounts to and the method used to account for those assets, and the expected disposal date
- The operation's income or loss during the reporting periods that have been excluded from the consolidated income statement and a schedule reconciling the excluded income or loss to the earnings received or losses funded by the parent that have been accounted for as an adjustment to the carrying amount of the assets—allocated interest cost should be identified separately
- Gain or loss on the ultimate disposition that has been reported as an adjustment of the original purchase price allocation
- Discussion in Management's Discussion and Analysis (MD&A) of Financial Condition and Results of Operations of any material effect on results of operations, liquidity, capital resources and known trends, commitments, or contingencies

In 1990, the EITF addressed accounting for several situations in which an operation to be sold is not sold as expected in EITF Issue 90-6, *Accounting for Certain Events Not Addressed in Issue No. 87-11 Relating to an Acquired Operating Unit to Be Sold.* If the operation is not sold by the end of the holding period and the acquirer still intends to sell, the acquirer should discontinue the accounting of EITF 87-11 after the holding period and should report results of operations and interest expense (if applicable) in its consolidated operations. The operating results, interest, and gain or loss on disposal should be reported as part of income from continuing operations if the operation is a portion of a segment of a business. If the operation is a segment of a business, it should be reported pursuant to the guidance for reporting the disposal of a segment of a business contained in APB Opinion 30, *Reporting the Results of Operations—Reporting the Effects of Disposal of a Segment of a Business, and Extraordinary, Unusual, and Infrequently Occurring Events and Transactions.*

If the acquirer during the holding period decides not to sell the operation, the purchase price should be reallocated as if the operation was never held for sale and the effects of applying the accounting of EITF 87-11 should be reversed as a cumulative adjustment to income in the period in which the decision is made. If a decision not to sell the operation is made after the holding period, there is no reallocation of the purchase price. The carrying value of the operation that was to be sold is allocated to its assets, based on their fair values, and any excess carrying value is allocated to goodwill and amortized over its remaining useful life.

The EITF indicated in EITF 90-6 that the accounting of EITF 87-11 may be used for up to one year following the acquisition date, provided that the acquirer is actively attempting to find a buyer and remains committed to a formal plan consistent with Opinion 30. An exception would be that the accounting of EITF 87-11 could be continued for a short time after the one-year period if a firm contract exists for the sale of the operation soon after the end of the one-year period.

In 1995, the EITF (in EITF Issue 95-21, *Accounting for Assets to Be Disposed of Acquired in a Purchase Business Combination*) considered the question of whether EITF 87-11 was still applicable because in the FASB's October 16, 1995, exposure draft on consolidation policy and procedures, the FASB proposed that a temporarily controlled entity acquired in a purchase-method acquisition should be valued at its fair value less cost to sell. The EITF discussed whether the guidance of EITF 87-11 was still applicable in light of the FASB exposure draft. The EITF discussed various issues related to accounting for assets acquired in a business combination that will be sold. The EITF removed Issue 95-21 from its agenda because Statement 121 addresses implementation issues.

See section 10.3(c)(x) for a discussion of related areas in EITF 95-3, *Recognition of Liabilities in Connection with a Purchase Business Combination.*

(h) INTANGIBLE ASSETS AND GOODWILL AT ACQUISITION DATE.

Statement 141 places significantly greater emphasis on allocating cost of acquisition to identifiable intangible assets. Paragraph 39 of Statement 141 requires that

> *An intangible asset shall be recognized as an asset apart from goodwill if it arises from contractual or other legal rights (regardless of whether those rights are transferable or separable from the acquired entity or from other rights and obligations). If an intangible asset does not arise from contractual or other legal rights,*

it shall be recognized as an asset apart from goodwill only if it is separable, that is, it is capable of being separated or divided from the acquired entity and sold, transferred, licensed, rented, or exchanged (regardless of whether there is an intent to do so). For purposes of this Statement, however, an intangible asset that cannot be sold, transferred, licensed, rented, or exchanged individually is considered separable if it can be sold, transferred, licensed, rented, or exchanged in combination with a related contract, asset, or liability. For purposes of this Statement, an assembled workforce shall not be recognized as an intangible asset apart from goodwill.

(i) INTANGIBLE ASSETS AND GOODWILL AFTER ACQUISITION DATE. Under Statement 141, after initial recognition in the purchase accounting allocation, goodwill and other intangible assets acquired in a business combination are accounted for in accordance with the provisions of FASB Statement No. 142, *Goodwill and Other Intangible Assets.*

Statement 142 bases the accounting for a recognized intangible asset on its useful life to the acquirer. Intangible assets with a finite useful life are amortized; intangible assets with an indefinite useful life are not amortized. Useful life is the period over which the asset is expected to contribute directly or indirectly to the future cash flows of the acquirer. The estimate of the useful life of an intangible asset to an entity shall be based on an analysis of all pertinent factors.

Paragraph 11 of Statement 142 lists these as factors to consider:

- The expected use of the asset by the entity
- The expected useful life of another asset or a group of assets to which the useful life of the intangible asset may relate (such as mineral rights to depleting assets)
- Any legal, regulatory, or contractual provisions that may limit the useful life
- Any legal, regulatory, or contractual provisions that enable renewal or extension of the asset's legal or contractual life without substantial cost (provided there is evidence to support renewal or extension and renewal or extension can be accomplished without material modifications of the existing terms and conditions)
- The effects of obsolescence, demand, competition, and other economic factors (such as the stability of the industry, known

technological advances, legislative action that results in an uncertain or changing regulatory environment, and expected changes in distribution channels)
*   The level of maintenance expenditures required to obtain the expected flows from the asset (e.g., a material level of required maintenance in relation to the carrying amount of the asset may suggest a very limited useful life)

If there are no legal, regulatory, contractual, competitive, economic, or other factors that limit the useful life of an intangible asset to the acquirer, the useful life of the asset is considered to be indefinite. The term "indefinite" does not mean infinite. Appendix A of Statement 142 includes illustrative examples of various intangible assets and how they should be accounted for, including determining whether the useful life is indefinite.

Unless an intangible asset is determined to have indefinite useful life, under Statement 142 it is amortized over its useful life. If there is a finite useful life, but the precise length is not known, amortization is recognized over the best estimate of useful life. The method of amortization should reflect the pattern in which the economic benefits of the intangible asset are consumed or otherwise used up. If that pattern cannot be reliably determined, a straight-line amortization method is used. An intangible asset is not written down or off in the period of acquisition unless it becomes impaired during that period.

Amortization is based on the amount initially assigned to an asset less any residual value. The acquirer should evaluate the remaining useful life of an intangible asset each reporting period to determine whether events and circumstances warrant a revision to the remaining period of amortization. If the estimate of remaining useful life is changed, the remaining carrying amount should be amortized prospectively over the revised remaining useful life. If an intangible asset that is being amortized is subsequently determined to have an indefinite useful life, the asset should be tested for impairment and should no longer be amortized and accounted for as other intangible assets not subject to amortization.

Statement 142 requires that intangible assets subject to amortization be reviewed for impairment in accordance with Statement 121. In August 2001, the FASB issued Statement No. 144, *Accounting for the Impairment or Disposal of Long-Lived Assets,* which supersedes

Statement 121 but retains its fundamentals by applying the recognition and measurement provisions in paragraphs 4 to 11 of Statement 121. In accordance with Statement 144, an impairment loss should be recognized if the carrying amount is not recoverable and exceeds fair value.

Intangible assets determined to have an indefinite useful life are not amortized until useful life is determined to be no longer indefinite. An acquirer must evaluate the remaining useful life each reporting period to determine whether events and circumstances continue to support indefinite useful life. If a finite useful life is then determined, the asset shall be tested for impairment and then amortized prospectively over its estimated remaining useful life. Intangible assets not subject to amortization must be tested for impairment annually, or more frequently if events or changes in circumstances indicate possible impairment.

Under Statements 141 and 142, goodwill is not amortized, but tested for impairment at a level of reporting referred to as a reporting unit. A two-step impairment test discussed in paragraphs 19 to 22 of Statement 142 should be used to identify potential goodwill impairment and to measure the amount of any goodwill impairment loss to be recognized.

The first step is to identify potential impairment by comparing fair value of a reporting unit with its carrying amount, including goodwill. Fair value of a reporting unit is determined using paragraphs 23 to 25 of Statement 142. If the fair value of a reporting unit exceeds its carrying amount, goodwill of the reporting unit is considered not impaired, and the second step is unnecessary. If the carrying amount exceeds fair value, the second step is performed to measure the amount of impairment loss, if any. The second step is used to measure the amount of impairment loss by comparing the implied fair value of reporting unit goodwill with the carrying amount used to estimate the implied fair value of goodwill. Implied fair value of goodwill is determined the same way as goodwill recognized in a business combination. This allocation is only for testing goodwill for impairment; an acquirer does not write up or down a recognized asset or liability or recognize a previously unrecognized intangible asset.

If the second step is not complete before financial statements are issued and a goodwill impairment loss is probable and can be reasonably estimated, the best estimate of that loss shall be recognized with disclosure that the impairment loss is an estimate. Any subsequent adjustment to the estimated loss based on the completion of the measurement is recognized in the subsequent reporting period.

Fair value for these purposes is the amount at which an asset or liability may be bought, incurred, or settled in a current transaction between willing parties other than in a forced sale or liquidation. The fair value of a reporting unit is the amount at which the unit as a whole may be bought or sold in a current transaction between willing parties. Quoted market prices in active markets are usually the best evidence of fair value and are used for the measurement, if available. However, the equity market price may not be representative of the fair value of a reporting unit as a whole and therefore may not need to be the sole measurement of fair value.

If quoted market prices are not available, the estimate of fair value is based on the best information available, including prices for similar assets and liabilities and the results of using other valuation techniques, such as a present value technique. Cash-flow estimates should incorporate assumptions that marketplace participants would use in their estimates of fair value. If that information is not available without undue cost and effort, an acquirer may use its own assumptions. If a range is estimated for the amounts or timing of possible cash flows, the likelihood of possible outcomes should be considered. A valuation technique using multiples of earnings or revenue or a similar performance measure may be used if that technique is consistent with the objective of measuring fair value, such as when the fair value of an entity that has comparable operations and economic characteristics is observable and the relevant multiples of the comparable entity are known.

Goodwill should be tested for impairment at the reporting unit level on an annual basis and between annual tests in certain circumstances. The test may be performed at the same time every fiscal year. Individual reporting units may be tested at different times.

The determination of the fair value of a reporting unit can be carried forward if the assets and liabilities of the reporting unit have not changed significantly, the most recent fair value determination resulted in an amount that exceeded the carrying amount of the reporting unit by a substantial margin, and based on an analysis of events that have occurred and circumstances that have changed since the most recent fair value determination, the likelihood that a current fair value determination would be less than the current carrying amount of the reporting unit is remote.

Goodwill should be tested between annual tests if an event occurs or circumstances change that would *more likely than not* reduce the fair value of a reporting unit below its carrying amount. Examples include a significant adverse change in legal factors or business climate; an adverse action or assessment by a regulator; unanticipated competition; loss of key personnel; a more likely than not expectation that a reporting unit or a significant portion of a reporting unit will be sold or otherwise disposed of; testing for recoverability under Statement 121 of a significant asset group within a reporting unit; recognition of a goodwill impairment loss in the financial statements of a subsidiary that is a component of a reporting unit; or if a portion of goodwill has been allocated to a business to be disposed of.

Public or nonpublic subsidiary separate financial statements prepared in accordance with generally accepted accounting principles (GAAP) must be accounted for in accordance with Statement 142, including goodwill testing. If a goodwill impairment loss is recognized by the subsidiary, goodwill of the reporting unit or units at the related higher consolidated level must be tested if the event would more likely than not reduce the fair value of the reporting unit at the higher consolidated level below carrying amount.

If there is a continuing noncontrolling or minority interest and goodwill is initially recognized based only on the interest of the acquirer, the fair value of the reporting unit used in the impairment test is based only on the acquirer's interest and does not reflect the portion of the fair value attributable to the noncontrolling or minority interest.

If goodwill and another asset or asset group are tested for impairment at the same time, the other asset or asset group is tested first. If the asset group is impaired, the impairment loss is recognized prior to testing goodwill.

(j) REPORTING UNITS. A reporting unit is an operating segment or one level below an operating segment, referred to as a *component*. A component is a reporting unit if it is a business for which separate financial information is available and received by segment management. Two or more *components* of an operating segment are aggregated and considered a single reporting unit if they have similar economic characteristics. An *operating segment* is a reporting unit if all its components are similar, if none of its components is a reporting unit, or if it comprises only a single component. Statement 131 and related interpretations should be used to determine reporting units.

Companies not required to report segment information by Statement 131 must test goodwill for impairment at the reporting unit level and should use paragraphs 10 to 15 of Statement 131 to determine operating segments for purposes of determining reporting units.

For goodwill testing, acquired assets and assumed liabilities are assigned to a reporting unit as of the acquisition date if the asset will be employed in or the liability related to the operations of a reporting unit, and if the asset or liability will be considered in determining the fair value of the reporting unit. Assets or liabilities an entity considers to be corporate assets or liabilities should also be assigned to a reporting unit if both the preceding criteria are met. For example, environmental liabilities that relate to an existing operating facility or a pension obligation would be included in the fair value of the reporting unit to which they relate. Assets or liabilities that relate to the operations of more than one reporting unit should be allocated to the different reporting units.

For testing goodwill, *all* goodwill acquired in a business combination is assigned to one or more reporting units at the acquisition date, based on reporting units of the acquirer that are expected to benefit from the synergies of the combination, even if other assets or liabilities of the acquired entity are not to be assigned to that reporting unit.

The amount of goodwill assigned to a reporting unit is determined similarly to the way in which goodwill is recognized in a business combination. Fair value for each reporting unit representing a *purchase price* is determined and allocated to the assets and liabilities of the unit. If purchase price exceeds the amount assigned to net assets, the excess is goodwill assigned to that reporting unit. If goodwill is assigned to a reporting unit that has not been assigned any of the assets acquired or liabilities assumed in an acquisition, the amount of goodwill to be assigned could be determined by a "with and without" computation, using the difference between the fair value of the reporting unit before and after the acquisition, which would represent the amount of goodwill to be assigned.

If an entity reorganizes its reporting structure resulting in a change in the composition of one or more of its reporting units, the guidance of paragraphs 32 and 33 of Statement 142 should be used to reassign assets and liabilities to the reporting units. Goodwill is reassigned to the reporting units using a relative fair value allocation similar to that used if a portion of a reporting unit is to be disposed of, as set forth in paragraph 39 of Statement 142.

If a reporting unit is to be disposed of in its entirety, goodwill of that reporting unit is included in the carrying amount in determining gain or loss on disposal. If a portion of a reporting unit that constitutes a business is to be disposed of, goodwill associated with that business shall be included in the carrying amount in determining gain or loss on disposal. The amount of goodwill shall be based on the relative fair values of the business to be disposed of and the portion of the reporting unit to be retained.

(k) EFFECTIVE DATES AND TRANSITION FOR STATEMENTS 141 AND 142. Statement 141 is effective for all business combinations initiated after June 30, 2001. Use of the pooling-of-interests method for transactions initiated after June 30, 2001, is prohibited. Initiation is defined in paragraph 46 of Opinion 16 as:

> *A plan of combination is initiated on the earlier of (1) the date that the major terms of a plan, including the ratio of exchange of stock, are announced publicly or otherwise formally made known to the stockholders of any one of the combining companies or (2) the date that stockholders of a combining company are notified in writing of an exchange offer. Therefore, a plan of combination is often initiated even though consummation is subject to the approval of stockholders and others.*

Statement 141 applies to all business combinations accounted for by the purchase method for which the date of acquisition is July 1, 2001, or later. For combinations between two or more mutual enterprises, Statement 141 will not be effective until related interpretative guidance is issued.

For business combinations with acquisition dates before July 1, 2001, that were accounted for using the purchase method, the carrying amount of acquired intangible assets that do not meet the criteria in paragraph 39 of Statement 141 for recognition apart from goodwill (and any related deferred tax liabilities if the intangible asset amortization is not deductible for tax purposes) are reclassified as goodwill on the date at which Statement 142 is initially applied in its entirety. Also, the carrying amount of any recognized intangible assets that meet the recognition criteria in paragraph 39 of Statement 141 or any unidentifiable intangible assets recognized in accordance with paragraph 5 of FASB Statement No. 72, *Accounting for Certain Acquisitions of Banking or Thrift Institutions,* that have been included in the amount reported as goodwill (or as goodwill and intangible assets) are reclassified and accounted for as an asset apart from goodwill as of the date Statement 142 is initially applied in its entirety. Acquirers do not change the purchase price assigned to the assets acquired and liabilities assumed in a business combination for which the acquisition date was before July 1, 2001, except for these items.

On the earlier of the first day of the fiscal year beginning after December 15, 2001, or the date Statement 142 is initially applied in its entirety, any unamortized deferred credit related to an excess of fair value over cost arising from a business combination for which the acquisition date was before July 1, 2001, or an investment accounted for by the equity method acquired before July 1, 2001, is written off and recognized as a change in accounting principle. The effect, net of tax, is presented in the income statement between the captions *extraordinary items* and *net income.* The per-share information presented in the income statement should separately state the per-share effect.

Statement 142 should be applied in fiscal years beginning after December 15, 2001, to all goodwill and other intangible assets recognized in a statement of financial position at the beginning of that fiscal year, regardless of when those assets were initially recognized. Early application is permitted for fiscal years beginning after March 15, 2001, if the first interim financial statements have not been previously issued. In all situations, the provisions of Statement 142 must be initially applied at the beginning of a fiscal year. Retroactive application is not permitted.

Certain provisions of Statement 142 are applied to goodwill and other acquired intangible assets for which the acquisition date is after June 30, 2001, even if an entity has not adopted Statement 142 in its entirety. These are described in paragraphs 50 and 51 of Statement 142.

Statement 142 is not applied to previously recognized good-will and intangible assets acquired in a combination between two or more mutual enterprises, acquired in a combination between not-for-profit organizations, or arising from the acquisition of a for-profit business entity by a not-for-profit organization until interpretative guidance related to the application of the purchase method to those transactions is issued.

Goodwill acquired in a business combination with an acquisition date after June 30, 2001, is not amortized. An acquirer with a December 31, 2001, fiscal year-end would initially apply the provisions of Statement 142 on January 1, 2002. If an acquirer completed a business combination on October 15, 2001, that gave rise to goodwill, it would not amortize the goodwill acquired in that business combination even though it would continue to amortize until January 1, 2002, goodwill that arose from any business combination completed before July 1, 2001. Intangible assets other than goodwill acquired in a business combination or other transaction for which the date of acquisition is after June 30, 2001, are amortized or not amortized in accordance with paragraphs 11 to 14 and 16 of Statement 142.

Goodwill and intangible assets acquired with an acquisition date after June 30, 2001, but before the date that Statement 142 is applied in its entirety must be reviewed for impairment in accordance with Opinion 17 or Statement 121 (as appropriate) until the date that Statement 142 is applied in it entirety. The financial statement presentation and disclosure provisions of Statement 142 are not applied to those assets until Statement 142 is applied in its entirety.

In applying Statement 142 to intangible assets acquired if the acquisition date is on or before June 30, 2001, the useful lives of those previously recognized intangible assets must be reassessed using the guidance in paragraph 11, with remaining amortization periods adjusted prospectively. The reassessment must occur prior to the end of the first interim period of the fiscal year in which Statement 142 is initially applied. Previously recognized intangible assets determined to have indefinite useful lives must be tested for impairment as of the beginning of the fiscal year of applying Statement 142. Any resulting impairment loss is reported as a change in accounting principle and presented net of tax in the income statement between the captions *extraordinary items* and *net income.* The per-share information presented in the income statement should separately state the per-share effect.

When Statement 142 is initially applied, reporting units are determined based on the reporting structure at that date. Recognized net assets, excluding goodwill, are assigned to reporting units, and all goodwill recognized in the statement of financial position at the date Statement 142 is initially applied is assigned to one or more reporting units. The sources of previously recognized goodwill should be considered in the initial assignment as well as reporting units to which the related acquired net assets were assigned.

Goodwill of each reporting unit must be tested for impairment as of the beginning of the fiscal year in which Statement 142 is initially applied in its entirety, with six months allowed from the date of initial adoption of Statement 142 to complete the first step of that transitional goodwill impairment test. Amounts used in the transitional goodwill impairment test should be measured as of the beginning of the year of initial application. If the carrying amount of the net assets of a reporting unit (including goodwill) exceeds fair value of the reporting unit, the second step of the transitional goodwill impairment test must be completed as soon as possible, but no later than the end of the year of initial application.

Impairment losses recognized as a result of a transitional goodwill impairment test are accounted for as a change in accounting principle and presented separately, net of tax, in the income statement between the captions *extraordinary items* and *net income.* The per-share information presented in the income statement should state separately the per-share effect. A transitional impairment loss for goodwill should be recognized in the first interim period, irrespective of the period in which it is measured, consistent with paragraph 10 of FASB Statement No. 3, *Reporting Accounting Changes in Interim Financial Statements.* Financial information for interim periods of the fiscal year that precede the period in which the transitional goodwill impairment loss is measured should be restated to reflect the accounting change.

If there are indicators that goodwill might be impaired before completion of the transitional goodwill impairment test, goodwill must be tested when the impairment indicator arises. An impairment loss that does not result from a transitional impairment test should *not* be accounted for as a change in accounting principle. Also, it is necessary to perform the required annual goodwill impairment test in the year that Statement 142 is initially applied in its entirety, unless an entity designates the beginning of its fiscal year as the date for its annual goodwill impairment test.

Upon initial application of Statement 142, the portion of excess of cost over underlying equity in net assets of an investee accounted for by the equity method that is attributed to goodwill is no longer amortized. However, equity method goodwill is not tested for impairment in accordance with Statement 142.

10.5 INCOME TAX ACCOUNTING

(a) GENERAL.   Accounting for the effects of income taxes in purchase-method acquisitions is covered by FASB Statement 109, *Accounting for Income Taxes,* which was issued in 1992. Prior to the issuance in 1987 of FASB Statement 96, *Accounting for Income Taxes,* accounting for income taxes in purchase acquisitions had been governed by Opinion 16. Statement 96 significantly changed the approach of Opinion 16 with respect to income taxes, and Statement 109 essentially continues the new methods established in Statement 96.

(b) DEFERRED TAXES

(i) General.   Statement 109 requires that deferred taxes be established in a purchase-method allocation for tax effects of temporary differences between amounts to be used for financial reporting of assets and liabilities and their tax bases. That approach is quite different from previous accounting under Opinion 16, which required that tax effects of differences between book and tax bases be recognized as an adjustment of the fair market value of applicable individual assets and liabilities.

Statement 109 provides that deferred taxes are not established for book-tax differences for goodwill to the extent that goodwill is not deductible for tax purposes. Deferred taxes are also not established for negative goodwill that is recorded as a deferred credit to the extent it is not amortizable for tax purposes. Deferred taxes are also not established for leveraged leases acquired in a purchase acquisition.

Statement 109 also indicates that deferred taxes should not be discounted to present value from the date the tax effect is expected to be realized. Under Opinion 16, discounting of the tax effect was appropriate in determining the adjustment to be made to the fair market value of the applicable asset or liability.

(ii) Deferred Taxes in Goodwill Situations.   If the acquisition cost exceeds the fair value of net identifiable assets, Statement 109 requires use of the *gross* method of purchase price allocation. Under the gross method, purchase price is allocated in this way:

- Determine the fair market values of identifiable assets and liabilities.
- Identify temporary differences related to identifiable assets and liabilities.
- Determine and recognize deferred tax assets and liabilities for deductible and taxable temporary differences.
- Determine and recognize deferred tax assets for net operating loss and tax credit carryforwards.
- Determine and recognize a valuation allowance to reduce the value of deferred tax assets using the *more-likely-than-not* criterion of Statement 109.
- Recognize goodwill for the difference between the total purchase price and the sum of net fair values of identifiable assets and liabilities and the deferred taxes that have been determined, net of valuation allowance.

Computation of deferred taxes in a goodwill situation is illustrated as part of Exhibit 10.5.

(iii) Deferred Taxes in Negative Goodwill Situations.   Statement 109 requires that deferred taxes be established for temporary differences related to the allocation to long-term assets of an excess of fair values of net identifiable assets over total acquisition cost, commonly referred to as *negative goodwill*. To compute the amounts to be assigned to the long-term assets and the deferred taxes, it is necessary to use a simultaneous equation. The simultaneous equation, which follows, will apply to most acquisitions, although it may need modification if an acquiree has operations in more than one tax jurisdiction or if the acquirer's and acquiree's temporary differences, net operating loss carryforwards, tax credit carryforwards, and valuation allowances

interact so as to require modification to the simultaneous equation approach.

$$\text{Net temporary difference} \times \frac{\text{Tax rate}}{(1-\text{tax rate})} =$$

Adjustment to deferred tax assets and liabilities and noncurrent assets

If tax benefits are recognized as a result of interaction of the tax positions of an acquirer and an acquiree, goodwill is reduced in the allocation of acquisition cost. If goodwill is reduced to zero, then other long-term assets are reduced as described in section 10.5(b)(ii).

(c) POSTACQUISITION RECOGNITION OF NET OPERATING LOSS AND TAX CREDIT CARRYFORWARDS.

Some or all of the tax benefits of an acquiree's net operating loss or tax credit carryforwards may be recognized in accounting for an acquisition if the *more-likely-than-not* criterion is met at the acquisition date. The result is a reduction of goodwill in the allocation of acquisition cost. If the benefit is not recognized, subsequent recognition of the tax benefits of an acquiree's net operating loss or tax credit carryforwards should be accounted for in this way:

- Goodwill from the acquisition is reduced.
- If goodwill is completely eliminated, then other noncurrent intangible assets are reduced until fully eliminated.
- Any further tax benefits are recorded as a reduction of the provision for income taxes.

If tax benefits of an acquired company have been recognized at the acquisition date and it is later determined that a valuation allowance is needed for the applicable items, the establishment of the valuation allowance is recorded as an increase in the provision for income taxes. Retroactive increases to goodwill are not permitted.

If an acquired net operating loss or tax credit carryforward is utilized in a future period but is offset by a new temporary difference, *and* the tax benefit of the new temporary difference is in turn recognized in a future period, the benefit is viewed as attributable to the acquired net operating loss or tax credit carryforward. Goodwill is reduced, even though there was an intervening temporary difference that delayed the ultimate tax effect of the net operating loss or tax credit carryforward.

Applicable tax law should be followed in determining the order in which net operating loss and tax credit carryforwards are utilized. The order in which they are utilized has accounting significance because postacquisition realization of an acquirer's net operating loss or tax credit carryforwards is recorded as a reduction of the provision for income taxes. Realization of an acquiree's net operating loss or tax credit carryforwards is recorded as a reduction of goodwill. If applicable tax laws do not provide the order of utilization, then the utilization should be prorated based on the proportion of the acquirer's and acquiree's respective shares of the carryforwards utilized.

If a tax benefit from an excess of tax basis of an acquired asset over the amount assigned to the asset (excess tax basis) in a purchase-method allocation is not recognized in the acquisition accounting at acquisition date, subsequent recognition of that tax benefit is accounted for the same as a postacquisition recognition of an acquiree's net operating loss or tax credit carryforward, as described previously.

(d) GOODWILL.   In taxable acquisitions, sometimes an allocation to goodwill for accounting purposes relates partly to amounts allocated to another asset that for tax purposes are deductible through amortization or otherwise. In that situation, the other asset is viewed as having excess tax basis, resulting in a temporary difference. The tax benefit of the tax deduction attributable to that other asset is accounted for as purchased excess tax basis at either the acquisition date or after the acquisition date.

Temporary differences are not recognizable for goodwill for which deductions may not be taken for tax purposes. Likewise, temporary differences are not recognized for negative goodwill.

For taxing jurisdictions in which goodwill is deductible for taxes, book and tax goodwill is divided into two categories:

1. The lesser of book- or tax-deductible goodwill
2. The remainder of any book or tax goodwill

For category 1, goodwill, any basis difference (e.g., from different amortization amounts or write-downs) that arises in postacquisition periods is accounted for as a temporary difference.

For category 2, if tax-deductible goodwill exceeds book goodwill, there will be no category 2 book goodwill, and category 2 tax goodwill will be equal to the excess of tax-deductible goodwill over book goodwill. If book goodwill exceeds tax-deductible goodwill, there will be no category 2 tax goodwill, and category 2 book goodwill will be equal to the excess of book goodwill over tax-deductible goodwill. Deferred taxes are not recognized for category 2 goodwill. If category 2 goodwill consists of tax-deductible goodwill, when the benefits are realized, they are first recognized as a reduction of book goodwill, then as a reduction of other acquired noncurrent intangible assets, and last as a reduction of the provision for income taxes.

The Omnibus Budget Reconciliation Act of 1993 changed previous tax rules that did not allow deductions for goodwill. Now goodwill may be amortized over 15 years for tax purposes. How to account for the new aspect of tax-deductible goodwill from business combinations is described in EITF Issue 93-12, *Recognition and Measurement of the Tax Benefit of Excess Tax-Deductible Goodwill Resulting from a Retroactive Change in Tax Law.* Also of interest on this subject is the fact that one of the reasons indicated for not establishing deferred taxes related to goodwill in an acquisition was that goodwill, by its nature, was not tax deductible. Even though goodwill can be deductible under the law, deferred taxes should not be established and goodwill increased as an ultimate balancing amount if goodwill will not be deductible because the inside tax basis of an acquired corporation is not changed in the acquisition.

(e) AGGRESSIVE TAX POSITIONS. Deferred taxes established at the date of an acquisition should be determined using management's estimate of tax positions that will be ultimately accepted by tax authorities, notwithstanding the fact that more aggressive positions may be reported on tax returns.

The same approach should be used in determining deferred taxes in postacquisition periods. Changes to management's estimate or final resolution by closing of tax years should be accounted for first by adjusting goodwill, then by adjusting other acquired noncurrent intangible assets, and finally by adjusting the provision for income taxes.

(f) MISCELLANEOUS.

(i) Identifiable Intangibles. Deferred taxes are established for all identifiable intangible assets, both at the acquisition date and for postacquisition temporary differences.

(ii) LIFO Inventories.   A difference between the book and tax basis of LIFO inventories is a temporary difference and should be included in the computation of deferred taxes at the acquisition date.

(iii) Tax Rates.   Under Statement 109, enacted tax rates should be used in computing deferred taxes at the acquisition date even if rate changes are anticipated. Postacquisition rate changes would result in changes to the deferred tax balances, which would be reported as an adjustment of the provision for income taxes.

(g) EFFECTS OF CONSOLIDATED TAX IMPLICATIONS.   If an acquired company will be included in the acquirer's consolidated tax return, deferred taxes attributable to the acquisition are determined based on the consolidated tax position after the acquisition using the *more-likely-than-not* criterion. The interaction of an acquirer's and acquiree's temporary differences, net operating loss carryforwards, and tax credit carryforwards can result in the elimination of a valuation allowance for deferred tax assets that would have been required without the acquisition. Filing a consolidated return may qualify as a *tax strategy* that enables the realization of tax benefits.

In determining whether the *more-likely-than-not* criterion is met, consideration should be given to the rules related to separate return limitation year (SRLY) restrictions, limitations on built-in gains, and limitations on usage of net operating loss and tax credit carryforwards.

10.6 RECORD KEEPING FOR PURCHASE ACCOUNTING ACQUISITIONS

If the stock of a company has been purchased, two approaches for the record-keeping aspects of the revaluations required by purchase accounting are:

1. The accounting records of the acquired company are left the same as prior to the acquisition, and the revaluations and related effects on future income and expenses are recorded as consolidation adjustments.
2. The revaluations are recorded directly in the accounts of the acquired company to establish a new basis of accounting.

The term "push-down accounting" refers to preparing separate postacquisition financial statements of the acquired entity that include the purchase accounting adjustments arising from the acquisition. The first approach can be used if separate financial statements of the acquired company are prepared using historical amounts. However, the books of an acquirer can be kept on a historical basis, and financial statements of the acquiree can be prepared using push-down accounting by adjusting the acquiree's historical general ledger balances for purchase accounting adjustments on a worksheet basis and then using the adjusted amounts in preparing the financial statements. The second approach takes the effects of push-down accounting and records them in the books of the acquired company and may be sensible to use only if historical financial statements of the acquired company are not needed.

Also, in deciding whether to push the purchase accounting adjustments into an acquiree's primary books, an acquirer should consider whether historical amounts will be needed for preparation of tax returns. If the acquisition has not resulted in a change to the *inside basis* of the acquired company for tax purposes or if there is a continuing minority interest, the author recommends using historical balances in the books and worksheet adjustments in preparing separate financial statements of the acquired company if push-down accounting financial statements are to be prepared.

10.7 FINANCIAL REPORTING OF A PURCHASE ACQUISITION

An acquirer includes the assets, liabilities, and results of operations of an acquired company in its financial statements, from the date of acquisition. Notes to the acquirer's financial statements should include these disclosures, required by Opinion 16, paragraph 95, for the period in which an acquisition accounted for by the purchase method is completed:

- Name and a brief description of the acquired company
- Method of accounting for the combination—that is, by the purchase method
- Period for which results of the acquired company's operations are included in the income statement of the acquiring corporation
- Cost of the acquired company and, if applicable, the number of stock shares issued or issuable and the amount assigned to the issued and issuable shares

- Description of the plan for amortization of acquired goodwill, the amortization method, and the period
- Contingent payments, options, or commitments specified in the acquisition agreement and their proposed accounting treatment

Opinion 16, paragraph 96, as amended by FASB Statement 79, *Elimination of Certain Disclosures for Business Combinations Accounted for by the Purchase Method,* requires that if an acquirer is a publicly held company, notes to the financial statements for the period in which a purchase-method acquisition occurs must also include, as supplemental pro forma information:

- Results of operations for the current period as if the companies had combined at the beginning of the period, unless the acquisition was at or near the beginning of the period
- Results of operations for the period immediately preceding, as if the companies had combined at the beginning of that period if comparable financial statements are presented

The pro forma information must be presented for the period of combination and the period immediately preceding. Information required includes revenues, income before extraordinary items, net income, and earnings per share. In computing the pro forma results, purchase accounting adjustments should be assumed to have taken place at the beginning of the period prior to the acquisition. The pro forma amounts should include any required changes to interest, income taxes, preferred stock dividends, depreciation, and amortization.

Exhibit 10.4 illustrates disclosure of a purchase-method acquisition in notes to a publicly held acquirer's financial statements.

The preceding disclosures are required by Opinion 16. Statement 141 adds certain other disclosure requirements, including primary reasons for an acquisition, such as a description of the factors that contributed to a purchase price that results in recognition of goodwill; the basis for assigning amounts to equity interests issued or issuable; a condensed balance sheet disclosing the amount assigned to each major asset and liability caption of the acquired entity at the acquisition date; the amount of purchased R&D assets acquired and written off in the period and the line item in the income statement in which the amounts written off are included; and for any purchase price allocation that has

NOTE 5. Acquisition of Company B

On June 1, XXX7, the Company A acquired all the stock of Company B, a manufacturer of automotive acessories, for $12 million in cash. The acquisition has been accounted for as a purhase, and the net assets and results of operations of Company B have been included in the consolidated financial statements since the acquisition date. The excess of cost over net assets acquired amounted to $670,000 and is being amortized over 40 years. Following are unaudited pro-forma consolidated results of operations assuming the acquisition had occurred on January 1, XXX6, including the effects of all significant adjustments related to the acquisition. Interest expense has been assumed from January 1, XXX6, on $5 million of 12% subordinated debentures issued by Company A on May 1, XXX7, to obtain funds for the acquisition.

	XXX7	XXX6
Net sales	$84,500,000	$77,600,000
Net income	6,750,000	6,200,000
Net income per common share	1.93	1.77

EXHIBIT 10.4 ILLUSTRATION OF A FOOTNOTE FOR A PURCHASE-METHOD ACQUISITION

not been finalized, that fact and the reasons why. In subsequent periods, the nature and amount of any material adjustments made to the initial allocation of the purchase price should be disclosed.

Statement 142 also adds new disclosures for purchased intangible assets and goodwill. These require that the notes to the financial statements disclose the next information for the period in which a material business combination is completed if the amounts assigned to goodwill or to other intangible assets are significant in relation to the total cost of the acquired entity:

- For intangible assets subject to amortization
  - The total amount assigned and the amount assigned to any major intangible asset class
  - The amount of any significant residual value, in total and by major intangible asset class
  - The weighted-average amortization period, in total and by major intangible asset class
- For intangible assets *not* subject to amortization, the total amount assigned and the amount assigned to any major intangible asset class

- For goodwill:
  - The total amount of goodwill and the amount that is expected to be deductible for tax purposes
  - The amount of goodwill by reportable segment (if the combined entity is required to disclose segment information in accordance with FASB Statement No. 131, *Disclosures about Segments of an Enterprise and Related Information*), unless not practicable

Statement 141 also requires that in the period in which an extraordinary gain is recognized under the new rules, the notes to the financial statements should provide the information required by paragraph 11 of Opinion 30.

If a business combination occurs after the balance sheet date but prior to issuance of the financial statements, these disclosures should be provided in the footnotes if a material business combination is completed after the balance sheet date (unless not practicable).

Goodwill is recognized only after allocation of cost to other intangible assets. Appendix A of Statement 141 provides an illustrative list of intangible assets that may exist apart from goodwill. They are detailed in Exhibit 10.5.

Marketing-related intangible assets
1. Trademarks, trade names*
2. Service marks, collective marks, certification marks*
3. Trade dress (unique color, shape, or package design)*
4. Newspaper mastheads*
5. Internet domain names*
6. Noncompetition agreements*

Customer-related intangible assets
1. Customer lists†
2. Order or production backlog*
3. Customer contracts and related customer relationships*
4. Noncontractual customer relationships†

EXHIBIT 10.5   INTANGIBLE ASSETS OTHER THAN GOODWILL (PER STATEMENT 141)

Artistic-related intangible assets
  1. Plays, operas, ballets*
  2. Books, magazines, newspapers, other literary works*
  3. Musical works such as compositions, song lyrics, advertising jingles*
  4. Pictures, photographs*
  5. Video and audiovisual material, including motion pictures, music videos, television programs*

Contract-based intangible assets
  1. Licensing, royalty, standstill agreements*
  2. Advertising, construction, management, service or supply contracts*
  3. Lease agreements*
  4. Construction permits*
  5. Franchise agreements*
  6. Operating and broadcast rights*
  7. Use rights such as drilling, water, air, mineral, timber cutting, and route authorities*
  8. Servicing contracts such as mortgage servicing contracts*
  9. Employment contracts*

Technology-based intangible assets
  1. Patented technology*
  2. Computer software and mask works*
  3. Unpatented technology†
  4. Databases, including title plants†
  5. Trade secrets, such as secret formulas, processes, recipes

Exhibit 10.5 (*continued*)
*Meets the contractual or legal criterion.
†Does not meet the contractual or legal criterion but does meet the separability criterion.

10.8 ILLUSTRATIONS OF PURCHASE ACCOUNTING

(a) POSITIVE GOODWILL SITUATION.   Exhibit 10.6 illustrates purchase accounting in a positive goodwill situation.

(b) NEGATIVE GOODWILL SITUATION.   Exhibit 10.7 illustrates the computation of deferred taxes and amounts to assign to long-term assets in a negative goodwill situation.

Company A acquired all the stock of Company B for $12.3 million cash. Company A also incurred other related costs of $200,000, resulting in a total acquisition cost of $12.5 million. For tax purposes, the basis of assets and liabilities of Company B is carried over but for accounting purposes, the assets must be revalued using the purchase accounting method. The balance sheets of Company B for book and tax purposes at the date of acquisition follow. Independent appraisals indicated fair values of identifiable assets as: fixed assets, $10 million; other assets (including trademarks and patents), $1 million. Inventories are valued at $3 million in accordance with purchase accounting. Assume a combined U.S. federal and state tax rate of 37%. A discount rate of 8% is considered appropriate for present value computations.

	HISTORICAL COMPANY B BOOK VALUE	TAX BASIS
Cash and receivables	$1,000,000	$1,000,000
Inventory	2,500,000	2,500,000
Fixed assets	5,000,000	2,500,000
Other assets	600,000	300,000
	$9,100,000	$6,300,000
Current liabilities	$1,200,000	$1,200,000
Deferred taxes	1,000,000	
Long-term debt	2,000,000	2,000,000
Stockholders' equity	4,900,000	3,100,000
	$9,100,000	$6,300,000

	HISTORICAL COMPANY B BOOK VALUE	FAIR MARKET VALUE OF IDENTIFIABLES	PURCHASE ACCOUNTING ADJUSTMENT	ACQUISITION COST
Cash and receivables	$1,000,000	$ 1,000,000		$ 1,000,000
Inventory	2,500,000	3,000,000	$500,000[a]	3,000,000
Fixed assets	5,000,000	10,000,000	5,000,000[b]	10,000,000
Other assets	600,000	1,000,000	400,000[f]	1,000,000
Good will			3,120,000[d]	3,120,000
	$9,100,000	$15,000,000	$9,020,000	$18,120,000
Current liabilities	$1,200,000	$1,200,000		$1,200,000
Unfavorable lease		200,000	200,000[e]	200,000
Deferred taxes	1,000,000		1,220,000[f]	2,220,000
Long-term debt	2,000,000	2,000,000		2,000,000
Stockholders' equity	4,900,000	11,600,000	7,600,000[g]	12,500,000
	$9,100,000	$15,000,000	$9,020,000	$18,120,000

EXHIBIT 10.6 ILLUSTRATION OF PURCHASE ACCOUNTING IN A POSITIVE GOODWILL SITUATION

Purchase Accounting Adjustments:

[a]Inventory:

Fair market value including seller's profit	$3,000,000
Historical book value	2,500,00
Purchase accounting adjustment	$ 500,000

[b]Fixed assets:

Appraised value of fixed assets	$10,000,000
Historical book value	5,000,000
Purchase accounting adjustment	$5,000,000

[c]Other assets:

	TRADEMARKS	MISCELLANEOUS	TOTAL
Appraised value	$400,000	$ 600,000	1,000,000
Historical book value	—	600,000	600,000
Purchase accounting adjustment	$400,000	—	$400,000

[d]Goodwill is the amount needed to balance the purchase accounting adjustments

[e]Unfavorable lease:

Present value (8% discount) of excess of future lease obligations over market value	$200,000

[f]Deferred taxes:

	ACQUISITION COST ALLOCATION	TAX BASIS	TEMPORARY DIFFERENCE	DEFERRED TAX (37%)
Inventory	$3,000,000	$2,500,000	$ (500,000)	$ (185,000)
Fixed assets	10,000,000	5,000,000	(5,000,000)	(1,850,000)
Other assets	1,000,000	300,000	(700,000)	(259,000)
Unfavorable lease	(200,000)		200,000	74,000
			$(6,000,000)	(2,220,000)
Historical deferred tax balance				(1,000,000)
Purchase accounting adjustment				$(1,220,000)

[g]Equity:

Acquisition cost	$12,500,000
Historical equity of Company B	4,900,00
Purchase accounting adjustment	$7,600,000

EXHIBIT 10.6 (*continued*)

Company A acquired all of Company B's stock for $7.3 million cash. Company A also incurred other related costs of $200,000, resulting in a total acquisition cost of $7.5 million. For tax purposes, the basis of assets and liabilities of Company B is carried over, but for accounting purposes, the assets must be revalued using the purchase accounting method. Company B's balance sheet for book and tax purposes at the date of acquisition follow. Independent appraisals indicated fair values of identifiable assets as: fixed assets, $10 million; other assests (including trademarks and patents), $1 million. Inventories are valued at $3 million in accordance with purchase accounting. Assume a combined U.S. federal and state tax rate of 37%. A discount rate of 8% is considered appropriate for present value computations.

	HISTORICAL COMPANY B BOOK VALUE	TAX BASIS
Cash and receivables	$1,000,000	$1,000,000
Inventory	2,500,000	2,500,000
Fixed assets	5,000,000	2,500,000
Other assets	600,000	300,000
	$9,100,000	$6,300,000
Current liabilities	$1,200,000	$1,200,000
Deferred taxes	1,000,000	
Long-term debt	2,000,000	2,000,000
Stockholders' equity	4,900,000	3,100,000
	$9,100,000	$6,300,000

	HISTORICAL COMPANY B BOOK VALUE	FAIR MARKET VALUE OF IDENTIFIABLES	PURCHASE ACCOUNTING ADJUSTMENT	PURCHASE PRICE ALLOCATION
Cash and receivables	$1,000,000	$ 1,000,000		$ 1,000,000
Inventory	2,500,000	3,000,000	$500,000[a]	3,000,000
Fixed assets	5,000,000	10,000,000	3,622,000[b]	8,622,000
Other assets	600,000	1,000,000	262,000[b]	862,000
	$9,100,000	$15,000,000	$4,384,000	$13,484,000
Current liabilities	$1,200,000	$1,200,000		$1,200,000
Unfavorable lease		200,000	$200,000[c]	200,000
Deferred taxes:				
Current			111,000[d]	111,000
Long-term	1,000,000		1,473,000[b]	2,473,000
Long-term debt	2,000,000	2,000,000		2,000,000
Stockholders' equity	4,900,000	11,600,000	2,600,000[a]	7,500,000
	$9,100,000	$15,000,000	$4,384,000	$13,484,000

EXHIBIT 10.7   ILLUSTRATION OF PURCHASE ACCOUNTING IN A NEGATIVE GOODWILL SITUATION

Purchase Accounting Adjustments:

[a]Inventory:

Fair market value including seller's profit	$3,000,000
Historical book value	2,500,000
Purchase accounting adjustment	$ 500,000

[b]Purchase accounting adjustments for long-term assets and related deferred taxes:

	TOTAL	FIXED ASSETS	OTHER ASSETS
Acquisition cost	$ 7,500,000		
Tax basis	3,100,000		
Temporary differences before adjustment	4,400,000		
Factor (see calculation below)	.5873		
Total adjustment	$ 2,584,000		
Fair value of identifiable net assets (not intended to foot across)	$11,600,000	$10,000,000	$1,000,000
Total acquisition cost	7,500,000		
Unadjusted negative goodwill	$ 4,100,000	3,727,000)	(373,000)
Unadjusted acquisition cost allocation (to fixed assets and other assets only)	$ 6,900,000	6,273,000	627,000
Adjustment	2,584,000	2,349,000	235,000
Adjusted acquisition cost allocation	9,484,000	8,622,000	862,000
Historical book value	5,600,000	(5,000,000)	(600,000)
Purchase accounting adjustment	$ 3,884,000	$ 3,622,000	262,000
Adjusted acquisition cost allocation	$ 9,484,000	$ 8,622,000	$ 862,000
Tax basis	2,800,000	2,500,000	300,000
Temporary difference	$ 6,684,000	$ 6,122,000	$ 562,000
Deferred taxes at 37%	$ 2,473,000	$ 2,265,000	$ 208,000
Less, historical deferred taxes	(1,000,000)		
Purchase accounting adjustment	$ 1,473,000		

Calculation of adjustment factor:

$$\frac{37}{(1-.37)} = .5873$$

Cross-check by application of complete simultaneous equation:

$$\text{Net temporary difference} \times \frac{\text{Tax rate}}{(1-\text{tax rate})} =$$

Adjustment to deferred tax assets and liabilities and noncurrent assets

$$\$4,400,000 \times \frac{37}{(1-.37)} = \$2,584,000$$

EXHIBIT 10.7　(*continued*)

CHAPTER 11

SECURITIES AND EXCHANGE COMMISSION AND OTHER REGULATORY REQUIREMENTS

The author would like to thank Robert J. Puls, who wrote the version of this chapter that appeared in the last edition.

11.1 OVERVIEW OF REGULATORY ENVIRONMENT

In the United States, various regulatory bodies have jurisdiction over mergers, acquisitions, and other forms of business combinations, depending on the specifics of the transaction. The determination of what laws and requirements apply is a complex legal matter and must be considered carefully in each and every situation. Some of the more critical requirements are listed next.

- If securities are to be issued or exchanged for public companies, registration statements may need to be filed with the Securities and Exchange Commission (SEC). Also, a proxy statement must be prepared if shareholders need to vote on a possible acquisition or merger. Even if no securities are exchanged, a Form 8-K current report may be required to be filed. Further, certain filings are required if a tender offer is made to acquire shares of another company.
- If public shares are issued or issuable in an acquisition or merger, a stock listing application usually would have to be filed with the stock exchange on which the company is listed.

- If certain conditions are met, contemplated mergers and acquisitions must be reported to the Federal Trade Commission and the U.S. Department of Justice prior to consummation. Further, the parties to the transaction must wait at least 30 days after reporting before completing the transaction to allow these organizations to consider the related antitrust implications.

The primary objective of this chapter is to provide the reader with a general awareness of the major regulatory requirements related to mergers or acquisitions. It is not intended to provide a comprehensive treatment or a complete presentation of the form or content of the various filings and regulations referred to.

11.2 SECURITIES LAW REQUIREMENTS UPON MERGER OR ACQUISITION

(a) PRIMARY FILING REQUIREMENTS. Various filings with the SEC can be required if a public company engages in a merger, acquisition, or other form of business combination. The primary filings under both the Securities Act of 1933 (the 1933 Act) and the Securities Exchange Act of 1934 (the 1934 Act) are listed next.

- A 1933 Act registration statement on Form S-1 or Form S-4. Either of these forms may be used to register securities offered in exchange for the securities of a *target* company. Form S-4 may also be used when a vote is required—either by the security holders of the acquiring company or by those of the target company, or both—and a proxy statement is supplied in connection with the solicitation of proxies.
- A proxy statement under Regulation 14A of the 1934 Act.
- A current report (Form 8-K) under the 1934 Act.

In addition, if a company's securities are listed on a national securities exchange, a stock listing application usually would have to be filed for any securities issued or issuable in the transaction.

(b) PRIVATE SALE EXEMPTIONS. In some situations, a company may be relieved of the registration requirements of the 1933 Act through Rule 144A if an acquisition does not involve a public offering. The most important factors to assess in determining whether an acquisition involves a public offering are size of the offer (i.e., the number of offerees), the offerees' relationship to the issuer, and whether the offerees will make a secondary distribution of the securities.

(i) Size of Offer.   Although not in itself determinative, the SEC has in many cases agreed that, under ordinary circumstances, an offering to less than 35 persons presumably does not involve a public offering.

(ii) Relationship to Issuer.   The relationship of offerees to an issuer has taken on greater importance since the Supreme Court decided that the basic test of the availability of the private sale exemption was "whether the particular class of persons affected needs the protection of the 1933 Act." In other words, if the offerees of the company to be acquired, because of their relationship as officers, directors, controlling stockholders, or the like, have access to the same type of information that would be available in a 1933 Act registration statement, they need not be regarded as members of the investing public.

(iii) Secondary Distribution.   Equally important is whether an offeree who is to receive the securities will make a secondary distribution of them, thereby falling within the 1933 Act definition of a *statutory underwriter.* If that is the case, the private sale exemption would be unavailable to the issuer. To protect against this, the issuer should obtain from each offeree an *investment letter* in which the offeree represents that he or she is purchasing the securities for investment and not for redistribution. However, although the issuer requests investment letters in a transaction, the courts have made it clear that such letters are of little value to the issuer if they are not adhered to. Some methods that may be used to guard against the possibility of a subsequent sale of the securities nullifying the exemption are:

- Require registration of the securities by the issuer if the offeree wants to make a public offering
- Provide for restrictions on transfer of the securities, such as stamping the face of the securities as unregistered or requiring that the transfer agent not transfer them without instructions from the issuer

(c) FORM S-1 FILINGS.   If Form S-1 is used in an *exchange offer,* potential investors (i.e., offerees) must be provided with sufficient information regarding both companies to enable them to arrive at an informed decision.

The most important requirement of Form S-1 is General Instruction III, which reads:

> *If any of the securities being registered are to be offered in exchange for securities of any other issuer, the prospectus shall also include the information which would be required by Item 11 if the securities of such other issuer were being registered on this Form. There shall also be included the information concerning such securities of such other issuer which would be called for by Item 9 if such securities were being registered. In connection with this instruction, reference is made to Rule 409.*

This means that, in registering securities to be offered in an exchange or other form of acquisition, the financial statement requirements of the company to be acquired are the same as those of the registrant. However, in some circumstances, management of the target may not cooperate in supplying all of the necessary information, such as if management does not approve of the offer. In those situations, an issuer can rely on rule 409 and include in the registration statement only information about the target that is available from public sources, such as annual reports to stockholders and other SEC filings. If a company is to avail itself of this rule, copies of correspondence between the two companies evidencing the request for and the refusal to furnish the necessary financial information must be provided to the SEC.

(d) FORM S-4 FILINGS. Form S-4 was developed to further simplify the 1933 Act registration of securities to be issued in a merger or acquisition. Since, in most situations, a shareholder vote is required for approval of the transaction, Form S-4 is designed to permit use of a proxy statement for the prospectus portion of the registration statement, eliminating the duplication of disclosures otherwise necessary in both a proxy statement and a separate 1933 Act registration statement.

Nonetheless, both a proxy statement and any 1933 Act form that a registrant might be eligible to use in a business combination transaction require a significant level of disclosure for all parties involved in the merger or acquisition.

11.3 SOLICITATION AND PREPARATION OF PROXIES

(a) **GENERAL.**   The SEC regulations do not require the solicitation of proxies but do govern procedures for their solicitation through Regulation 14A of the 1934 Act. This regulation sets forth requirements for form and content of a proxy if it is determined that one is required. A proxy can be required by:

- Statutory provisions of the jurisdiction under which a corporation is organized
- Regulations of the stock exchange on which the company's shares are listed
- The company's bylaws
- Provisions contained in a company's certificate of incorporation or similar controlling instruments

Both the New York and the American Stock Exchanges require that shareholder approval be obtained through a proxy solicitation if a business is acquired from an *insider* or if the number of shares to be issued in the acquisition or the market value thereof would exceed 20% of the respective amounts related to presently outstanding shares.

Even though companies may not be required to obtain stockholder approval for a merger or acquisition, they sometimes obtain such approval to avoid potential legal difficulties and criticism in the future.

(b) **INFORMATION INCLUDED IN PROXY STATEMENTS.**   As mentioned, information to be included in a proxy statement relating to acquisitions and mergers is governed by Item 14 of Regulation 14A, which requires:

- *Summary term sheet.* In bullet form, list a brief description of the most significant terms of the proposed transaction.
- *Contact information.* Provide name, address, and phone number of the principal executive offices.
- *Business conducted.* Give a brief description of the general nature of the business.
- *Terms of the transaction:*
  - Brief description of it
  - Consideration offered

- ○ Reasons for the transaction
- ○ Vote required
- ○ Any material differences in rights of security holders
- ○ Accounting treatment, if material
- ○ Tax consequences, if material

- *Regulatory Approvals.* Detail whether any regulatory requirements must be complied with or approvals obtained (if so, the status of such).
- *Reports, Opinions, and Appraisals.* If any obtained, material to the transaction and referred to in the proxy statement. Furnish the information required by Item 1015(b) of Regulation M-A.
- *Past Contacts, Transactions, or Negotiations.* If applicable, provide the information required by Items 1005(b) and 1011(a)(1) of Regulation M-A during the periods for which financial statements are presented or incorporated.
- *Selected Financial and Pro Forma Data.* Provide information as required by Item 301 of Regulation S-K.

As previously discussed, if an acquiring company cannot obtain all the required information from the target, it may rely on Rule 409 and provide whatever it is able to obtain.

11.4 TENDER OFFERS

(a) GENERAL. A tender offer is an active and widespread solicitation of public shareholders for the shares of a company. While there is currently no exact definition of what constitutes a tender offer, the next six characteristics are common.

1. The solicitation is made for a substantial percentage of the company's stock.
2. The offer is made at a premium over the prevailing market price.
3. Terms of offer are firm rather than negotiable.
4. The offer is contingent on receipt of a fixed number of shares and often is subject to a maximum.
5. The offer is open for a limited period of time.
6. The offeree is subjected to pressure to sell his or her stock.

Tender offers fall into two general types:

1. Those made by a company to purchase its own securities
2. Those made by unrelated third parties

Special disclosure requirements pertain to tender offers to acquire shares of public companies if certain conditions are met. The specific rules regulating tender offers are dependent on the type of offer. Some general guidelines and basic disclosure requirements of certain types are discussed next.

In 1999, the SEC adopted comprehensive revisions to the rules and regulations applicable to takeover transactions, including tender offers, mergers, and/or acquisitions. These revisions:

- Relax restrictions on communications with security holders by permitting the distribution of more information on a timely basis.
- Balance the treatment of stock and cash tender offers.
- Simplify and integrate the various disclosure requirements in a new series of rules within Regulation S-K, called Regulation M-A.
- Combine the existing schedules for tender offers into one schedule, titled Schedule TO.
- Require a plain English summary term sheet in all such transactions.
- Update the financial statement requirements for such transactions.
- Permit an optional subsequent offering period after completion of a tender, during which shares can be tendered without withdrawal rights.
- Clarify Rule 13-e1, which requires issuers to report intended repurchases of their own securities once a third-party tender has commenced.
- Conform security holder list requirements in tender offers with proxy rules.
- Clarify Rule 10b-13, which prohibits purchases outside a tender offer, and redesignates it Rule 14e-5.

(b) PURCHASE OF OWN SECURITIES.   Section 13(e) of the 1934 Act contains the rules regulating purchases or tender offers by a company for its own equity securities. These rules also apply when an affiliate makes the purchase or tender. An *affiliate* is a person or entity that, directly or indirectly through one or more intermediaries, controls, is controlled by, or is under common control with such company. Section 13(e) covers three types of transactions:

1. Purchases of securities by a company during a third-party tender offer
2. *Going-private* transactions
3. Other cash tender and exchange offers

Section 13(e) also specifies disclosures required to be disseminated to security holders for each of these transactions. Additionally, if the tender offer involves the solicitation of a proxy or distribution of an information statement, the transaction would also be subject to either Regulation 14A or Regulation 14C of the 1934 Act.

Regulation M-A incorporates all the current disclosure requirements for the company and third-party offers and going-private transactions.

(i) Purchase during a Third-Party Tender Offer.   Once a company has received notice of a third-party tender offer filed with the SEC, it can purchase its own securities during the period of the tender only if a *disclosure document* has been filed with the SEC that contains information regarding the nature of the securities, the purpose of the purchase, the source and amount of funds used or to be used in making the purchase, and so on (no specific form or schedule must be filed).

(ii) Other Self-Tenders.   A company that makes a tender offer for its own securities for any other purpose is subject to Rule 13e-4. For this catchall, Schedule TO must be filed with the SEC disclosing information regarding the security, the source and amount of funds or other consideration, the purpose of the tender offer and plans or proposals of the company or affiliate, and other similar information.

In addition, a company making the tender must also disclose:

- The scheduled termination date of the tender offer and whether it may be extended
- Withdrawal rights of persons who tender their shares

- If the tender offer is for less than all the securities of a class, the exact dates of the period during which securities will be accepted on a pro rata basis and the company's intentions if the offer is oversubscribed

(iii) Financial Statement Requirements.   Schedules 13E-3 and TO each require five financial information disclosures concerning the issuing company (any information that has been included in a document previously filed with the SEC may be incorporated by reference):

1. Audited financial statements for the two fiscal years required to be filed with the company's most recent annual report
2. Unaudited balance sheets and comparative year-to-date income statements and statements of cash flows required to be included in the company's most recent quarterly report
3. Ratio of earnings to fixed charges for the two most recent fiscal years and the interim periods provided under item 2
4. Book value per share as of the date of the latest balance sheet provided
5. Pro forma data, if material, disclosing the effect of the transaction on:
   - The company's balance sheet as of the date of the most recent balance sheet provided
   - The company's statement of income, earnings per share, and ratio of earnings in fixed charges for the most recent fiscal year and the late interim period provided under item 2
   - The company's book value per share as of the date of the most recent balance sheet provided

(c) THIRD-PARTY TENDER OFFERS.   Third-party tender offers are one of the most common methods used to acquire control of a target company in a takeover attempt. These offers are subject to SEC requirements (Section 14(d) of the 1934 Act) whenever the bidder, upon consummation of the tender offer, would be the beneficial owner of more than 5% of the security of the target.

(i) Tender Offer Commencement.   A tender offer generally is deemed to commence when a bidder makes a public announcement through a press release, newspaper advertisement, or public statement or when such information is sent or given by the bidder to the security holders of the target company. The information required to be included in the announcement or advertisement is dependent on the type of offer.

If it meets the 5% rule discussed previously, the bidder is required to file Schedule TO with the SEC as soon as practicable after commencement of the offer and is also required to deliver a copy of it to:

- The subject company's principal executive office
- Any other bidder that has filed a Schedule TO
- Each national securities exchange on which the security is registered and the National Association of Securities Dealers (NASD), if applicable

Schedule TO requires disclosure of the security and subject company, source and amount of funds or other consideration, purpose of the tender offer, plans or proposals of the bidder, and so forth.

(ii) Financial Statements of Certain Bidders.   If a bidder is other than a natural person and its financial condition is material to an investment decision, current adequate financial information of the bidder is required.

The financial condition of the bidder is usually considered material if a security holder of the target company receives a security of the bidder as part of the tender offer consideration. If a security of the bidder is part of the consideration, a 1933 Act registration statement must be filed by the bidder. Financial statements are not considered material when:

- The consideration offered consists entirely of cash
- The offer is not subject to any financing conditions and either:
    - The bidder is a public reporting entity under Sections 13(a) or 15(d) of the 1934 Act that files reports on EDGAR or
    - The offer is for all outstanding securities of the subject class

The financial statements required to be included are determined by the nature of the bidder. Generally, financial statements prepared in compliance with Form 10 are appropriate for a domestic bidder and financial statements prepared in accordance with Item 17 of Form 20F are appropriate for a foreign bidder. If the bidder is subject to the periodic reporting requirements of the 1934 Act, the financial statements may be incorporated by reference.

11.5 SEC FINANCIAL REPORTING REQUIREMENTS

(a) HISTORICAL FINANCIAL STATEMENTS OF REGISTRANTS.   For filings related to business combinations, Form S-1, Form S-4, and proxy statements must include or incorporate by reference the registrant's financial statements and supplementary financial information required by Regulation S-X. These principally are audited balance sheets as of the end of each of the two most recent fiscal years and audited statements of income and changes in cash flow for each of the three fiscal years preceding the date of the most recent audited balance sheet.

Depending on the date of the filing, interim financial statements may also be required. These interim statements need not be audited.

(b) HISTORICAL FINANCIAL STATEMENTS OF ACQUIRED ENTITIES.
Audited financial statements of a business acquired or to be acquired (if probable) are required if either the combination is accounted for as a purchase (including an investment to be accounted for by the equity method), or the combination is to be accounted for as a pooling. Note that Financial Accounting Standards Board (FASB) Statement 141, *Business Combinations,* eliminated pooling-of-interests accounting for transactions initiated after June 30, 2001. In recognition that acquisitions come in all sizes, Rule 3-05 utilizes a sliding scale to determine the period(s) for which financial statements are required. Regardless of significance, audited financial statements of a business to be acquired must be furnished if securities are being registered (e.g., on Form S-4) in connection with the acquisition of *that* business.

The SEC's requirements for financial statements of businesses acquired or to be acquired are set forth in Rule 3-05 of Regulation S-X. Its requirements for pro forma financial information are included in Article 11 of Regulation S-X. The SEC's interpretive views on such statements are included at Financial Reporting Releases (FRR) Section 506.

In the SEC's integrated disclosure system, Form 8-K is intended to provide investors with timely information, including that of businesses acquired. The inability to provide the financial statements or pro forma information within the required time period (generally 15 days, although an automatic 60-day extension to file is provided for) can limit current access to the securities markets.

In Release No. 33–7355, the SEC adopted amendments to its disclosure rules regarding significant business acquisitions, which will eliminate, in most circumstances, the requirement to include in Securities Act registration statements audited financial statements for probable business acquisitions or for business acquisitions that were consummated 74 or fewer days before a registered offering of securities. However, financial statements of probable and recently consummated business acquisitions will continue to be required if the acquisition is significant above the 50% level, using the tests that have been previously established (see section 11.5(d)).

(c) PROBABLE ACQUISITIONS. The SEC guidance regarding probable acquisitions states that "consummation of a transaction is considered to be probable whenever the registrant's financial statements alone would not provide investors with adequate financial information with which to make an investment decision." The SEC has not attempted to provide definitive guidance as to when consummation is deemed probable because of the many variables involved. Each situation must be evaluated based on the specific facts and circumstances.

(d) PERIODS TO BE PRESENTED. Except as discussed in the following text, the sliding scale test determines the number of years audited annual financial statements must be furnished for a business acquired or to be acquired. When audited annual statements are presented, unaudited interim financial statements must also be furnished (Rules 3-01 and 3-02).

If securities are being registered on Forms S-4 or F-4 to be offered to the security holders of the business to be acquired (an exchange offer) or an acquisition/merger proxy statement is being prepared, the sliding scale is not used; rather, three-year audited financial statements of the acquired business are usually required to be furnished or incorporated by reference, as appropriate. In all other cases, the financial statements to be filed for a significant business acquired or to be acquired should be determined based on the sliding scale test.

The test for significance is based on a comparison of the most recent annual financial statements of the business acquired or to be

Any Comparison Criteria	Number of Fiscal Years Required	
	Balance Sheet	Statements of Income and of Cash Flows
Greater than 20% but less than 40%	1	1
Greater than 40% but less than 50%	2	2
Greater than 50%	2	3

EXHIBIT 11.1   S-X Rule 3-05(B) Summarization for Acquired Businesses

acquired with the registrant's most recent annual consolidated financial statements or, in certain instances, with the registrant's pro forma financial information. Specific items compared are net book value (after considering the purchase price), total assets, and pretax income. The largest percent relationship derived from these specific comparisons should be compared with Exhibit 11.1, which is a summarization of S-X Rule 3-05(b). This exhibit indicates the number of years for which audited financial statements of the acquired entity are required.

Any required audited financial statements of the acquired businesses are for its most recent fiscal year(s). Pursuant to Rule 3-06, the SEC will accept for the acquired business the filing of audited financial statements covering a period from 9 to 12 months as satisfying a requirement for filing financial statements for a period of 1 year. However, no period shorter than 9 months will be accepted.

(e) ACQUISITIONS OF INDIVIDUALLY INSIGNIFICANT SUBSIDIARIES.   Rule 3-05 provides that all individually insignificant entities acquired in a fiscal year (i.e., those which do not exceed at least one of the aforementioned tests at the 20% threshold) that have not been included in the audited statement of operations of the registrant for at least nine months shall be aggregated in the test for significance.

If these aggregated insignificant entities exceed the 50% threshold in the year of acquisition, then financial statements covering at least the *substantial majority* of the businesses acquired shall be furnished. SEC staff believes that a *substantial majority* of the businesses acquired have been furnished when the aggregate of the entities not audited do not exceed any of the tests at the 20% level. Audited financial statements shall be provided for *at least* the most recent annual period and any interim periods required by Rules 3-01 and 3-02.

With respect to registration statements, the SEC staff believes the aggregate impact of all acquired and to-be-acquired businesses for which financial statements have not been included in the registration statement should not exceed 50%. Once the 50% threshold has been exceeded, financial statements of individually insignificant businesses must be furnished in registration statements. In that case, financial statements of the substantial majority of the businesses would be required. The SEC will accept audited financial statements of at least a mathematical majority of the acquirees (i.e., more than 50% of combined assets, pretax income, and investment) as satisfying the audit requirement.

The financial statements of insignificant entities may be combined, if appropriate. However, financial statements could not be combined, for example, for entities with different year-ends if there were significant intercompany transactions that would not be eliminated because of the timing of such transactions.

(f) WHAT CONSTITUTES A BUSINESS.   Since inception of the Securities Acts, there has been a continuing dialogue within and without the SEC as to the appropriate definition of a *business*. It has not yet been defined, nor is it likely to be in the near future. Registrants often contend that a business has not been acquired (i.e., only assets have been acquired) and that audited financial statements therefore are not required. In relatively few cases, the staff has agreed. In the overwhelming majority, the SEC considers a business acquisition to have occurred.

The SEC concluded in Financial Reporting Release No. 2 (FRR 2) that it was impracticable to provide a precise definition of *business*. Notwithstanding that position, they provided certain Rule 11-01 guidelines, which they deemed relevant to that determination. In 1991, the SEC issued some guidance in Staff Accounting Bulletin 89 regarding troubled financial institutions acquired or to be acquired. Additional guidance in this determination can be found in the consensus of Emerging Issues Task Force Issue No. 98-3; however, where conflicts exist between this guidance and that contained in Article 11-01, the Article 11-01 guidance should be followed.

The acquisition of *related businesses* should be treated as a single business combination for purposes of determining significance under Rule 3-05 and the periods for which financial statements are required.

Related businesses are defined as businesses under common ownership or management or whose acquisitions are conditioned on each other or on a single common condition.

Many acquisition-minded companies make audited financial statements a condition of closing. If the buyer is willing to close without audited amounts, a subsequent audit becomes an unavoidable cost of the acquisition. Until the audits are performed, the buyer has the choice of delaying the acquisition or forgoing the 1933 Act securities offerings.

(g) STOCK EXCHANGE REQUIREMENTS.   If securities are to be issued in connection with an acquisition and listed on the New York or American Stock Exchange, the latest available balance sheet and related statements of income, changes in financial position, and retained earnings (including supplemental interim statements) are required to be audited by independent accountants or certified by the company's principal accounting officer.

(h) PRO FORMA FINANCIAL STATEMENTS.   Pro forma financial statements are required in SEC registration statements and proxy statements where business combinations have occurred, are in progress, or are probable. Pro forma financial statements show the results of operations and financial position on an *as-if* basis, which assumes the separate entities had always been combined.

In the case of an SEC registration presenting financial statements, including a period for which a purchase-method acquisition was made, the pro forma financial statements will present a historical *as-if* combining of the previously separate entities prior to the date of the business combination. Where a combination accounted for as a pooling has already occurred, pro forma financial statements are not necessary, because the historical financial statements will have been restated.

(i) Article 11 Presentation of Pro Forma Information.   Rule 11-02 contains instructions for presentation of pro forma information. The rules allow flexibility in order to tailor pro forma information to individual facts and circumstances. The requirements for the pro forma statement of income clearly distinguish between the one-time impact and the ongoing impact of the transaction. Items with a one-time impact should be excluded from the pro forma income statement.

Article 11 requires introductory language, a condensed pro forma balance sheet, condensed income statement, and explanatory notes. The introductory headnote(s) should describe the transaction and the entities involved. The purpose of the pro formas should also be described.

The most recent annual and interim pro forma income statements must be presented. The interim presentation must cover the period from the most recent fiscal year-end to the date of the interim balance sheet required. Optionally, a pro forma income statement for the corresponding period in the preceding year may be filed.

Pro forma income information should be presented only through income (loss) from continuing operations. Any amounts relating to discontinued operations, extraordinary items, or the cumulative effect of accounting changes are to be excluded. Material nonrecurring charges or credits that result from the transaction and that will impact the income statement during the next 12 months should not be included in the pro forma income statement. These amounts should be discussed separately in a note or table with a clear indication that they are not reflected in the pro forma income information. For example, if an acquirer decided to shut down an existing plant because it was made redundant by an acquired facility, any resulting charge should only be included in a pro forma footnote disclosure.

Basic and diluted earnings per share from continuing operations and the number of shares used in each computation must be shown on the face of the pro forma income statement. In computing the weighted average shares outstanding, effect would be given to shares issued or to be issued as if issuance had taken place at the beginning of the period presented. If any convertible securities are issued as part of the transaction, their dilution must be considered in the basic earnings per share (EPS) (if a common stock equivalent) and in the diluted EPS calculation.

The pro forma balance sheet should be as of the date of the most recent balance sheet included or incorporated by reference in the registration statement. A pro forma balance sheet is not required if the transaction is reflected in the most recent historical balance sheet filed.

As already noted, only items with an ongoing impact (i.e., those that will continue to affect the income statement 12 months after the transaction) should be income statement adjustments. These typically include items such as goodwill amortization, depreciation charges, estimated changes in interest expense due to debt assumed or retired, and tax provision adjustments due to changes in tax allocation methods. Pro forma adjustments to conform an acquired entity's accounting policies should be made as if the acquisition occurred at the beginning of the year.

(ii) Multiple Presentation for Some Transactions. A single pro forma presentation may be inadequate in circumstances where a transaction is subject to several different outcomes with a wide range of possible effects. In this case, several pro formas may be needed to give effect to the range of possible results.

A common example is a tender offer where the seller has options to receive cash or available stock. In this example, the amounts of cash and stock to be ultimately exchanged cannot be accurately determined until consummation of the tender offer. In these situations, two pro forma presentations are usually made to portray the two ends of the spectrum of the offer (the effect of issuing the maximum cash and minimum stock and vice versa). Occasionally another pro forma presentation is made which represents the outcome considered most probable by management.

(i) UNIQUE SITUATIONS INVOLVING IPOS. Recently there has been increased activity in industry consolidations and roll-ups, for which Staff Accounting Bulletin 80 (Topic 1-J) may apply. It is the SEC staff's view that initial public offerings (IPOs) involving registrants that have been built by the aggregation of discrete businesses were not contemplated during the drafting of Rule 3-05 of Regulation S-X. In such situations, the significance of an acquired entity might be better measured in relation to the size of the registrant at the time the registration statement is filed rather than at the time the acquisition was made. Therefore, for a first-time registrant, the use of Topic 1-J in lieu of a literal application of Rule 3-05 is optional. The significance tests in Rule 3-05 (for this purpose, 10%, 20%, and 40% should be used, and not the higher percents allowed in normal 3.05 situations) generally can be measured against the combined entities, including those to be acquired, which comprise the registrant at the time the registration statement is filed.

The staff's policy is intended to ensure that the registration statement will include not less than three, two, and one year(s) of audited financial statements for not less than 60%, 80%, and 90%, respectively, of the constituent businesses that will comprise the registrant on an ongoing basis. In all circumstances, the audited financial statements of the registrant are required for three years, or since its inception if less than three years. The requirement to provide the audited financial statements of a constituent business in the registration statement is satisfied for the postacquisition period by including the entity's results in the audited consolidated financial statements of the registrant.

(j) SIGNIFICANT FOREIGN EQUITY INVESTEES AND ACQUIRED FOREIGN BUSINESSES OF DOMESTIC ISSUERS. In Release 33–7718, the SEC amended the requirements of domestic issuers that are required to provide financial statements for significant foreign equity investees or acquired foreign businesses. The proposals address the age of financial statements, nature of reconciling information, and thresholds for providing such reconciliations. The amendments also eliminate certain financial schedules that were previously required to be filed by both domestic and foreign issuers.

(k) FOREIGN PRIVATE ISSUERS. In Release 33–7719, the SEC streamlined the financial statement reconciliation requirements for foreign private issuers that have entered into business combinations. The amendments eliminated the requirement to reconcile certain differences attributable to the determination of the method of accounting for a business combination and the amortization period of goodwill and negative goodwill, provided that the financial statements comply with International Accounting Standard 22, *Business Combinations,* as amended, with respect to these items.

(l) SEC STAFF POSITION ON FINANCIAL STATEMENTS OF BUSINESSES ACQUIRED OR TO BE ACQUIRED. The SEC staff has clarified its position on when interim period preacquisition financial statements of an acquiree are required to be audited in an IPO. Specifically:

- In an IPO where Topic 1-J is applied (i.e., when the IPO involves a business that has been built up by the aggregate of discrete businesses that remain substantially intact after the acquisition), when audited preacquisition financial statements of an acquiree are presented and the registrant's audited financial statements give effect to the acquisition, the SEC requires that financial statements of the acquiree be audited for the interim period between the acquiree's latest preacquisition year-end and the date of its acquisition by the registrant. Comparable financial statements for the corresponding interim period of the preceding year should also be presented but may be unaudited.

- In an IPO where Topic 1-J is not applied (e.g., when a company with an operating history makes an acquisition), the SEC does not require the financial statements of the acquiree for the interim period following the acquiree's latest preacquisition fiscal year-end to be audited, unless the acquiree is of such significance that it is deemed to be the predecessor to the registrant. For nonpredecessor situations, interim financial statements can be unaudited and should be presented through the date of the acquiree's most recent quarterly interim period prior to acquisition and for the corresponding period in the preceding year. Predecessor financial statements would need to be audited for the current-year interim period through the date of acquisition. Comparable financial statements for the corresponding period of the preceding year may be unaudited.

11.6 ANTITRUST REGULATIONS

The Hart-Scott-Rodino Antitrust Improvement Act of 1976 requires that certain mergers and acquisitions be reported to the Federal Trade Commission (FTC) and the U.S. Department of Justice prior to consummation. The parties involved must wait at least 30 days before completing the acquisition to allow the governmental agencies time to consider the antitrust implications of the proposed transaction. Premerger notification is made on *Notification and Report Form for Certain Mergers and Acquisitions,* and must be made when:

- Either of the acquiring or acquired companies is involved in commerce or in any activity affecting commerce.
- The annual net sales or total assets of one company are $10 million or more and of the other company are $100 million or more.
- The acquiring company would gain one of:

- 15% or more of the voting securities or assets of the acquired company or more than $15 million worth of both the assets and the voting securities of the acquired company
- 15% or more of the issuer's outstanding voting securities, which are valued in excess of $15 million
- 25% of the issuer's outstanding voting securities
- 50% of the issuer's outstanding voting securities

Additional notifications must be filed when 15%, 25%, and 50% of the outstanding voting securities of an issuer are about to be acquired. Smaller acquisitions are exempt if the acquiring company will not hold voting securities and assets aggregating more than $15 million.

Information included in the Premerger Notification Form applies only to operations conducted within the United States, including its commonwealths, territories, possessions, and the District of Columbia. Information requested includes a description of the acquisition, assets to be acquired, voting securities to be acquired, and dollar revenues by Standard Industrial Classification (SIC) Code.

If the FTC or Department of Justice believes the merger or acquisition violates antitrust laws, it must file for an injunction requiring the parties to *cease and desist* from consummation of the merger or acquisition. However, these parties do not have the power to stop the merger or acquisition; only a court of law can render a decision on whether antitrust laws would be violated.

11.7 OTHER REGULATIONS

(a) BLUE SKY LAWS.   If an acquisition involves the issuance or *sale* of the buyer's securities, the buyer must also comply with *blue sky laws* in all states where its securities are being offered to selling shareholders.

Sales or exchanges of stock or other securities are regulated by various state and federal laws. Generally, it is illegal to sell or exchange unregistered securities, unless they meet specific exemptions. The burden of proof as to qualifying under the various exemptions lies with the issuer of the security. Exemptions to the federal laws prohibiting transactions in unregistered securities generally apply to limited sales or exchanges of securities by corporations if:

- The company is incorporated or is doing business in one state and the security is offered or sold only to residents of that state.
- The issue is a private placement. A private placement is where the offer to acquire securities is made to no more than 35 persons. In addition, the purchaser of securities in a private placement must represent that he or she has purchased the securities for investment and not for secondary distribution.

(b) ERISA FILINGS.   The Employee Retirement Income Security Act (ERISA) was enacted to protect the interest of participants in employee benefit plans. Filings must be made with the Pension Benefit Guaranty Corporation (PBGC) and the Internal Revenue Service (IRS) if pension plans are merged or partially or completely terminated.

(c) IRS RULINGS.   With a tax-free transaction (see Chapter 8), IRS approval should be sought before a deal is completed. Final approval typically takes several months.

(d) OTHER FILINGS.   When buying or selling a business in a regulated industry such as banking, public utilities, transportation, or communications, filing and obtaining the necessary approval(s) with applicable regulatory agencies, such as the Federal Reserve Board, Interstate Commerce Commission, Public Utility Commission, or Federal Communications Commission, are usually required.

SIGNIFICANT SEC REGULATORY AND ACCOUNTING PRONOUNCEMENTS

THE SECURITIES ACT OF 1933

- Rule 409 Exemption from Requirements for Information Unknown or Not Reasonable
- Available Rule 145 Mergers and Acquisitions Rule 3-05 Financial Statements of Businesses Acquired or to Be Acquired

THE SECURITIES EXCHANGE ACT OF 1934
Regulation 14A   Solicitation of Proxies
Section 13(e)   Purchases or Tender Offers by a Company for Its Own Securities
Section 14(d)   Third-Party Tender Offers
SEC RELEASES
Accounting Series Releases (ASRs):
ASR 135   Revised Guidelines for the Application of ASR No. 130
ASR 146   Effect of Treasury Stock Transactions on Accounting for Business Combinations
ASR 146-A   Statement of Policy and Interpretations in Regard to ASR No. 146
Financial Reporting Releases (FRRs):
FRR 2 Guidance as to What Constitutes a "Business"
Staff Accounting Bulletins (SABs):
SAB 54   Pushdown Accounting
SAB 89   Financial Statement Requirements of Certain Troubled Financial Institution Acquisitions

INDEX